OPTIMIZING
FACTORY
PERFORMANCE

OPTIMIZING FACTORY PERFORMANCE

Cost-Effective Ways to Achieve Significant and Sustainable Improvement

JAMES P. IGNIZIO, Ph.D.

New York   Chicago   San Francisco   Lisbon   London
Madrid   Mexico City   Milan   New Delhi   San Juan
Seoul   Singapore   Sydney   Toronto

1 2 3 4 5 6 7 8 9 0   DOC / DOC   0 1 0 9

ISBN: 978–0–07–163285–0
MHID: 0–07–163285–9

McGraw-Hill books are available at special quantity discounts to use as premiums and sales promotions, or for use in corporate training programs. To contact a representative please e-mail us at bulksales@mcgraw-hill.com.

This book is printed on acid-free paper.

Disclaimer
The 15 case studies in this book represent a work of fiction. Names, characters, places, and incidents are either the product of the author's imagination or are used fictitiously, and any resemblance to actual persons, living or dead, business establishments, events, or locales is entirely coincidental.

Library of Congress Cataloging-in-Publication Data

Ignizio, James P.
   Optimizing factory performance : cost-effective ways to achieve significant and sustainable improvements / James P. Ignizio.
      p. cm.
   Includes bibliographical references and index.
   ISBN 978–0–07–163285–0 (alk. paper)
1. Production management. 2. Quality control. 3. Industrial management. I. Title.

TS155.I39 2009
658.5—dc22   2009022282

The author dedicates this book to
the memory of his mother:
Nora Ignizio

Après moi,
le déluge.

motto of the Royal Air Force
617 Squadron: "The Dambusters"

Contents

Chapter 14 The Elements of Success   329

Chapter 15 Summary and Conclusions   347

Bibliography   355

Index   359

Foreword

This book takes a major step forward in establishing a science of manufacturing systems. Dr. Ignizio begins the book by citing three principal causes of poor performance of manufacturing systems; namely, complexity, variability, and lackluster leadership. He then proceeds to lay out a prescription for overcoming these obstacles based on the three dimensions of manufacturing: (1) the *first dimension of manufacturing,* which focuses on the physical dimensions of the factory itself, including its location, size, layout, the processes it employs, and the products it manufactures; (2) the *second dimension of manufacturing,* which addresses the physical components housed within the factory; and (3) the *third dimension of manufacturing,* which encompasses the protocols used to manage the factory, with the objective of increasing productive capacity, reducing cycle time, and eliminating uncertainty. In his own words, Ignizio seeks to "fill the gap between the theory and practice of factory performance improvement." In filling that gap, the author advances the science of manufacturing systems in ways no other author has even attempted. This book is replete with developments that would, in themselves, merit a series of archival journal articles.

The material presented in this book describes, discusses, and illustrates the politics, art and science of manufacturing. It identifies the factors that hamper optimum performance—the aforementioned complexity, variability, and lackluster leadership—and describes methods by which the debilitating influences of these factors can be reduced or eliminated. Another purpose of the book is to introduce previously unpublished methods and concepts for the improvement of factory performance, as well as that for supply chain, business processes, and organizational performance.

It is these newly introduced methods and techniques that represent the core concepts of this book. They include such topics as:

- Improved metrics for the measurement and comparison of factory performance
- Optimal allocation of the maintenance function to factory workstations
- Methods for the de-clustering of factory starts or preventive maintenance activities
- Contrasting "workstation-centric and process step-centric" perspectives of factory performance
- The so-called "Waddington Analysis," a methodology for improving both operations and maintenance performance

These are novel concepts developed by the author over the last two decades, and they represent a significant departure from any of the other prominent texts in the field of manufacturing systems.

A brief summary of this book will uncover its uniqueness. Chapters 1 and 2 introduce the reader to the purposes and terminology of the book. Chapter 3 gives two very useful definitions of a factory:

1. A factory is a processing network through which jobs and information flow and within which events take place.
2. A factory is a nonlinear, dynamic, stochastic system with feedback.

It is these two definitions that tell the reader the perspective from which the author proposes to develop an entire science of manufacturing. In Chapter 4 Ignizio introduces the use of a simple spreadsheet simulation model of a 12-workstation factory for the purpose of evaluating the performance of a factory in two dimensions; i.e., the first two dimensions of manufacturing given above. He demonstrates that it is more effective, and far less costly, to balance the production line than to acquire additional machines (the second dimension) or expand the factory (the first dimension). In Chapter 5 the author introduces the three fundamental equations of manufacturing performance that are applied to running a factory. He demonstrates how variability in process step cycle time affects overall factory performance. Chapter 6 focuses on running a factory in three dimensions. Here the author demonstrates that it is easier and far less costly to invoke the third dimension of manufacturing (i.e., increasing the effective process rates of the several workstations, reducing the variability of factory starts, or reducing the variability of process times for one or more workstations) than to increase the physical capacity of the factory or any workstation. Chapter 7 introduces three factory performance curves that afford the opportunity to evaluate factory performance, while Chapter 8 describes a variety of factory performance metrics, including some that are widely used but nonetheless flawed. In summary, the first eight chapters serve to describe the fundamental methodology for analyzing manufacturing systems.

Chapter 9 sets the stage for the remainder of the book. Chapters 10 through 15 illustrate how the application of the science-based principles discussed in Chapters 1 through 8 can lead to improved production line performance. These principles are dedicated to mitigating complexity, reducing variability, and gaining a more accurate determination of workstation and factory capacity. Chapter 10 focuses on reducing the complexity of the protocols employed within the factory. Chapter 11 discusses ways to reduce variability. Chapter 12 presents a simple example—using a modification of the 12-workstation factory model introduced in Chapter 4—to illustrate how applying the methodology introduced in earlier chapters will substantially improve factory performance. Chapter 13 shows how to determine a true upper bound on workstation and factory capacity. Chapter 14 fashions a systematic approach for developing a vision, a plan, a work organization, and the leadership necessary for implementing all of these elements.

Little has been made here of the third demon of manufacturing systems management, that of "lackluster leadership." Dr. Ignizio employs an interesting and highly effective device to portray the disastrous influence of lackluster leadership on factory performance by using a series of chapter-ending case studies. Actually, these 15 case studies are themselves chapters in the continuing saga of several figures in various levels of management in a fictional manufacturing enterprise, "Muddle, Inc" (the very name speaks to the many tawdry management practices that inhibit effective factory performance in this company). I gave these case studies to my class in a graduate course in engineering management, with the assignment to write a series of four essays on how the managers and engineers of Muddle, Inc. would benefit from a basic understanding of the management concepts in my course. Reading four essays from each of the 60 students was an onerous task, but I was gratified that my students were able to quickly identify the flaws in Muddle's management practices and recommend appropriate organizational and policy changes.

Widespread adoption of Dr. Ignizio's book would do much to improve factory management in the United States and around the world. More than a century ago, Frederick W. Taylor—the father of scientific management—wrote that three groups of people should, ideally, share in the financial benefits derived from improved productivity; namely, workers, management, and owners. The industrial world would be a better place if twenty-first century managers were adherents of Ignizio's philosophy of manufacturing management and practiced the precepts that Taylor advanced so long ago.

Professor William E. Biles, Ph.D.
Department of Industrial Engineering University of Louisville

Preface

Nations with the resolve and skill to produce high-quality goods, and which do so efficiently, prosper and grow. Manufacturing is a crucial component of the foundation that maintains the security, health, and wealth of any country. One of the most important measures of manufacturing performance is that of factory cycle time— the time between the introduction of a job into the factory and its completion. Firms whose factories deliver the right product to the right customer at the right time ultimately dominate those that are merely runner-ups. Manufacturers that are fast and agile will be the survivors in the highly competitive world of making "things."

Over the past 50 years, more than 50 management and manufacturing fads and fashions have been proposed for the achievement of improved organizational and factory performance. Almost all have failed to live up to their hype. Today, in fact, the principal performance measure of a factory—load-adjusted cycle-time efficiency—is either the same or marginally better than that of factories of a half-century ago. While the goods produced by factories have grown in sophistication and have, in general, improved in terms of reliability, the time spent in their actual production continues to represent but a small fraction (on the order of 5 to 20 percent) of the total time they are in the factory. Consequently, there is enormous room for improvement in the running of almost any factory— in any country.

While methods such as *lean manufacturing, reengineering, theory of constraints,* and *Six Sigma* may—*when and if applied properly*— improve factory performance, they represent just one part of the solution. To achieve significant and, in particular, sustainable performance improvement, an approach that balances the art and science of manufacturing while taking into account the culture and politics of the organization must be employed. The attainment of this balanced approach will require more than lean, more than Six Sigma and—when implemented—will result in much more than what was once considered an acceptable level of factory performance. It will necessitate, however, a paradigm shift—a shift akin to that which occurred when the third dimension of warfare was realized by means of exploitation of the airplane.

In this book I examine the importance of manufacturing, its history, and its terminology. I show that to improve factory performance cost-effectively, one must venture beyond the traditional first and second dimensions of manufacturing—the dimensions that rely almost exclusively on physical changes to the factory or its components. Instead, the most effective approach to improved factory performance may be achieved by means of the third dimension of manufacturing—the dimension involving changes to factory operating and maintenance protocols (i.e., the strategies and tactics employed to actually run a factory).

I introduce the operating and maintenance protocols best suited for effectively dealing with the three main enemies of factory performance, that is, the obstacles of complexity, variability, and lackluster leadership. While the approaches illustrated have a scientific basis and rely on the three fundamental equations and one fundamental model of manufacturing, the material is presented in such a way as to minimize the need for expertise in mathematics beyond that of a high school student. However, those who wish to avoid virtually all mathematics may do so by covering just Chapters 1 and 2, Chapters 7 through 12, and Chapters 14 and 15.

Finally, as a means to indicate the impact of organizational politics and dysfunctional cultures, case studies (of a strictly fictional nature) appear at the end of each chapter. In these vignettes, the trials and tribulations of employees of the fictional Muddle Corporation are observed.

James P. Ignizio
Placitas, New Mexico

Acknowledgments

The author wishes to acknowledge the reviewing efforts and subsequent input provided by Laura Burke and Bill Biles. He also wants to express his appreciation to Judy Bass, senior editor, and Daina Penikas, senior editing supervisor, of McGraw-Hill for their faith in and assistance with the production of the book you hold in your hands. Finally, thanks are given to all those who helped to educate me in the complexities and politics of real world manufacturing. Most prominently figuring in that endeavor were Gene Minder, Ben Niebel, Inyong Ham, Katsundo Hitomi, Ken Knott, Jonathan Matthews, Peter Tag, Mike Gannon, and Sam Mouck.

OPTIMIZING

FACTORY

PERFORMANCE

Introduction

MANUFACTURING AND ITS IMPORTANCE

At one time in America's history, manufacturing was considered the nation's primary mission. The period from 1800 until 1932 was, in fact, denoted as the time of the "American system of manufacturing" (Hounshell, 1984). Industrial tourists from all over the world (and particularly Japan) traveled to America in an attempt to learn and copy the methods employed.

Beginning in the latter half of the twentieth century, the emphasis in America on making things was seemingly changed to that of making deals. Students who would, in the past, have sought degrees in science and engineering shifted their attention to careers in business, banking, politics, venture capital, law, finance, and other components of the service sector. American manufacturing firms, mostly in an attempt to reduce their costs—and mitigate the impact of regulations—either outsourced much of their production or moved entire factories to other nations. Included among the U.S. firms that have either (1) moved all or the majority of their production elsewhere, or (2) are considering such a move, or (3) actually have closed operations in the United States are Ford, Chrysler, Levi-Strauss, Bethlehem Steel, Boeing Commercial Aircraft, IBM's Personal Computers, RCA, Schwinn Bicycles, Maytag, OshKosh, Carrier Air Conditioning, several semiconductor manufacturing firms, approximately 96 percent of all clothing producers, and many of this nation's manufacturers of wood furniture, lighting fixtures, batteries, and household appliances.

Not only did the manufacturers of items for household consumption move elsewhere, so did much of the production critical to national defense. Just a few of those vital products that are now wholly or primarily outsourced include

- *Bearings.* These are key components to everything from automobiles to spy satellites.
- *Metal castings.* China and other countries are now the major suppliers to the U.S. military.
- *Roller cutters.* Only one firm is left in the United States that produces roller cutters for armored plate or heavy steel.
- *Chemicals.* The United States now must depend on a foreign company's facilities to supply the chemicals used for binding windows and aluminum panels to aircraft.
- *Military clothing.* As one example, an order actually was placed with Chinese manufacturers to produce the U.S. military's black berets (this order was later recalled after protests were raised).

Until quite recently, conventional wisdom held that the "smart thing to do" was for a firm to either outsource a portion of its operations or move entire factories to lower-cost developing nations. Management gurus recommended such measures, and Wall Street analysts quickly upgraded the ratings of the firms that followed this advice. The long-term impact of such decisions, however, was either ignored or not comprehended. More specifically, plans apparently were made in the naive belief that "tomorrow will be exactly like today." The illusion under which decisions were made was that in the developing nations to which factories were being moved

- Labor costs would remain low.
- Regulations (e.g., construction, financial reporting, and environmental) would remain loose to nonexistent.
- The value of the dollar would remain stable.
- Shipping costs would remain constant.
- The cost of oil, natural gas, and other commodities would not increase appreciably.
- The economy would remain constant (e.g., inflation would remain low and there would be no economic meltdown).

Beginning in 2008, manufacturing firms discovered that the premises for many of their decisions as to outsourcing and relocation of factories were no longer valid. As developing nations became wealthier—mostly by means of increasing their manufacturing sector—labor costs rose, regulations were imposed or strengthened, and the cost of production increased. The impact of these changes on the economics of outsourcing was magnified by the decrease in the value of the U.S. dollar coupled with an increase in the cost of oil (along with most other basic resources).

Suddenly, the benefits of outsourcing and moving factories to developing nations were either substantially reduced or simply vanished. As just one reason for this change, the cost of shipping a 40-foot container from Shanghai to San Diego increased by 150 percent from 2000 to 2008.

The developing nations to which much of America's manufacturing was outsourced now have their own problems. With a rise in *their* standard of living and subsequent increase in *their* cost of labor and a tightening of *their* regulations, they have begun to outsource their own manufacturing efforts to even less expensive countries. One can only wonder when the outsourcing cycle will end.

In the United States, some of the firms that have maintained at least some manufacturing capacity and capability are now busy reactivating moth-balled factories and rehiring production personnel. Some of the advantages of maintaining manufacturing capabilities in one's home country, wherever that may be, include

- Reduced transportation costs for shipment to home-country customers
- Mitigation of the risk of the unauthorized transfer of intellectual property
- Maintenance of a trained, experienced home-country workforce
- Maintenance of state-of-the-art factories within the home country
- Reduction of the threat to national security if a need arises to produce critical products locally

There's yet another reason to maintain, to whatever degree possible, manufacturing within one's own country—economics. There are only four economic sectors that generate material wealth:

- Agriculture
- Mining
- Manufacturing
- Construction

Other sectors, such as service and trade, only distribute wealth. It has been estimated, in fact, that manufacturing within the United States generates $1.37 of additional economic activity for every $1 of goods produced. This is more than any other economic sector. Manufacturing is also a country's source—often its primary source—of innovation. In the United States, for example, nearly 60 percent of all private-sector research and development is conducted by manufacturers (Popkin and Kobe, 2006).

Despite the advantages of manufacturing in one's home country, there remains a belief that outsourcing will always reduce costs. This is simply not the case. Factories in America, as well as elsewhere, are, for the most part, not nearly as efficient as they could be—and should be. While a massive amount of money is spent on development of new products, facilities, and machines, little regard is given to the importance of manufacturing protocols—the policies and procedures employed to actually run a factory. While this deficiency has been mitigated in part by the introduction of such concepts as lean manufacturing, far more improvement in factory performance is possible by means of taking an even broader view of factory protocols and, in particular, the crucial importance of fast cycle time.

Unfortunately, in both the United States and elsewhere neither the art nor the science of manufacturing is fully exploited or appreciated. Consequently, when faced with the need to improve factory performance, the typical reaction is to build bigger, more expensive factories and purchase bigger, more expensive, and more complex machines—and perhaps do so somewhere else than in one's home country. As we shall see, there is a better way. First, however, it may be of benefit to provide some background and details that should serve to explain the motivation for this book.

BACKGROUND AND MOTIVATION

By way of introduction and as a means to explain the rationale behind certain opinions expressed in the text (some of which may be viewed, in some quarters, as controversial), allow me to provide a brief overview of my background and experience. This may serve as both an explanation and a warning.

I was a university professor for 30 years. During that time, I also served as a consultant to more than 100 firms and governmental agencies—mostly for assistance with or direction of the improvement of factory, supply-chain, business process, and organizational performance. Prior to and following my academic career, I was employed in industry as a senior-level manager (five years) and internal consultant and scientific advisor (six years). While I don't claim to have seen it all, I've seen a lot.

Over that period (i.e., of more than four decades), I came to the conclusion that courses in manufacturing and management (including those in production management, operations management, management science, manufacturing engineering, industrial engineering, and MBA programs), as taught in universities or via the training programs offered to industry and government by management gurus and motivational speakers, do not necessarily provide an adequate, comprehensive, or even accurate portrait of the environment faced in industry, government, or any real-world organization. In too many cases, the picture presented is naive, overly simplistic, and subsequently limited in scope and value. Even the case studies presented in most courses and textbooks fail to reflect the complexity, confusion, and outright chaos one typically faces in the real world.

Students in engineering, science, and business programs receive an education that often ignores the most important aspects of real-world problems. But those are the factors that must be understood and dealt with effectively if the full potential of the organization is to be achieved. If not, any remedies that are implemented most likely will achieve, at best, only transient improvements—akin to the counterintuitive effect observed in the famous Hawthorne experiments (Roethlisberger and Dickson, 1939).

The most important finding in the Hawthorne experiments was identification of the *Hawthorne effect*. In brief, it was observed that the behavior of people changes when they recognize—consciously or subconsciously—they are part of an "experiment." This may explain why so many pilot studies or full-blown implementations of management fads and fashions result in a transient improvement in performance, only to be followed (weeks, months, or even a year or more afterward) by a disappointing return to the status quo. The Hawthorne effect points out the danger in relying on the short-term impact of any method implemented for the purpose of any type of performance improvement. Even a seriously flawed concept may, when first introduced into the organization or factory, produce a short-lived improvement in performance.

Ignorance of the Hawthorne effect, as well as a failure to recognize other symptoms of a dysfunctional culture (and its accompanying dysfunctional policies, procedures, and values), is exhibited in those organizations in which one management fad after another is embraced, implemented, and ultimately, abandoned. Such routine failures are in part a consequence of deficiencies in both the classes taught in universities and the training courses provided within business and government. When these shortcomings are combined with a short-term planning horizon and a desire for quick and easy solutions by management (particularly, alas, American management), the result is depressingly predictable—disappointing results and lowered morale.

To illustrate the point, consider the skills required to achieve a significant and sustainable improvement in the operation of a real-world factory. Industrial and manufacturing engineering students, for example, are schooled in a number of topics, some of which serve as an important and necessary basis for a (limited) understanding of the science of manufacturing. Rarely, however, is time devoted to two other equally important (and, in some cases, more important) aspects of manufacturing. Yet these factors can make or break any plan for factory performance improvement.

The missing ingredients are the politics and art that must be considered, understood, and dealt with if any method for improved factory, supply-chain, business process, or organizational performance is to be accepted, implemented, and (equally if not more important) sustained. More specifically, without adequate appreciation of the politics and art associated with performance improvement, it is doubtful that the student, on entering the workforce, will have the positive influence on either organizational or factory performance that one would (and should) expect.

It is also my belief that the typical science, engineering, or business school graduate may not have an adequate appreciation of certain of the unique features of the fundamentals required to obtain significant and sustainable improvement in factories, supply chains, business processes, or the organization as a whole. This is particularly true with regard to an understanding and appreciation of the role played by complexity and variability, two of the three primary enemies of performance that must be dealt with if measurable and sustainable improvement is to be ensured.

Complexity, for example, is rarely discussed to the degree it deserves in either academia or industry despite its pervasive negative impact on performance. Variability has received limited attention [mainly owing to its exposition in such texts as Gross and Harris (1998) and Hopp and Spearman (2001)], but the crucial importance of the reduction of variability has, for the most part, failed to reach the middle to upper levels of management.

Furthermore, only a limited number of methods for the mitigation of variability, in either the organization or its factories, have been considered (e.g., the variability induced by reentrancy—a phenomenon prevalent in high-tech factories such as semiconductor manufacturing—has not received nearly the attention it is due).

The third enemy of performance improvement—and often the most damaging—is lackluster leadership or even the virtual absence of leadership coupled with a lack of vision. The recent college graduate ultimately will discover that in most any organization there is an abundance, if not overabundance, of managers. The typical manager in the typical organization busies himself or herself with scheduling and holding meetings, attending meetings, overseeing employee performance evaluations, replying to a never-ending stream of (mostly unimportant) e-mails, listening to complaints, presenting PowerPoint presentations to his or her superiors, serving as a conduit between senior management and the individuals who report to him or her, and endorsing the organization's formal mission plan.

But those are tasks that merely support the perpetuation of the status quo. Leaders and visionaries, on the other hand, are rare and unappreciated commodities.

THE THREE DIMENSIONS OF MANUFACTURING

Hand in hand with a lack of appreciation of complexity, variability, and lackluster leadership is the failure to recognize the fact that there are three dimensions to manufacturing (Ignizio, 1980). As a consequence, factory engineers and managers are likely to consider only the first two dimensions and overlook the third in their decision making. To clarify this point, each of the three dimensions of manufacturing is summarized briefly.

The first dimension of manufacturing addresses the attributes of and decisions made with regard to the physical features of the factory itself, for example,

- Factory location
- Factory size
- Factory layout
- Factory processes and products selection

The second dimension of manufacturing is focused on the physical components housed within the factory, including

- Factory workstations and their machines
- Factory floor operations and maintenance personnel
- Factory support personnel
- Material handling systems
- Inventory storage of in-process jobs
- Spare parts and supplies storage
- Pass-through and dispatch stations
- Maintenance equipment and replacement parts
- Inspection/testing equipment
- Emergency response centers
- The equipment dedicated to the automation of operations

The third dimension of manufacturing encompasses the protocols (e.g., policies, practices, and procedures) employed to actually manage and run the factory. The emphasis in this dimension is on changes in strategies and tactics as opposed to physical changes. Included among these protocols are

- Factory starts protocol (e.g., how many jobs to introduce into the factory and when to schedule these starts)
- Preventive maintenance event protocols (e.g., both the scheduling and content of such events)
- Declustering[1] protocols (e.g., the declustering of jobs started into a factory, the declustering of preventive maintenance events)
- Batching protocols (e.g., the determination of batch sizes supported by the machines that employ batching)
- Development and validation of operation and maintenance specifications
- Establishment of run rules (e.g., which job to run on a machine at any given time, i.e., "WIP management") for each of the factory's workstations

---

1 The term *declustering* is used to represent the "smoothing out" of events. For example, rather than clustering preventive maintenance events at the beginning of a work shift, they should be evenly spread out over the entire shift if factory variability is to be reduced.

- Protocols for minimization of wait time (e.g., time spent waiting for a technician to conduct a maintenance event, or waiting for a spare part to be delivered to a workstation, or waiting for an operator to introduce a job into a machine, or waiting for a decision to be made, or filling out forms, or waiting for committees to reach a consensus)
- Protocols for determining how to best allocate personnel (either operations or maintenance personnel) to workstations
- Protocols for identifying and reducing excessive complexity (e.g., unnecessary process steps, unnecessary maintenance steps, or unnecessarily complex run rules)
- Protocols employed in the ordering, location, and dispatch of spare parts and factory supplies

Note again that the first two dimensions of manufacturing are those that deal mainly, if not exclusively, with the physical elements of the factory. The primary emphasis of these first two dimensions is that of the achievement of changes to factory capacity—where any changes in capacity are confined to those accomplished by physical means (e.g., adding or deleting machines, adding or deleting personnel, or adding or deleting factory floor space).

As mentioned, most factory managers confine their interest and decisions to just these first two dimensions. One reason for this self-imposed affliction is that physical alterations to the factory are changes the manager can easily see, count, and even touch. As a consequence, managers who restrict their decision space to just the first two dimensions of manufacturing will, for example, purchase expensive machines in an attempt to increase factory capacity when a far less costly and more effective alternative may exist (and likely does exist) within the third dimension of manufacturing (Ignizio, 1998).

The third dimension of manufacturing employs changes to protocols not only to improve capacity (i.e., the main emphasis of the first two dimensions) but also—and chiefly—to reduce factory cycle time and the uncertainty about that time. Perhaps the main reason the third dimension is overlooked so routinely is that changes in protocols are difficult to discern.

While you can see, touch, and count machines (or tool bins, supplies, or people), a change in protocols is virtually invisible—at least to the untrained eye. The fact that changes to protocols are not nearly as transparent as physical changes makes life difficult for those who wish to extend decision making in the factory to the third dimension. But it is this dimension that usually enables one to achieve faster, cheaper, and more sustainable improvements to factory performance.

Ignoring the third dimension of manufacturing is analogous to—and as foolish as—trying to fight a modern-day war within just two dimensions—land and sea—while ignoring the third—the air. It is for this reason that the coverage of this book will focus on all three dimensions of manufacturing—and particularly the third.

PURPOSE OF THIS BOOK

My primary purpose in writing this book is to attempt to fill the gap between the theory and practice of factory performance improvement—and in doing so to reveal crucial aspects of the world of manufacturing rarely touched on in classrooms, textbooks, and training courses. More specifically, my purpose is to provide readers with the concepts, techniques, and understanding necessary to achieve significant and sustainable improvement in the complex, confusing, and perplexing environment of a real-world factory, an atmosphere clouded with and influenced by interpersonal relationships, oversized egos, turf battles, in-house politics, resistance to change, and—often—a resistance even to listening. While my focus will be on the factory, it should be understood that the concepts presented apply as well to supply chains, business processes, and the organization as a whole.

The material presented will describe, discuss, and illustrate the politics, art, and science of manufacturing. In support of this, the three enemies of factory performance—complexity, variability, and lackluster leadership—will be identified, discussed, and illustrated. Methods for most effectively eliminating or at least mitigating their negative impact will be presented. Avoidance of these three enemies should diminish the need to consider a move of a firm's production facilities to other, seemingly lower-cost countries.

In keeping with the goal of reducing unnecessary complexity, the mathematical prerequisites of readers are minimal. In fact, as readers will discover, the only mathematics employed within the text are addition, subtraction, multiplication, and division. Even the discussions that involve mathematics are illuminated by means of straightforward numerical illustrations.

If, however, a reader insists on avoiding any level of mathematical and technical detail, this is possible by restricting his or her focus to Chapters 1 and 2, 7 through 12, and 14 and 15. Hopefully, however, you will decide to read the chapters in order because, once again, the level of mathematics employed (with the possible exception of Chapter 13) has been reduced to that which a high school student should be able to follow.

A secondary purpose of the book is to introduce a number of original and previously unpublished methods and concepts for the improvement of factory, supply-chain, business process, and organizational performance. While many of these methods have been presented via short courses to my clients, I have refrained—until now—from disseminating most of these ideas in a public forum. Among these are such topics as

- New, holistic, and robust metrics for the measurement and comparison of factory performance
- Optimized allocation of maintenance or operations personnel to factory workstations
- Methods for the declustering of either factory starts or preventive maintenance events
- The Waddington analysis, an effective and practical methodology for improving both operations and maintenance
- An improved method for the estimate of workstation or factory capacity
- Achievement of C^4U-compliant specifications (i.e., complete, correct, concise, clear, and unambiguous specifications) for the conduct of operations or maintenance events
- Process-step decoupling (a method for dealing with the variability and complexity induced by reentrant process steps, e.g., workstations that must support multiple operations as fed back from downstream processing)
- A process-step-centric perspective of factories as opposed to the conventional workstation view presented in the literature[2]

Finally, case studies, in the form of an ongoing novelette, accompany each chapter. These serve to accompany and illustrate the concepts introduced, particularly their political and interpersonal

---

2 The use of a process-step-centric perspective is vital when dealing with real-world factories, particularly those that are reentrant and/or use machine-to-operation (i.e., machine-to-process-step) assignments. This will be made clear in the chapters to follow.

aspects. These yarns center around incidents that occur within a strictly fictional—but, alas, representative—company.

The firm in question manufactures a high-tech product and has belatedly come to recognize that its upstart competitors are eating into the firm's profits and market share. Each case study reveals how good ideas can be torpedoed while flawed concepts are embraced. By means of these stories, readers, hopefully, should learn how to avoid the same mistakes this unfortunate firm makes.

The name of the fictional firm is Muddle, Inc. While the firm and all the characters discussed in these case studies are purely fictional, the situations and politics are, unfortunately, representative of those found in many real-world situations. A detailed introduction to the Muddle Corporation is provided in the next section.

INTRODUCTION TO MUDDLE, INC.

The Muddle Corporation is a large multinational manufacturing firm. The company is replete with examples of mediocre to poor to simply atrocious business practices and decision making—factors that induce waste and diminish the firm's profit and market share. The problems Muddle must cope with, as well as the mistakes it makes, are—unfortunately—typical of those that may be observed in many real-world manufacturing firms. These problems and mistakes will, however, provide lessons that readers may learn from and hopefully avoid repeating.

The present CEO of Muddle is Marvin Muddle, the son of Peter Muddle. Peter, in turn, was one of the firm's founders, its previous CEO, and now serves as chairman of the board.

Marvin, sporting an MBA from a prestigious Ivy League university and 10 years' experience with the firm, is faced with a company whose profits, market share, and stock price are in decline. Since the tech bubble burst in 2001, Muddle's stock price has plummeted a whopping 80 percent. The morale of Muddle's employees, most of who rely on their stock options to augment an unimpressive level of compensation, has plunged even lower.

One of the most pressing problems facing the Muddle Corporation is that of poor factory performance. This problem is, in fact, much worse than comprehended by the firm's senior management—managers far more interested in the development of an improved or more "jazzy" product than the mundane matter of improved factory performance.

At one time, the firm virtually owned the market for its high-tech product despite its outdated, mostly intuitive, and thoroughly substandard manufacturing practices. That product, however, has now become more or less a commodity, and a number of firms have surfaced with equal or even superior versions of the artifact, along with manufacturing processes, policies, and procedures that allow them to often beat Muddle to the market. As a consequence, customers for Muddle's product have, of late, been shifting their business to Muddle's competitors.

Marvin Muddle is convinced that the glory days of the firm can be recaptured if he can just reduce costs. Cost reduction is and always has been, in fact, his main, if not only, concern. Certainly, thinks Marvin, reductions in manufacturing costs coupled with introduction of the latest and greatest management and motivational methods will enable Muddle to crush its competition.

If that doesn't work, Marvin simply will engage in a cutthroat price war that should drive the competition out of business. This approach may reduce the firm's profit margin significantly, but considering the deep pockets of the company, it is bound to be effective. In fact, one of his father's favorite sayings is: "If you can't compete, destroy." Satisfied that he has an answer to the firm's predicament, Marvin returns to the business at hand—consideration of yet another change in the company's logo.

In the meantime, while Muddle's costs have indeed been reduced—mostly via layoffs of employees, shutting down of domestic factories, transfer of manufacturing facilities to offshore (and lower labor cost) countries, and the sale of a plethora of poorly performing companies purchased during the ill-fated tech bubble—the firm's market share hasn't improved appreciably. Just as disappointing, the introduction of a long line of management fads and fashions launched over the past several decades hasn't produced the results promised by a series of glib and high-priced management consultants. In fact, despite Muddle's embrace of reengineering, one-minute management, total quality control, quality circles, management by objectives, management by walking around, management by positive thinking, management by the Ouija board, management practices of Hannibal Lecter, management via blind faith, management by intimidation, theories A through Z, and a host of other celebrated concepts, matters have only gotten worse. In particular, average product cycle time actually has increased—substantially.

Some weeks ago, the perky and persuasive Sally Swindel, the very same management consultant who previously sold the firm on reengineering (promising that it would be the answer to all the firm's problems), returned with what she guaranteed to be an even better approach: lean manufacturing.[3] Sally assured the members of Muddle's Management Review Committee (MRC) that lean manufacturing—a concept she claimed originated in Japan with the Toyota Company—will "turn the fortunes of the firm around." All it will take to get started, she insisted, is a two-week training course. Sally added that if Muddle sends enough people to that course, the fee will be dropped from the normal $40,000 down to $30,000 per attendee. She even guaranteed a discount in the room rates of the plush seaside resort hotel in which the attendees will be housed.

Desperate for a quick and easy solution to Muddle's problems, Marvin Muddle ignored his Management Review Committee's timid recommendation for "further investigation" as well as a "proof of concept." One member of the MRC actually had the temerity to remind Marvin of the drastic consequences the firm endured—and is still trying to recover from—after implementing reengineering, the previous "final solution" recommended by Sally Swindel.

Brushing those concerns aside, Marvin demanded the MRC make plans to introduce lean manufacturing into the firm's factories—and do so ASAP. He concluded the meeting with a warning that he expects results within 6 to at most 12 months.

We'll see how that works out.

OVERVIEW OF THE MATERIAL TO FOLLOW

Chapter 2 provides a brief summary of the history of manufacturing, focusing on some of the most important concepts and developments that have been introduced over the decades (and even centuries) to improve factory performance. While an impatient reader may be tempted to skip this chapter (e.g., "Who cares about history?" or "I already know this"), please read it. You may discover that the history of manufacturing you were taught in school has some serious deficiencies and oversights. (As just one example, the first moving assembly line for the assembly of vehicles was

---

3 Before drawing the *erroneous* conclusion that I'm bashing such concepts as lean manufacturing, do take the time to read the rest of the book. In the chapters that follow, both the scope and the limitations of lean manufacturing will be covered.

developed long before Henry Ford or Ransom Olds was born—several centuries before to be exact.) More important, if you are acquainted with the history of manufacturing, you'll reduce your chances of falling victim to those who would try to sell you one fad after another—and who, in most instances, are actually marketing some very old ideas under different and more clever names.

Perhaps most important of all, Chapter 2 concludes with a preliminary analysis of why some firms succeed in attaining improved performance while others quickly or ultimately fail to achieve any lasting benefits. Why, for example, has Toyota managed to so successfully implement and exploit its production system while, at the same time, scores upon scores of firms that have tried desperately to emulate Toyota's practices have either failed to do so or have experienced only transient improvement? To answer this question, one must have some familiarity with the history of manufacturing.

Chapter 2, as well as all the chapters that follow, concludes with a case study that deals with the situation at the Muddle Corporation. Will the Muddle Corporation change its ways? Will lean manufacturing be implemented properly, and will it make a significant and lasting difference? Will Marvin Muddle lose weight? Will Sally Swindel change her last name? You'll find out the answer to at least some of these cliff-hangers in the end-of-chapter case studies.

In Chapter 3, certain crucial notation, terminology, and definitions are presented. In addition, two approaches for constructing a factory flowchart (e.g., value-stream process flow and process flowchart) are presented and illustrated. This chapter serves to introduce readers to the important difference between a workstation-centric perspective and a process-step-centric view of a factory. While I can't promise you that this chapter will be a riveting read, the material covered is essential to an understanding of the notions that form a basis for an appreciation of the technical factors that determine factory performance.

Chapter 4 provides you with an opportunity to test out your own theories or intuition with regard to running a factory. You are presented with a simulation model of an exceptionally simple factory and are invited to expend a limited budget for adding machines, improving machine availability, or increasing machine process rates (e.g., run rates). Your goal is to improve a particularly important aspect of factory performance, the average product factory cycle time (i.e., the average time between the introduction of a job into the factory and its exit, in finished form, from the factory). Those of you with some familiarity with the theory of constraints (Goldratt and Cox, 1984; Hitomi, 1996) or lean manufacturing (Arthur, 2007; Bodek, 2004; George, 2002; Hirano and Furuya, 2006; Ignizio, 2008b, 2008c; Levinson, 2002; Liker, 2004; Standard and Davis, 1999; Womack and Jones, 2003; Womack, Jones, and Roos, 1991) may find this chapter to be of particular interest.

About 99.9 percent of those who attempt to improve this factory ultimately will discover that their intuition and what they have been taught may be insufficient, ineffective, or even inappropriate when it comes to dealing with a very typical factory situation. For example, how many readers would believe that you can inadvertently increase overall factory cycle time simply as a consequence of balancing the workload (i.e., the so-called fundamental premise of lean manufacturing) across factory workstations? Or that adding machines and/or increasing their availability can, under certain circumstances, degrade overall factory performance? Or that any effort that focuses on the components of the factory rather than on the factory as a whole may cause more problems than it cures?

Moving on, it is essential to appreciate that there are three fundamental equations and a single fundamental model that together serve to determine factory performance. In informal surveys conducted over the past two decades, I found that fewer than 10 percent of factory engineers or factory managers are familiar with these three equations—and none were aware of the fundamental model. This is not entirely their fault because most university programs do not cover the three fundamental equations, and none, until recently, have taught (or been aware of) the fundamental model.

Unfortunately, a failure to cover these equations and model serves to severely diminish an engineer's or manager's ability to either understand or most cost-effectively solve problems that exist within the factory. Instead of correcting the real source of problems, what is too often done is to focus on the symptoms—leading to an ineffective, counterproductive, and wasteful "Band-Aid approach" to problem solving.

It is odd that while one would never consider hiring a physicist who is unaware of the equation relating force, mass, and acceleration ($f = m \cdot a$) or an electrical engineer who is ignorant of the equation relating voltage, current, and resistance ($V = I \cdot R$), it is standard practice to run a factory without any acquaintance whatsoever with the fundamentals that dictate its performance. As such, it is no wonder that so few factories achieve anywhere near the level of performance of which they are capable.

In Chapter 5, the omission with respect to the three fundamental equations of manufacturing is corrected (in a later chapter, the fundamental model of manufacturing is presented and illustrated). Once this is accomplished, readers will be prepared to reconsider the factory demonstration of Chapter 4. One of the most important matters covered in Chapter 5 is that of the adaptation of the three fundamental equations to a process-step-centric view of the factory.

Chapter 6 provides readers with a second opportunity to improve the performance of the simulated factory of Chapter 4. You will discover that when armed with some appreciation of the three fundamental equations of manufacturing—and by means of exploiting the third dimension of manufacturing—you can improve factory performance at a fraction of the cost (and time) necessary under the conditions set forth in Chapter 4.

Chapter 7 reflects on the findings produced in the factory demonstration model of Chapters 4 and 6. Three important plots of factory performance are introduced and illustrated. These are the factory operating curve, the load-adjusted cycle-time efficiency curve, and the profit versus factory loading curve. These curves provide the three most valuable indications of overall factory performance available. Each curve is illustrated by means of generating it from the factory demonstration models of Chapters 4 and 6.

Chapter 8 deals with the metrics that should be employed to evaluate the performance of a factory—and/or to compare the performances of two or more facilities fairly and objectively. In addition to the three curves covered in Chapter 7, you will be introduced to the Waddington effect plot, the M-ratio (the ratio of scheduled to unscheduled downtime), the availability profile plot, the cycle-time contribution factor, and the degree-of-reentrancy (DoR) metric.

Equally important, metrics commonly used but actually of little or no value—or even counterproductive—will be identified. Among these (and this discussion may be disconcerting to some readers) are such widely employed performance measures as moves, utilization, and inventory turnover (or WIP turns). This material, as well as the three curves presented in Chapter 7, will provide the factory engineer or factory manager—or, in particular, senior management—with useful and valid measures of factory performance.

To quote Lord Kelvin, "If you cannot measure it, you cannot improve it." A restatement of this quote serves to succinctly summarize the purpose of Chapter 8; that is, "If you don't employ a meaningful metric, you not only can't improve factory performance, but you are likely to only worsen it."

Chapter 9 serves to summarize the material presented in the previous eight chapters. More specifically, the scope and limitations of the methods and models that have been introduced are discussed. This allows us to focus our attention on practical, pragmatic, and cost-effective methods for improving factory performance, that is, the material to be presented in the remaining chapters of this book. In short, Chapter 9 permits us to transition from history, concepts, and equations to a straightforward and practical approach to factory performance improvement.

The material in Chapter 10 addresses the matter of the reduction of complexity in the factory. Some of the usual sources of unnecessary complexity (e.g., batching, excessive and/or unnecessary inspection steps, disorganized and cluttered work areas, excessive steps in the conduct of a preventive maintenance or repair event, and unclear and ambiguous specifications) are discussed, and means for reducing complexity are presented and illustrated. As a side benefit, you'll even learn how to properly perform the musket drills used in the Napoleonic War period. As you will discover, effectively firing a musket during the heat of battle involves many of the same protocols necessary to run a factory. You can learn a lot from some odd and seemingly ancient practices.

Chapter 11 addresses the reduction of variability within a factory. Typical sources of variability and their symptoms are discussed. Practical methods for dealing with variability cost-effectively then are introduced and illustrated. The typical obstacles imposed on the introduction of measures for variability reduction are also discussed. Since variability reduction is usually the fastest, cheapest, most effective, and most sustainable means for improving performance, this is a particularly critical topic and chapter.

The guidelines listed in the previous chapters, particularly those of Chapter 10 and 11, are employed in Chapter 12 to deal with a revised version of the 12-workstation factory. Here, your objective will be to maximize profit and reduce factory cycle time. In other words, Chapter 12 serves as a means of both summarizing and illustrating the art and science of manufacturing.

The fundamental model of manufacturing is the subject of Chapter 13. This model allows the factory engineer or manager to compute the capacity of each factory workstation more accurately (even in the face of reentrancy and multiple product types) as well as more precisely predict factory bottlenecks. When the fundamental model is combined with the material of Chapter 11 (i.e., variability), a reasonably accurate estimate of workstation or factory performance is possible. The painful fact is that most factory engineers and managers have no idea as to their facility's true capacity and, as a consequence, cannot determine whether or not they are under- or overloading their factory.

Chapter 14 provides recommendations for the establishment of an effective approach for the implementation of methods for the achievement of significant and sustainable factory performance improvement. The crucial role of management, at all levels up to and including the firm's CEO, is discussed. Of particular importance is the need for management, at every level, to be involved in performance improvement. This chapter continues and elaborates on the discussion initiated in Chapter 2, an analysis of why a few firms (e.g., Toyota) manage to achieve significant and sustainable improvement in factory performance, whereas most others, apparently using the same approach, fail. Among the other topics covered are

- Leaders versus managers
- The selection of factory performance-improvement personnel
- The education and training of factory performance-improvement personnel
- The need for and establishment and role of a "center for factory performance improvement"
- An overview of decisions and actions that can make or break any factory performance-improvement effort
- A list of dos and don'ts

A summary, conclusions, and recommendations form the material covered in Chapter 15, the final chapter of the book. In this chapter, the attributes of the ideal factory are cited, along with a succinct summary of the most promising methods that may be used to strive for that goal. For those who may wonder if the concepts outlined in this book actually work, a brief discussion of a Spanish firm, Inditex, is provided in this chapter. Inditex, an apparel manufacturing firm (its most well-known retail outlet is Zara, a women's clothing store chain), has demonstrated that by overcoming the three enemies of factory (and corporate) performance, you can become the biggest, fastest growing, and most profitable clothing manufacturing firm in the world—without outsourcing production, chasing fads, or having a fixation on cost cutting. Also included in this chapter is the final installment of the case studies involving the Muddle Corporation.

CHAPTER SUMMARY

In this chapter, the three primary enemies of factory (or supply-chain or organizational) performance were identified. These are

- Complexity
- Variability
- Lackluster leadership

It also was noted that significant and sustainable factory performance improvement can only be obtained by means of a proper balance between the art and science of manufacturing—along with an appreciation of the office politics and corporate culture that must be overcome so as to achieve acceptance of any method or methods proposed for improvement. In this book, I address the art and science of manufacturing within the main sections of each chapter. The corporate politics and culture are covered by means of the case studies presented at the conclusions of the chapters. Given an appreciation of all three elements (i.e., politics, art, and science) of manufacturing, the likelihood of success in factory performance-improvement efforts is vastly increased. This, in turn, should lead to the achievement of our primary goal: *greater and sustainable factory performance improvement*.

Again, for the sake of readers who may wish to skip over material dealing with technical details, the recommended reading assignment consists of Chapters 1 and 2, 7 through 12, and 14 and 15. The Muddle case studies are meant, however, to be read sequentially from Chapters 1 through 15.

CASE STUDY 1: LITTLE THINGS MEAN (AND INDICATE) A LOT

With apologies to the songwriters, Edith Lindeman and Carl Stuz, I've made a few revisions to the lyrics of "Little Things Mean a Lot" to fit a typical factory scenario:

Bring me a spare part from across the room
And don't say it's been inspected if it's not
Sign the release form as you pass my desk
Little things mean a lot

The case study to accompany these lyrics may seem too bizarre to be real, but they do say that truth is stranger than fiction. I'll let the reader decide whether or not any real-world firm could have such an extraordinarily poor system for the delivery of parts and supplies to its factory floor or such a dysfunctional culture. Perhaps the most important point made, however, is that deficiencies in even the most seemingly minor aspect of manufacturing may have grave consequences on both performance and morale.

As indicated earlier, the Muddle Corporation has several multi-billion-dollar factories located in sites scattered across the globe—wherever labor is cheap and regulations are loose. The performance of these factories, when compared with Muddle's competitors, is, however, definitely subpar. Marvin Muddle, the firm's reclusive and extremely well-compensated CEO, demands that something be done about this. "No way," warns Marvin in a Webcast to his employees, "is my company content with being second best."

Actually, Marvin exaggerates his firm's standing. The performances of its factories are in reality worst in class. Marvin has "tried everything" to improve the situation, from bringing in high-paid motivational speakers, to holding pep rallies, to instituting challenge goals, to issuing edicts, to embracing every management and manufacturing fad conceivable. Last month he even went so far as to change the firm's logo and slogan—for the fifth time in seven years.

The most recent attempt by Marvin to improve his firm's standing and bottom line has been the adoption of lean manufacturing. Marvin has been informed that lean manufacturing is the hottest and most fashionable management technique since reengineering and business process reengineering.

Ignoring or oblivious to the harmful impact that the latter two concepts had on the firm a few years back, and despite the fact that Marvin hasn't taken the time necessary to actually understand what lean manufacturing is all about and (in particular) what is required for a successful implementation, he issues an edict that states that all of Muddle's middle and lower-level managers must attend Sally Swindel's two-week lean manufacturing training courses (of course, he sees no reason why he or the members of the

MRC should spend their valuable time in such a course) and that lean must and will become the focus of the firm—at least until something better comes along.

Marvin's most recent change in the firm's slogan is *"LEAN Forward."* The change is intended to reflect the firm's new emphasis on lean manufacturing. Despite his edict, change in slogan, change in company logo, and millions of dollars and thousands of personnel hours spent on training in lean, the situation only gets worse.

When, however, one takes a close look at just one (apparently) small part of the operations of Muddle's factories, one reason for the firm's last-place position becomes clearer. Not only is maintenance an afterthought at Muddle, but the role played in dispatching replacement parts and supplies to its multimillion-dollar machines is hardly given any thought.

Let's consider one brief observation of life on the factory floor. We'll limit our focus to a few hours of the trials and tribulations of Dan Ryan, a recently hired day-shift factory floor supervisor. Dan is responsible for operation of the machines in a single workstation (workstation 107) within one of Muddle's largest and most important factories, designated by the firm as "Factory 7." Unfortunately for Muddle and its shareholders, it is also the firm's poorest performing factory in terms of such matters as getting the product to the customer on time and the predictability of product lead time.

Today, two of the dozen or so (complex and extremely expensive) machines in Dan's workstation suddenly and without warning break down. Dan's of the opinion that the frequency and magnitude of the unscheduled downtimes of the machines in his workstation have something to do with the way in which preventive maintenance (PM) events are performed. Following his review of some of the major PM event documents for his machines, he's not convinced that the PM specifications are written properly.

Dan is even beginning to believe that the misconduct of PM events is causing the majority of the unscheduled downtimes, more so than any shortcomings in the design or operation of the machines themselves. Last week, Dan even complained, to no avail, to his department head about the ambiguity and lack of clarity of the PM specifications.

That meeting didn't go well. Donna Garcia, Factory 7's assertive factory floor operations department head, advised Dan to shut up and just follow the darn specifications. After all, she hissed, the same PM specifications are being used across all of Muddle's factories. This is part of a program designated "NO DEVIATIONS" (i.e., based on a belief that every factory should follow precisely the same factory layout, selection of machines, policies, procedures, and processes). Donna emphasized that the effort required to obtain approval for even the slightest change in any specification would be enormous and generate some mighty unfavorable feedback from William "Wild Bill" Barlow, Muddle's director of manufacturing. And the possibility of everyone in every factory reaching a consensus on a specification change was nigh on to impossible. Furthermore, with Wild Bill's latest edict on cost cutting, there would be zero chance of spending any funds on the improvement of PM specifications.

"Besides," Donna added, "I've been out of the office for a two-week training course on lean manufacturing, and tons of work have piled up during my absence. Do run along, Danny Boy, I'm already late for Muddle's refresher course on employee motivation. So, case closed; get back to your workstation."

But let's get back to Dan's immediate problem. Two of his machines have broken down, and the impact of those failures will soon be felt across the factory—and firm. Dan and his crew quickly identify the failed parts in each machine. Repairs can be made if Dan is able to acquire two screws for one machine and a vacuum pump for the other. Dan's sure those parts must be on hand—somewhere in the bowels of one of the two parts and supply warehouses that serve the factory.

Dan hurries to the computer terminal that supports his workstation. A few agonizing minutes later, the parts and supplies order software package, code named *Broken Arrow*, is finally up and apparently running. Dan initiates a search for the vacuum pump by typing in "vacuum pump" in the program's search engine.

But nothing happens!

Sorry, change that to nothing happens except that Dan is unceremoniously kicked out of the *Broken Arrow* program. Three more times Dan tries to run a search on "vacuum pump," and three more times he fails. Perhaps, thinks Dan, I should be typing in "vacuum pumps." But this too results in a string of time-consuming failures.

Brad Simmons, one of Dan's coworkers and the factory floor supervisor for the adjacent workstation, has been observing Dan's desperate attempts to place an order and the even more desperate look on the poor man's face. "Dan, old boy," says Brad, "what's the problem?"

Dan, sweating profusely, explains his predicament. "Brad, what the heck is wrong? I know how to spell 'vacuum pump,' yet every time I type in those words, I get kicked out of *Broken Arrow* and have to bring the program up again. The same thing happens when I type in 'vacuum pumps.' Am I losing my mind?"

"No," says Brad, "you aren't losing your mind, old boy, and you're definitely using the correct spelling. The problem is that the sad little lunatics who created *Broken Arrow* may have been fair to decent programmers, but they weren't all that hot at spelling. If you want to search for vacuum pump, you'll need to type in 'vacum pump'! That's v-a-c-u-m. Just type in one 'u' instead of two."

Dan shakes his head and types in "vacum pump" rather than "vacuum pump." Sure enough, just as Brad promised, he is taken to the portion of *Broken Arrow*'s database that stores information on the availability of the various vacuum pumps used by the factory's machines. He manages to locate the particular one he needs and types in the order—despite the program's incessant demands for unnecessary and redundant entries (e.g., he has to type his work-station location in five different places on the order form, his employee identification number in three other slots, and then complete a survey to determine his satisfaction with the process).

Finished with the vacuum pump order, Dan is ready to search for the specialty screws needed for repair of the other failed machine. After a few unsuccessful attempts, he discovers that he can't just change the search word and hit the ENTER key. Instead, he has to close *Broken Arrow,* reopen the program, wait a few minutes for the start screen to appear, and then begin the entire search process over.

Dan types "Type 107X" screws in the search menu. This brings up what should be a photograph of the screws—a means to visually check the screw type shown on the screen with the one that is needed. Instead of showing the screws, however, the photo that appears is of a paper bag. A handwritten note on the bag reads, "Type 107X screws." Shaking his head, Dan can only assume that the team who designed *Broken Arrow* had taken a photo of a bag containing the screws rather than of the screws themselves.

Growing ever more frustrated, Dan places a request for 10 Type 107X screws. Even though he has been on the factory floor just a few weeks, he has learned to always request more of anything than is actually needed. If he just orders two screws, he reasons, the maintenance tech might lose, misplace, or strip the threads on one or two. And if he ever needs the miserable Type

107X screws again, he can hide the excess in one of his technicians' tool boxes and avoid the need to order them via *Broken Arrow.*

Pressing the ENTER key, Dan is dismayed to discover that the screen reads, "REQUIRED ITEM NOT AVAILABLE." Dan's cursing and frantic hand waving attract the attention of Brad, who hurries over to see if he can help.

"Brad, *Broken Arrow* is telling me that there aren't any Type 107X screws in-house for the repair of Machine 107. We can't get Machine 107 up and running until we get those screws from the vendor, and that could take a day or more. Is it really possible that there are none of those screws in stock? It's my understanding that they are constantly failing. I thought we had tons of those screws."

"Sorry, Dan, someone must have forgotten to tell you about another quirk of *Broken Arrow.* You can't just type in "10" for the number of screws. Some screws come in packages of two, six, a dozen, or some other number. I'm guessing that Type 107X screws simply don't come in packages of 10."

"Good grief," Dan replies, "so how do I order 10 screws?"

"You're going to have to try ordering one, two, three, and so on. Sooner or later, the number you enter will—hopefully—coincide with the number in the packaging of Type 107X screws as originally entered in *Broken Arrow*'s database. I know it's crazy, but *Broken Arrow* is, according to management, a 'finalized, tested, tried and true' software support package. Heck, it even won a corporate award. So, if you're thinking about it, I'd forget trying to escalate the issue. Believe me, it will only cause grief. Take it from a guy who knows first hand. Besides, management claims to have saved $200,000 a year by terminating all support for revisions to the program. Welcome to Muddle, Incorporated, old boy. Here, cost savings overrides everything, including common sense."

Dan follows Brad's advice and finally determines that Type 107X screws come in packages of four each. To accomplish an order for the 10 screws, he has to place three separate orders for four screws each. Based on the throbbing in his head, Dan is beginning to wonder if he is experiencing a migraine—or a stroke.

Two hours later, Dan receives a visit from Ben Arnold, the universally despised technical assistant for Factory 7's senior plant manager. Even though Dan has been on the job only a few weeks (having previously endured three agonizing and seemingly point-less weeks of new employee indoctrination), he has heard about Ben—and had hoped and prayed never to meet the man.

Ben, eyes narrowed and a permanent sneer imprinted on his face, informs Dan that his workstation has become the factory con-straint. Jobs are piling up in front of the workstation, and it won't be long until they will have to decommit factory starts. That, Ben advises, is something that simply will not be tolerated. A decom-mit of factory starts is, according to Ben, the absolute worst thing that can happen in a Muddle factory. "Why," Ben demands, his face now just inches from Dan's, "haven't you ordered the replace-ment parts?"

Dan explains his situation and stresses that the parts have been ordered, but he has yet to be paged with a confirmation that the parts are located and available for pickup. "Procedures dic-tate," pleads Dan, pointing to the parts ordering policy promi-nently posted next to the workstation, "that no one is to attempt to retrieve any parts order until they have been paged. The penalty for that offense is immediate termination."

"Idiot," says Ben through clenched teeth, "our pagers only work about half the time on the factory floor. They probably sent you a communication you didn't receive. That happens all the time. So move your butt to the dispatch station and see if the parts are there!"

Dan decides that it may be best not to mention the fact that company policy also dictates that he, as a factory floor supervisor, must not leave his workstation except for lunch breaks, bathroom breaks, training sessions, and scheduled meetings. Instead, he rapidly walks (company policy prohibits running on the factory floor, another cause for immediate termination) to the nearest parts dispatch station, the one to which he had transmitted the parts order.

Reaching the station, Dan is shocked to see that its customer window is closed. A small, handwritten sign is taped to the win-dow. It states that, as a part of the lean manufacturing program and in support of the *LEAN* Forward effort, the station has been "decommissioned," and its staff "redeployed" (the latter term being the firm's code word for being laid off). A ceremony recognizing the lean *kaizen* team that recommended the closing is to be held in the company cafeteria later that day. Attendance is mandatory.

Muttering a particularly inappropriate obscenity, Dan turns on his heel and speed walks to the one remaining dispatch station, located a 20-minute hike from the closed station. Reaching the station, he is relieved to learn that the parts he ordered, some three hours ago, are there. The dispatcher, a crusty old fellow with bad teeth, informs Dan that he had paged him over two hours ago, and it wasn't his responsibility to make sure that the page was received.

Deciding not to argue the point, Dan reaches over the desk to take the box containing the screws and vacuum pump. The dispatcher, displaying the swift reflexes of a wild west gunslinger, moves to block his path.

"No you don't," says the dispatcher, grasping Dan's arm. "Those parts were ordered under the name of John Wilson. The name on your badge is Dan Ryan. We only allow the person who ordered the parts to pick them up. And Pard, you ain't that person!"

"But I'm the floor supervisor who replaced John Wilson. They haven't changed the auto-population program on my computer, the one Wilson used to use. So, naturally, everything I've been sending out has been under the name of John Wilson. Don't you understand? I ordered those parts, and I'm picking them up. This nonsense is impacting factory performance. I'm begging you, please, just give me the parts."

"Sorry, Pard, that would be a serious violation of company policy. You need to escalate this matter to the senior plant manager. If he says you can have the parts, then they're yours. Otherwise, they stay right here. And by the way, the escalation procedure takes—on average—about a week. Good luck, Pard."

We'll conclude this case study with a brief discussion and a few observations. The situation Dan Ryan experienced reflects all three major obstacles to improved factory—or organizational—performance. You may recall that these are (1) lackluster leadership, (2) complexity, and (3) variability.

Muddle's lackluster leadership is reflected in its impact on company politics, specifically the politics characterized by the firm's actual (as opposed to its formal) culture. This culture serves to dissuade any change to the status quo. For example, the "NO DEVIATIONS" program may have been well intended but only places a roadblock in front of any proposal for a change in existing policies, procedures, or processes. Those who have attempted, despite this obstacle, to propose changes have been branded as heretics and accused of trying to "rock the boat." The message transmitted to all Muddle personnel is to live with "NO DEVIA-TIONS" rather than stick one's neck out. This "shoot the messenger" attitude permeates the firm and cripples its effectiveness.

Marvin Muddle confides in and takes advice from a small, closed circle of subordinates. Jealous of their position and influence, these individuals—members of the firm's Management Review Committee—do everything possible to shelter Marvin from any complaints or criticism (constructive or not) from the firm's employees and lower-level managers. Thus, even though the "NO DEVIATIONS" program has seriously degraded both factory performance and morale, word of this is kept from Marvin.

Real-world illustrations of this type of behavior have been exhibited by the manner in which bad news was kept from such infamous "CEOs" as Saddam Hussein, Adolf Hitler, and Joseph Stalin. The subordinates of those men quickly learned that even if it required lies and deception, any revelations of bad news to their leader just might result in worse news for them. The members of Muddle's MRC, as well as most of those in a management position at the firm, would rather run their tongue through a paper shredder than mention anything that might conflict with the comfortable and limited view of the world held by Marvin Muddle.

Further evidence of the negative impact of the firm's lackluster leadership, although not explicitly cited in the case study, exists in the atmosphere of fear and intimidation that permeates the entire company. Proclamations such as the "NO DEVIATIONS" program and *"LEAN* Forward" slogan only motivate the firm's managers and employees to cut costs—even when such cost cutting actually results in significantly degraded factory performance (as in the instance of closure of the dispatch station and the redeployment of its personnel). However, when a firm's managers are only interested in reducing the expenditures that appear on their accounting sheets, and ignore the hidden costs of inefficient operations (and the subsequent reduction in a firm's profit and share of market), cost reductions will be rewarded, whatever the true consequences.

Lackluster leadership and the company politics engendered also play a role in the metrics employed by Marvin Muddle and his Management Review Committee. Marvin and the MRC are presented each week with charts and plots that allegedly indicate the performance of each factory in the firm. Those plots focus mainly on costs per unit of product produced, factory floor personnel utilization, machine utilization, factory starts, and factory cycle time. They are also used (again, allegedly) to compare the performance of Muddle's factories. A few of the firm's more courageous senior engineers have sent e-mails to Marvin noting that none of these plots or metrics are useful and, in fact, that they present a flawed and misleading picture of performance. Since, however, all e-mail to Marvin is routed through his technical assistant, those concerns never reach the CEO.

Another aspect of the impact of the company politics that result as a consequence of poor leadership may be observed by Donna Garcia's (Factory 7's factory floor operations department head) reaction to Dan's recommendation to improve PM specifications. Donna has recognized that a particularly effective road to promotion and salary increases at Muddle is to simply fill her outlook calendar with as many meetings as humanly possible—not a hard thing to do with a firm afflicted with "obsessive-compulsive meeting disorder" (OCMD). Donna's discovered that the thankless task of dealing with problems on the factory floor just gets in the way of attending meetings.

Next, let's examine the issue of complexity. The unnecessary extent and degree of complexity imposed on Dan and his coworkers simply for ordering spare parts should be evident in the story. Not only are the policies, procedures, and processes overly and unnecessarily complex, there is no clear picture of if and when they can be ignored. The "NO DEVIATIONS" program is but one example of unnecessary complexity—and inflexibility. While on the surface the program may appear reasonable to higher management, such dictates add many additional—and complex and unnecessary—impediments to the acceptance and implementation of methods that provide for improved efficiency.

At Muddle, as well as at many real-world firms, thousands of good ideas are never put forward simply because of the red tape required for their recommendation. To make matters worse, the practice of rewarding bad ideas (e.g., the recognition being given to the lean *kaizen* group that recommended closing down the spare parts dispatch station in the Muddle factory) is all too prevalent.

Another example of unnecessary complexity is evident in the problems involved in using the *Broken Arrow* parts and supplies ordering system. That system took years and many millions of dollars to develop (even though a far better off-the-shelf program could have been purchased for a fraction of the cost from an outside vendor). The *Broken Arrow* effort was initiated by means of a slick marketing program introduced by Muddle's senior vice president for automation and information technology. He promised that automation, in any aspect of factory procedures, always would lead to reduced costs of operation. *Broken Arrow,* he assured Muddle's MRC, would enable the firm to eliminate the "primitive" job positions of parts and supplies runners. (The runners had been used, prior to *Broken Arrow* and their "redeployment," to dispatch orders from the parts and supplies warehouses directly to the factory floor supervisors. On receipt of the parts or supplies that had been ordered, a runner would deliver them to the appropriate factory floor supervisor. Many of the runners were even capable of assisting in the repair or PM event. Primitive, perhaps, but extremely efficient.)

When the "primitive" runner system was in effect, the average time between requesting and receiving a spare part for an unscheduled machine down event was on the order of 30 minutes. After the introduction of *Broken Arrow,* that time skyrocketed to three or four hours and often more. Even worse, the variability about the wait-for-spares times increased dramatically, resulting in decreased machine availability and increased factory cycle time.

Just one more example of unnecessary complexity will be mentioned. This source of complexity exists within the PM specifications employed by Muddle. These specifications were provided by the machine vendors to Muddle on delivery of the machines. The unspoken intention was that they be used during the first few months of the machines' operation and then revised to adapt to actual factory conditions. The cost-cutting obsession at Muddle serves to ignore that fact. Revising a PM specification takes, after all, time and resources. As a consequence, the specifications are seldom, if ever, changed (any changes, by the way, require numerous approvals and a degree of red tape seldom seen anywhere outside a government agency).

The result is that the PM specifications delivered by the vendor, no matter how poorly written and ambiguous, are accepted as the "best known method" for conducting the PM—even when many of the steps involved are unnecessary and even (and often) serve to cause unscheduled machine down events.

The induction of unscheduled machine down events by unnecessary PMs is, in fact, the reason for the need for replacement of the Type 107X screws cited in the case study. It so happens that PM events are being conducted too frequently. This, in turn, results in the subsequent stripping of the threads on the screws—and the unscheduled downtime required to replace the screws.

Let's turn our attention to evidence of excessive variability indicated by the case study. Look closely and you'll find that this brief case study is replete with examples of excessive variability. There are, for example, clear indications of excessive human-induced variability at the CEO level. Marvin Muddle has changed the firm's logo and slogans five times in seven years. The message transmitted to his employees, as well as to any sharp-eyed business analyst, is that Marvin is indecisive and grasping for straws. A CEO or manager who is indecisive and vacillates between the emphasis of one goal over another—or who frequently changes the metric or metrics by which the firm or factory is measured—is a source of excessive and damaging variability. The practice of flip-flopping—in politics or in business—ultimately leads to a condition known as *decision paralysis* (i.e., the fear of making any decision) among all levels of the workforce.

Another example of variability is the random adherence to company policies. As we noted, even though company policy stated that Dan should not attempt to retrieve an ordered part until after the receipt of a page, the senior plant manager's technical assistant demanded that Dan ignore that dictate, as well as ignore the written policy that floor supervisors should not leave their workstations for other than lunch, training sessions, meetings, and short biobreaks.

When a firm announces that the violation of a policy is enforceable by termination or other serious consequences and then allows (or encourages) infringements to happen, variability and confusion reign supreme. One of the prime written directives of Muddle is to "encourage and embrace change and always challenge the status quo." Any employee naive enough to believe this could receive an unpleasant surprise.

Roughly a third of the time the person proposing any recommendation for a change or a challenge of the status quo will be reprimanded or even punished (as a consequence of the "shoot the messenger" culture) for "rocking the boat." Another third of the time the individual's manager will take credit for the proposal. The final third of the time the recommendation simply will be ignored. The latter response, it should be noted, is possibly the most insulting and demoralizing of all.

The final illustration of variability that will be discussed is one that is—like most variability—not visible to the untrained eye. The practices inherent in Muddle's flawed parts ordering process lead to increased downtime, increased wait for spare parts, and a subsequent increase in the variability of maintenance and repair times. As you will learn in later chapters, the variability induced by the existing parts ordering and delivery practice (and limitations of *Broken Arrow*) serves to increase factory cycle time and uncertainty in job completion dramatically.

By the way, in a situation somewhat similar to the fictional one described in this case study, it was proven (via a detailed simulation model of the factory in question) that overall factory performance could be improved significantly by adding more dispatch stations (rather than closing any) and using the "primitive" runner system. I'll leave it to readers to guess whether or not management accepted that recommendation.

CHAPTER 1 EXERCISES

1. The spare parts ordering process that Dan Ryan has to go through is obviously flawed. Discuss the following matters:
   - Why do you believe the process has been tolerated rather than changed?
   - What revised process (in general, brief terms) would you propose to improve the process?
   - How would you measure any improvement in the revised process—and objectively compare it with the original method?
2. It is the author's observation that high-tech manufacturing firms (e.g., semiconductor manufacturers, solar cell manufacturers, etc.) actually have more primitive and less effective manufacturing protocols than many lower-tech companies (e.g., producers of incandescent light bulbs, manufacturers of crown molding, etc.). Assuming that this is true, what would your explanation be as to why?
3. List the problematic features of the Muddle culture that were identified in the case study. Discuss how these may have originated and why they haven't been addressed.

CHAPTER 2

History—and Implications

DON'T KNOW OR CARE MUCH ABOUT HISTORY?

Some of the remarks I often must endure whenever I begin any discussion of the history of manufacturing in either my university classes or training courses include

- "Let's just get to the meat of things!"
- "Who cares about history? I just want to learn how to improve factory performance!"
- "How long is this going to take?"
- "Gee whiz, Doc! We all know that the Toyota Company invented manufacturing; we're not stupid."
- "Why don't we just copy Toyota's methods and cut to the chase?"

So how does one respond to such complaints? To answer this question, it is necessary to understand why such questions are asked. One reason, I believe, is an almost frenzied desire on the part of some individuals to be provided with a quick and easy solution to their current problem. They have a problem, and they want an "answer" ASAP. It's as simple to them as that. Any discussion other than that which will solve their problem *du jour* immediately is considered irrelevant. Another—even more troubling—reason is that some people simply do not appreciate how a discussion of the history of manufacturing, no matter how brief, could be of any conceivable value to them.

My response to such individuals consists of two parts. The first part addresses the current interest in the Toyota production system, a.k.a. *lean manufacturing*. At the time this book is being written, lean manufacturing is being touted as the answer to improved factory performance (as well as improved health care, accounting, etc.). Tutorials and presentations on lean manufacturing now dominate most conferences held by professional societies having anything to do with manufacturing—much like reengineering tutorials and presentations did a decade or so ago.

The efficiency and effectiveness of the Toyota Company, however, cannot and should not be ignored or underestimated. Toyota became so superior in terms of profit per car, customer satisfaction, product reliability, and almost any other ingredient leading to dominance in an industry that it is now the role model other firms desperately hope to emulate. Such firms typically do so by copying what they see (e.g., via visits to a Toyota factory) and even employing the same Japanese words and phrases that Toyota uses to describe its methods. But these firms remain blissfully unaware of or simply choose to ignore the equally if not more important aspects of the firm that they don't see.

The result is that most firms that attempt to copy the Toyota production system (i.e., implement lean manufacturing) either fail to attain or are ultimately unable to sustain performance improvement. The failure/disillusionment rate of lean manufacturing has been estimated to range from 70 to 90 percent. In fact, even some of the strongest advocates of the methodology go so far as to claim a 95 percent failure/disillusionment rate. (This is, by the way, very much the same failure rate incurred by the firms that adopted reengineering—the alleged answer to either organizational or factory performance improvement in vogue a decade or so ago.)

However, if you are familiar with the history of manufacturing, there is an answer—or at least a partial answer—to why so few firms are able to implement the Toyota production system successfully, whereas most others ultimately fail in their attempt. The question as to why Toyota has been successful and most other firms have not is addressed later in this chapter. Next, however, allow me to continue my response to those who doubt the need for an introduction to the history of manufacturing.

The second part of my answer to the question of a need for an appreciation of the history of manufacturing is to employ an analogy—one dealing with warfare. I ask the skeptics if they would have faith in a general or admiral who had little or no (real, factual) knowledge of the history of warfare, particularly the history of both the successful and failed strategies and tactics that have been employed in battles. If a person's answer to this question is, "Yes" (i.e., he or she has no problem with relying on a military leader who is ignorant of the history of warfare), then such an individual is probably beyond help.

If, on the other hand, one can comprehend the need for a military leader (and his officer corps) to have an appreciation of the history of military strategy and tactics, then that person should be equally receptive to the belief that it is just as vital for the factory engineer or manager to have an appreciation of the history of the strategies and tactics that have been introduced into the "battle-ground" of the factory. That person should want to know which of these produced successful results and which failed—and, just as important, why.

Despite this argument, I sometimes encounter factory engineers and managers who continue to rely on strategies and tactics that have failed in the past—and who stubbornly resist any argument for change. An ignorance of the history of manufacturing makes you easy prey for the voracious herds of management gurus, management consultants, and motivational speakers who too often want to sell you old ideas under a newer, fancier, and more expensive "wrapper."

Beware, in particular, of consultants and gurus who "dumb down" concepts and methods so as to suggest to factory engineers or managers that performance improvement is possible simply by means of a few clever-sounding rules and guidelines. While certain rules and guidelines are (when understood) useful, they are not sufficient. Management fads and fashions, however, may rely almost totally on slogans, rules, principles, and guidelines while failing to explain the "why" and "how" of their methodology. In a factory, however, that "why" and "how" require an appreciation of the science of manufacturing.

While conducting a survey of management books and articles, I found that more than 50 management fads and fashions have been introduced over the past 50 years.[1] The failure and/or

---

1 A *fad* or *fashion* is a concept (e.g., a diet plan for the obese) that is enthusiastically embraced by a specific group of individuals (e.g., people concerned about their weight) for a relatively short period of time—followed by waning interest. The typical lifetime of a *management* fad ranges from 5 to 10 years, although a small group of "true believers" may never abandon their faith in a given fad. The similarity between the adoption and abandonment of management fads and diet fads is uncanny.

disillusionment rate of these fads and fashions typically ranges from 70 to 90 percent—or more.

In almost every case, these fads and fashions are based on concepts that originated decades or even centuries ago. In many cases, they actually have a kernel of truth. They disappoint, however, mainly because of

- A failure to provide the support necessary for success—particularly the essential support and engagement of top management.
- A failure to appreciate the limitations of the concepts—that is, there are no magic wands that can easily, quickly, and effectively address or solve every problem.
- A failure to appreciate that the majority of the problems induced by years of bad decisions cannot be rectified in just a few days, weeks, or even months.
- A failure to appreciate that it takes far more than a week or two of "training classes" to become an expert in the politics, art, and science of manufacturing.
- A failure to appreciate that you simply cannot turn just anyone into an expert.[2]
- A focus on the symptoms of the problems within the factory rather than an identification and appreciation of their causes.
- An outright misapplication of the concept embraced—that is, failing to use the right people, having the right training, supported by the right methods, on the right problem.

With this background in mind, let's move on to an abbreviated discussion of the history of manufacturing. This history has been divided into three parts: (1) from ancient times up to and including World War II, (2) post–World War II until now, and (3) the present. After completing these sections, you will be better able to intelligently discuss why the Toyota Company has been so successful and most of its imitators have not.

---

2 I continue to be dismayed that so many firms have such a disquieting ability to pick possibly the very worst person or persons to lead their factory performance-improvement efforts. This may be yet another example of how politics and personalities sabotage even the best intentions.

HISTORY UP TO AND INCLUDING WORLD WAR II

While the scope and purpose of this text do not allow for in-depth coverage of each and every development in or influence on the evolution of manufacturing, a few of the more important events will be introduced. In reading this material, you will see clearly that there has been and continues to be—like it or not—a significant influence on manufacturing as a consequence of the needs, nature, and evolution of warfare.

Sun Tzu; the Battle of Thermopylae

In 480 BC, the Greek city-states were faced with an invasion by the Persian emperor Xerxes. The Greeks were vastly outnumbered by Xerxes' forces, but a small and determined band of warriors, some 300 Spartans and several hundred Thespians, attempted to hold them off (a delaying action evidently intended to allow other Greek forces time to regroup) at a choke point at Thermopylae. Outnumbered by at least 10 to 1 (some say 50 or even 100 to 1), the small Greek force, led by King Leonidas of Sparta, kept the enemy at bay for three days and even inflicted enormous casualties on the numerically superior Persian invaders.

During those three days, the forces of Xerxes attempted one frontal assault after another—suffering horrific losses each time. The Persian forces were only able to capture the pass after a local resident betrayed the Greeks and showed the Persians a little-known mountain path (i.e., a way to bypass the choke point on the battlefield) that led to a position behind the troops of Leonidas.

Centuries before the battle of Thermopylae, the importance of choke points (termed *bottlenecks* or *constraints* within the environment of a factory) was well known and documented. For example, *Sun Tzu's Art of War* (Barnes & Noble Classics, 2003), a volume written more than 2,000 years ago, cites the use of choke points in both offensive and defensive situations. Military leaders in relatively more recent times (e.g., Henry V of England, Napoleon, Wellington, Mao Zedong, and the British Admiralty in both World War I and World War II) have been equally aware of the crucial importance of choke points.

The lessons learned with regard to choke points in warfare were carried over into the environment of the factory. For example, the existence of choke points in the Model T factory was recognized and dealt with effectively by Henry Ford's advisors roughly 100 years ago.

The technical aspects of choke points within a factory were addressed in the mid-twentieth century by a number of academicians, including Katsundo Hitomi (Hitomi, 1996). Their papers and books, however, were thought to be written at such an esoteric level of mathematics that they received little attention outside academia.

In the 1980s, the existence and importance of choke points within a manufacturing environment were reintroduced by Eliyahu Goldratt and Jeff Cox (Goldratt and Cox, 1984) in their best-selling book, *The Goal*. Rather than employing the off-putting mathematical treatment of academicians on this subject, Goldratt and Cox provided a simple analogy (i.e., a group of Boy Scouts on a hike) and a set of straightforward steps for the identification and "elevation" of choke points (i.e., factory constraints). As a result of the simplicity of their treatment of bottlenecks, coupled with the employment of a simple analogy, a sizable number of factory engineers and managers who had previously overlooked or ignored factory choke points suddenly became true believers in what Goldratt and Cox term the "theory of constraints."[3]

The Arsenal of Venice

One of the most prominent examples of the influence of warfare on manufacturing occurred at the Arsenal of Venice (Wills, 2001). From about the twelfth through the nineteenth century, the most important manufacturing effort of the arsenal was the assembly of ships and cannons, particularly those used for naval warfare.

The Arsenal's most famous warship was the *galea sottile* (a thin or long galley). In addition, the Arsenal produced a variety of other ships, including the *galea grossa* (a large merchant ship).

The first moving assembly line for the production of vehicles (the vehicles being ships in this case) was implemented at the Arsenal of Venice—centuries before the moving automobile assembly lines of Ransom Olds and Henry Ford. Beginning with the keel,

---

3 It must be noted, however, that the choke points in warfare (e.g., mountain passes and narrow ocean passageways) are *fixed*. Their position is both known and constant. In a factory, on the other hand, there are *multiple and migrating* choke points/constraints. Unfortunately, these aspects of the real-world factory are often overlooked or downplayed—resulting in an overly simplistic treatment of factory constraints. More will be said about this in subsequent chapters.

the work in progress (a.k.a. *WIP*) was floated down a canal. At points along the route, warehouses were strategically located, and a specifically trained subset of Arsenal workers would perform a predetermined set of steps of the assembly process. At the end of this moving assembly line, a completely outfitted and manned ship sailed into the Mediterranean, ready for duty. As is the case of the Toyota assembly line of today (and unlike the less flexible assembly line employed for the Model T), a variety of types of ships could be produced at any given time.

Documentation indicates that by the sixteenth century, the art of manufacturing at the Arsenal of Venice had advanced to the point where it was possible to assemble a warship in as little as an hour (e.g., King Henry III of France is said to have witnessed such a feat of moving-assembly-line manufacturing in 1574). The more typical (but still impressive) production rate, however, was on the order of one to three ships a day. When compared with the several months of assembly time required per vessel by shipbuilders in other countries, the Arsenal of Venice's factory performance was a marvel of its time.

The Arsenal is said to have employed as many as 16,000 workers in its heyday, each housed in publicly owned accommodations close to their work. The Arsenal was considered such a miracle of shipbuilding that "industrial tourists" from all over the world visited the site—very much akin to the manner in which wide-eyed modern-day industrial tourists make their pilgrimages to Toyota factories.

Nor did the methods employed by the Arsenal of Venice escape the eyes of the scientists, mathematicians, and engineers of that time. Galileo (who moved to the Venetian Republic in 1592) credits his visits to the Arsenal and discussions with the workers there with the establishment of his two new sciences: the strength of materials (e.g., as required in the construction of ships) and an understanding of accelerated motion (e.g., as exhibited by the cannons built at the Arsenal) (Galileo, 1638).

Even Dante Alighieri, author of the *Divine Comedy* ("Dante's Inferno") mentions the maintenance activities conducted at the Arsenal in his verses. The excerpt from Canto 21 that describes this follows:

As in the Arsenal of the Venetians
Boils in the winter the tenacious pitch
To smear their unsound vessels o'er again,

For sail they cannot; and instead thereof
One makes his vessel new, and one recaulks
The ribs of that which many a voyage has made;

One hammers at the prow, one at the stern,
This one makes oars, and that one cordage twists,
Another mends the mainsail and the mizzen;

Thus, not by fire, but by the art divine,
Was boiling down below there a dense pitch
Which upon every side the bank belimed.

Based on records that survive, it would appear that such methods and concepts as just-in-time manufacturing, modular manufacturing, flexible manufacturing, preventive maintenance, standardized parts, inventory control, waste control, employment of external setups,[4] establishment of worker pensions, and efficient methods for staffing, training, accounting, and production control were employed. The end result of these developments (of what are now considered to be the basis of modern manufacturing) was a moving-assembly-line process that approached the ideal state, that is, a single-unit continuous-flow assembly process. In fact, it was not until Ford's assembly line for the Model T that any other assembly-line factory came close to the efficiency of the Arsenal.

Despite the advances in manufacturing developed at the Arsenal of Venice, these concepts were not transferred to any significant degree to other types of manufacturing. Possibly it was believed that they only applied to shipbuilding. As a consequence of this limited perspective, these concepts, now so vital to efficient modern-day manufacturing, had to be reinvented decades and even centuries later.

Matthew Boulton and the Soho Factory

Skipping ahead several centuries, let's consider the impact that the Englishman, Matthew Boulton (and his business partner, James Watt—whose refinements served to vastly improve the steam engine), had on manufacturing. Boulton was an inventor, a

---

4 Externalized setups consist of the conduct of setup activities that may be performed *while a machine is still running* rather than shutting the machine down (a concept developed independently by Frank Gilbreth and termed *SMED* by the Japanese).

businessman, and—most important—a leader and visionary. In 1765, his most advanced factory was completed.

Boulton's Soho factory was three stories high and included workshops, showrooms, offices, and inventory stores. Boulton even provided accommodation for his employees (Encyclopedia Britannica, 2008; Cooke-Taylor, 1886; Usher, 1920).

The Soho factory was a model of manufacturing efficiency and employed (contrary to the bleak images of more typical factory conditions provided by Charles Dickens) a safe and clean work environment. Boulton employed interchangeable components and a variety of advanced manufacturing methods. Accompanying these technical advances was the use of well-lit, clean, orderly, and properly ventilated facilities, as well as an obsession with regard to the reduction of waste. Boulton went so far as to have the walls of the Soho factory painted a clean, bright white—all the better to quickly identify dirt and clutter or any other form of waste.

Boulton even provided his workers with accident and death benefits. Their contributions of 1/60th of their compensation provided benefits of up to 80 percent of their wages. In addition, and unlike the majority of factory owners of the time, Boulton refused to hire young children.

Boulton and his partner, James Watt, had a major influence on the first industrial revolution. With Boulton's encouragement and assistance, Watt's steam engine was converted from its original vertical movement (e.g., as used to pump water from mines) to a rotary-motion machine. This provided factories with a means to run their machines (e.g., an alternative to the use of water wheels). The steam engine in factories led to the first industrial revolution and the (steam-driven) railroads led to the second.

The American System of Manufacturing

The period from 1800 to 1932 has been designated as the time of the American system of manufacturing (Coman, 1930; Hounshell, 1984). The practices that distinguished this system from those used previously or by other countries were the employment of machine tools and templates (a.k.a. *jigs*)[5] in place of hand-crafted production. The machine tools increased the processing speed of the factory,

---

5 The importance of templates, or jigs, for the achievement of tight tolerances is possibly the least appreciated of the concepts developed for the achievement of mass production.

and the jigs provided the foundation for tighter parts tolerances (which led to the practicality, as opposed to just the theory, of interchangeable parts).

Since parts were interchangeable, it was possible to separate manufacture (e.g., the forming of each individual part of a product) from assembly. The simplified assembly process, in turn, permitted the use of semiskilled (and lower-cost) workers in place of skilled craftsmen.

As with many other advances in manufacturing, the American system came about as a consequence of the needs and funding of the military. America's armories were encouraged to produce muskets with interchangeable parts. While Eli Whitney is erroneously given credit for the development of interchangeable parts, the first practical and successful development of methods for the production of high-precision interchangeable parts (for muskets) was accomplished in 1820 by Captain John H. Hall (Hall served as a contractor to the Armory at Harper's Ferry).[6]

The methods developed in America for the practical and cost-effective introduction of interchangeable parts soon migrated to the factories of that time. Early adopters included firms that produced clocks, sewing machines, bicycles, and woodworking and farm equipment. The most prominent of these adopters was, of course, the Ford Motor Company in the first two decades of the twentieth century (Ford, 1922; Hounshell, 1984; Levinson, 2002).

Scientific Management

Concurrent with the development and refinement of the American system of manufacturing was the advancement of the philosophy, concepts, and methods of scientific management (Alford and Beatty, 1951; Gilbreth, 1909, 1911; Taylor, 1911; Walton, 1986). Some of the pioneers of this field and a very brief sample of the concepts they conceived and introduced are listed in Table 2.1. In the far right-hand side of the table are some alternative words or phrases used to describe some of these notions—words and phrases sometimes

---

6 As noted in the discussion of the Arsenal of Venice, the use of interchangeable parts was evident there, centuries prior to the accomplishment of Captain Hall. Matthew Boulton also employed interchangeable parts in his Soho factory. The assembly of muskets, however, required levels of parts tolerances beyond those employed in the construction of the ships by the Arsenal of Venice or the variety of artifacts (e.g., buttons and toys) manufactured by Boulton.

TABLE 2.1

Scientific Management pioneers and their contributions

Name of Scientific Management Pioneer	Contributions	Alternative Word or Phrase
Frederick Taylor	Scientific management and industrial engineering Preventive Maintenance Time study Piece-rate incentives	Japanese production system Total productive maintenance
Henry Gantt	Graphic aids (Gantt chart) Extensions of Taylor's work	–
Frank Gilbreth	Process step mapping Externalized setups Motion study "Seventeen basic motions"	Value stream maps SMED
A.K. Erlang	Queuing theory and models	–
Walter Shewhart	Continuous improvement PDSA (plan, do, study, act) or PDCA (plan, do, check, act); a.k.a. the "*Shewhart Cycle*" Total quality management Statistical-based quality control Control charts	*Kaizen* Ishikawa circle
Ford Motor Company and American grocery stores (early twentieth century)	Just-in-time manufacturing Fast cycle time	Taiichi Ohno's JIT
Ford Motor Company (early twentieth century)	Error proofing Assembly line signals/alarms Waste walks "Go and see" CANDO (reduction of clutter in the workspace and factory floor) Machines organized according to the sequence of operations Design for manufacturability Sorenson proxy (the assignment of jobs to machines in a given workstation that must support several process steps)	*Poka-Yoke* Andon Muda elimination Genchi Genbutsu 5S or CANDO

employed by those teaching the topic of lean manufacturing (or the Toyota production system).

The last two segments of Table 2.1 list just a few of the many protocols of scientific management either introduced or developed within the Ford Motor Company by Henry Ford's staff. The lessons learned by Ford's people in automobile production ultimately led to the introduction of analogous concepts into the production of military equipment during World War II.

The impact of these methods on wartime manufacturing is something that should not be forgotten by factory engineers or managers. The implementation that received the most attention, particularly in Japan, was the "bomber an hour" effort directed by Charles Sorenson of the Ford Motor Company (Nolan, 1997).

Bomber an Hour

In World War II, the crucial role of aircraft in warfare was finally recognized. The need for aircraft by the Allies, however, far out-stripped existing manufacturing capabilities—at least until techniques originally developed for the manufacture of automobiles were introduced into the assembly lines for aircraft.

One of the most important and effective aircraft of World War II, particularly in the battle against Japan, was the B24 bomber, known as the *Liberator.* At the start of hostilities, the U.S. Army Air Corps had hoped to assemble one B24 a day at the Willow Run factory. In support of this seemingly overly ambitious goal, the assistance of Henry Ford's best and brightest advisors was sought. Charles Sorenson (Ford's production chief) and his team devised a set of manufacturing protocols—based on their success with the rapid assembly of Ford automobiles—that enabled the Willow Run facility to vastly exceed the bomber-a-day goal. Once the bugs were ironed out, the procedure enabled the assembly of a bomber an hour.

Operational Research in World War II

During World War II, the academician C. H. Waddington (a pioneering figure in both operational research and genetic algorithms) maintained a diary that detailed the efforts of an operational research (OR) team in support of the British Air Coastal Command. That command was, in turn, dedicated to the battle against the German U-boat. Waddington's diary was declassified in 1973 and released by Elek Science Publishing under the title, *OR in World War 2: Operational Research Against the U-Boat* (Waddington, 1973).

Waddington's book should be mandatory reading not just for military officers but also for managers, engineers, and scientists of all stripes—including in particular factory managers and engineers. Waddington describes methods employed successfully for the solution of a host of military problems ranging from maintenance to personnel staffing and training to flight assignments to the strategies and tactics employed in actual combat. He also describes the push-back the OR groups received from the military and the political climate that had to be dealt with. Strikingly similar problems—and politics and resistance to change—exist in the factory.

While the scenario (i.e., World War II) may seem like ancient history to some readers, the same problems encountered then are still faced in both the military and industrial sectors of today. Our aircraft may now be jet propelled and our factories might be automated and populated by robots, but the methods employed by OR groups more than six decades ago apply equally well today.

For example, factories that have adopted the methods described in Waddington's journal have experienced improved performance. This has been particularly true in the area of maintenance—one of the most overlooked factors determining factory performance.

Several of the methods described by Waddington will be discussed in detail in subsequent chapters. These include

- *The Waddington effect plot.* This is a means to determine if preventive maintenance events are actually doing more harm than good.

- *Waddington analysis.* A procedure for the development of C^4U-compliant operating or maintenance specifications[7]— and reduction of complexity.

- *Maintenance personnel staffing and training.* The assignment of maintenance personnel to workstations so as to reduce the "wait for tech" time in the factory.

More to the point, Waddington's book illustrates the importance of protocols, the core of the third dimension of manufacturing. This crucial point is made evident in the graph of Figure 2.1

---

7 Recall that C^4U-compliant specifications are those that are "complete, clear, concise, correct, and unambiguous."

FIGURE 2.1

Percent lethality of attacks on U-boats.

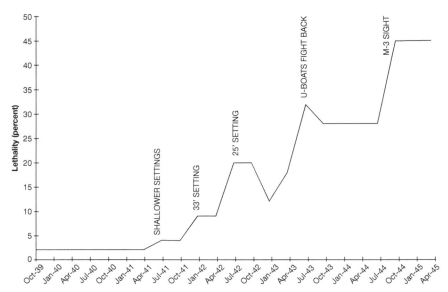

(based on a plot in Waddington's text). Note that the horizontal axis is in years, whereas the vertical axis represents the percent lethality of attacks on U-boats.

Despite the crucial importance of dealing with the German U-boats, the lethality of air attacks (i.e., probability of sinking or severely damaging a U-boat first detected on the surface) was pathetically small during the first two years of World War II. As may be seen in Figure 2.1, the probability of a lethal air attack on a U-boat was only about 1 or 2 percent—and possibly less (i.e., the claims by some pilots may have exaggerated their successes).

The military brass of the British Air Coastal Command believed that the degree of lethality could be improved most effectively by means of predominantly physical changes, specifically changes involving the manufacture of more aircraft and the development and implementation of improved weapon systems. Just like many factory managers of today, they restricted their focus to changes they could see, count, and touch—matters with which they felt most comfortable.

The members of the British OR group supporting the Air Coastal Command proposed, instead, the adoption of a variety of controversial (to the British Admiralty) protocols (i.e., policies and procedures). Possibly the most important of these was the recommendation that the depth charges (known as *sticks*) dropped from its planes be set to explode at a level of 25 feet below the surface as opposed to the much deeper settings (100 to 200 feet) usually used.

The reaction of the British Admiralty was, in a word, contempt. What, after all, could a bunch of silly academicians teach the military about warfare?

In light of the damage inflicted by the German U-boats, however, the Air Coastal Command ultimately and reluctantly agreed to reduce the depth-charge setting. Rather than the 25-foot setting recommended, though, the charges were set to explode at about 50 feet. The impact of this reduced setting is evident in the increase in lethality beginning in the spring of 1941. This success motivated the Air Coastal Command to implement an additional reduction in the setting to about 33 feet in the summer of 1941.

The impact of this decision is also obvious in Figure 2.1. The original 25-foot setting was finally implemented in the summer of 1942—and resulted in yet an additional increase in lethality.

By the conclusion of the war, the probability of a lethal attack on a German U-boat by an Air Coastal Command aircraft was on the order of 40 to 45 percent (the physical and psychological impact of this attrition rate on German U-boat crews is captured in the movie, *Das Boot*). While not all the improvement in lethality was due to changes in operational protocols, the overall impact of protocols in the battle against the U-boat is unmistakable.

In addition to the OR group's recommendations for reduced depth-charge settings, an investigation of aircraft maintenance events and their scheduling was conducted. It was discovered that the preventive maintenance (PM) events themselves were inducing unscheduled downs. Unscheduled downtime, in turn, significantly reduced the number of hours that a plane could be airborne and searching for a U-boat.

Waddington describes both the impact of these problematic PM events and the approach employed (i.e., a change in protocols) to alleviate the situation. The overall result was an increase in the effective size of the Air Coastal Command's air fleet on the order of 60 percent![8]

---

8 Think about what such an increase in the effective capacity of the machines in a factory could provide in terms of factory performance improvement. In other words, instead of spending money on buying more machines, a quicker and far less costly alternative may be to simply reduce unscheduled downtime.

Unfortunately, many of the lessons learned with regard to the use of protocols for performance improvement as developed by the OR group were either forgotten or ignored after World War II. Since these can play a major role in factory performance improvement, some of them will be covered and illustrated in subsequent chapters. Next, however, I briefly discuss an important but overlooked methodology for performance improvement (particularly for sustaining improvement) designated *Training Within Industry.*

Training Within Industry (TWI)

The demand for ships by the Allied forces during World War II was enormous, particularly in light of the damage inflicted on them by German U-boats (a matter discussed previously). The same was true for every other weapon or weapon support system. While America had vast natural resources, its capability for producing these essential items was severely limited as a consequence of inefficient manufacturing practices. In response to the need for improved production performance, a training program, labeled *Training Within Industry* (TWI), was developed.

The TWI program, implemented by means of a straightforward set of lessons, served as a catalyst for significant improvements in factory production within the United States. An illustration of this is captured in the plot provided in Figure 2.2 (War Production Board, Bureau of Training, 1945).

Quite simply, over the period from May 1943 through September 1945, the percentage of American plants reporting increases in production of more than 25 percent rocketed from 37 to 86 percent. Much of this improvement was credited to TWI.

While the reference (War Production Board, Bureau of Training, 1945) fully describes and discusses TWI, the most pertinent point is that TWI was introduced into Japan following World War II. Not only was it introduced there, but it also was eagerly embraced—particularly by the Toyota Company, where it has been credited with forming the "roots of lean manufacturing." Unfortunately and ironically, at almost the same time Toyota adopted TWI, it was virtually abandoned (as well as conveniently forgotten) in the United States.

Manufacturing firms in America saw no need for TWI at the end of the war. Even with inefficient production methods and obsolete factories, they could produce shoddy goods that were eagerly purchased by American consumers. With the rise of a new type of American CEO—focused on short-term results and cost

FIGURE 2.2

Impact of TWI program.

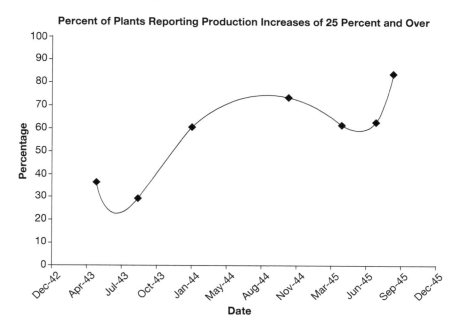

Percent of Plants Reporting Production Increases of 25 Percent and Over

cutting—it was left to the Japanese, particularly the Toyota Company, to adopt and benefit from the TWI lesson plans provided to them by American trainers.

TWI may be considered a missing link between what is termed *lean manufacturing* and its successful and sustainable implementation. The failure to employ or even be aware of TWI might be a key reason for the huge failure rate of lean manufacturing efforts in the United States—and this is yet another illustration of the need to be aware of the history of manufacturing.

HISTORY: POST–WORLD WAR II TO PRESENT

Following World War II, the Japanese economy and industry were in shambles. General Douglas MacArthur, supreme commander of the Allied Powers in Japan from 1945 to 1951, took actions that would forever change both the social structure and manufacturing methods of Japan. One of the most significant of these was to encourage and buttress the rebirth of Japan's manufacturing sector.

In support of MacArthur's goals, the Japanese Union of Scientists and Engineers (JUSE) invited a number of American academicians and consultants to provide educational and training programs in support of the reengineering of Japanese manufacturing. Prominent among these Americans were W. Edwards Deming and Joseph Juran (Walton, 1986), two men who could—and probably should—be called the "fathers of Japanese manufacturing."

In 1950, Deming trained scores of factory engineers and managers in Japan. Among the attendees of Deming's classes were a large number of senior-level managers, including CEOs. Deming remarked that when his classes were offered in the United States, virtually no interest was shown on the part of management. Yet, when offered in Japan, the very same classes attracted Japanese managers at all levels.

Deming's lectures were focused on three primary areas: (1) the employment of Walter Shewhart's PDCA (plan-do-check-act) cycle, (2) an appreciation of the causes of variability, and (3) process control via Shewhart's control charts. At roughly the same time, other Americans were training the Japanese in the methods of TWI.

In 1954, Joseph Juran was invited to lecture the Japanese on management's role in the promotion, support, and implementation of quality control programs. Juran emphasized that managers had the responsibility to lead such efforts (in sharp contrast to most American managers at the time, who took no part—or interest—in leading any type of factory performance-improvement programs). It was emphasized that managers, up to and including the CEO, had to be involved in factory performance improvement—rather than delegate that responsibility to their people.

As a consequence of such lectures and advice, Japanese managers and factory workers became involved in the reincarnation of manufacturing in that country. Henry Ford's book on manufacturing became a Japanese best-seller there (much like books on Japanese management have now become best-sellers in America). There was even a popular weekly radio program that served to train both factory managers and workers in statistics.

In the United States, however, virtually no interest in Deming's and Juran's efforts was exhibited by American management. It was, in fact, not until the unanticipated and unwelcome "invasion" of Japanese automobiles in the 1970s and 1980s that any significant attention was paid to the Japanese production system (Pegals, 1984).

Examining the accomplishments of the Japanese or Toyota production system, readers should note that the foundations of Japanese success rested on the introduction and employment of manufacturing protocols—most of which, ironically, originated in America and were either ignored or abandoned by American management following World War II. Instead, as mentioned, the emphasis of American management was (and, for the most part, still is) focused almost exclusively on cost cutting and short-term performance.

Apollo Manned Moon Landing Program

My own introduction to the importance of protocols came as a consequence of my responsibilities as an engineer and, later, a manager in America's manned moon landing program. The manned moon landing mission required the construction and assembly of an enormous three-stage booster rocket (the Saturn V launch vehicle), the three-person Apollo space capsule, and the Lunar Excursion Module (LEM).

To successfully fulfill President John F. Kennedy's promise to land our astronauts on the moon by the end of the decade (i.e., by 1969), a combination of physical developments (e.g., the design and production of the components of the launch vehicle, spacecraft, and ground support systems) and protocols was required. Ignorant of the methods described in Waddington's book (which was not declassified until 1973), we went about revising, refining, and reinventing protocols for the development and validation of what are now termed C^4U-compliant specifications.

In addition to the development of a methodology for C^4U-compliant specifications, protocols were introduced for

- Optimized deployment of antennas on the vehicles (Ignizio, 1962) [which may be used in a factory to locate workstations and parts and supply centers (Ignizio, 2003a)]
- Complexity reduction in the steps of the launch countdown procedure
- Mitigation of the Waddington effect (e.g., although the term *Waddington effect* was not used at the time, we became aware that many of our well-intentioned maintenance, test, and inspection methods actually caused more problems than they solved)

- Improved methods for both the scheduling and declustering of events

While there is little, if any, mention of such protocols in the articles and books on the history of the Saturn/Apollo program, I can assure you that they played a significant role in its success. More important to this text, however, is the fact that lessons learned in that effort are directly transferable to factory performance improvement—as will be illustrated in chapters to follow.

THE PRESENT: LEAN MANUFACTURING

Over the past 50 or so years, numerous concepts (e.g., reengineering, quality circles, total quality management, total productive maintenance, Six Sigma, zero defects, management by objectives, management by walking around, etc.) have been proposed for the improvement of factories and entire organizations and industries. Some of these have shown promise, whereas others have been relegated to the dustbin of history. Lean manufacturing, one of the most recent methodologies (at least in terms of interest), has exhibited—*when employed by the right people, in the right manner, to the right problem*—the potential to fulfill the promises of its advocates. Despite this, lean manufacturing's failure and disillusionment rate, as mentioned, has been extraordinarily high. The primary reason for the 70 to 90 percent failure/disillusionment rate has been mainly due to three problems: (1) the lack of support and involvement by management, (2) the failure to balance the rules and guidelines of lean manufacturing with the science of manufacturing, and (3) employment by the wrong people in the wrong manner on the wrong problem.

One artifact of lean manufacturing that has seemed to have a significant and positive impact on at least some factory managers and engineers has been the citation of the so-called seven wastes (Liker, 2004). This listing, by itself, has made many people more aware of the impact of certain behaviors on factory performance. The seven wastes are

- *Overproduction.* Producing items for which there are no orders or market.
- *Waiting.* Waiting for batches to form or waiting for spare parts.
- *Unnecessary transport.* Excessive transit time and unnecessarily long transport paths.

- *Overprocessing or improper processing.* Employing unnecessary operations (steps) in the processing of jobs or using inefficient processes.
- *Excessive inventory.* Excess raw materials or using inventory as a buffer to mitigate inefficient factory protocols.
- *Unnecessary movement.* Wasted motion or excessive walking.
- *Defects.* Producing an excessive number of defective parts and the possible scrapping of the defects or the corresponding need to correct those defects.

While all of the seven wastes were pointed out previously by the pioneers of scientific management, Toyota compiled these and brought them to the attention of a much more receptive audience. To these seven wastes, I would add five more:

- *Wasted opportunities.* The opportunities to reduce factory cycle time are, in any firm, enormous. Unfortunately, the enormous benefits of fast cycle time are often ignored.
- *Time wasted in meetings.* Anywhere from 50 to 70 percent of the time spent in meetings is wasted. This is particularly true when the meetings are used as a means for some of the attendees simply to gain "face time."
- *Time wasted chasing fads.* Instead of expending time, energy, and resources on every management or manufacturing fad that happens to be in the news, first perform a rigorous assessment of the validity of these notions.
- *Suboptimization.* Suboptimization (e.g., a focus on the attainment of optimal performance at one workstation in the production line while ignoring the impact on the entire factory) is a major source of waste. Rewarding efforts that only serve to suboptimize amplify their negative impact.
- *The waste of human creativity.* The most serious waste of all is that of human creativity, that is, ignoring the concepts, ideas, and enthusiasm of your best and brightest employees.

I might even add a thirteenth waste, that of ignoring the lessons of history. Why, for example, has Toyota been so successful, whereas the bulk of its imitators have not? This question will be dealt with in a later section. First, however, let's discuss a recent concept that is often associated with lean manufacturing—the Six Sigma process.

SIX SIGMA

At this point in time (i.e., 2009), the two approaches receiving the biggest buzz in the manufacturing sector are lean manufacturing and Six Sigma (and a combination known as *Lean Six Sigma*). The preceding section has dealt with lean manufacturing. Here, I provide a brief description and assessment of Six Sigma.

A Google search produced the following definitions of Six Sigma:

- "A method or set of techniques . . . focused on business process improvement."
- ". . . a failure rate of 3.4 parts per million, or 99.9997 percent."
- "A systematic method for improving the operational performance of an organization by eliminating variability and waste."
- "A quality management and process improvement methodology particularly well suited to process-intensive industries like manufacturing."
- "An invention of Motorola in the 1980s . . . ."
- ". . . a management philosophy developed by Motorola that emphasizes setting extremely high objectives, collecting data, and analyzing results to a fine degree as a way to reduce defects."

Other than the fact that Six Sigma cites a very specific goal (3.4 parts per million) for failure rate and its practice of assigning belts of various colors to it advocates, one would be hard pressed to distinguish the concept and its tools from those of the fields of either operations research or industrial engineering. Joseph Juran, one of the handful of people responsible for the rebirth of Japanese manufacturing, stated that "there is nothing new here" when referring to Six Sigma. He went on to say that "they've adopted more flamboyant terms, like belts with different colors" (Paton, 2002).

While, as is the case with lean manufacturing, there is nothing fundamentally wrong with Six Sigma—when applied by the right people to the right problem in the right manner—its early hype has been subdued by recognition that it is not necessarily the answer. This is particularly true when it is implemented by those seeking a quick and easy fix. An article in *Industrial Engineering* (Del Angel and Pritchard, 2008) discusses "the rising concern across industry sectors regarding the failure of many Six Sigma and Lean projects."

A couple of quotes from that article follow:

- "Nearly 60 percent of all corporate Six Sigma initiatives fail to yield desired results."
- ". . . many corporations are pulling back on specific change initiatives realizing that the Six Sigma methodology by itself is not the cure-all for corporate ills."

The authors recommend, as a means to avoid this high failure rate, the use of a "behavior-focused approach."

Unfortunately, the typical approaches employed in the implementation of Six Sigma lead, as noted by Del Angel and Pritchard, to a 60 percent failure rate—close to the 70 percent failure rate of lean manufacturing. Returning, however, to our earlier discussion; why is it that Toyota evidently has managed to avoid this failure rate and disappointment? What exactly is Toyota doing right and its imitators doing wrong? I return to this important matter in the following section.

A QUESTION: WHY TOYOTA?

The preceding discussion indicates that much of what is considered new and original with regard to approaches (particularly protocols) to factory performance improvement is actually just a reinvention or refinement—or renaming—of methods that originated decades or even centuries ago. This should not be surprising. Perhaps it is true that "there is nothing new under the sun."

What is surprising, however, is the fact that so few manufacturing firms have been able to adapt these methods—under whatever name—to achieve significant and (particularly) sustainable improvement in the manufacturing process. In fact, apparently only the Arsenal of Venice (for several centuries), Toyota (for about a half century), and Ford (for less than three decades) have been able to achieve truly noteworthy factory performance improvement over any significant period of time.

Even the Ford Motor Company, where many of the concepts now credited to the Toyota production system or lean manufacturing were developed, was able to sustain its heralded production system for Model T assembly for only a few decades. A host of companies in the United States and elsewhere have recently—or relatively recently—adopted (or claimed to have adopted) the Toyota production system/lean manufacturing, but the jury is out as to whether or not they can sustain, for any appreciable length of time, any real or alleged improvements provided by their implementation of that system. In fact, as has been noted, the failure/disillusionment rate for lean manufacturing is estimated to be in the range of 70 to 90 percent—a failure rate eerily similar to that of earlier performance-improvement attempts such as reengineering, total quality management, management by objectives, and quality circles.

In the introduction to this chapter I stated that an appreciation of the history of manufacturing may provide answers—or at the least some understanding—as to why Toyota has been so successful, whereas the vast majority of firms that seek to copy its approach fail to see significant and, in particular, sustained factory performance improvement. Let's now address, in a preliminary form, this issue.

Consider first those factors that enabled the Arsenal of Venice and Ford and now permit the Toyota Company to achieve their success. The most prominent among these are

- Leadership and vision
- A long-term perspective accompanied by the decision making necessary to support that perspective
- The support and involvement of top management, up to and including the CEO
- The establishment of and adherence to meaningful and realistic goals
- A willingness to listen—even to proposals that may happen to be critical of the existing culture and its protocols
- The support of a society that values and promotes real education, particularly in mathematics and science
- A continuing education in the art and science of manufacturing (i.e., rather than expecting a few weeks of training to turn just anyone into an expert)
- A recognition of the need to change coupled with the will to change
- A recognition that it may take years to see any significant and sustainable improvement—and that the journey to improved performance must never end
- The appointment of performance-improvement team leaders who are the firm's best and brightest—and the avoidance of political appointments
- Allowing the appointment of performance-improvement team members to be selected by the team leaders (see previous bullet)

- An appreciation of the history of manufacturing and a knowledge of what has worked . . . and what has not
- Patience and perseverance
- An emphasis on speed (i.e., fast cycle time)

A more detailed recipe for success in factory performance improvement is provided in Chapter 14. Next, however, the importance of fast factory cycle time is discussed.

THE NEED FOR SPEED

Pausing for a moment, consider one essential point—a point too often overlooked by today's factory engineers, managers, and owners. Whether it is the assembly of ships at the Arsenal of Venice, the manufacture of Model T's at the Ford Motor Company, the production of B24 bombers at Willow Run, the assembly of automobiles at the Toyota Company, or the fabrication of computer chips in the semiconductor industry, there is—or should be—one particular goal in common. That goal is *speed.* The focus on speed (i.e., fast factory cycle time) was—and is—paramount to success (Clason, 2003; Meyer, 1993).

Fast factory cycle time enabled Henry Ford to pay his workers more than twice the wages of his competitors and still capture the majority of the market for automobiles. Fast factory cycle time provided the Arsenal of Venice with the foundation necessary to maintain its position as a powerful city-state for centuries. Fast cycle time wins wars. Fast factory (and supply-chain) cycle time is the foundation on which the success of the Toyota Company has been achieved. The benefits of fast factory cycle time include

- Decreased levels of inventory (and reduced inventory holding costs)
- Decreased time to market (and increased net present value)
- Increased opportunities (e.g., freeing funds tied up in inventory)
- The fact that excursions may be identified and corrected in less time
- Increased knowledge turns
- Increased opportunities to run or expedite priority jobs
- Increased yield—or the ability to run cost-effectively with decreased yields
- Increased burst capacity

- Opportunity to trade off increased velocity for increased capacity
- Increased flexibility (e.g., the ability to change production policies faster and with quicker results)
- Opportunity to establish a disciplined and accountable approach to manufacturing
- Increased customer satisfaction—and a subsequent increase in market share

The fact is that in any competitive situation, only the fast and agile will survive and prosper.

Achievement of the goal of fast factory cycle time can be accomplished only if the factory, its organization, personnel, business processes, and manufacturing protocols are all efficient and effective. Of course, fast factory cycle time must deliver products of high (but not unnecessarily high) quality. [A recent example of how firms can achieve unnecessarily high quality was made evident in a report entitled, "Japanese Computer Chips Made at Too High Quality to be Competitive on World Market." Any reader not convinced that you can overdo an emphasis on quality is invited to read this report (TECHNEWS, 2006).] Thus, in this discussion, it is assumed that achievement of a sufficient level of quality (or level of defects or yield) is a given.

Fast factory cycle time requires the identification and reduction of both visible and hidden waste throughout the entire system. Traditional methods for factory performance improvement, including the bulk of the methods encompassed within lean manufacturing, focus primarily on visible waste (e.g., clutter on the factory floor, unnecessary motion, excessive inventory, and disorganized work areas).

As we shall see, however, it is equally if not more important to develop methods that deal with the hidden waste within a factory. This hidden waste is almost always due to the employment of inferior protocols (e.g., inefficient protocols employed for factory starts, the clustering of starts, the clustering of preventive maintenance events, inappropriate run rules, improper batch sizes, etc.).

The importance of identification and reduction of hidden waste is illustrated by the cycle-time components plot of Figure 2.3. This plot was developed for an actual factory prior to the introduction of improved protocols. The numbers above each block (e.g., "8.4" for "Processing") indicate the average number of days that an average job spends in a given state.

FIGURE 2.3

Components of factory cycle time.

8.4	5.6	20.3	35.7

Processing	Moves & Inspection	Batch Forming	Queue Time

For example, the average time a job spends in transit ("moves") and inspection is 5.6 days. Adding up the numbers in Figure 2.3, we find that the average factory cycle time for this facility is 70 days (i.e., 8.4 + 5.6 + 20.3 + 35.7). This happened to be about twice the cycle time of one of the firm's competitors.

Certain physical limitations (e.g., machine process rates and AMHS [Automated Material Handling System] speed) and quality requirements determine the amount of time spent in processing, moves, and inspection (i.e., for a total of 14 days, on average, per job for the factory of Figure 2.3). The bulk of factory cycle time, however, is consumed by batch forming [i.e., the time required to form a batch of jobs in front of each batching machine (Hopp and Spearman, 2001; Khade and Ignizio, 1990; Sato, Ignizio, and Ham, 1978)] and queue time (i.e., the average time that jobs or batches simply must sit and wait in the queues formed in front of workstations). To be more precise, the two most significant contributors to factory cycle time (i.e., batch forming and queue time) are a consequence primarily of the protocols employed in the running of the factory.

The most important message imparted by Figure 2.3 is that the biggest lever in the reduction of factory cycle time is that of the reduction of batch forming and—*in particular*—queue time. Factory managers who dwell only in the first two dimensions of manufacturing, however, most likely will limit improvement efforts to the reduction of process time, transit time, and possibly inspection time.

Unless you have an effective means to identify and reduce hidden waste, the more traditional methods of factory performance improvement will produce only limited results. This is so because traditional approaches (including lean manufacturing, or the Toyota production system) rely primarily on art and experience and involve only a limited degree of science.

Figure 2.4 depicts the cycle-time components of the same factory illustrated in Figure 2.3. The 70 days of factory cycle time have been reduced to 24.5 days. This was accomplished by means of a combination of the methods to be described in subsequent chapters. The time required to achieve this improvement (which has been sustained for more than five years) was approximately 15 months.

When one realizes that the reduction of just a single day of factory cycle time in certain industries (e.g., semiconductor wafer fabrication) can result in millions of dollars of increase in the firm's bottom line, the need for fast cycle times becomes or should become even clearer. Improvement in factory cycle time is best achieved by combining the best features of the art of manufacturing with the science of manufacturing while maintaining, at all times, an awareness of the political environment.

CHAPTER SUMMARY: THE PATH FROM ART TO SCIENCE

This chapter has presented a very brief summary of the history of manufacturing. Taking a closer look, it becomes apparent that the evolution of manufacturing has been achieved primarily via empirical and intuitive means. It has, in fact, been only relatively recently that science—particularly advanced scientific methods and models—has been introduced.

One of the definitions—and the most pertinent for our purposes—found in the *Merriam-Webster OnLine Dictionary* for *empirical* is "relying on experience or observation alone, often without due regard for system and theory." This definition sums up, aptly, the art of manufacturing as well as the evolution of that art. That is, the art of manufacturing has relied on empirical evidence, intuition, and analogies while ignoring, for the most part, science.

FIGURE 2.4

Components of factory cycle time after an improvement effort.

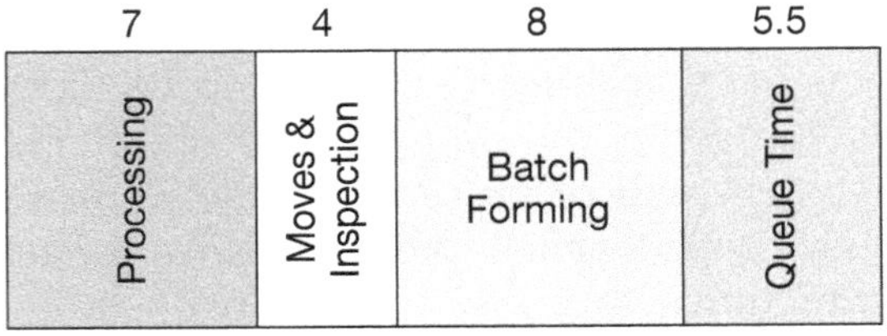

The scientific management movement of the late nineteenth and early twentieth centuries advanced manufacturing by means of the employment of experiments coupled with rather basic descriptive statistics. For example, such people as Frederick Taylor and Frank Gilbreth relied on the statistics (e.g., averages and variances) gleaned from their experiments. These results could be summarized visually by means of histograms and other plots. In this way, one approach to performance improvement could be compared with another.

Such approaches, while advances over purely intuitive efforts, still do not provide a quantitative model of the system (e.g., factory and workstation) that lends itself to an improved and scientifically valid understanding of the actual causes (and the confounding of multiple events) of problems or an indication of the optimal approach to the resolution of problems. A more advanced scientific basis for the evolution of manufacturing requires the development of mathematical models [e.g., queuing theory, stochastic processes, and optimization (Buzacott and Shanthikumar, 1993; Goldberg, 1989; Gross and Harris, 1998; Hillier and Lieberman, 2005; Hopp and Spearman, 2001; Ignizio and Gupta, 1975; Ignizio and Cavalier, 1994; Taha, 2006)] that are specifically adapted to the representation of factories and their production processes.

The Ford production system provided the foundation for the Toyota production system, now popularly designated as *lean manufacturing*. Lean manufacturing, in turn, consists mainly of the art of manufacturing, that is, methods developed empirically and refined over years of experimentation, observation, and statistical analysis. For the most part, however, lean manufacturing does not rely on the models and methods developed via a more advanced scientific approach. This can be—as we shall see—both an advantage (in terms of ease of acceptance) and a disadvantage (in terms of lesser power, robustness, and understanding).

Let's now consider Case Study 2, in which some historical facts with regard to the characters in the Muddle Corporation story are provided.

CASE STUDY 2: A LITTLE BIT OF HISTORY

As mentioned earlier, politics play a major role—sometimes *the* major role—in either the success or failure of factory performance-improvement efforts. Politics, in fact, often represent the most complex human element in such efforts. One way in which to gain a better appreciation of the politics—and culture—of any organization is to learn as much as you can about the background, motivation, beliefs, and experience of its management. So let's first address the background and experience of the managers having the most significant impact on the culture, goals, and values within the Muddle Corporation.

As discussed previously, Peter Muddle was one of the founders of Muddle, its previous CEO, and is presently chairman of its board. His imprint on the culture, goals, and value system of the firm is significant. As such, we'll begin with a brief overview of his history.

Peter Muddle was born, some 70 years ago, in the American Midwest. While he may have been a mediocre student, Peter was clever—sometimes a bit too clever. After his expulsion from college (for plagiarism), Peter teamed up with a former university roommate to establish a firm for the preparation of small-business income tax forms.

Two years later Peter was discovered by the Internal Revenue Service (IRS) to have been submitting bogus income tax forms for several of his clients and splitting the subsequent bogus tax refunds with those clients. A guilty plea and a lenient judge allowed Peter to pay a fine and escape jail time.

Following this misstep, Peter decided to move to California. Shortly thereafter, Peter met a bright young Stanford University student, Harold Smith. Harold had a brilliant idea for the production of what was then a new and novel device. Peter convinced Harold to become his partner, and together they established a firm for the manufacture of the item. Peter was able to obtain venture-capital funding for the firm that became the foundation of what is now the Muddle Corporation—although its original name was S&M (short for Smith and Muddle) Enterprises.

Over the next several years, the unsuspecting Harold allowed Peter to file the patents for his inventions—inventions that moved S&M into the forefront of its field. All the patents, however, were filed under the name of Peter Muddle.

Without any further need for Harold's services, Peter and his carefully selected board of directors pushed the young and gullible Harold out the door. It was then that Peter renamed the firm Muddle, Inc.

Marvin Muddle, Peter's son and present CEO, was a so-so student but did manage (with some considerable help from a large donation to the university by his father) to obtain an MBA degree. Marvin is a chip off the old block in many respects. His motto—written in Latin on his coat of arms—is, in fact, *"Aufero absque dedecus."*[9] This may explain the atmosphere within Muddle that permits and even encourages the co-opting of ideas.

Jack Gibson, whom we have yet to encounter, is a plant manager for Muddle's Factory 2, the firm's smallest facility. Jack is determined to move up the corporate ladder and has his eyes on the position of director of manufacturing—the position presently held by William "Wild Bill" Barlow. What Jack may lack in brains, he more than makes up for in cunning.

Tommy Jenkins, another individual whom we have yet to encounter, is—like Jack Gibson—also a plant manager. Tommy is "three-in-a-box" with two other plant managers for the factory (Factory 7) in which Dan Ryan and Brad Simmons work.[10] He happens to be the senior plant manager (i.e., the top rung of the management ladder at a given factory site).

Tommy takes his job very seriously—so seriously, in fact, that he insists on being involved in virtually every aspect of the factory, no matter how trivial. Tommy is what is known as a *micromanager.* Micromanagers have little or no faith in their subordinates and insist on being involved in each and every decision. Another aspect of Tommy's personality is his disdain for science. He's convinced that as a consequence of his 20 years of experience with Muddle, there is nothing that anyone can teach him about running a factory.

I also should provide some mention of the histories of other characters in these case studies. Sally Swindel, as discussed earlier, has recently convinced Muddle to implement lean manufacturing. Previously, she was responsible for Muddle's unsuccessful attempt at the adoption of reengineering. Sally works for Hyperbola, Ltd., a major consulting firm with a worldwide presence. Although her only previous work experience was that of an order taker at a fast-food franchise, Sally has been able to persuade a long line of CEOs to adopt the methods promoted by Hyperbola.

Hyperbola provided Sally with a two-week training course in lean manufacturing before sending her out to spread the message

---

9 In English, this means "Steal shamelessly."
10 The firm has a practice that involves, despite its obsession with cost cutting, the assignment of two or more people to almost every low- to middle-level management position. Thus, "three-in-a-box" means that there are three plant managers at this particular site. Tommy Jenkins is the senior of the three in his "box."

that "Lean is *the answer.*" Hyperbola furnishes its clients with books on each of the methods it espouses.

The company's latest text is a slim volume entitled, *Lean Is the Answer.* This book is a revision of an earlier book entitled, *Reengineering Is the Answer* (which, in turn, was a revised version of earlier books such as *Total Quality Management Is the Answer, Quality Circles Are the Answer, Theory of Constraints Is the Answer,* etc.). Most managers at Muddle have at least one copy of every book produced by Hyperbola. The irony of their titles evidently has escaped them.

We also met Dan Ryan in Chapter 1. Dan was employed previously by a small manufacturing firm, ToraXpress. That firm had struggled for years and was on the edge of bankruptcy until a retired professor, Aristotle Leonidas, turned its fortunes around. Professor Leonidas introduced a program and training courses that enabled ToraXpress not only to recover but also to become a leader in its field.

A few years later, ToraXpress was purchased by Muddle. Two years after that the company, then a division of Muddle, was but a shell of its former self and was closed on the orders of Marvin Muddle. Of its 300 employees, only a handful were offered positions in Muddle's other factories. Among this select group was Dan Ryan.

Brad Simmons, the factory floor supervisor for the workstation adjacent to Dan's, has been with Muddle his entire career—some 12 years. Brad is resigned to the fact that the performance of Muddle's factories will never improve without a major change in the practices and procedures employed on the factory floor. When Brad heard about adoption of the lean manufacturing effort, he pulled as many strings as he could to obtain a full-time position with Muddle's *LEAN* Forward team. Based on his recommendation, Dan Ryan also was given—and accepted—a similar position on the team.

Donna Garcia, as you may recall, was (until their appointment to the *LEAN* Forward team) Dan and Brad's department head. Donna is the factory floor operations manager for Factory 7 and is responsible for all operations and maintenance activities in the factory. Donna is a compulsive tattletale and makes it a practice to meet regularly with Tommy Jenkins. As with other characters in this story, Donna wants desperately to climb Muddle's career ladder.

Ben Arnold, whom Dan Ryan had the unfortunate opportunity to meet earlier, is Tommy Jenkins' technical assistant (i.e., technical advisor). Ben previously worked at Muddle's Factory 2, at which time he became friends with Jack Gibson. It's rumored that Ben may have played some role in the promotion of Jack to Factory 2's (junior) plant manager position.

Julia Austen is another person we have yet to meet. Julia is a Muddle Fellow (a position allegedly based on the individual's "world class" technical expertise). Unlike most Muddle Fellows, Julia actually is an expert, albeit in one rather narrow aspect of manufacturing. Julia, like Brad and Dan, is beginning to question the decisions being made with regard to improving factory performance.

Let's now listen in on the conversation between Brad and Dan in the company cafeteria.

"Dan, old man," says Brad, "before we start the *LEAN* Forward training course, I have a few words of advice."

"No problem, I'm all ears."

"I strongly recommend that you don't let anyone know you've had training in factory performance improvement; you know, the stuff you said that professor guy, Leonidas, taught you when you were at ToraXpress."

"Actually," replies Dan, "I wasn't hired into ToraXpress until after Professor Leonidas had almost finished his training courses. In fact, I was only able to attend two of his lectures. But that was enough to convince me that he was spot on about how to achieve factory performance improvement."

"That doesn't really make any difference," says Brad. "You still need to keep quiet about anything you may have learned."

"Okay," replies Dan, raising his eyebrows, "but why on earth should I keep that a secret?"

"Because, in this company, it can be dangerous to let people know you have any expertise whatsoever in whatever topic may be on the agenda. Unless you're a member of a fairly select group—and trust me, you ain't—just keep your mouth shut and nod your head. Agree with whatever is said in the *LEAN* Forward class, no matter how foolish or misguided you think it might be."

One can conclude from this case study that the Muddle family has a checkered past and a habit of taking credit for the ideas of others. And if the advice of Brad Simmons is to be believed, it's best to keep your mouth shut unless it is to express agreement.

CHAPTER 3

Terminology, Notation, and Definitions

A PROPER FOUNDATION

To most fully appreciate and effectively exploit the art and science of manufacturing, you should be familiar with the terminology, notation, and definitions that allow you to intelligently discuss and employ these concepts. It is advisable, therefore, that you read this chapter because much of what follows is based on the material covered here. This recommendation holds true even if you may have had a previous introduction to the art (e.g., lean manufacturing) and/or science (e.g., industrial engineering, manufacturing engineering, operations research, stochastic systems, or production control) of manufacturing because the treatment presented in this text differs, in some cases considerably, from that found in other works.

Once the definitions, terminology, and notation have been covered, these concepts will be further clarified by means of an end-of-chapter numerical illustration. The illustration employed—that of an extremely simple factory—indicates just how to "pull together" and implement the material presented in this chapter.

Our discussion begins, however, with the definition and purpose of a factory—a topic that should not be taken lightly. Factories, as you shall see, are considerably more complex than the stereotypical "noisy, big building with lots of smoke belching out."

THE FACTORY: DEFINITION AND PURPOSE

We've certainly all seen factories, and some readers may have worked or perhaps are presently working on a factory floor or are otherwise employed by a manufacturing firm. A widely held and overly simplistic view of a factory is that of a building that houses machines and people and produces an end product that is delivered to its customers. A considerably more useful definition of a factory is provided below:

> A factory is a processing network through which jobs and information flow and within which events take place.

The jobs (i.e., items requiring processing) within a factory are assembled (e.g., automobile assembly, cell phone assembly, or laptop computer assembly) or otherwise transformed (e.g., the implant of transistors within a silicon wafer or the annealing process employed in the manufacture of metals) from the raw materials entering the factory into the final product that ultimately leaves the factory. These jobs flow through a network of predetermined process steps. Job process steps (a.k.a. *operations*) include

- *Assembly* or *transformation*—an activity resulting in or directly supporting a physical and measurable change to the job
- *Transit* of the job from one machine to the next
- *Inspection* of the job

In addition, a job may have to undergo rework. While this is not part of a predetermined process-step flow, it is a state in which a given job might exist at a specific time.

Concurrent with the flow of jobs through a factory are events that occur within the factory's workstations. These events serve to reduce the availability of the machines that form the workstation and, subsequently, the overall availability of the workstation itself. The degradation imposed by such events on the workstation—and the factory—in turn, will have an impact on factory performance.

Workstation events may occur either randomly, according to a schedule (e.g., perform a maintenance event every week), or according to usage (e.g., perform a maintenance event on the completion of every 500 jobs). Included among the most common workstation events are

- Maintenance of a machine
- Repair of a machine
- Inspection of a machine

- Qualification of a machine
- Setup of a machine

From a more scientific perspective, an alternate and more revealing definition of a factory may be developed, specifically:

> A factory is a nonlinear, dynamic, stochastic system with feedback.

The implication of this definition is that even a seemingly simple factory is a very complex system. It involves all the features (i.e., nonlinear, dynamic, stochastic, and feedback) that serve to define a system so complex as to defy human intuition (Forrester, 1999). A corollary to this finding is that your intuition, when it comes to a factory, is almost always wrong.[1] This may come as a surprise to those who believe that they can manage and run a factory effectively using just their experience and "gut feel." While many factories are indeed managed and run in such a seat-of-the-pants manner, their performance is invariably far below their true potential.

Another insight that may be gained from the second definition of a factory is that a manufacturing facility shares the same features as several other important and related systems. Specifically, the models and methods that may be employed to represent and solve problems within a factory (i.e., within a nonlinear, dynamic, stochastic system with feedback) apply equally as well to supply chains and business processes. In fact, these same models and methods can, with but modest effort, even be adapted to such a seemingly unrelated problem as the design of multicore computer chips (which, like factories, also involve flows and bottlenecks). In short, there are numerous important real-world problems having essentially the same mathematical model as that of a "simple factory."

While mathematical models of a factory play a vital role in factory performance-improvement efforts, process-flow models provide the best means for visualizing the flow of jobs through a factory. These models also serve as a basis for the definitions, terminology, and notation to be covered in the sections that follow. Two versions of these models are described and illustrated below.

---

1 To quote Francis Bacon, "Beware the fallacies into which undisciplined thinkers most easily fall." Among them is to "assume more order than exists in chaotic nature."

FACTORY PROCESS-FLOW MODELS

Every factory (or supply chain or business process) supports a process flow. There are several ways to represent this flow, but this chapter will deal with only two of these. The first is a representation of the process flow in a factory by means of a workstation-centric model. The second is a representation via a process-step-centric model.

To clarify, a workstation consists of one or more machines that support identical or nearly identical processing functions. For example, there may be workstations that support polishing, those that support etching, those that support photolithography, and those that support a specific inspection step.

A process step, on the other hand, is an operation conducted within a workstation (and, quite possibly, by means of the support of only a subset of the machines in the workstation) or is a transit step between workstations. Some process steps add value to the final product (i.e., from the perspective of the customer), whereas others (such as transit and inspection) are considered non-value-added operations (again, from the perspective of the customer).

The workstation-centric flow model (and its variants) is the most widely employed representation of a factory—and it has its uses. In fact, there may be instances in which the factory under consideration is so simple and straightforward that a workstation-centric model will suffice. The process-step-centric model, however, while not as well known, is more robust, often more useful, and in many cases may be essential if a complete and accurate appreciation of the factory is to be obtained. Our discussion begins, however, with the conventional workstation-centric model.

WORKSTATION-CENTRIC MODEL—AND REENTRANCY

The workstation-centric model is best explained by means of an illustration. In so doing, the concept of reentrancy also will be introduced.

Figure 3.1 depicts a simple factory consisting of three workstations (A, B, and C), designated in the drawing as WS-A, WS-B, and WS-C. In a workstation-centric model, workstations (and their devices, e.g., conveyor belts, monorails, carts, etc.) that support transit operations, as well as the transit operations themselves, are not explicitly depicted. Within each workstation are its

FIGURE 3.1

Three-workstation factory with reentrancy.

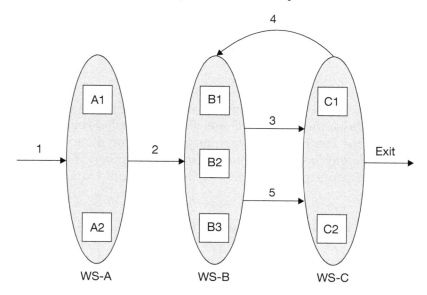

machines. In workstation A, these machines are designated as A1 and A2; in workstation B, as B1, B2, and B3; and in workstation C, as C1 and C2.

The arrows and arcs in the figure represent the flow of all process steps (a.k.a. *operations*) other than those of the transit type. The arrow emanating from workstation C and labeled as "Exit" serves simply to indicate the departure of the job from the factory.

Since workstations B and C each support more than a single operation and are coupled (the coupling is indicated in the figure by the manner in which operation 4 forms a deterministic feedback loop from WS-C to WS-B), this particular factory is considered to be reentrant.[2] The *degree of reentrancy* (DoR) of a factory is found by dividing the total number of operations (excluding process steps that involve only transit) it supports by the total number of work-stations in the factory.

---

2 If the feedback loop is *probabilistic* (e.g., jobs are, only when necessary, sent back to earlier workstations for rework), the loop is technically not considered reentrant. To be reentrant, the feedback loop must form part of the *predetermined* process flow. If not, the feedback loop is probabilistic.

The factory in Figure 3.1 supports five operations (not count-
ing transit operations), as depicted by the arrows and arcs labeled
from 1 to 5, and consists of three workstations. Thus its DoR is
given by

$$DoR(factory) = 5/3 = 1.67$$

It also may be observed that this factory has a single reentrant
nest. A *nest*, in turn, is a contiguous series of directly coupled workstations. Workstations B and C are directly coupled (because they
are part of the feedback loop formed by operation 4), and the DoR
of this nest may be found by dividing the number of nontransit
operations supported by the nest by the number of workstations in
the nest:

$$DoR(\text{of nest formed by workstations B and C}) = 4/2 = 2$$

For the record, automobile assembly lines have little, if any,
reentrancy (the ideal assembly line has none), whereas other, more
complex factories (such as semiconductor wafer fabrication facilities, or "fabs") typically have factory DoR values ranging from 3 to
5 or even more—with individual nests that may have DoRs in the
double digits. Attempting to treat a reentrant factory with methods
developed for nonreentrant systems, by the way, may lead to either
overestimates or underestimates of the facility's capability and performance. Furthermore, the ideal factory should not contain any
reentrant loops.

We next consider two other, more traditional (in that they do
not include reentrancy) workstation-centric models. In Figure 3.2, a
flowshop is depicted (again, transit process steps and their associated "machines" are omitted). For simplicity, the machines in each
workstation have not been drawn. A *flowshop* is a factory in which
each job follows precisely the same pathway, that is, from entry into
the first workstation (WS-A in the figure) and movement through
all the workstations and exit from the final workstation (WS-F).

Each workstation, in turn, supports just one process step, and
every machine in the workstation is assumed to be qualified to
support that step. Moreover, it is usually assumed that there is no
passing of jobs. That is, if four jobs enter the factory in, say, the job
sequence J1, J2, J3, and J4, they must enter and leave each workstation in that same sequence. As you might guess, pure flowshop factories usually are found only in textbooks.

Another type of factory, one somewhat more realistic than a flowshop, is a *jobshop* facility. For sake of discussion, the factory in Figure 3.2 may be converted into a jobshop facility if certain restrictions of the flowshop are relaxed. Figure 3.3 presents one of many possible representations. Notice that in a jobshop, each job that enters the factory may follow a different process flow path. For example, job J1 follows a path (the *dashed line*) from WS-A to WS-B to WS-E to WS-F and then exits the factory. Job J2, on the other hand, follows a path (the *solid line*) from WS-A to WS-C to WS-D to WS-E and then leaves the factory.

An even more general-case factory could be formed by including reentrancy (i.e., deterministic feedback loops) as well as rework (i.e., probabilistic feedback) and allowing job passing (i.e., relaxing the requirement that jobs must proceed through every workstation in the same sequence) in the jobshop factory model. At any rate,

FIGURE 3.2

Flowshop factory in workstation-centric form.

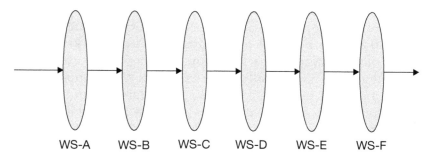

FIGURE 3.3

Jobshop factory in workstation-centric form.

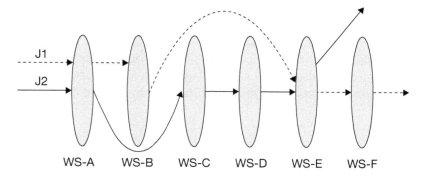

real-world factories are usually more complex than those in these figures. Furthermore, most factories contain many more workstations, machines, job types, process steps, and process flows. As just one example, the typical semiconductor wafer fabrication facility may contain a hundred or more workstations, with possibly up to a thousand or so individual machines, and support hundreds of process steps.

Factories of such size and, in particular, complexity (especially the complexity imposed by reentrancy) are a far cry from the ideal single-unit, continuous-flow factory.[3] This fact alone serves to help explain why so many real-world factories perform so poorly—a fact that is true even if they are assumed by management to be performing "adequately."

PROCESS-STEP-CENTRIC MODELS

The workstation-centric model in Figure 3.1 may be converted into a process-step-centric representation (this is true of any workstation-centric model). To accomplish this, however, we must first know which machines are capable of supporting (e.g., qualified to conduct or be assigned to) each process step. Stated another way, it may be that only a subset of the machines in a workstation are capable of or assigned to a given process step supported by the workstation (e.g., as generally is the case with photolithography or implant machines in a semiconductor wafer fabrication facility).

Therefore, we shall assume that we know the specific process step to machine assignments (a.k.a. *dedications*) for the workstation depicted in Figure 3.1. Specifically, we assume that any machine in workstation A can support process step 1 and that any machine in workstation C can support either process step 3 or process step 5.

On the other hand, we will assume that only machines B1 and B2 are capable of supporting process step 2, whereas only machines B2 and B3 can deal with process step 4. Given these assumptions, the conversion of the workstation-centric model in Figure 3.1 results in the process-step-centric model in Figure 3.4.

In this figure, the circles represent the operations, or process steps—excluding those that simply support a transit operation. The transit process steps, in turn, are indicated by the arrows leading

---

3 *Single-unit flow* means that the jobs flow as single units (e.g., in the extreme case, a silicon wafer used to fabricate a computer chip would flow as a single chip rather than as a wafer with hundreds of chips on its surface).

FIGURE 3.4

Process-step-centric representation.

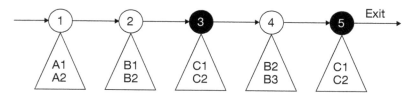

from one (nontransit) process step to another. For our purposes, nontransit process steps that are non-value-added steps are depicted as black circles (i.e., process steps 3 and 5, which may be, for example, inspection steps that every job must endure). As is the case with inspection process steps, the transit steps represented by the arrows are also non-value-added steps. It should be noted that an important goal of either scientific management, classic industrial engineering, or more recently, lean manufacturing is to eliminate or at least reduce the number of non-value-added process steps.

Underneath each process step is a triangle, and within each triangle is a list of the machines that support the given process step. For example, process step 1—based on the assumptions mentioned previously—is supported by machines A1 and A2 (of workstation A).

But (as based on our previous assumptions) notice that process step 2 is supported by only a subset of the machines in workstation B, that is, machines B1 and B2. Further, process step 4 is also supported by only another subset of workstation B's machines, that is, machines B2 and B3.

This is a crucial point and serves to indicate to some degree why a process-step-centric representation, particularly of a reentrant factory, is so important. Specifically, the process-step-centric model indicates not only the process step flow but also the precise support responsibilities of each machine in the factory.

The DoR of a factory also may be determined from the process-step-centric representation. As before, we divide the number of nontransit process steps (five) by the number of workstations (three) to arrive at a factory DoR of $5/3 = 1.67$.

We also may determine the DoR of any nests, just as done previously with the workstation-centric model. From Figure 3.4, it should be clear that operations flow from workstation B to workstation C and then back to workstation B and ultimately return to workstation C. In other words, workstations B and C form a nest. Consequently, two workstations, B and C, support four operations (i.e., 2, 3, 4, and 5), and the DoR of the nest is simply 4/2, or 2.

The importance of the process-step-centric model will be made even more apparent in Chapter 13 when the matter of determining the capacity of workstations and factories is covered. As you shall see, it is often more important to be aware of the capacity of the specific subset of machines that supports each process step than the composite capacity of the entire workstation. With this discussion of factory flow models now behind us, we can move on to other definitions, notation, and terminology.

FACTORY DEFINITIONS AND TERMINOLOGY

A factory possesses certain important features. I begin the list of definitions and terminology with those pertinent to such factory attributes.

Factory Types

The types of factories that one may encounter include

- Flowshops
- Jobshops
- Factories without reentrancy (i.e., DoR = 1)
- Factories with reentrancy (i.e., DoR > 1)
- Synchronous factories (e.g., every job flows through the factory at the same constant speed, such as bottles in a beverage bottling plant)
- Asynchronous factories (e.g., each job—as in semi-conductor fabrication—may flow through the factory at different speeds and in addition may remain temporarily held in a queue)
- High-mix factories (e.g., those that process numerous job types)
- Low-mix factories (e.g., those that process only a limited number of job types)
- Low-volume factories (e.g., those that process only a relatively limited number of jobs per time period, such as aircraft manufacturers or research and development factories that produce only prototypes of a product)

- High-volume factories (e.g., those that process a large number of jobs per time period, such as high-volume semiconductor wafer fabrication facilities)
- High-mix, low-volume factories
- High-mix, high-volume factories
- Low-mix, low-volume factories
- Low-mix, high-volume factories
- Factories involving various combinations of the preceding features

Included within a factory are its workstations (and their associated machines), jobs, supplies, spare parts, dispatch centers, operational personnel, maintenance personnel, automation equipment and personnel, transit equipment (e.g., either manual or automated material handling systems), transit support personnel, and all the associated information and documentation believed necessary for the operation of the facility. Accompanying the information and documentation are (or should be) the metrics by which each important aspect of the factory is measured.

I now proceed to list the terminology and definitions employed for the jobs processed and events performed within a factory.

JOBS AND EVENTS

The activities that occur within the factory consist primarily of the processing of jobs and the conduct of workstation-associated events. The processing of jobs (including rework) provides the firm with the potential for profit—assuming that the jobs are not scrapped or otherwise disposed of owing to defects or obsolescence.

Events, on the other hand, consume time in which a workstation or machine otherwise might be available for the processing of jobs. Events also consume resources (e.g., maintenance personnel time) that otherwise might be allocated more effectively.

Job Types and Configurations

Jobs may require either assembly (as in the case of an automobile assembly line), transformation (as in the case of an oil refinery, chemical processing plant, or woodworking facility), or some combination of assembly and transformation (as in the case of the manufacture of computer chips). Furthermore, a job may flow through the factory as a single unit (e.g., as an automobile), as a *lot* (e.g., as a "container" consisting of a number of silicon wafers), or as a *batch* (e.g., a group of either individual jobs or lots).[4]

There are two primary types of batches of interest. The first is a *conventional batch,* sometimes designated as a *parallel batch.* A parallel batch is composed of two or more jobs, and each job (or lot) in the batch is processed simultaneously on the machines that support batching operations. Furthermore, each job in a given parallel batch typically requires the same process time for a given process step. For example, a factory furnace might support batches of 12 jobs each and require six hours of heat treatment.

Once the batch has been processed, six hours later, the jobs within the batch typically move as an ensemble to the machines supporting the next process step (the machines supporting the next operation may or may not use batching). The purpose of parallel batching supposedly is to reduce setup time; that is, each batch undergoes just one setup in front of the batching machine.

Another type of batching is known as *series batching* or *cascading.* The jobs within a cascade are processed sequentially by the cascading machine or workstation. Each job in a cascade must wait for the preceding job in its cascade to finish before entering the machine or workstation. Once a job in a cascade finishes processing, it moves—usually by itself—to the machines supporting the next process step. The purpose of cascading supposedly is to reduce setup time because each cascade undergoes just one setup prior to entry into the cascading machine or workstation.

Other versions of batching may exist, wherein the jobs in a batch might be *split* so as to allow a portion of the batch to be sent to the next process step prior to completion of the entire batch. Whether this is the case or not, batching of any type serves to complicate the process-step flow as well as induce variability into the factory. The ideal (i.e., utopian) factory should not employ batching.

Event Types

As mentioned previously, events are activities that are conducted within a workstation rather than on a job. While conventional wisdom may hold that some of the events to be described are "essential,"

---

4 The silicon wafers in a semiconductor wafer facility typically are transported in *cassettes* or *front-opening unified pods* (FOUPS). At a particular process step, the entire lot might be processed either simultaneously or as individual wafers. Some process steps, in fact, employ machines that process batches or cascades of lots. Despite this complexity, a *job* in such a facility typically is considered to be a single lot.

the goal of the ideal factory is to eliminate each and every one. First, however, it is useful to distinguish between preemptive and nonpreemptive events.

Preemptive Events   A *preemptive event* is one that occurs during the processing of a given job (or batch). The processing of the job must stop and cannot proceed until recovery from the preemptive event. In some cases, the preemptive event even may cause the job to have to restart the interrupted process step. In others, the event could cause the job to be scrapped or require rework. Among the most common types of preemptive events are

- Unscheduled downs
- Power outages or voltage/current spikes
- Unanticipated supply outages and replenishment

Nonpreemptive Events   A *nonpreemptive event* is one that occurs (or can be scheduled to occur) during a period in which the machine is not processing a job. Such events include

- Scheduled maintenance [e.g., preventive maintenance (PM) events]
- Unscheduled downs (i.e., those that happen to not occur during processing)
- Inspections and engineering tests
- Qualifications
- Setups
- Scheduled operator breaks (e.g., biobreaks or meetings)

Whether an event is preemptive or nonpreemptive, it still serves to increase the variability and decrease the capacity of the machines within the factory. Consequently, significant improvement in factory performance may be achieved by eliminating or at least mitigating these events.

Job States

During its journey through a factory, a job will exist in one of a finite number of states at any given time. Specifically, it may be engaged in

- Value-added processing, that is, an actual assembly or transformation operation

- Non-value-added processing, including
  - Rework
  - Transit
  - Inspection/test
  - Waiting, including
    - Waiting as an individual job for processing at a nonbatching/noncascading process step
    - Waiting for a batch (or cascade) to form in front of a batching/cascading process step
    - Waiting in a batch (or cascade) as part of the queue formed in front of a batching/cascading process step
    - Waiting in a "set aside" state (e.g., the job is removed temporarily from the production line)

Note that rework has been classified as a non-value-added job state. The rationale for this is that rework increases cycle time and reduces capacity and should not be required unless there is a deficiency in the operators, machines, or process flow. In an ideal factory, there would be no need for rework. Consequently, attempts should be made to avoid circumstances leading to the need to rework a job.

Each of the states in which a job may exist contributes to the average overall job cycle time (i.e., the average factory cycle time for the given job type). Figure 3.5 provides a graphic depiction of the percentage of time spent by an average job within an actual factory in its various job states. In this particular factory, there happened to be no rework (job rework simply was not possible), nor was there any waiting in a set-aside state. Despite this bit of "good news," it should be clear from the figure that there was considerable waste, mostly in terms of wait times, in this factory.

As may be noted from this figure, wait time (of all types) consumed slightly more than 80 percent of factory cycle time! Non-value-added processing consumed about 8 percent of the cycle time. Only 12 percent of the factory cycle time was used for value-added processing. In other words, this factory was operating at just 12 percent efficiency.[5] In short, this factory was performing

---

[5] I've actually encountered real-world factories operating at much lower levels of efficiency. One, in fact, was found to be operating at slightly less than 5 percent efficiency (i.e., non-value-added processing and wait consumed about 95 percent of the average job's cycle time).

FIGURE 3.5

Job states (factory cycle-time components).

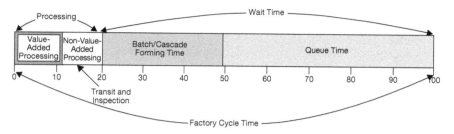

extremely poorly. Unfortunately, many real-world factories perform at this level—and some are even less efficient.

A minimally efficient factory (i.e., one involved in assembly
operations) should operate at 35 percent or (preferably) more efficiency when running at full capacity (*full capacity* will be defined in
a subsequent section). Stated another way, wait times and non-
value-added processing should consume no more than 65 percent of
the cycle time. When the methods to be discussed in subsequent
chapters were implemented in the factory associated with Figure 3.5,
its factory cycle time—for the same level of factory loading and without adding machines or personnel—was decreased by 65 percent.
(In the five years since then, this reduction in factory cycle time has
been sustained.)

WORKSTATIONS, MACHINES, AND PROCESS STEPS

Process steps are supported by the factory's workstations and
machines. Events, of the type discussed previously, occur within
the workstations and machines. As a consequence, a given machine
will find itself in one of a finite number of states. Before listing
these states, it is necessary to review and further elaborate on the
notions of workstations and machines.

Workstations

A given workstation consists of one or more machines, each dedicated to an identical or nearly identical processing function. For
example, a workstation may support the function of polishing,
grinding, etching, moving, or inspecting the jobs entering the

workstation. Some workstations exist within close proximity (i.e., grouped areas, or *cells*). Others may be geographically distributed in quite possibly an ad hoc manner. Then there are workstations located according to the precise sequence of the functions to be performed (as in an automobile assembly line or as was the case of the moving shipbuilding assembly line at the Arsenal of Venice).

A given workstation may support

- A single process step
- Multiple process steps
- A value-added process step or steps
- A non-value-added process step or steps
- Some combination of the preceding

In addition, a workstation may be a part of a factory nest (i.e., coupled with other workstations via reentrant loops).

Machines

The fundamental physical, nonhuman component of any workstation is its machines. Some of the types of machines that may be found in a workstation include

- Machines dedicated to any and all process steps supported by the workstation
- Machines dedicated to just a portion of the process steps supported by the workstation
- Machines employing batching or cascading
- Machines that are fully or partially automated
- Machines that consist of a "cluster" processing mechanism (e.g., machines that consist of multiple chambers, such as those employed in wet etching in semiconductor wafer manufacturing)

Machines also may be categorized by cost, size, and complexity. It should be noted that a rule of thumb for machine size is that it ideally should not be more than four times the size of the job (or lot or batch) it processes—unless otherwise dictated by the laws of physics. While some factory managers may delight in bragging about the cost and complexity of their machines, the ideal factory should have small, inexpensive, and simple machines.[6]

Machine States

At any given time, a machine will exist in one of a finite number of states. Specifically, the machine may be in the

- *Processing state.* Busy in support of job processing; that is, the machine is engaged in the support of a process step for a potentially marketable job. This includes the time spent in such job process steps as
  - Those involving assembly or transformation
  - Those involving rework
  - Those involving transit
  - Those involving inspection/test (i.e., of a job)

The average time spent by a machine in these states is termed *processing time*, or *busy time*.

- *Blocked state.* Engaged in the conduct of a machine event; that is, the machine is up and running but engaged in an event that either precludes (i.e., blocks) or could preclude the support of an actual process step. Such events include
  - Those involving inspection/test (i.e., of the machine)
  - Those involving qualification
  - Those involving setup
  - Those machines on hold waiting for the arrival of a priority job

The average time spent in these states is termed *blocked time.*[7]

---

6 After being subjected to what seems to have been literally hundreds of factory tours, I never cease to be amazed by the statistics quoted by some plant and factory managers. They brag that their factory and its machines are (1) big, (2) expensive, and (3) complex when the ideal factory and its machines should possess precisely the opposite of these attributes.

7 Another type of blocked state is termed *warm bagging.* For example, one or more machines in a workstation may be up and running but removed from the process flow.

- *Idle state.* The machine is up, running, and qualified, but there are no jobs either in the machine or waiting for the machine—or alternately, the only jobs in queue in front of the machine cannot be processed until a specific minimum batch size has been formed. The average time spent in this state is *idle time.*
- *Down state.* The machine may be down owing to either a scheduled or unscheduled event. The average time spent in this state is *downtime.*

Note that the primary difference between blocked time and downtime lies in the fact that a machine is actually "up and running" in the blocked state, whereas it is not running in the down state. Be careful to realize that if a machine is in a blocked state, it is not available for the processing of a job.

Previously, in Figure 3.5, a plot of factory cycle time from the perspective of the states taken on by the average job was presented. If we assume the perspective of a machine, the states it encounters may be depicted via Figure 3.6.

Again, it must be emphasized that blocked time (e.g., engagement in machine events including test, qualification, and setup) detracts—just as downtimes do—from machine availability. A failure to recognize this (or to not even consider the average amount of machine blocked time) will result in an overestimate of the machine's true capacity.

Despite this, there are firms that fail to factor in blocked time in their determination of availability. As a consequence, they may overestimate (sometimes dramatically) their machine capacity while underestimating its cycle time.

FIGURE 3.6

Machine states (percentages).

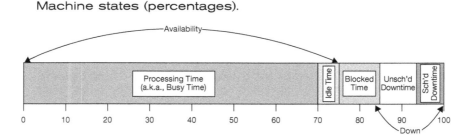

Process Steps

Earlier in this chapter we discussed two versions of factory flow models. As mentioned, the process-step-centric flowchart provides more information and generally is the most useful. This focus on the process step is considerably different from the traditional treatment of a factory, where the level of interest may stop at the workstation or machine. However, if we wish to determine the most effective means to improve factory performance, the process step is where our interest should lie. For example, in many factories—and virtually all factories that involve reentrancy—the key attributes of capacity and cycle time are determined by the support provided to each individual process step rather than each functional area. As such, the very notion of the cycle time of a workstation may be meaningless.

More specifically, the cycle time of a factory is found via Equation (3.1):

$$CT_f = \sum_{ps=1}^{P} CT_{ps} \qquad\qquad (3.1)$$

where CT_f = cycle time of the entire factory
$\quad CT_{ps}$ = cycle time of a given process step (including transit steps)
$\quad\quad P$ = total number of process steps in the factory

Furthermore, the *capacity* (i.e., maximum sustainable throughput) of a factory is determined by the bottleneck (i.e., constraint or choke point) process step, not necessarily a bottleneck workstation. A more general model used to determine the capacity of a process step will be presented in Chapter 13.

PERSONNEL

Factory personnel may be divided into those who work (primarily) on the factory floor and those who otherwise support the firm's manufacturing efforts. The latter are sometimes referred to as *carpet dwellers* or—even less kindly—*cubicle creatures*. For our purposes, discussion will be restricted to factory floor workers.

Factory Worker Assignments

The most typical job assignments found on the factory floor include

- Operations (e.g., forming job queues, performing machine setups, inserting jobs into machines, and removing completed jobs from machines)
- Maintenance and repair (e.g., performance of maintenance and repair events)
- Inspection/test
- Material handling
- Automation support
- Dispatch of spares and supplies
- Safety and emergency response

In some instances, factory floor personnel may be trained to support multiple assignments (e.g., cross-trained). In others, they may be assigned to just a specific task in a specific workstation.

Factory Worker States

At any given time, a specific factory floor worker may be in one of a finite number of states. These include

- Performing assigned duties
- Idle owing to lack of work
- Idle owing to either slacking off or being unaware of the need for his or her services
- In a meeting
- In a training session
- On a break (e.g., biobreak, rest break, or meal break)
- Absent from the factory (e.g., owing to illness, jury duty, vacation, or simply AWOL)

Factory managers too often rely on estimates or nothing more than "educated guesses" as to the *availability* (i.e., for the conduct of assigned duties) of an average factory floor worker. Desired levels (or minimum required levels) of personnel availability often are estimated by assuming a certain average rate of the occurrence of activities requiring worker support and multiplying that by the average time assumed necessary to conduct these activities—and then adding in a buffer of time supposedly (or hopefully) to account for breaks, meetings, absences, etc.

In one factory it was decided that factory floor maintenance personnel should be available to perform their assigned duties for two-thirds of each shift. Or, stated another way, the number of maintenance personnel should be established so that they would, on average, be idle or otherwise unavailable no more than one-third of the time. The decision was made on the basis of the average time required to perform their maintenance (and repair) events and the average rate of occurrence of those events.

Unfortunately, the maintenance and repair specifications used by factory floor personnel (plus an unevenness in skills and training) induced an extremely high degree of variability about the time required to perform a maintenance or repair event. As a consequence, given the subsequent inadequate number of maintenance personnel assigned to the floor, this factory's cycle-time goal was never attained. In fact, average factory cycle time was more than double the cycle-time goal. The factory manager had four choices, either (1) do nothing and suffer the wrath of corporate management, (2) hire enough maintenance personnel to increase their average idle time to 40 percent, (3) take the measures necessary to reduce the variability induced by poor maintenance specifications and training, or (4) purchase additional machines.

Blissfully unaware of the importance of variability, and evidently unable to compute the number of workers actually required to achieve the cycle-time goal, the factory manager chose the worst possible course of action (in terms of time and cost) and purchased a significant number of (large, costly, and complex) machines.

The moral of this story is that the number of factory floor workers required to achieve any particular performance goal is a function of both the average time required and (in particular) the variability about that time.

Another message that should be transmitted is that a reliance on averages is a very dangerous thing. For example, consider a news story that appeared during the housing slump problems of 2008. The story stated that although the sales of preexisting houses in a city had dropped by 40 percent, the average price of homes for sale had increased by 10 percent. The conclusion was that even with the burst of the housing bubble, the prices of homes were rising.

The actual fact was that about the only homes in the area that were selling at that time were those on the lower end of the price range. This left (unsold) much higher-priced houses. Consequently, the composition of the population of houses listed had changed dramatically, resulting in a higher value for the subsequent average house price listing.

PERFORMANCE MEASURES

As mentioned in Chapter 1, I am convinced that if you don't employ a meaningful metric, not only can you not improve factory performance, but you are also likely to worsen it. This section provides a listing and discussion of potential performance measures. Following this is a numerical illustration that pulls together as many as possible of the topics covered in this chapter. (Chapters 7 and 8 provide further coverage of these measures and recommends those that should be used as well as those that should be avoided.)

There are performance measures to gauge the performance of an entire firm, a firm's factories, an individual factory, a workstation, a machine within a workstation, a process step, and personnel and documentation (e.g., maintenance specifications). The discussion here, however, will be limited to factory, workstation, machine, and process-step performance measures. I begin, however, with an explanation of the notation that will be employed.

Notation

To discriminate between performance measures at the process-step, machine, workstation, and factory levels, the notation employed must be clarified. Specifically, in instances in which I am discussing a performance measure for an entity, I will usually employ the following format:

$$\text{Measure}_{\text{entity}}(\text{specific entity designation})$$

In addition, the subscripts that will be used and the limits on each specific entity will be defined as

$$ps = \text{process step, where } ps = 1, \ldots, P$$
$$m = \text{machines, where } m = 1, \ldots, M$$
$$ws = \text{workstations, where } ws = 1, \ldots, W$$
$$f = \text{factory}$$

For example, if I am discussing the cycle time CT of process step ps number 9, the notation will be

$$CT_{ps}(9)$$

And should I be referring to the process rate PR of machine 3 in workstation B (i.e., B3), I will use

$$PR_m(B3)$$

We begin our discussion of performance measures with those at the process-step level.

Process-Step Performance

Measures associated with the performance of a given process step include

- Process-step average throughput rate TH_{ps}
- Process-step maximum sustainable capacity SC_{ps}
- Process-step maximum theoretical capacity EPR_{ps}
- Process-step cycle time CT_{ps}
- Arrival rate at the process step AR_{ps}
- Departure rate from the process step DR_{ps}

Process-Step Throughput Rate   The throughput rate of a process step is the average rate of flow (e.g., jobs per unit time) through the process step over a given time period. For example, if two jobs per hour on average flow through a process step each week and the factory operates 168 hours per week, its weekly throughput rate is 336 jobs, that is,

$$TH_{ps} = 336 \text{ jobs/week}$$

Process-Step Maximum Sustainable Capacity   The capacity of a given process step is determined by the capacity (in terms of jobs per unit time) of the machines that support the process step.[8] The maximum sustainable (i.e., practical) capacity of a given process step (i.e., of the machines supporting that step) is determined by the maximum acceptable cycle time permissible as imposed by the associated throughput rate of the process step. I denote the maximum sustainable capacity as SC_{ps}.

---

8 A model for determination of the capacity of those machines for any general case (e.g., multiple products, reentrancy, job-machine dedications, etc.) is provided in Chapter 13.

Process-Step Maximum Theoretical Capacity   The maximum theoretical capacity of a given process step (i.e., of the machines supporting that step) is the capacity (in terms of jobs per unit time) of
the machines supporting that step *in the absence of any variability*.
This is also known as the *upper bound of the process-step capacity* as
well as the *effective process rate*. I denote this capacity level as EPR_{ps}.

To further clarify the difference between maximum sustainable and maximum theoretical capacity (i.e., SC_{ps} versus EPR_{ps}),
consider a process step that, ignoring variability, can (theoretically)
support a maximum throughput rate of 30 jobs per day. In this case,
by ignoring variability as well as the associated cycle time, EPR_{ps}—
the maximum theoretical capacity—is given as 30 jobs per day.

This is the case even though the cycle time for a throughput
rate of 30 jobs per day will approach infinity. This may be seen in
Figure 3.7, where the maximum theoretical capacity of a process
step is depicted (the same discussion also holds true for machines,
workstations, or factories).

FIGURE 3.7

Maximum sustainable versus maximum theoretical capacity.

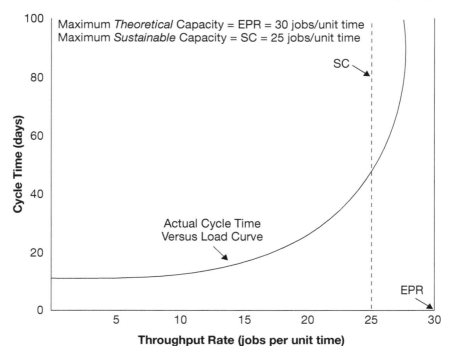

Maximum *Theoretical* Capacity = EPR = 30 jobs/unit time
Maximum *Sustainable* Capacity = SC = 25 jobs/unit time

On the other hand, assume that for a throughput rate of 25 jobs per day the actual, real-world cycle time of the process step is 48 days (see Figure 3.7), and further assume that this is the practical limit on the cycle time that may be tolerated for that process step. Thus, in this case, the maximum sustainable capacity is given as SC_{ps} = 25 jobs per day.

Process-Step Cycle Time   The cycle time of a process step is the average time required to conduct a given operation on a job, that is, the elapsed time between the arrival of the job at the queue (if one exists) in front of the process step (i.e., at the queue in front of the machines supporting the subject process step) and its departure on completion of the operation. If, for example, the average time a job spends in queue or waiting for a batch to form in front of a process step is 1.5 hours and the average time required to process the job is 0.75 hours, then its process-step cycle time is given by the sum of these two times, that is,

$$CT_{ps} = 1.5 + 0.75 = 2.25 \text{ hours}$$

The general form of the equation that will be employed to compute this cycle time is presented in Chapter 5.

Process-Step Arrival Rate   The process-step arrival rate is simply the average number of jobs arriving at the queue in front of a process step over a given time period. For example, if five jobs arrive, on average, each hour, then the process-step arrival rate is given as

$$AR_{ps} = 5 \text{ jobs/hour}$$

Process-Step Departure Rate   The process-step departure rate is the average number of jobs departing from a process step over a given time period. If the average number of departing jobs is five per hour, then

$$DR_{ps} = 5 \text{ jobs/hour}$$

Machine Performance

Measures associated with the performance of a machine include

- Machine throughput rate TH_m
- Machine maximum sustainable capacity SC_m

- Machine availability A_m
- Machine raw process rate PR_m
- Machine maximum theoretical capacity EPR_m, where EPR_m = effective process rate of the machine
- Machine busy time, busy time rate B_m
- Machine downtime, downtime rate DT_m
- Machine occupancy rate ρ_m
- Machine production control channel width PCC_m
- Mean time between machine down events $MTBE_m$
- Mean time to recover from machine down events $MTTR_m$

Machine Throughput Rate   The throughput rate of a machine is the average rate of flow (e.g., jobs per unit time) through the machine over a given time period. For example, if, on average, five jobs per hour flow through a machine each week and the factory operates 80 hours per week, its weekly throughput rate is 80 times 5, or 400 jobs, that is,

$$TH_m = 400\ \text{jobs/week}$$

Machine Maximum Sustainable Capacity   The practical (as opposed to theoretical) capacity of a given machine is given by its maximum sustainable capacity and is denoted as SC_m. For example, if it would be irrational (i.e., owing to a subsequent unacceptably high level of machine cycle time) for more than six jobs per hour to flow through a machine and the factory operates 80 hours per week, then its maximum sustainable capacity is given as

$$SC_m = 6\ \text{jobs/hour} \bullet 80\ \text{hours} = 480\ \text{jobs/week}$$

Machine Availability   The availability of a machine is denoted as A_m and is found by determining the average amount of time the machine is up, running, and qualified to process jobs per unit of time (e.g., per week). One form of the equation for the determination of machine availability is provided by Equation (3.2):

$$A_m = \frac{T - (DT_m + BT_m)}{T} \tag{3.2}$$

where T = number of hours per week the factory operates

DT_m = total average downtime (scheduled and unscheduled) of the machine per week

BT_m = total average blocked time per week of the machine

For example, if over a 168-hour week a machine is, on average, up, running, and qualified to support jobs for 120 hours (which implies that it is down for blocked time and scheduled or unscheduled down events for a total of 48 hours per week, on average), then

$$A_m = \frac{T - (DT_m + BT_m)}{T} = \frac{168 - 48}{168} = 71.4 \text{ percent}$$

An alternative equation for estimation of the availability of a machine is

$$A_m = \frac{MTBE}{MTBE + MTTR} \tag{3.3}$$

where $MTBE$ is the mean time between down and blocked events and $MTTR$ is the mean time to recover from down and blocked events.

To illustrate, assume that the average time between either blocked and down events (i.e., scheduled or unscheduled downs) is 90 hours and that the average time required to recover from such events is 10 hours. Using Equation (3.3), the machine's availability is

$$A_m = \frac{90}{90 + 10} = 90 \text{ percent}$$

Machine Raw Process Rate   If a machine supports more than a single process step, its process rate may vary according to the specific process step of interest. For the sake of discussion, I shall restrict attention at this point to a machine having a single process rate (a.k.a. *run rate*). The raw process rate is the maximum number of jobs per unit time the machine can process under ideal conditions. By *maximum possible* I mean that there are no preemptive events that occur during processing (e.g., no down events during processing) and that the machine is up, running, and qualified 100 percent of the time. If, under these assumptions, a machine could process five jobs per hour, then its raw process rate is

$$PR_m = 5 \text{ jobs/hour}$$

The inverse of a machine's raw process rate is its raw process time, that is, the time required to process a lot under ideal conditions. Using PT_m to represent a machine's raw process time, we have

$$PT_m = \frac{1}{PR_m} \tag{3.4}$$

and thus

$$PR_m = \frac{1}{PT_m} \tag{3.5}$$

Machine Effective Process Rate Machine effective process rate equals machine maximum theoretical capacity. Again, for sake of discussion, I shall restrict attention to a machine having a single process rate. Its maximum theoretical capacity, that is, its effective process rate, is given by multiplying the machine's raw process rate by its availability. That is,

$$EPR_m = A_m \bullet PR_m \tag{3.6}$$

Consider, for example, a machine with a raw process rate of five jobs per hour and an availability of 80 percent. Its effective process rate is simply

$$EPR_m = 0.8 \bullet 5 = 4 \text{ jobs/hour}$$

The inverse of a machine's effective process rate is its effective process time, that is, the time required to process a lot when availability is considered. Thus, using EPT_m to represent a machine's effective process time, we have

$$EPT_m = \frac{1}{EPR_m} \tag{3.7}$$

and thus

$$EPR_m = \frac{1}{EPT_m} \tag{3.8}$$

Machine Busy Rate Earlier we discussed the various states of an individual machine. One state was that denoted as its *processing,* or *busy, state.* When engaged in the busy state, a machine is actually processing jobs. Recall that the amount of time spent in this state (e.g., over a given period of time) is denoted as *processing*, or *busy, time*. The busy rate of a machine is simply the percent of time, over a given time period, spent in the busy state. For example, if the factory operates 168 hours a week and the machine is busy supporting its process step (or steps), on average, 135 hours, then its busy rate, denoted as B_m, is

$$B_m = \frac{135}{168} = 80.4 \text{ percent}$$

An alternative equation for the busy rate of a machine is given by Equation (3.9):

$$B_m = \frac{AR_m}{PR_m} = AR_m \bullet PT_m \tag{3.9}$$

where AR_m = arrival rate of jobs at the machine
PR_m = raw process rate of the machine
PT_m = raw process time of the machine

Machine Occupancy Rate The occupancy rate of a machine is the percentage of its available time that it is in the busy state. Designated ρ_m, the machine occupancy rate is given by

$$\rho_m = \frac{AR_m}{EPR_m} \tag{3.10}$$

or alternately (by means of Equation 3.9) as

$$\rho_m = \frac{B_m}{A_m} \tag{3.11}$$

Machine Production Control Channel A machine (or workstation or factory) has, associated with it, a production control channel PCC_m.[9] The cycle time of the machine is determined in part by the normalized width of this channel (i.e., the narrower the channel, the longer is the cycle time).

9 The production control channel is sometimes referred to as the *gap* of a machine—the *normalized* gap between its occupancy (utilization) and its capacity. *If the machine's utilization and capacity are computed correctly,* then the production control channel and the gap are equivalent.

Equations for determining PCC_m include

$$PCC_m = 1 - \rho_m \qquad (3.12)$$

and

$$PCC_m = \frac{A_m - B_m}{A_m} \qquad (3.13)$$

Workstation Performance

Measures associated with the performance of a workstation include

- Workstation throughput rate TH_{ws}
- Workstation maximum sustainable capacity SC_{ws}
- Workstation maximum theoretical capacity EPR_{ws}
- Workstation availability A_{ws}
- Workstation busy rate B_{ws}
- Workstation occupancy rate ρ_{ws}
- Workstation production control channel width PCC_{ws}

A discussion of the performance measures of a workstation will make sense in general only if the workstation supports a single process step and every machine in the workstation is qualified to support that process step and only that process step. If the workstation satisfies these assumptions, then its performance measures follow directly from the measures employed to assess each of its machines. For the cases in which these assumptions do not hold, discussions and illustrations will be provided in later chapters.

Therefore, under the assumption of a workstation that supports just one process step and in which every machine in the workstation supports that step, its performance measures will be described. I begin with workstation throughput.

Workstation Throughput Rate   The throughput rate of a workstation, under the assumptions just listed, is the sum of the average throughputs (i.e., rate of flow of jobs) of each of the machines in the workstation. Using TH_{ws} to designate workstation throughput, and assuming M machines in the workstation, we may state that

$$TH_{ws} = \sum_{m=1}^{M} TH_m \qquad (3.14)$$

For example, if a workstation has three machines ($M = 3$) and their throughput rates are 3, 3.4, and 4 jobs per hour, on average, respectively, the throughput of the entire workstation is simply $3 + 3.4 + 4 = 10.4$ jobs per hour.

Workstation Maximum Sustainable Capacity   The practical capacity of a workstation is given by its maximum sustainable capacity and is denoted as SC_{ws}. For example, consider the case in which it would be irrational (i.e., owing to an unacceptably high level of workstation or factory cycle time) for more than 12 jobs per hour to flow through a workstation. Thus, if the factory operates 80 hours per week, then the workstation's maximum sustainable capacity is given as

$$SC_{ws} = 12 \text{ jobs/hour} \bullet 80 \text{ hours}$$
$$= 960 \text{ jobs/week maximum sustainable}$$
$$\text{workstation capacity}$$

Workstation Maximum Theoretical Capacity   The upper bound on workstation capacity is the absolute maximum workstation capacity possible under strictly theoretical conditions. These conditions would exist if there were no variability whatsoever in the factory. If this were the case, you would be able to increase the flow of jobs through a workstation to its upper bound. The upper bound on workstation capacity (i.e., the effective process rate of the entire workstation under the assumptions cited) is equal to the sum of the effective process rates of its machines. That is,

$$\text{Workstation capacity upper bound} = EPR_{ws} = \sum_{m=1}^{M} EPR_m \qquad (3.15)$$

or

$$EPR_{ws} = \sum_{m=1}^{M} \frac{1}{EPT_m} \qquad (3.16)$$

Workstation Availability   The availability of a workstation is denoted as A_{ws} and is the average amount of time the workstation is up, running, and qualified to process jobs per unit of time (e.g., per week). Given the determination of the availability of each of the workstation's machines, and given M machines, an equation for workstation availability is provided by

$$A_{ws} = \frac{\sum\limits_{m=1}^{M} A_m}{M} \tag{3.17}$$

Workstation Busy Rate   The busy rate of a workstation is given by determining the arrival rate of jobs at the queue in front of the workstation and the raw process time of the workstation. Equation (3.16) serves to determine the effective process rate of the workstation, and if it is divided by the workstation availability (Equation 3.17), the workstation's raw process rate PR_{ws} may be found. Thus the equation for the busy rate of a workstation is

$$B_{ws} = \frac{AR_{ws}}{PR_{ws}} \tag{3.18}$$

Workstation Occupancy Rate   The occupancy rate of a workstation is the percentage of time it is in the busy state per time period. Designated as ρ_{ws}, the workstation occupancy rate is given by

$$\rho_{ws} = \frac{AR_{ws}}{EPR_{ws}} \tag{3.19}$$

or alternately (using Equation 3.18) as

$$\rho_{ws} = \frac{B_{ws}}{A_{ws}} \tag{3.20}$$

Workstation Production Control Channel   The production control channel of a workstation is denoted as PCC_{ws}. Equations for the determination of PCC_{ws} include

$$PCC_{ws} = 1 - \rho_{ws} \tag{3.21}$$

and

$$PCC_{ws} = \frac{A_{ws} - B_{ws}}{A_{ws}} \tag{3.22}$$

Factory Performance

Metrics that have been used in an attempt to measure the performance of an overall factory include but are definitely not limited to

- Factory cycle time CT_f

- Factory cycle-time efficiency CTE_f
- Factory throughput rate TH_f
- Factory maximum sustainable capacity SC_f
- Factory maximum theoretical capacity EPR_f
- Product lead time
- Factory moves
- Factory inventory WIP_f

Factory Cycle Time   If computed properly, factory cycle time is one of a handful of important performance metrics. Unfortunately, some firms fail to compute or interpret this measure correctly. Equation (3.1) is needed to compute raw factory cycle time and is repeated here:

$$CT_f = \sum_{ps=1}^{P} CT_{ps}$$

where CT_f = cycle time of the entire factory
CT_{ps} = cycle time of a given process step
P = total number of process steps in the factory

Note that the cycle time of all process steps, including those involving transit and inspection/test (if a predetermined operation in the process flow), must be summed to arrive at the value of raw factory cycle time. As you will discover, however, the cycle time of a factory will vacillate, often dramatically, with its loading. For example, a factory operating close to its maximal capacity may have a cycle time of, say, 100 days. However, simply by reducing the loading a small amount, say, 5 or 10 percent, the cycle time could—depending on the specific scenario—fall to just 50 days. Remember this the next time you attempt to compare the performance of two factories or evaluate the impact on cycle time of any changes within a particular factory!

Factory Cycle-Time Efficiency   As with factory cycle time, factory cycle-time efficiency can be an extremely useful measure, but only if it is computed and interpreted correctly. A means to determine raw factory cycle-time efficiency is given by Equation (3.23):

$$CTE_f = \frac{Process\ Time_f}{CT_f} \tag{3.23}$$

Recall from Figure 3.5 that a factory's process time includes the time devoted to all value-added as well as non-value-added process steps. Alternative representations of factory cycle-time efficiency may omit any non-value-added process step time (e.g., time consumed by transit, inspection, or test). As long as you are consistent, however, either definition may suffice. (The inverse of cycle-time efficiency, by the way, is a metric that has been denoted as the *X-factor*.)

The problem with the factory cycle-time efficiency metric (and the X-factor) is precisely the same as pointed out for factory cycle time. Specifically, unless this metric is normalized for the loading imposed on the factory, it fails to provide valid information.

Factory Throughput Rate   A factory's throughput rate is the average, over a specific time period, of the rate of flow of jobs through the entire factory. For example, if the number of jobs exiting the factory averages 900 units per week, the throughput rate is given as 900 units per week. It must be stressed, however, that the average number of jobs started into the factory each week over the period of interest might be considerably more than 900 units per week. This will happen if either there is a high scrap rate or—and more likely—if the factory capacity limits factory throughput to just 900 units per week.

Factory Maximum Sustainable Capacity   Some firms assume that a factory's capacity is the *maximum* theoretical capacity (e.g., upper bound on throughput in terms of jobs per unit time) of the factory's bottleneck workstation (or workstations). If, however, the factory actually operated at the theoretical limit of its bottleneck (or even close to it), its cycle time would approach infinity. Consequently, a factory's maximum sustainable capacity is determined by the maximum factory cycle time that the firm can tolerate. Stated another way, *factory cycle time determines factory capacity.*

Note that this statement is the converse of conventional wisdom, which says that factory capacity determines factory cycle time. Figure 3.8 serves to confirm the fact that, in practice, cycle time determines capacity. Two factory operating curves (labeled *"Cycle Time A"* and *"Cycle Time B"*) have been developed using a simulation model of a real-world factory. A factory operating curve, in turn, is simply a plot of factory loading (i.e., the ratio of starts to capacity) versus the associated factory cycle time (Aurand and Miller, 1997).

FIGURE 3.8

Factory operating curves.

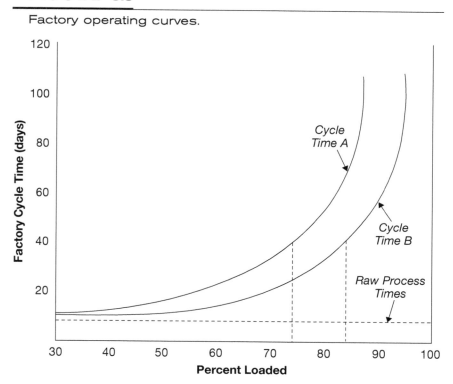

The sum of all raw process times for all process steps in the factory (including such non-value-added steps as inspection and transit) has been determined and is indicated by the dashed horizontal line. This value is approximately eight days.[10]

The operating curve labeled "*Cycle Time A*" was developed for the factory when it operated under its original level of variability. The curve labeled "*Cycle Time B*" was developed for the same factory after some reduction in variability.

At a low factory loading (i.e., low factory throughput rate), the cycle time for the factory under condition A is close to its raw process time (only loadings from 30 to 100 percent of the maximum theoretical factory loading have been plotted). Once the loading

---

10 As mentioned previously, some analysts define the sum of all raw process times to be the sum of only all value-added process times (i.e., transit and inspection times are not included). The choice is one of personal preference, and either may be used if employed in a consistent manner.

increases, however, the factory cycle time increases. At a loading of 74 percent, for example, factory cycle time is 40 days (about five times its raw process time). At a loading of 87 percent, the cycle time has *gone ballistic;* that is, it is increasing exponentially with loading.

With a reduction in factory variability, however, cycle-time performance is improved significantly. For example, while factory A, at a loading of 74 percent, had a 40-day cycle time, factory B had the same 40-day cycle time at 84 percent loading. Furthermore, at a loading of 87 percent (the same loading that "broke" factory A), the cycle time of factory B is just 43 days. Factory B's cycle time does not, in fact, go ballistic until its loading (i.e., throughput) reaches about 95 percent of its maximum theoretical capacity.

Returning to the notion of factory capacity and its relation to factory cycle time, it is hopefully obvious that the maximum permissible value of cycle time determines (or should determine) factory capacity. For example, and using factory A as a basis, if our firm (and our customers) cannot tolerate more than a 60-day cycle time, then the maximum sustainable factory loading must be 82 percent or less.

Factory Lead Time   The *lead time* for a given product type is the time allotted for its production. For example, if we have promised a customer his or her delivery in 20 days, then 20 days is the lead time. Clearly, one should have a good estimate of factory cycle time (both the average cycle time and the variability about that time) before making a lead-time promise.

Factory Moves   The *moves* within a factory are given by the sum of the number of jobs that have flowed through each factory workstation over a given time period. I've encountered some factory managers who rely on factory moves as their favorite measure of factory (or workstation or machine) performance. This attraction is based on the belief that the more moves within the factory, the better it must be performing. There is, however, no basis for this belief, and moves—as will be discussed in more detail in Chapter 8—are actually one of the worst ways to evaluate a factory.

Factory Inventory   Factory inventory, known as *work in progress* (WIP), is determined by the factory throughput rate and its cycle time. Little's equation (a.k.a. *Little's law*) states that

$$WIP_f = TH_f \bullet CT_f \qquad (3.24)$$

Little's equation is the first of the three fundamental equations necessary for determining a factory's performance. The equation also may be used to estimate the amount of inventory in a given workstation. This level of WIP may be found simply by multiplying the throughput of jobs through the workstation by the workstation's cycle time. Little's equation and the two other fundamental equations will be covered in detail in Chapter 5.

PUTTING IT ALL TOGETHER

I've listed and briefly discussed a fair number of terms and concepts in this chapter. The best way to both clarify and reinforce the material just covered is by means of a numerical example. Figure 3.9 depicts a factory with three workstations that will be employed to support the illustration. Jobs arrive at this factory at a constant rate of three jobs every two hours, or 1.5 jobs per hour. Table 3.1 serves to indicate most of the pertinent data associated with the factory.

It is obvious from the figure that the DoR value of the factory is 2 (i.e., six operations divided by three workstations). There is one nest, composed of all three workstations, with the same DoR. As noted previously, the throughput rate into the factory (i.e., jobs arriving at workstation A from outside the factory) is 1.5 jobs per hour. We shall assume that the factory operates 168 hours per week.

From Table 3.1, we may compute the effective process rate EPR_m of each machine in the example. To accomplish this, we must

TABLE 3.1

Factory Data, Phase 1

Workstations	A		B				C			
Machines	A1	A2	B1	B2	B3	B4	C1	C2	C3	C4
Block time (hours/week)	6.8	6.8	5.2	5.2	5.2	5.2	2	2	2	2
Downtime (hours/week)	10	10	20	20	20	20	6.4	6.4	6.4	6.4
Downtime plus block time (hours/week)	16.8	16.8	25.2	25.2	25.2	25.2	8.4	8.4	8.4	8.4
Process rate (jobs/hour)	2	2	1	1	1	1	0.9	0.9	0.9	0.9

FIGURE 3.9

Reentrant factory illustration.

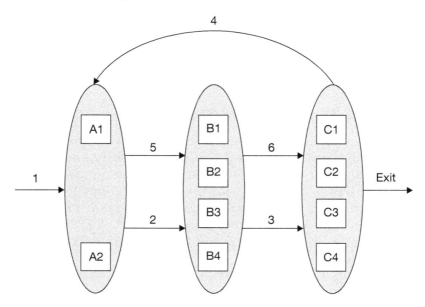

first determine the availability of each machine by means of Equation (3.2), that is,

$$A_m = \frac{T - (DT_m + BT_m)}{T}$$

The sum of the downtime and blocked time for each machine is provided in the row of Table 3.1 labeled "Downtime plus block time," and the total time T is simply 168 hours. To keep matters simple, it has been assumed that each machine in a workstation is identical and has identical performance.

The calculations for the availability of two of the machines, A1 [designated as $A_m(\text{A1})$] and B1 [designated as $A_m(\text{B1})$], are shown below and serve to illustrate the procedure employed to determine the availability of all the machines in the factory.

$$A_m(\text{A1}) = \frac{T - (DT_{A1} + BT_{A1})}{T} = \frac{168 - (16.8)}{168} = 0.90 = 90 \text{ percent}$$

$$A_m(\text{B1}) = \frac{T - (DT_{B1} + BT_{B1})}{T} = \frac{168 - (25.2)}{168} = 0.85 = 85 \text{ percent}$$

We repeat this process to develop the availabilities of all 10 machines. Then, using Equation (3.6), we may compute the effective process rates of the machines.

For example, the effective process rates (i.e., the maximum theoretical capacity) of machines A1 and B1 are given by

$$EPR_m(A1) = A_m(A1) \bullet PR_m(A1) = 0.90 \bullet 2 = 1.80 \text{ jobs/hour}$$

and

$$EPR_m(B1) = A_m(B1) \bullet PR_m(B1) = 0.85 \bullet 1 = 0.85 \text{ jobs/hour}$$

This is repeated for all 10 machines, and the results have been inserted into Table 3.2.

At this point we might wish to conduct a "sanity check." Specifically, is the factory configuration and capacity of Figure 3.9 sufficient to accommodate the throughput rates imposed on each workstation? To answer this, we must determine the total throughput imposed on each workstation and compare that with the workstation's maximum theoretical capacity.

Assuming that there are no losses (e.g., no scrap) in the network, the throughput rate imposed on each workstation is 1.5 + 1.5, or 3, jobs per hour. For this simple factory, the maximum theoretical capacity of each workstation may be computed by adding up the EPR_m values of the machines in the workstation. That is,

$$EPR_{ws}(A) = 1.8 + 1.8 = 3.6 \text{ jobs/hour}$$
$$EPR_{ws}(B) = 0.85 + 0.85 + 0.85 + 0.85 = 3.4 \text{ jobs/hour}$$
$$EPR_{ws}(C) = 0.855 + 0.855 + 0.855 + 0.855 = 3.42 \text{ jobs/hour}$$

TABLE 3.2

Factory Data, Phase 2

Workstation	A		B				C			
Machine	A1	A2	B1	B2	B3	B4	C1	C2	C3	C4
Downtime plus block time (hours/week)	16.8	16.8	25.2	25.2	25.2	25.2	8.4	8.4	8.4	8.4
Availability	0.9	0.9	0.85	0.85	0.85	0.85	0.95	0.95	0.95	0.95
Process rate (jobs/hour)	2	2	1	1	1	1	0.9	0.9	0.9	0.9
Effective process rate (jobs/hour)	1.8	1.8	0.85	0.85	0.85	0.85	0.855	0.855	0.855	0.855

Since the maximum theoretical capacities (i.e., upper bound on capacity) of each workstation exceeds the throughput rate of three jobs per hour, we may assume, at least for now, that each workstation is capable of supporting the job flow.

Next, let's consider a transformation of the workstation-centric model of Figure 3.9 into a process-step-centric model. To accomplish this, we must first determine the specific machine-to-process-step dedications in each workstation. We'll begin by assuming that every machine in a workstation is capable of supporting any process step that flows through that workstation. This leads to the process-step-centric flowchart in Figure 3.10. (I've assumed, for sake of simplicity, that every process step is a value-added operation, and thus the process-step numbers are enclosed by white circles.)

The throughput rate imposed on each process step is listed, in parentheses, above the arrows leading into the process step. The total capacity (i.e., maximum theoretical capacity) of the machines supporting each of the process steps flowing through each workstation (as shown in the triangles) is listed below the triangles.

Now examine what would happen if we were to reallocate machines to process steps in each workstation. Specifically, consider the following allocations:

- Process step 1→ machine A1
- Process step 2→ machines B1 and B2
- Process step 3→ machines C1 and C2
- Process step 4→ machine A2
- Process step 5→ machines B3 and B4
- Process step 6→ machines C3 and C4

FIGURE 3.10

Process-step-centric representation.

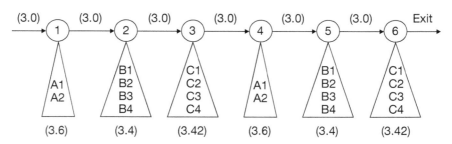

Employing these allocations, we may configure a new process-step-centric flow model for this factory. This model is depicted in Figure 3.11.

Notice that by simply changing machine to process-step assignments, a new factory configuration has been created. This new configuration supports precisely the same process-step flow but now reflects a complete decoupling of the factory involved. This is evident if we construct the workstation-centric flow model for the factory configured in Figure 3.11. This model is shown in Figure 3.12. The factory of Figure 3.12 has no reentrant loops (and thus a DoR value of 1) but is equivalent, in terms of the process-step flow, to the original reentrant factory of Figure 3.9.

The decoupling of the factory leads to new designations for the workstations. Now, rather than having three workstations (A, B, and C), we have six (virtual) workstations (A, B, C, A', B', and C'). Beneath each workstation is listed the upper bound on its capacity (i.e., the sum of the EPR_m values of the machines in the

FIGURE 3.11

Fully decoupled factory in process-step-centric form.

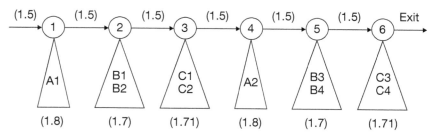

FIGURE 3.12

Fully decoupled factory in workstation-centric form.

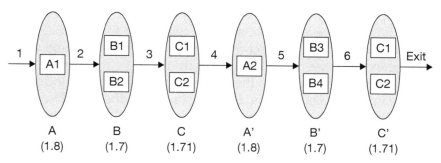

workstations). Since the arrival rate is the same for every workstation, that is, 1.5 jobs per hour, we can determine their occupancy
rate by means of Equation (3.19). These values are listed below.

$$\rho_{ws}(A) = \frac{1.5}{1.8} = 0.8333 = 83.33 \text{ percent} = \rho_{ws}(1)$$

$$\rho_{ws}(B) = \frac{1.5}{1.7} = 0.8824 = 88.24 \text{ percent} = \rho_{ws}(2)$$

$$\rho_{ws}(C) = \frac{1.5}{1.71} = 0.8772 = 87.72 \text{ percent} = \rho_{ws}(3)$$

$$\rho_{ws}(A') = \frac{1.5}{1.8} = 0.8333 = 83.33 \text{ percent} = \rho_{ws}(4)$$

$$\rho_{ws}(B') = \frac{1.5}{1.7} = 0.8824 = 88.24 \text{ percent} = \rho_{ws}(5)$$

$$\rho_{ws}(C') = \frac{1.5}{1.71} = 0.8772 = 87.72 \text{ percent} = \rho_{ws}(6)$$

From these values we can identify (under some very restrictive assumptions that will be relaxed in Chapter 5) the bottleneck
(i.e., choke point or constraint) process steps and workstations.
Specifically:

- Process steps 2 and 5, having the highest occupancy rates,
  are the bottleneck operations.
- Workstations B and B', because they are composed of the
  machines supporting the bottleneck process steps, are the
  bottleneck workstations.

In addition (and under the same restrictive assumptions), we
may determine the capacity of the entire factory—the upper bound
on the throughput supported by the bottleneck process steps. This
upper bound on factory throughput is determined by finding the
lowest upper bound of process-step effective process rates. This is
1.7 jobs per hour (for either process steps 2 or 5). Thus, given ideal
conditions and the assumptions to be relaxed in Chapter 5, at this
point we will assume the factory capacity to be its maximum theoretical capacity, that is, 1.7 jobs per hour.

Finally, let's determine the cycle time of the factory under the
same restrictive assumptions. If we assume that there is absolutely
no variability in the machines, process rates, and throughput rate,
the cycle time of the factory may be determined by adding the cycle
times of all the process steps—including those of transit times.

Assuming that the time required to move from one nontransit process step to another is five minutes (0.0833 hours) and that the transit process steps are $CT_1, CT_2, \ldots, CT_6$, then the factory cycle time is given by

$$CT_f = CT_1 + CT_{ps}(1) + CT_2 + CT_{ps}(2) + CT_3 + CT_{ps}(3) + CT_4$$
$$+ CT_{ps}(4) + CT_5 + CT_{ps}(5) + CT_6 + CT_{ps}(6)$$

We know that $CT_1, CT_2, CT_3, CT_4, CT_5$, and CT_6 are each 0.0833 hour in duration, and thus the transit portion of the factory cycle time is 6 • 0.0833, or 0.5, hours. We next determine the nontransit process-step times, which are given by finding the inverse of their effective process times, that is,

$$CT_{ps}(1) = \frac{1}{EPR_{ps}(1)} = \frac{1}{1.8} = 0.5556$$

$$CT_{ps}(2) = \frac{1}{EPR_{ps}(2)} = \frac{1}{1.7} = 0.5882$$

$$CT_{ps}(3) = \frac{1}{EPR_{ps}(3)} = \frac{1}{1.71} = 0.5848$$

$$CT_{ps}(4) = \frac{1}{EPR_{ps}(4)} = \frac{1}{1.8} = 0.5556$$

$$CT_{ps}(5) = \frac{1}{EPR_{ps}(5)} = \frac{1}{1.7} = 0.5882$$

$$CT_{ps}(6) = \frac{1}{EPR_{ps}(6)} = \frac{1}{1.71} = 0.5848$$

Adding these process-step cycle times (which total 3.4572 hours) to the total transit time, we determine the cycle time of the factory to be 3.4572 + 0.5 = 3.9572 hours.

Employing Equation (3.24), we also could determine the total inventory in the factory, that is, the product of the factory throughput (1.5 jobs per hour) times the job cycle time (3.9572 hours). The total factory inventory at any given time thus is predicted to be 5.9358 jobs.

There are two matters in particular that should be clarified at this point. First, while under perfect conditions the cycle time of the factory might be 3.9572 hours (or something on the order of 4 hours), under more realistic circumstances, the actual factory cycle time could be several times this value. For example, in a less than ideal environment, this factory's cycle time easily could exceed 25 hours! The reason for this is variability, a factor ignored thus far.

Second, the transformation of the factory of Figure 3.9 (a fully coupled system with a DoR of 2) into that of Figure 3.12 (a completely decoupled system with a DoR of 1) is not nearly so easy to accomplish in a real factory—nor necessarily practical. However, for purpose of illustration, the factory, its throughput, and effective process rates were carefully selected so as to permit the development of a completely decoupled system without the need to add more machines.

This does not diminish, however, the importance of at least attempting to reduce the DoR of any real factory. In fact, as we shall see, it actually may be worthwhile to buy some additional machines simply for the sake of DoR reduction. The cost of those machines could well be more than made up for by improved factory performance.

CHAPTER SUMMARY

A number of important concepts—and terminology, definitions, and notation—have been covered in this chapter. But it must be recognized that the discussion has been restricted to metrics measured by their average values. Variability, one of the three enemies of factory performance, has been ignored. This omission will be rectified in Chapter 5.

One of the most important messages contained in this chapter is that there are two ways to measure the capacity of process steps, machines, workstations, or factories. Specifically, there is a significant practical difference between an entity's maximum *sustainable* capacity *SC* and its maximum *theoretical* capacity *EPR*.

Chapter 4 will allow you to combine what has been covered in this chapter with your experience, judgment, intuition, and insight so as to determine how to improve the performance of a simple factory. First, though, let's check into the happenings at Muddle, Inc. More specifically, just how do Dan and Brad feel about their one week of training in lean manufacturing?

CASE STUDY 3: DAN IS NOT AMUSED

In Case Study 2 we left Dan Ryan and Brad Simmons in the company cafeteria. Brad warned Dan not to mention that he had some (limited) previous schooling in factory performance improvement prior to attending Muddle's *LEAN* Forward training class. It's now Friday, and the week-long class (the two-week off-site class at the ritzy resort was restricted to management), as taught by Sally Swindel, is over. The purpose of this class allegedly was to "train the trainer"; that is, each person who has taken the class is assumed to know, at its conclusion, enough about lean manufacturing to teach it to other factory personnel. They, in turn, are then assumed to know enough to teach it to the personnel in their departments.

Once again we encounter Dan and Brad in the company cafeteria, now mulling over the lean manufacturing training course.

"Brad, I kept my mouth shut this entire week, just as you advised. But now that the course is over, I've got to say that it was a joke. A really bad joke. I've . . ." Dan pauses as a well-dressed woman (an oddity in the casual atmosphere of a Muddle factory site) takes a seat at their table. Brad introduces her.

"Dan," says Brad, "I'd like you to meet Julia Austen. You may recall that Julia also was in this week's course. She was sitting in the back of the room."

"How do you do," says Dan, warily.

"I'm doing quite well," replies Julia, "but do go on. You were saying that the course was a joke . . . a really bad joke."

"Dan, old boy," interjects Brad, "not to worry. Julia shared her thoughts on the course with me this morning. I'd say that the three of us are at least somewhat in agreement as to our impressions of the course. It was pretty much a pep talk coupled with lots of slogans and some rather obvious advice on how to do some rather elementary things, like clean up the factory floor and put tools where they belong. But, if I do say so, it really wouldn't hurt to follow that advice. We've got some real messy people out there." Julia nods in agreement.

"I agree that several of the ideas that were presented made sense," says Dan. "And I sure as heck agree that there is a lot of waste and sloppiness in the factory. But, for heaven's sake, how can we now be expected to 'go forth and teach the masses.' Good grief, we've only had a week of training—some rather dubious training I might add. Furthermore, based on the lessons my former colleagues learned at ToraXpress, there's a whole lot more to factory performance than what Sally Swindel covered. Frankly, we could clean up the clutter and polish every machine in this factory until we see our reflections, but I'm not convinced that's all this company needs to obtain real, significant, and sustainable performance improvement."

"I absolutely agree that a week is hardly enough to become an expert in lean, but the instructor did provide us with a book," replies Brad, pointing to a copy of *Lean Is the Answer.*

"ToraXpress, you say," Julia says, changing the subject. "That's the firm Muddle bought and had to shut down. How about sharing the lessons you say you learned from your time there?"

"Sure," says Dan. "But let me say that I was working as an intern in ToraXpress's finance department at the time and not directly involved in factory performance improvement. So a lot of what I'm going to tell you is second hand."

"That's alright," says Julia, "I'm just curious as to how ToraXpress managed to so quickly improve itself and why things went sour so soon afterward."

"Well," Dan replies, "here's what I believe happened. As you may know, ToraXpress was in a bad way for years. The owner of the company brought in consultant after consultant. They tried every management and manufacturing fad you could think of. In fact, they even implemented lean manufacturing based on the recommendation of Sally Swindel, the very same Sally Swindel who just spent this week telling us that lean would cure this company's ills."

"So," says Brad, "what happened? Did lean turn things around? Was it really the answer?"

"Actually," says Dan, "I'm told that things just went from bad to worse. Every once in a while, there would be a brief period of improvement—something Professor Leonidas calls the Hawthorne effect—but then things would return to the norm or worse. For example, the lean teams would conduct waste walks and *kaizen* events and what not. They'd clean up work areas and take lots of before-and-after photographs. By the way, I was told that management really liked those pictures; they gave them the feeling that all the firm's problems would go away. But, within a few weeks or months, the work areas would revert back to the same old mess, and you'd see the same old sloppy habits reappear. In the meantime, factory cycle time just got worse. As Professor Leonidas told us later, you've got to change the company's culture and get the involvement and engagement of everyone up to and including the CEO. And you've got to provide an explanation for doing things, and that requires some knowledge of the science of manufacturing."

"That fits in with my reaction to Sally's course," replies Julia. "I kept wondering how you maintain performance improvement, and most of all, I wondered how cleaning up a workplace, or reducing batch sizes, or whatever directly and indirectly affected such things as cycle time and capacity. But first, Dan, who is this Professor Leonidas you mentioned?"

"Yeah," Brad agrees, "who is this guy, and when can we meet him?"

"Professor Leonidas, Professor Aristotle Leonidas to be exact, has a ranch about 30 miles from here. He's a retired professor. The owner of ToraXpress happened to meet the professor on a fishing trip. He was so impressed that he asked Leonidas to present a one-week course on what the professor called the science of manufacturing to the top management at ToraXpress. Shortly after that, the professor was asked to present the same course to all our managers and engineers. He went on to teach several four-week courses to our factory engineers. Within a year, factory cycle time was reduced by 75 percent, we increased our capacity—without buying any new equipment—and we improved the accuracy of our lead-time forecasts. Of course, that's when Muddle bought out ToraXpress and put in its own methods for manufacturing. And that's when our performance went down the drain."

"Those were pretty impressive results," remarks Brad, "but our senior plant manager, Tommy Jenkins, is definitely adverse to science. He's said more than once that you can't replace experience and gut feelings with science."

"I imagine," says Dan, "that's why he didn't resist the introduction of the lean manufacturing courses in this factory. The way that Sally Swindel presented the material, you'd be hard pressed to find much in the way of science."

"So," remarks Brad, frowning, "I take it that your professor friend doesn't think much of lean manufacturing."

"No, you're absolutely wrong about that," replies Dan, "Professor Leonidas is a firm believer in most of the concepts and methods that are now included in what is called lean manufacturing. He simply told us that lean manufacturing is only part of the solution, not *the* solution."

"Interesting," says Julia. "When can we meet this gentleman? Do you think we could convince him to present his lectures on the science of manufacturing at this site? How about it, fellows?"

"Hold on," replies Brad. "I'd like to meet the professor myself, but before we bring this matter up to management—particularly

Tommy Jenkins—we need to get real. As I mentioned before, Tommy doesn't even want to hear the word *science*. We might all wind up 'redeployed' or—at the least—sent to Room 101[11] if we ask Tommy to invite some guy here to talk about the science of manufacturing."

"Agreed," says Julia. "But what's stopping the three of us from talking to the professor? If we do so on our own time and keep our mouths shut, we should be okay. How about it, Dan, would you be able to arrange a meeting with the professor?"

"I can try, but like I said, he's retired and only presented the courses to ToraXpress as a favor to the firm's owner. I'll give it a shot; I've got his e-mail address somewhere. I'll let the two of you know what he says once I contact him."

"Great," says Brad, "I sure hope we can meet with the gentlemen. In the meantime, I hope to learn a little more about Sally Swindel; she's quite attractive, don't you think?"

We can conclude from the preceding discussion that Brad, Julia, and—particularly—Dan haven't yet been convinced that lean manufacturing is the answer—at least in the format being presented by Sally Swindel. Neither are they convinced that they, after just a one-week slide show, are now experts on lean manufacturing and ready and able to teach their coworkers—and, in particular, to provide intelligent answers to any questions that might be raised. Perhaps they're just wrong. Perhaps lean manufacturing is so simple that you can learn everything you need to know in a week of training, followed by a reading of *Lean Is the Answer*.

Then again, perhaps you can become a world-class brain surgeon or fully qualified rocket scientist in a week. Sarcasm aside, perhaps it takes just a bit more. Perhaps Professor Aristotle Leonidas can fill in the blanks. Then again, what does an old, retired professor know about how to improve Muddle? After all, isn't every factory different? Doesn't it take years of actual experience in the factory even to begin to think about improving its performance?

---

11 Many of Muddle's employees would rather be fired than be sent to the firm's infamous Room 101. As we'll discover later, Julia Austen has had the unfortunate experience of being sent to Room 101. As did Winston Smith, a man we'll meet later.

Tommy Jenkins, the senior plant manager, is convinced that all it takes to run a factory is about 10 years of experience coupled with a "gut feel." In fact, many of the firm's plant and department managers are convinced that all it takes to manage a factory is intuition. If this is true, then you, dear readers, just might be able to improve the performance of the simple factory discussed in Chapter 4.

By the way, just what did Brad Simmons imply by his mention of hoping to learn more about Sally Swindel? And just who is he meeting for dinner tonight?

CHAPTER 3 EXERCISES

1. Given the factory workstation-centric model shown in Figure 3.13, develop its process-step-centric representation under the following set of job/machine dedications:
   - Process step 1→ machines A1 and A2
   - Process step 2→ machines B1, B2, and B3
   - Process step 3→ machines C1 and C4
   - Process step 4→ machine A2

FIGURE 3.13

Exercise 1.

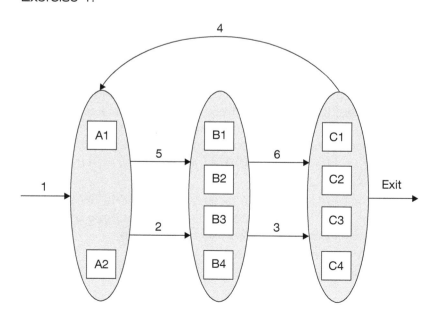

TABLE 3.3

Exercise 2 Data

State	Average Time (hours)	Percentage of Time
Waiting for a batch to form	1.3	13.68
Waiting in queue as part of a completed batch	2.2	23.16
Rework	0.5	5.26
Inspection	0.4	4.21
In processing (excluding rework)	3.9	41.05
In transit	1.2	12.63
Average cycle time	9.5	100

TABLE 3.4

Exercise 4 Data

State	Average Time in Hours per Week
Scheduled downtime	12
Up and running but being qualified	7
Processing (busy) time	96
Up and running but under inspection	6
Unscheduled downtime	25
Idle time	22

- Process step 5→ machines B2, B3, and B4
- Process step 6→ machines C2 and C3

2. A typical job flowing through a factory spends, on average, the amount of time in certain states as listed in Table 3.3. Construct the equivalent factory cycle-time components plot (in terms of percentages) for this factory.
3. What is the cycle-time efficiency of the factory described in Exercise 2?
4. A machine located in a factory with a 168-hour workweek spends the following amounts of average time in the states listed in Table 3.4. Given this information,
   - Plot the machine states.
   - Determine the availability of this machine.

Running a Factory: In Two Dimensions

In this chapter you are provided with the opportunity to manage and run a simulated factory. More specifically, you are asked to improve the cycle time of the factory (i.e., reduce its cycle time subject to certain budget limitations). There are no tricks to this problem, nor is there any attempt to mislead you. Simply employ what you have learned from whatever source to date (e.g., your real-world experience, your education or training, or simply your intuition and "gut feel") to achieve the cycle-time reduction goal.

THE ATTRIBUTES OF THE FACTORY

The factory you will manage—and seek to improve its performance—is an exceptionally simple facility. Its attributes may be summarized as follows:

- Twelve workstations connected in series (see Figures 4.1 and 4.2).
- Each workstation consists of a number of identical machines running at identical effective process rates (e.g., with identical maximum theoretical capacities).
- Neither batching nor cascading is employed.
- A single product type flowing from the first workstation to the second and so on until it exits the final (twelfth) workstation is being processed.
- There is zero transit time between workstations.

FIGURE 4.1

Workstation-centric flowchart for a 12-workstation factory.

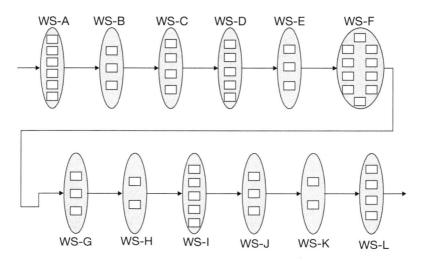

FIGURE 4.2

Process-step-centric flowchart for a 12-workstation factory.

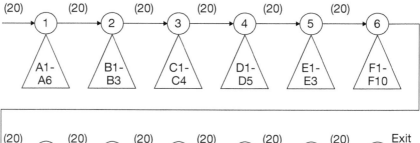
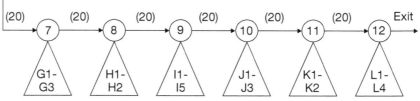

- There is no inspection or monitoring (i.e., the product simply moves from one value-added workstation to the next via the zero-time-transit process).
- There is no reentrancy (i.e., each workstation and its machines support a single operation in the process-step flow).

- There is no rework or scrap (i.e., it is assumed that the product flows directly from one workstation to the next without the need for any rework and no loss in yield).

Figure 4.1 presents the workstation-centric flowchart of the 12 workstations. The blocks within each workstation indicate the number of machines that initially exist in the associated workstation. For example, workstation A (WS-A) presently has six machines, whereas workstation F (WS-F) has 10. The direction of job flow from workstation to workstation is depicted by the arrows.

Assuming that every machine in a given workstation is qualified to support the process step conducted by that workstation, an equivalent process-step-centric model may be constructed for the 12-workstation factory. This model is shown in Figure 4.2. In this figure, the machines supporting each process step are listed in the triangle under the associated process step. For example, process step 2 is supported by machines B1, B2, and B3 (i.e., B1 through B3, designated in the figure as B1–B3) of workstation B.

The numbers in parentheses above each transit-step arrow indicate that the throughput flow rate of jobs through the factory and through each workstation in the factory is, on average, 20 units per day. Additional details as to the attributes of the factory are presented in the next section.

PROBLEM STATEMENT

Presently, the cycle time of this factory is 90.42 days—which is much, much worse than your hypothetical competition. Your job is to reduce the cycle time by means of either

- Adding additional machines to one or more of the workstations, or
- Improving the effective process rate EPR_{ws} (see Chapter 3 for a review of this parameter) of the existing machines in one or more workstations, or
- Using some combination of the preceding

Since additional machines or the improvement of effective process rates (either by increasing availability or by increasing run rates) cost money, you must achieve your goal within a limited budget. Specifically, the total amount you are permitted to spend is limited to $13M. (These funds may be allocated, up to the total amount of $13M, to the darkened cells of the 12-workstation simulation

FIGURE 4.3

Twelve-workstation factory simulation model, initial scenario.

File Edit View Insert Format Tools Data Window Help OM_IE OR_MM

Initialize

Copyright ©: 1994-2009 James P. Ignizio & Laura I. Burke

	$6	$4	$4	$10	$6	$6	$4	$10	$6	$4	$10	$4
Workstation	WS_A	WS_B	WS_C	WS_D	WS_E	WS_F	WS_G	WS_H	WS_I	WS_J	WS_K	WS_L
Add $M to increase EPR_{ws}	0.00	0.00	0.00	0.00	0.00	0.00	0.00	0.00	0.00	0.00	0.00	0.00
Original EPR_m	4.00	10.00	8.00	4.10	9.50	2.50	11.00	10.20	5.20	10.00	10.20	10.00
New EPR_m	4.00	10.00	8.00	4.10	9.50	2.50	11.00	10.20	5.20	10.00	10.20	10.00
Add $M to increase machines	0.00	0.00	0.00	0.00	0.00	0.00	0.00	0.00	0.00	0.00	0.00	0.00
Orignal Machine Count	6.00	3.00	4.00	5.00	3.00	10.00	3.00	2.00	5.00	3.00	2.00	4.00
New Machine Count	6.00	3.00	4.00	5.00	3.00	10.00	3.00	2.00	5.00	3.00	2.00	4.00
Original TH capacity (EPR_{ws})	24.00	30.00	32.00	20.50	28.50	25.00	33.00	20.40	26.00	30.00	20.40	40.00
New TH capacity (EPR_{ws})	24.00	30.00	32.00	20.50	28.50	25.00	33.00	20.40	26.00	30.00	20.40	40.00
Workstation "Utilization" (ρ_{ws})	0.83	0.67	0.62	**0.98**	0.70	0.80	0.61	**0.98**	0.77	0.67	**0.98**	0.50

Factory Throughput (lots per day)	**20**
Factory Cycle Time (CT_f)	**90.42**
Factory Inventory (WIP_f)	**1808**

0.00% Percentage Reduction in CT

Additional Cost for Cycle Time Reduction **$0.00 millions**

model.) Figure 4.3 summarizes in matrix form the existing condition of the factory.

Note in Figure 4.3 that such attributes as factory throughput (i.e., the rate of flow of jobs through the factory), factory cycle time, factory inventory, number of machines in each workstation, and the capacity (i.e., $EPR_{ws,}$ the maximum theoretical capacity) of each workstation are listed. The cells associated with these parameters are indicated in Table 4.1.

Next, we need to determine how much it will cost either to increase the maximum theoretical capacity (i.e., *EPR*) of each machine in a workstation or to add more machines to a workstation. The cost of an additional machine in each workstation is shown in Table 4.2. For example, if you wish to add one machine to those already existing in WS-A, it will cost $6M. Adding a machine to workstation B (WS-B) will require the allocation of $4M.

Next, consider what it will cost to improve the *EPR* of each and every machine in a given workstation. We know that the effective process rate of a machine is found by multiplying its availability by its raw process rate (i.e., ideal run rate in jobs per unit time). This means that to increase a machine's effective process rate, you can either (1) increase its availability, (2) increase its process speed, or (3) attempt to increase both the availability and process rate. To keep matters simple, we'll use Equation (4.1) to predict the impact of funds on increases in workstation *EPR* values by whatever means:

$$\$M = (\text{new } EPR_{ws} - \text{old } EPR_{ws})^5 \tag{4.1}$$

TABLE 4.1

Factory or Workstation Attributes

Attribute	Value	From Cell	Comments
Factory throughput	20 jobs/day	B14	Customer demand rate
Factory cycle time	90.42 days	B15	Average factory CT
Factory inventory	1808 jobs	B16	Average factory WIP
Effective process rate of each machine in WS-A	4 jobs/day	B5	This is the initial value of EPR per machine
EPR per machine in WS-A after improvement	4 jobs/day	B6	In initial matrix, no improvements have been made
Original machine count in WS-A	6 machines	B8	Initially, there are 6 machines in the workstation
Machine count in WS-A after improvement	6 machines	B9	In initial matrix, no additional machines have been added
Original workstation theoretical capacity for WS-A	24 jobs/day	B10	6 machines times 4 jobs/machine = 24 jobs/day
Theoretical capacity of WS-A after improvement	24 jobs/day	B11	No change from B10 because no improvement yet
WS-A workstation utilization (occupation rate)	0.83 (83 percent)	B12	Equals factory $TH/$ workstation capacity ρ_{ws}, or 20/24
Additional cost	$0.00M	M15	Cost incurred by improvements
Funds allocated to EPR improvement	$0.00M	B4:M4	No funds allocated
Funds allocated to adding machines	$0.00M	B7:M7	No funds allocated

TABLE 4.2

Machine Cost

Workstation	Cost of Each Additional Machine, in $M
A	6
B	4
C	4
D	10
E	6
F	6
G	4
H	10
I	6
J	4
K	10
L	4

This equation, for example, would predict that a change in the *EPR* of a workstation (a.k.a. *maximum theoretical capacity*) from a rate of 4 jobs per day to 4.5 jobs per day would require

$$\$M = (4.5 - 4)^5 = 0.5^5 = \$0.03125M, \text{ or } \$31,250$$

While this equation is merely a rough approximation used for purposes of illustration, it indicates the fact that an increase in the *EPR* of a workstation (i.e., by increasing the availability or run rates of the existing machines) requires funds that increase exponentially with the desired increase in the workstation's *EPR* value.

PROBLEM SOLUTION

Given the data and information in the preceding section, you now should be prepared to find a solution to the 12-workstation problem that will reduce factory cycle time subject to a budget limitation of $13M. You can try your skill, luck, gut feel, intuition, or prayers in solving this problem by using the simulation model provided at the following Web site:

www.mhprofessional.com/Ignizio/12WS_Ch4

Just one of the many approaches that have been employed is described below. It centers about the notion of *elevating the factory constraint.*

If you happen to be a fan of the theory of constraints (ToC), you might try to elevate the factory constraints one at a time. If, however, you examine the workstation utilization entries in cells B12 through M12, you will notice that there are *three* factory constraints, that is, workstation D, workstation H, and workstation K, each with utilization (i.e., occupation rate) of approximately 0.98. This raises some interesting questions—just some of which are listed below:

- Which factory constraint (i.e., workstation) should you begin with given a factory with multiple constraints?
- Should you add machines to the constraint?
- Or should you improve the *EPR* of the constraint (i.e., by using funds to increase the availability and/or run rate of the existing machines in the constraint workstation)?

- Or should you try some combination of adding machines and improving workstation *EPR*?

The decision you make with regard to each of these questions will make a difference—likely a big difference—in the solution you ultimately reach. This fact alone should be reason enough to give advocates of the theory of constraints some concern.

Once the theory of constraints advocate decides on which of the three factory constraints to begin with, the procedure employed is to add just enough resources (i.e., funds for either more machines or an increase in workstation *EPR*) so that the workstation selected for the allocation of funds is no longer a constraint. This is known as *elevation of the factory constraint*. The elevation procedure then is repeated for the new factory constraint. This process is continued until the budget limitation ($13M) is reached.

Any number of other approaches might be employed for the allocation of the $13M budget for factory performance improvement. Your task is to employ whatever method you prefer to accomplish a reduction in factory cycle time. So go ahead and see how you do. But don't look at the solution provided herein until after you've done your very best to reduce factory cycle time while staying within the $13M budget.

I've listed in Figure 4.4 one of the better solutions (i.e., most ToC-based solutions that have been generated by students and course attendees actually have been worse) arrived at by means of

FIGURE 4.4

Twelve-workstation factory simulation model with ToC-based solution.

	A	B	C	D	E	F	G	H	I	J	K	L	M
1					*Copyright © 1994-2008 James P. Ignizio & Laura I. Burke*								
2	Initialize		$6	$4	$4	$10	$6	$6	$4	$10	$6	$4	$10	$4
3	Workstation	WS A	WS B	WS C	WS D	WS E	WS F	WS G	WS H	WS I	WS J	WS K	WS L
4	Add $M to increase EPR_ws	0.00	0.00	0.00	1.00	0.00	0.00	0.00	2.00	0.00	0.00	0.00	0.00
5	Original *EPR_m*	4.00	10.00	8.00	4.10	9.50	2.50	11.00	10.20	5.20	10.00	10.20	10.00
6	New *EPR_m*	4.00	10.00	8.00	5.10	9.50	2.50	11.00	11.35	5.20	10.00	10.20	10.00
7	Add $M to increase machines	0.00	0.00	0.00	0.00	0.00	0.00	0.00	0.00	0.00	0.00	10.00	0.00
8	Original Machine Count	6.00	3.00	4.00	5.00	3.00	10.00	3.00	2.00	5.00	3.00	2.00	4.00
9	New Machine Count	6.00	3.00	4.00	5.00	3.00	10.00	3.00	2.00	5.00	3.00	3.00	4.00
10	Original TH capacity (*EPR_ws*)	24.00	30.00	32.00	20.50	28.50	25.00	33.00	20.40	26.00	30.00	20.40	40.00
11	New TH capacity (*EPR_ws*)	24.00	30.00	32.00	25.50	28.50	25.00	33.00	22.70	26.00	30.00	30.60	40.00
12	Workstation "Utilization" (*ρ_ws*)	0.83	0.67	0.62	0.78	0.70	0.80	0.61	0.88	0.77	0.67	0.65	0.50
13													
14	Factory Throughput (lots per day)	20											
15	Factory Cycle Time (*CT_f*)	21.84		*75.84% Percentage Reduction in CT*				Additional Cost for Cycle Time Reduction				$13.00	
16	Factory Inventory (*WIP_f*)	437											millions

the theory of constraints. First, a machine is added to workstation K (at a cost of $10M), then $2M is provided to improve the *EPR* of workstation H, and finally, $1M is allocated to workstation D for *EPR* improvement. The resulting cycle time is 21.84 days—a reduction of 75.84 percent over the initial value of 90.42 days. The degree of improvement is certainly impressive.

While the solution shown in Figure 4.4 achieved a 75.84 percent cycle-time reduction via the expenditure of $13M, consider the solution shown in Figure 4.5. Here, by means of optimization [i.e., genetic algorithms (Goldberg, 1989)], the factory cycle time has been reduced by an even more impressive 83.86 percent to 14.59 days!

Note that the optimal solution[1] in Figure 4.5 allocates funds across all 12 workstations.[2] These funds happen to be restricted solely to the improvement of workstation effective process rates rather than to the purchase of any machines.

The message one may take away from the ToC-based approach of Figure 4.4 and the optimization results [achieved via genetic algorithms (Goldberg, 1989)] of Figure 4.5 is that the theory of constraints is a strictly heuristic approach and as such cannot be

FIGURE   4.5

Twelve-workstation factory simulation model, optimized.

	A	B	C	D	E	F	G	H	I	J	K	L	M	O
1				*Copyright © 1994-2008 James P. Ignizio & Laura L. Burke*										
2	Initialize		$6	$4	$4	$10	$6	$6	$4	$10	$6	$4	$10	$4
3	Workstation		WS A	WS B	WS C	WS D	WS E	WS F	WS G	WS H	WS I	WS J	WS K	WS L
4	Add $M to increase EPR$_{ws}$		$1.52	$0.69	$0.83	$2.07	$0.05	$0.36	$1.70	$2.00	$0.52	$1.17	$1.93	$0.14
5	Original *EPR$_m$*		4.00	10.00	8.00	4.10	9.50	2.50	11.00	10.20	5.20	10.00	10.20	10.00
6	New *EPR$_m$*		5.09	10.93	8.96	5.26	10.06	3.31	12.11	11.35	6.08	11.03	11.34	10.67
7	Add $M to increase machines		0.00	0.00	0.00	0.00	0.00	0.00	0.00	0.00	0.00	0.00	0.00	0.00
8	Original Machine Count		6.00	3.00	4.00	5.00	3.00	10.00	3.00	2.00	5.00	3.00	2.00	4.00
9	New Machine Count		6.00	3.00	4.00	5.00	3.00	10.00	3.00	2.00	5.00	3.00	2.00	4.00
10	Original TH capacity (*EPR$_{ws}$*)		24.00	30.00	32.00	20.50	28.50	25.00	33.00	20.40	26.00	30.00	20.40	40.00
11	New TH capacity (*EPR$_{ws}$*)		30.53	32.79	35.86	26.29	30.17	33.14	36.34	22.70	30.39	33.09	22.68	42.69
12	Workstation "Utilization" (*ρ$_{ws}$*)		0.66	0.61	0.56	0.76	0.66	0.60	0.55	0.88	0.66	0.60	0.88	0.47
13														
14	Factory Throughput (lots per day)	20												
15	Factory Cycle Time (*CT$_f$*)	14.59	*83.86% Percentage Reduction in CT*					Additional Cost for Cycle Time Reduction				$13.00		
16	Factory Inventory (*WIP$_f$*)	292											millions	

---

1 Actually, this is the solution reached during just the first phase of an optimization procedure.

2 Obtaining accurate estimates of *EPR* improvement per dollar allocated and attempting to distribute these funds in the manner shown likely would be impractical in a real-world situation with imprecise real-world data.

guaranteed to reach an optimal solution or even a close to optimal solution. In fact, in any real-world factory, one can virtually guarantee that the theory of constraints will not achieve the best possible solution. Some of the reasons for the limitations of the theory of constraints include that

- Almost any real-world factory has multiple constraints.
- Factory constraints migrate (i.e., they change as a consequence of even slight changes in such things as product mix, starts policy, maintenance policies, etc.).
- The crucial impact of variability on factory—and bottleneck—performance is completely ignored.

This doesn't mean that the theory of constraints is "bad," only that there are usually more effective and less costly ways to improve factory performance. (More about this will be said in Chapter 6.)

Before proceeding to the next section, allow me to pose a question: Do you believe that it is possible to reduce the cycle time of a single workstation (while keeping all other factors in the factory constant) and actually wind up increasing *overall* factory cycle time? In other words, if you are an advocate of, say, lean manufacturing, would you believe that you actually could overdo the improvement of a single workstation at the expense of the factory? I will employ the 12-workstation model to investigate these matters.

YOUR INTUITION IS LIKELY TO BE WRONG

Return to the original 12-workstation factory scenario (accomplished by clicking on the icon labeled "Initialize" in the upper left-hand corner of the 12-workstation spreadsheet found on the Web site provided earlier). After initialization, the factory cycle time should revert to its original value of 90.42 days.

Now gradually increase the funds devoted to an increase in the effective process rate *EPR* of workstation A or, alternately, simply continue to add funding to increase the total number of machines in the workstation. (Feel free to ignore the $13M budget limit.) Either way, you are increasing the maximum theoretical capacity (i.e., EPR_{ws}) of the workstation. Figure 4.6 presents a graph that serves to indicate how factory cycle time changes with each increase in capacity (in terms of jobs per day) of either workstation A or workstation B.

FIGURE 4.6

Cycle times of workstations A and B as capacity is increased.

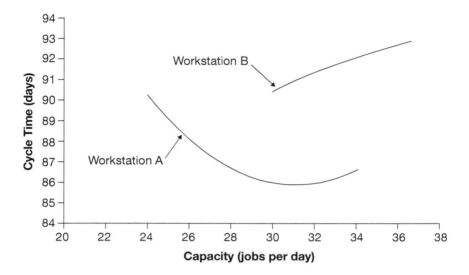

Notice in Figure 4.6 that as you increase the capacity of workstation A (while leaving all other workstations alone), the factory cycle time gradually drops to about 86 days. After that, however, any increase in the capacity of workstation A actually begins to increase factory cycle time. Increasing the capacity of workstation B (again, while leaving all other workstations alone), on the other hand, always results in an increase of factory cycle time over the range under consideration.

These results are counterintuitive to some people. I have, in fact, encountered individuals who refused to believe that the improvement of a single workstation (i.e., increasing its capacity) could possibly degrade a factory's overall performance. Once the three fundamental equations are covered in Chapter 5, it should become clearer, however, as to just when and how such results may happen. In the meantime, be wary of any methodology that fails to take a holistic view of the entire factory.

More specifically, recall that a real-world factory is a nonlinear, stochastic, dynamic system with feedback. When faced with such a system, you can rest assured that your intuition is almost always wrong. In short, factories are complex systems, and no matter how intelligent and experienced you might be, it is vital to avoid jumping to conclusions. Thankfully, there is a science that allows an objective analysis of such systems.

WHAT ABOUT LEAN MANUFACTURING?

The methods discussed thus far for the reduction of cycle time in a 12-workstation factory were based on guessing, intuition, the theory of constraints, and optimization. A lean manufacturing advocate may want to consider yet another approach. Specifically, a number of prominent lean manufacturing advocates have asserted that the workload in a factory should be *balanced*. More specifically, they state that the cycle time of each workstation ideally should be identical and that the factory must run at the customer demand rate (designated as the *takt rate*).[3]

Just a few of many statements of this belief are quoted below:

> A core principle of JIT [These authors state that just-in-time is synonymous with lean manufacturing] is that every operation within a production process should produce at the takt rate, regardless of the fact that most operations are capable of producing much faster [Hiroyuki Hirano and Makoto Furuya, *JIT Is Flow*, Vancouver, WA, PCS Press, 2006, p. 35].

> But what many companies fail to do is the more difficult process of stabilizing the system and creating "evenness"—a true balance lean flow of work. This is the Toyota concept of *heijunka*. . . . achieving *heijunka* is fundamental to eliminating *mura*, which is fundamental to eliminating *muri* and *muda* [Jeffery K. Liker, *The Toyota Way*, New York, McGraw-Hill, 2004, p 115].

> . . . work progresses from each station to the next in accordance with takt time and at the same rate as final assembly.

---

3 Examining Figure 4.5, wherein factory cycle time was minimized via optimization, note that the *EPR* values (and utilization) of the workstations differ considerably—indicating a production line that is most definitely *not* balanced. Yet we minimized factory cycle time via this procedure. Furthermore, factory inventory was minimized. This result, in itself, should give pause to a belief in balanced production lines.

> ... the work in each step has been carefully balanced
> with the work in every other step so that everyone is
> working to a cycle time equal to takt time [J. P. Womack
> and D. T. Jones, *Lean Thinking*, New York, The Free Press,
> 2003, p. 63].
> Level out the workload (*heijunka*) to the rate of cus-
> tomer demand or pull [Jay Arthur, "Core Ideas of Lean,"
> in *Lean Six Sigma Demystified*, New York, McGraw-Hill,
> 2007, p. 31].

As mentioned, a *balanced line* is achieved by having all workstations process jobs at the same rate as that of customer demand
(i.e., takt time). An alternate and equivalent definition of a balanced
line is one in which the cycle times of each workstation are identical. There are, in fact, numerous references in the lean manufacturing literature asserting that a balanced line will minimize factory
inventory. This assertion, if true, also would result in minimization
of factory cycle time. So, once again, what about using lean manufacturing to solve the 12-workstation problem?

Unfortunately, the simulation spreadsheet for the 12-worksta-
tion problem was not designed to accommodate attempts to balance the line. Specifically, it was developed so that one may only
increase the maximum theoretical capacity of the workstations.
I have, however, developed an even simpler factory model (one
consisting of just five workstations) that does permit line balancing
(Ignizio, 2008b, 2008c). And if a balanced line achieves the desired
cycle-time minimization on the 5-workstation model, it certainly
would achieve similar results for the 12-workstation model.

The five-workstation model is shown in workstation-centric
form in Figure 4.7. To keep things simple, as well as to permit the
development of a perfectly balanced production line, each workstation's effective process rate is assumed to be continuously variable over specific ranges.

In the five-workstation model, we shall assume that customer
demand rate is 20 jobs per hour. This is the rate (i.e., the takt rate)
at which the factory throughput shall be set. For simplicity, we
assume that all transit times are zero. The process rate of each of the
five workstations is continuously adjustable from a minimum to a
maximum speed (e.g., workstation A can be adjusted to a process
rate of from 10 to 25 jobs per hour, whereas workstation B can be
adjusted over the range of 10 to 40 jobs per hour). It would not be
wise, however, to set the workstation effective process rates below

FIGURE 4.7

The five-workstation model.

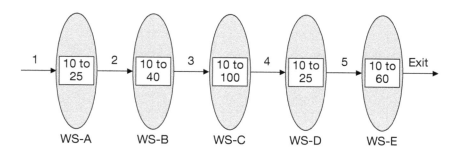

roughly 20.1 jobs per hour because, as a consequence of inherent factory variability, this would not allow for a sufficient gap between capacity and utilization. The factory simulation spreadsheet for this model may be found at

www.mhprofessional.com/Ignizio/5WS_Ch4

Readers are invited to observe what happens if the line is balanced according to the fundamental premise of lean manufacturing. The initial simulation scenario provided at the Web site for the factory is, in fact, a balanced line wherein every workstation has an effective process rate of 20.5 jobs per hour. The average cycle time and average inventory under this balanced scenario is 104.45 hours and 2088.98 units, respectively.

You are invited to try whatever scheme you believe might be superior, including running all workstations at their maximum effective process rate or balancing the line at effective process rates ranging from 20 to 25 jobs per hour (balancing at any higher rate than 25 jobs per hour is impossible owing to the limitations of workstations A and D).

The results of balancing the line using effective process rates from 20.1 (much lower and the factory will experience a near-infinite cycle time) to 25 units per hour (workstations A and D serve to determine this upper limit) are shown in Figure 4.8 (i.e., while the factory throughput is maintained at 20 units per hour.) One might assume from these results and from the statements in the lean manufacturing literature that cycle time and inventory are minimized via a balanced line in which all five workstations run at

FIGURE 4.8

Cycle times for balanced lines.

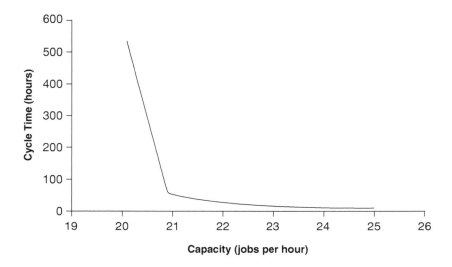

a rate of 25 jobs per hour. At this process rate, the balanced-line cycle time is 9.39 hours, and factory inventory is 187.76 units.

There is, however, a much better solution. Simply set the effective process rates of each workstation to their upper limit (e.g., 25, 40, 100, 25, and 60 jobs per hour, respectively) and note the results. In this (very) unbalanced line, both factory cycle time and factory inventory level are reduced over that of any balanced line. Cycle time is 5.03 hours, whereas factory inventory is 100.59 units. This is a reduction of more than 46 percent over the best balanced line.

In short, the factory performance of a balanced line, in terms of cycle time and inventory, is inferior to the performance of the five-workstation factory in which every workstation is set at its maximum speed. This should give pause to those who have accepted on face value assertions in the lean manufacturing literature that a balanced line running at the rate of customer demand is optimal (i.e., in terms of minimizing factory inventory and cycle time). Does this mean that what some denote as the fundamental basis of lean manufacturing is invalid? The answer is, "Not exactly."

The basis for the belief that a factory should employ a balanced line running at takt speed is a consequence of a narrow focus on *synchronous* factories. An ultimate example of a synchronous factory might be that of a soft-drink bottling plant. In such a plant, the flow of each job (i.e., each bottle) is synchronized with every other job. There is no extra room on the conveyor belt connecting one workstation to another, so balance and synchronization are essential.

Automobile assembly lines, while not necessarily strictly synchronous, are very close to being synchronized. In a moving automobile assembly line or a perfectly synchronized line, a balanced line makes sense. But this does not hold for *asynchronous* factories such as semiconductor wafer fabrication facilities.

The belief that balanced lines optimize factory performance originated in the study of traditional factories, specifically those with little or no automation. In such factories, it appeared to make sense to balance the workload. It simply did not seem fair to have the workers in one workstation almost always busy while the workers in another station were idle most of the time. In such a situation, a typical recommendation would be to move some of the workers from the mostly idle workstation to the much busier one, that is, balance the production line.

However, when one is dealing with factories that are highly automated, as in the case of the five-workstation factory demonstration, and particularly when the primary focus is on fast cycle time, it is almost always better to have every machine running at its maximum process rate—while factory throughput is maintained at the rate of customer demand. The caveat of "almost always" is employed because there are instances in which the cost (e.g., in terms of maintenance events or the provision for dealing with queues in front of slower workstations) may outweigh the advantage of faster cycle time.

The point is, however, that balanced lines may not be the best way (and quite often are most definitely *not* the best way) to configure and run a modern-day factory. Despite this, it has proven extremely difficult to convince some in the lean manufacturing community that there are situations in which science trumps lean. This simply does not fit the accepted narrative.

Before we leave this topic, it should be noted that while an unbalanced production line—with each workstation running at its maximum process rate—is almost always superior to a balanced line, it is not necessarily the case that such a line is optimal in terms of performance (i.e., in terms of minimal factory cycle time and inventory). This will be clarified and illustrated in Chapter 6.

CHAPTER SUMMARY

When I developed the 12-workstation model, more than 25 years ago, it was used to demonstrate methods for performance improvement in supply chains and business processes. With but minor changes in terminology, the model was changed to encompass performance improvement in factories. Whether the situation involves a factory, a supply chain, or a business process, the 12-workstation model illustrates the complexity inherent in even the most simple process flow. Moreover, the model has proven to be an extremely effective teaching tool.

In this chapter, our solutions to the 12-workstation model have been restricted, for the most part, to the first two dimensions of manufacturing, that is, to physical changes to workstations. That is, we were constrained to adding machines or increasing effective process rates.

The first alternative, adding machines, is definitely physical (and undeniably costly). The second, increasing machine EPR rates (i.e., increasing their maximum theoretical capacity—which also may be quite costly), may be achieved either by physical means or by dealing with complexity.

For example, we could change the physical nature of the machines in the workstation to increase their process rates. Or we could change the physical nature of the machines so as to increase their average availability (e.g., incorporate parts that are less likely to fail or require less frequent and less involved maintenance procedures). But we also could increase the EPR of the machines by other than physical means. That is, we could employ the approaches available in the third dimension of manufacturing to increase availability. This might be achieved by reducing the number of steps required to conduct a maintenance event, by reducing clutter in the workstation, by improving the training of the workstation operators and maintenance crew, or by improving the content and clarity of the maintenance specifications.

Alternately, we might employ a balanced line, a concept asserted to be the fundamental premise of lean manufacturing and to lead to minimized factory cycle time and inventory. As demonstrated by the five-workstation model, however, an unbalanced line may—and generally does for asynchronous factories—achieve superior performance.

The avenue thus far not open to us, however, was that of reducing the *variability* of the factory. In fact, thus far we have completely ignored variability—one of the three enemies of factory performance. Referring back to Figures 4.3 through 4.5, you may notice there were no data provided with regard to variability. The limited amount of data presented in those matrices served implicitly to restrict choices. Many firms, in fact, do not record data necessary to determine the variability existing in the factory.

Reduction of variability, however, is almost always easier and less costly to achieve—and has greater impact on factory performance—than any other approach. Before we proceed to exploitation of variability reduction, it is first necessary to introduce the concept of variability and then discuss and illustrate the three fundamental equations of manufacturing, the topics of Chapter 5.

CASE STUDY 4: PROFESSOR ARISTOTLE LEONIDAS

Dan Ryan contacted Professor Aristotle Leonidas via e-mail, just as he had promised. A meeting this weekend, at the professor's ranch, was agreed on. Dan, Brad, and Julia have arrived at the ranch and are presently engaged in a discussion with the professor.

"So let me get this straight," says the professor, "you'd like for me to present my course on the science of manufacturing to the members of Muddle's *LEAN* Forward team. More specifically, to those members of the team resident at your factory site. Is that correct?"

Julia, as the senior member of the visiting group, has been taking the lead in answering the professor's questions. "What we'd first like to have done," replies Julia, "is to have you present just a brief overview of the topic, say, at a brown-bag lunch meeting. That way the team, and our management, can get an idea of how we might include more science in our lean efforts."

"Ah," says the professor, "what you want is for me to convince your folks of the need for the science of manufacturing . . . over lunch. In other words, you'd like for me to put it all in a nutshell. Is that it?"

"That's right," says Julia. "Our management has a short attention span, and our senior plant manager isn't at all keen on science. Frankly, while he's a nice guy, he thinks all professors—or anyone with a Ph.D.—are 'eggheads.' It may be difficult to convince him, particularly if you use the word *science*. I'd suggest that you just call your work something like factory performance improvement."

Brad nods in agreement while Dan's eyes roll in disbelief.

"Children," replies the professor, "it sounds as if you have a bigger problem than the lack of science in your factory. Frankly, I'd be more concerned about your firm's managers, culture, and values. If what you say is any indication of your management's vision, my guess is that they want a quick and dirty solution—one that's void of anything as troublesome as needing to have an appreciation of science. So let me just say that I'm really not interested in being your managers' and the *LEAN* Forward team's lunchtime entertainment. If they're not willing to give me their full, undivided attention for at least eight hours, there's no point in wasting their time or mine."

At first, no one said a word on the drive back to the factory. After a few minutes, however, Dan breaks the silence.

"My recommendation is that we try to convince the *LEAN* Forward team and our management to attend an eight-hour presentation on the science of manufacturing. Good grief, our managers recently spent two whole weeks in training classes on lean manufacturing. So what's the big deal about rounding out their education with an eight-hour meeting? Why don't we . . ."

"Did you hear that old man?" Julia interrupts, ignoring Dan's question. "Your professor friend called us children!"

"Is that what's been bothering you?" asks Dan. "Julia, Professor Leonidas is 88 years old, for heaven's sake! He fought in World War II. The man worked with people like W. Edwards Deming and Joseph Juran after the war. He was involved with the training programs presented to the Japanese in the 1950s, the very same training programs that companies like Toyota admit to having had a major influence on their production systems. Besides, I don't think he meant anything by it, and if the professor wants to call us children, I've got no complaints. He's an educator, for heaven's sake, not a diplomat."

In response, Brad simply nods in agreement. Julia, for her part, stares straight ahead.

"Okay," says Dan, "what about my question? Why don't we at least try to convince the *LEAN* Forward team and our management to attend the professor's eight-hour talk? The worst that can happen is that they say no."

"Alright," replies Julia, "I'll do what I can to convince them. I've known and worked with Tommy Jenkins, our senior plant manager, for more than 10 years. We may not see eye to eye all the time, but he seems to respect my work. If I can get him to agree, the rest of the herd will follow, that I promise you."

"Besides," adds Brad, "if we can't get the three plant managers to attend, no one else will. That's standard operating procedure in this company. Unless management shows interest in this, no one else will—no matter how great the concept. So go ahead, Julia; give it your best shot."

"Agreed," Julia replies. "By the way, fellows, I just heard something very interesting last night. There's evidently a huge fight brewing between the *LEAN* Forward team leaders and the factory's quality control team."

"Really," says Brad, "tell us more."

"It seems," Julia continues, "that the quality control team intends to put up posters all over the factory and office areas next week. The posters have a slogan on the top and a warning on the bottom. The slogan states, 'Quality Is Priority One.' The wording beneath the slogan says, 'No matter how long it takes, you absolutely must achieve or exceed your quality goals,' and then they cite the maximum rate of defects they intend to impose as the goal."

"I'm not sure why that's a problem," says Brad, puzzled. "After all, it is important to reduce defects."

"It's a problem, *children*," says Julia, "because the *LEAN* Forward team leaders have prepared posters that state, 'Cycle Time Reduction Is Priority One.' Evidently the *LEAN* Forward team leaders are following Sally Swindel's advice to reduce the number of inspections. The quality control team, naturally, thinks that this will increase defects. The whole mess has been escalated to Tommy Jenkins. It should be interesting to see how he resolves it."

It would seem that Professor Aristotle Leonidas is abrasive as well as idealistic. He appears to believe that the members of the *LEAN* Forward team and, in particular, factory management are going to take eight hours out of their busy schedule to listen to an old man rave on about the need for science in factory performance-improvement efforts.

The fact that management was able to find two whole weeks to attend the lean manufacturing training was due, for the most part, to the dictate by Muddle's CEO. No such dictate has been issued—at least at this point—in regard to any training in the science of manufacturing.

It is also interesting to note that the *LEAN* Forward team and the quality control team are at loggerheads. The lean team wants to reduce non-value-added activities in the factory and believes that certain inspection steps do not add value. The quality control team wants to reduce defects and believes that the more inspections the better. Each team sees the other's goal as a threat to its effort.

Actually, several other shoes are about to fall. Tommy Jenkins has recently established a cost reduction team. He's also put in place a capacity improvement team. This means that at this point in time the following "factory performance" teams exist within Tommy's factory:

- *LEAN* Forward team (with an emphasis on the reduction of waste—or, as Sally Swindel insists on calling it, *muda*)
- CANDO team (responsible for cleaning up workplaces and reducing clutter)
- Quality control team (with an emphasis on the reduction of defects)
- Cycle-time reduction team (with an emphasis on the reduction of factory cycle time)
- Cost reduction team (with an emphasis on reducing funds expended)
- Capacity improvement team (with an emphasis on increasing factory capacity/maximum sustainable throughput)
- Equipment maintenance team (with an emphasis on increasing the availability of the factory's workstations)
- Factory utilization team (this team has been ordered to make sure that the utilization of every machine and every factory floor worker is 90 percent or more; that is, they cannot be idle any more than 10 percent of the time)
- Spare parts team (with an emphasis on determining the number of spare parts to keep in inventory subject to budget and space restrictions)
- Metrics team (with the responsibility of collecting data in support of the numerous factory performance metrics)

Tommy, like many other plant or factory managers, has failed to notice that the mission statements (and goals) of each and every one of these teams are in conflict. As mentioned, the *LEAN* Forward team wants to reduce inspection steps—to reduce what they consider waste—whereas the quality control team actually wants to add such steps—in the belief this will reduce defects.

Besides being in conflict, every one of the metrics by which the performance of these teams is being measured can be easily "gamed." For example, factory floor personnel have discovered that they can increase the utilization of their workstations simply by conducting unnecessary rework efforts. In turn, they can make themselves appear busier than they actually are by scheduling more meetings. Since meetings count toward personnel utilization at Muddle, this has been a particularly attractive means to "improve" their performance—and simultaneously have the firm provide them with lots of free pizza and soft drinks.

To worsen matters, there is no single point of oversight with regard to the activities of each of the teams. Each one remains focused on the metric by which it is measured, and each of these metrics is in conflict with what should be the goal of simply improving overall factory performance.

By the way, we've just learned that Tommy Jenkins has agreed (as a result of Julia's persuasion) to allow Professor Leonidas to give an eight-hour presentation to the plant managers, department managers, Muddle Fellows, and members of the *LEAN* Forward team. Tommy also has finalized the composition of the team. He's going to be the team's coach, and Donna Garcia (Dan and Brad's former boss) and Roger Durbin (a long-time Muddle employee and close friend of Tommy Jenkins) will serve as the two-in-a-box team leaders. Furthermore, even though he has not received an invitation to (and was intentionally omitted from the list of attendees invited to) Professor Leonidas' presentation, it's rumored that the mysterious Winston Smith might attend.

CHAPTER 4 EXERCISES

1. Using the 12-workstation factory simulation model of this chapter, perform the following exercises:
   - Initialize the simulation model and then change the factory throughput rate (cell B14) from 2 lots per day up to 20 lots per day (in 1 lot per day increments)

and develop a plot of factory cycle time versus throughput rate.

- Initialize the simulation model and then employ the theory of constraints to decrease factory cycle time. Do not, however, allocate any funds for the purchase of additional machines (i.e., allocate funds only to the increase in workstation effective process rates). Compare your results with those found in the chapter.

2. Explain why the 12-workstation model limits your decisions to (mainly) the first two dimensions of manufacturing.
3. Explain why the cost of increasing a machine's *EPR* rises exponentially.

CHAPTER 5

Variability

$\blacksquare$t was possible to improve the performance of the 12-workstation factory significantly in Chapter 4 "simply" by adding machines or by increasing the availability and/or process rate of workstations. By means of a theory of constraints (ToC)–influenced approach, cycle time was reduced by 75.84 percent. Using optimization (i.e., genetic algorithms), the reduction was an even better 83.86 percent.

Of course, those degrees of improvement were achieved only by consuming the entire $13M budget. In Chapter 6 you'll be asked to deal with this same factory once again. There will be two very significant differences, however. First, rather than being provided with $13M, you'll be permitted to expend only $500,000 (i.e., $0.5M). Second, a new avenue for improvement will be open to you—the reduction of variability. With the introduction of variability into the decision-making process, you will have at your disposal all three dimensions of manufacturing.

If you are to exploit variability reduction most effectively, however, you must first be able to

- Appreciate the role that variability plays in factory performance
- Locate the sources of variability
- Collect the data required to measure variability
- Properly interpret the data used to measure variability
- Compare the variability inherent in two or more machines, workstations, or factories
- Comprehend the three fundamental equations of manufacturing

We begin our discussion with a brief overview of variability and several variability metrics. Following that, the three fundamental equations of manufacturing will be presented and illustrated. Once this material has been covered (and understood), you will be armed with insight into the most powerful and cost-effective tools available for factory performance improvement.

MEASURING VARIABILITY

Thus far our attention has been focused on attributes and metrics based on averages, that is, average cycle time, average throughput rate, average process rate, average occupancy rate, etc. If, however, you wish to appreciate the scope and limitations of a factory (i.e., a nonlinear, dynamic, stochastic system with feedback), you absolutely must address variability.

We begin our discussion by first defining and illustrating the notion of the coefficient of variability (a.k.a. *coefficient of variation*). While certainly not perfect, the coefficient of variability CoV provides us with a practical and—for our purposes—reasonably effective means to compare the variability of two different populations (e.g., two different factories or the before and after performance of a given factory).

CoV = Coefficient of Variability

The equation for CoV is

$$CoV = \frac{\sigma}{\mu} = \frac{\text{standard deviation}}{\text{mean}} \quad (5.1)$$

For the sake of illustration, assume that we wish to compare the variability of the process rates of two different machines. Machine X has a mean process rate of 100 units per day and a standard deviation of 50, whereas machine Y has a mean process rate of 20 units per day and a standard deviation of 30.

The coefficients of variability of the process rates of each machine thus are

$$CoV[PR(X)] = \frac{50}{100} = 0.50$$

$$CoV[PR(Y)] = \frac{30}{20} = 1.50$$

Despite the fact that the value of the standard deviation of the process time of machine X is much larger in absolute terms than that of machine Y, the coefficient of variability of the process time of machine Y is greater (i.e., three times greater). The greater the variability (i.e., *CoV*) of a machine or factory, the worse will be its performance.

C_{AR} = Coefficient of Variability of Arrivals

I will use C_{AR} to represent the variability about the arrival rate of jobs *at a given process step*. More precisely, C_{AR} is the coefficient of variability about the interarrival times of those jobs entering the associated process step.

Since our focus is at the process-step level, it will be assumed that all variability metrics, including $C_{AR,}$ represent variability with respect to a given process step. When we need to discriminate between different process steps, the notation employed will be $C_{AR}(ps,)$ where *ps* will indicate the specific process step of interest.

Assume, for example, that we record the times at which individual jobs arrive at a particular process step, say, process step 7. Given these data, we may compute the interarrival times of the jobs by subtracting the time of arrival of one job from the time the preceding job arrived. To illustrate, the derivation of the coefficient of variability for a small sample of job arrival times is developed for the data shown in Table 5.1.

TABLE 5.1

Process Step 7 Job Arrivals (Assuming One Job per Batch)

Job	Arrival Time	Interarrival Time (in Minutes)
1	8:00 a.m.	—
2	8:15 a.m.	15
3	8:50 a.m.	35
4	8:56 a.m.	6
5	9:40 a.m.	44
6	9:48 a.m.	8
7	10:02 a.m.	14
8	10:50 a.m.	48
9	10:58 a.m.	8
10	11:33 a.m.	35
11	11:40 a.m.	7

Our interest lies in the third column, the times between arrivals of jobs (i.e., the interarrival rate) at the process step. We simply find the mean and standard deviation of the 10 values in that column (this is accomplished easily by means of entering the preceding data into a MicroSoft Excel spreadsheet and using a data analysis tool to determine the associated statistics), where

μ = 22 minutes (the mean of the interarrival times)

σ = 16.613 minutes (the standard deviation of the interarrival times)

The value of C_{AR} for this process step (recall that we have assumed that this is for process step 7) thus is

$$C_{AR}(7) = \frac{\sigma}{\mu} = \frac{16.613}{22} = 0.755$$

It must be emphasized that just 10 samples of interarrival times is highly unlikely to provide a sufficient sample size. This small number of samples has been used, however, simply to illustrate the mechanics of the process. Details on the determination of proper sample sizes may be found in the references (Ignizio and Gupta, 1975; Kennedy and Neville, 1964).

Before we leave this example, consider an extremely important matter—the employment of batches in place of individual jobs. In the example, it was assumed that the arrival times listed were for individual jobs (i.e., one job per batch). Now consider what happens if instead of individual jobs, the jobs arrive—simultaneously—in batches of four (i.e., of four jobs per batch). Employing the arrival-time data used previously, we note that at 8:00 a.m., the first batch arrives. At 8:15 a.m., the next batch arrives. At 8:50 a.m., the third batch arrives. The change from individual jobs to batches of jobs has a significant impact on the value of C_{AR}.

Table 5.2 lists the batch arrivals along with the interarrival rates of each individual job within the batch. Notice carefully that for the second batch (jobs 5, 6, 7, and 8), the first job in that batch arrives 15 minutes after the last job in batch 1 (jobs 1, 2, 3, and 4). The second job in batch 2 also arrives 15 minutes after the last job in batch 1, and the same is true for the third and fourth jobs of batch 2.

When the arrival of jobs is in batches, the coefficient of variability of arrivals increases. In this case, C_{AR} for the original

TABLE 5.2

Arrivals in Batches (of Four Jobs per Batch)

Job	Batch Arrival Time	Individual Job Interarrival Time (Minutes)	Job	Batch Arrival Time	Individual Job Interarrival Time (Minutes)
1	8:00 a.m.	0	25	10:02 a.m.	14
2		0	26		0
3		0	27		0
4		0	28		0
5	8:15 a.m.	15	29	10:50 a.m.	48
6		0	30		0
7		0	31		0
8		0	32		0
9	8:50 a.m.	35	33	10:58 a.m.	8
10		0	34		0
11		0	35		0
12		0	36		0
13	8:56 a.m.	6	37	11:33 a.m.	35
14		0	38		0
15		0	39		0
16		0	40		0
17	9:40 a.m.	44	41	11:40 a.m.	7
18		0	42		0
19		0	43		0
20		0	44		0
21	9:48 a.m.	8			
22		0			
23		0			
24		0			

data—where the batch size was one (i.e., one job per batch)—was 0.755. This is a relatively modest degree of variability. However, when the jobs arrive in batches of four, C_{AR} becomes 2.41—a very significant degree of variability. As we shall soon discover, the coefficient of variability of job interarrivals plays a significant role in processing entity performance.

We may conclude that as the batch size of the preceding workstation is increased, the coefficient of variability seen by the machines supporting the next process step increases. It should be noted that there are equations that allow computation of the optimal batch size for a given workstation. These serve to minimize the cycle time of the batching workstation. On the surface, this might seem to be a good thing.

Unfortunately, the optimal batch size of a workstation actually may impose significant arrival-rate variability on one or more downstream workstations. As a consequence, while the cycle time of the batching workstation might be reduced, the cycle time of the overall factory actually could increase. This is an illustration of *sub-optimization,* that is, the danger of focusing on the improvement of just one element of a system rather than the system as a whole.

C_{PT} = Coefficient of Variability of Raw Process Times

I will use $C_{PT}(ps)$ to represent the coefficient of variability of the raw process times *of a given process step* (i.e., actually, that of each of the machines supporting that process step). To determine $C_{PT,}$ we should record (or at least estimate) the raw process times of a given process step. Since these are the *raw* process times, we only measure the time that the entity supporting the step is actually processing a job (i.e., we ignore any blocked time or downtime occurring after the job is started or before it is finished).

The data for an example illustrating the derivation of C_{PT} is provided in Table 5.3. Assume, for sake of discussion, that the process step of interest is again step 7, and thus we seek the value of $C_{PT}(7)$. Specifically, for a sample of 10 jobs, the raw process times (of the machines supporting the given process step) have been listed.

T A B L E   5.3

Derivation of the Coefficient of Variability of Raw
Process Times

Job	Raw Process Time (in Minutes)
1	31
2	32
3	29
4	30
5	32
6	28
7	30
8	31
9	30
10	31

Given these data, the coefficient of variability of raw process times is

$$C_{PT}(7) = \frac{\sigma}{\mu} = \frac{1.265}{30.4} = 0.042$$

A *CoV* of 0.042 is extremely small but might be possible for the raw process times of some high-precision machines. What is far more important, however, is determination of the coefficient of variability of the *effective* process times, or C_{EPT}.

C_{EPT} = Coefficient of Variability of Effective Process Times

$C_{EPT}(ps)$ is used to represent the variability of the effective process times of a process step designated as *ps*. This particular *CoV* is a function of such factors as the coefficient of variability of both blocked and down events (either scheduled or unscheduled), designated here as $C_{DE,}$ as well as such parameters as availability of the entity, its raw process time, and the mean time required to recover *MTTR* from either a blocked or down event.

Equation (5.2) provides a means to approximate the square of the coefficient of variability of the effective process time (i.e., C_{EPT}^2) for a nonreentrant (*DoR* = 1), single machine (*M* = 1) workstation. It also may be employed to provide an even rougher (but, for our purposes, adequate) approximation of C_{EPT}^2 for a nonreentrant, multiple-machine workstation.

$$C_{EPT}^2(ps) = C_0^2 + A \bullet (1-A) \bullet \frac{MTTR}{PT} + C_{DE}^2 \bullet A \bullet (1-A) \bullet \frac{MTTR}{PT} \quad (5.2)$$

where C_0 = inherent variability of the process times of the machines supporting the process step of interest

C_{DE} = variability of the recovery times (from both blocked and down events) of the machines supporting the process step of interest

A = average availability of the machines supporting the process step of interest

$MTTR$ = mean time to recover from both blocked and down events of the machines supporting the process step of interest

PT = average raw process time of the machines supporting the process step of interest

For example, assume that a workstation in which all machines support a single process step (say, process step 7) has the following characteristics:

$$\text{Mean time between events } MTBE = 90 \text{ hours}$$
$$MTTR = 10 \text{ hours}$$

Thus the availability of those machines is given by Equation (3.3) as

$$A = \frac{MTBE}{MTBE + MTTR} = \frac{90}{90 + 10} = 0.90$$

In addition, assume for sake of discussion that we know that

- $C_{PT}(7) = 0.042$ (which typically is close to the value of C_0).
- $C_{DE}(7) = 1.5$ (i.e., the average CoV of the down event recovery times).
- $PT(7) = 1$ hour (i.e., the average process time of each of the machines).

These values may be substituted into Equation (5.2) to approximate C^2_{EPT} of the process step under consideration:

$$C^2_{EPT}(7) = 0.042^2 + 0.9 \bullet (1-0.9) \bullet \frac{10}{1} + 1.5^2 \bullet 0.9 \bullet (1-0.9) \bullet \frac{10}{1} = 2.93$$

Notice that even though the inherent (i.e., raw) variability of the process step (i.e., roughly that of the CoV of its raw process time) may have been small, because of blocked and down events, the CoV of the effective process time is rather large (i.e., the square root of 2.93, or 1.71). This is just one reason why you must consider the impact of blocked events, maintenance, and repairs if factory improvement is to be achieved.

There is yet another message to be gleaned from Equation (5.2). Specifically, given all other factors equal, the coefficient of variability of the effective process time may be reduced by dividing scheduled down events [preventive maintenance (PM)] into more frequent, smaller segments. To illustrate, assume that there are no blocked events and that the only down events are regularly scheduled PM events (i.e., events over which we have some control).

In the preceding illustration, the mean time to recover from a blocked or down event was 10 hours. Assume that these down events are solely PM events and may be divided into segmented PM events of 5 hours each and conducted every 45 hours. Thus

$$MTBE = 50 \text{ hours}$$
$$MTTR = 5 \text{ hours}$$

and

$$A = \frac{MTBE}{MTBE + MTTR} = \frac{45}{45+5} = 0.90$$

Even though we have segmented the PM events and halved the time between PM events, the availability of the workstation remains 90 percent. We assume that all other parameters (i.e., C_0, PT, and C_{DE} for the process step) have the same values as before.

Notice what happens to $C_{EPT}(ps)$ when we substitute the new value of $MTTR$ into Equation (5.2):

$$C_{EPT}^2(7) = 0.042^2 + 0.9 \bullet (1-0.9) \bullet \left(\frac{5}{1}\right) + 1.5^2 \bullet 0.9 \bullet (1-0.9) \bullet \left(\frac{5}{1}\right) = 1.464$$

In other words, simply by conducting shorter and more frequent PM events, we have reduced the squared CoV of effective processing time from 2.93 to 1.464. This degree of reduction may have, as we shall see, a significant positive impact on factory performance.

I now proceed to a presentation of the three fundamental equations of manufacturing. I begin with Little's equation (a.k.a. *Little's law*). It should be noted that it is the only one of the three equations that relies solely on averages. But first a warning:

The forms of the fundamental equations that follow are based on the assumption of a factory in which every workstation supports just one process step and every machine in the workstation supports only that process step. Furthermore, it is assumed that the machines within each workstation are identical, with identical raw and effective process rates. While these equations may be extended to encompass more complex factory configurations, we will still be able to identify the general characteristics of the factory phenomena of interest, if not their precise values, from the simplified models.

FUNDAMENTAL EQUATION ONE

Intuitively (although, as mentioned, you really need to be careful about relying on intuition), it would seem that factory inventory should increase as factory starts (i.e., factory throughput or loading) increase. This is, in fact, true. In 1961, John Little developed an equation—known as *Little's equation* or *law*—relating factory inventory, designated as work in progress *WIP* to factory cycle time *CT* and factory throughput *TH* (Little, 1961). The same equation may be used to relate workstation inventory to workstation cycle time and throughput. Little's equation is

$$WIP = CT \cdot TH \tag{5.3}$$

To demonstrate, consider a factory whose average cycle time is 50 days and whose average throughput (i.e., flow of jobs through the factory) is 700 units per week. Changing all units to days (and making sure that all parameters are indeed in the same units), the expected inventory of the factory at any given time will be

$$WIP = 50 \text{ days} \cdot 100 \text{ units/day} = 5,000 \text{ units}$$

Little's equation should provide a reasonably good approximation for either total factory inventory or the inventory existing at any given workstation or at an individual process step—under the assumptions stated previously. More important, however, is the fact that the equation serves to clearly relate cycle time and throughput to inventory. The equation is in some respects the factory equivalent of Newton's most famous law—force equals mass times acceleration.

FUNDAMENTAL EQUATION TWO

The second fundamental equation is more commonly known as the *P-K equation* (an abbreviation, for obvious reasons, of the *Pollaczek-Khintchine equation*). This equation typically is used to predict the cycle time of either a factory, a portion of a factory, or some individual workstation. However, here, we will focus on the cycle time at the process-step level. To determine total factory cycle time, we find the sum of all cycle times across all process steps.

The form of the second fundamental equation requires the determination of a number of the factors covered in Chapter 3 plus those just introduced in this chapter. These are

- $CT_{ps,}$ the cycle time of the process step. It is once again emphasized that in this text our interest extends to the process-step level rather than stopping with the workstation or machine.
- $C_{AR,}$ the coefficient of variability of arrivals at the process step.
- $C_{EPT,}$ the coefficient of variability of effective process times of the machines that support the process step.
- $EPR_{ps,}$ the effective process rate (maximum theoretical capacity) of each of the identical machines that support the given process step.
- A, the average availability of the machines that support the process step.
- ρ, the average occupation rate (a.k.a. *utilization*) of the machines supporting the process step.
- BS, the batch size—if any—of the machines supporting the process step.
- AR, the arrival rate of the jobs arriving at the process step.
- m, the number of (identical) machines supporting the process step.

The specific form of the P-K equation depends on the situation addressed (e.g., number of machines and existence or nonexistence of batching, cascading, or reentrancy). For the purpose of this discussion, we will restrict our interest, for the moment, to determination of the cycle time of a process step supported by m nonreentrant and nonbatching machines. Thus the equation for cycle time of a given process step, that is, the second fundamental equation of manufacturing, is

$$CT_{ps} = \underbrace{\left(\frac{C_{AR}^2 + C_{EPT}^2}{2}\right) \bullet \left[\frac{\rho^{\sqrt{2(m+1)}-1}}{m \bullet (1-\rho)}\right] \bullet \left(\frac{1}{EPR_{ps}}\right)}_{\text{wait in queue time}} + \underbrace{\left(\frac{1}{EPR_{ps}}\right)}_{\text{effective process time}} \quad (5.4)$$

If the process step is supported by only a single machine (i.e., $m = 1$), the form of the second fundamental equation of manufacturing is

$$CT_{ps} = \underbrace{\left(\frac{C_{AR}^2 + C_{EPT}^2}{2}\right) \bullet \left[\frac{\rho}{(1-\rho)}\right] \bullet \left(\frac{1}{EPR_{ps}}\right)}_{\text{wait in queue time}} + \underbrace{\left(\frac{1}{EPR_{ps}}\right)}_{\text{effective process time}} \quad (5.5)$$

Alternately, if the process step is supported by m machines and these machines employ batching, the form of the second fundamental equation becomes

$$CT_{ps} = \underbrace{\frac{BS-1}{2 \bullet AR}}_{\text{batch forming time}} + \underbrace{\left(\frac{\frac{C^2_{AR}}{BS} + C^2_{EPT}}{2} \right) \bullet \left[\frac{\rho^{\sqrt{2(m+1)}-1}}{m \bullet (1-\rho)} \right] \bullet \left(\frac{1}{EPR_{ps}} \right)}_{\text{wait in queue time}} + \underbrace{\left(\frac{1}{EPR_{ps}} \right)}_{\text{effective process time}} \quad (5.6)$$

If the process step is supported by nonreentrant, cascading machines, the form of the second fundamental equation must be revised accordingly [i.e., see Hopp and Spearman (2001) or Buzacott and Shanthikumar (1993) for these forms of the P-K equation]. For our purposes, however, it is not vital that the form for nonreentrant, cascading machines be discussed. In fact, we shall restrict our attention to just Equation (5.4), that is, m machines and no batching.

To illustrate, assume that we wish to determine the cycle time of process step 2 given the data provided in Table 5.4.

Substituting the values in Table 5.4 into Equation (5.4), we may find the cycle time of process step 2 as follows:

$$CT_{ps} = \underbrace{\left(\frac{C^2_{AR} + C^2_{EPT}}{2} \right) \bullet \left[\frac{\rho^{\sqrt{2(m+1)}-1}}{m \bullet (1-\rho)} \right] \bullet \left(\frac{1}{EPR_{ps}} \right)}_{\text{wait in queue time}} + \underbrace{\left(\frac{1}{EPR_{ps}} \right)}_{\text{effective process time}}$$

$$CT_{ps}(2) = \underbrace{\left(\frac{6.17^2 + 2^2}{2} \right) \bullet \left[\frac{0.67^{\sqrt{2(3+1)}-1}}{3 \bullet (1-0.67)} \right] \bullet \left(\frac{1}{10} \right)}_{\text{wait in queue time}} + \underbrace{\left(\frac{1}{10} \right)}_{\text{effective process time}} = 1.10 \text{ days}$$

TABLE 5.4

Data for Application of Second Fundamental Equation

Parameter	Parameter Description	Value
M	Number of machines supporting the process step	3
C_{AR}	CoV of interarrivals	6.17
C_{EPT}	CoV of effective process times	2.00
ρ	Occupancy rate of the m machines supporting process step 2	0.67
EPR	Effective process rate of each of the machines supporting process step 2 (jobs per day)	10

Since the 12-workstation model of Chapter 4 dealt with a series of nonreentrant workstations and batching was not employed, the cycle time of each of the workstations (each of which supports a single process step) may be (and was) determined by means of Equation (5.4) in conjunction, as we shall see, with the first and third fundamental equations of manufacturing.

FUNDAMENTAL EQUATION THREE

The third fundamental equation is known more commonly as either the *linking equation* or the *propagation of variability equation*. This approximating equation is employed to estimate the coefficient of variability of the jobs departing a given process step. Given m machines and no reentrancy, the form of the third equation of manufacturing is

$$C_{DR}^2 = 1 + \left(1 - \rho^2\right) \bullet \left(C_{AR}^2 - 1\right) + \left(\frac{\rho^2}{\sqrt{m}}\right) \bullet (C_{EPT}^2 - 1) \qquad (5.7)$$

If only a single machine ($m = 1$) supports the process step, the equation reduces to

$$C_{DR}^2 = \rho^2 \bullet C_{EPT}^2 + (1 - \rho^2) \bullet C_{AR}^2 \qquad (5.8)$$

To illustrate, consider a process step supported by three machines ($m = 3$) with an occupancy rate of 0.67 ($\rho = 0.67$), a coefficient of variability of interarrivals of 6.17 ($C_{AR} = 6.17$), and a coefficient of variability of effective process times of 2.0 ($C_{EPT} = 2.0$). Using Equation (5.7), we may determine the coefficient of variability of the jobs departing this process step:

$$C_{DR}^2 = 1 + \left(1 - 0.67^2\right) \bullet \left(6.17^2 - 1\right) + \left(\frac{0.67^2}{\sqrt{3}}\right) \bullet (2^2 - 1) = 22.21 \text{ and thus}$$

$$C_{DR} = \sqrt{2.221} = 4.7315$$

Given that process step 2 is supported by the machines in workstation B and that the next process step (i.e., process step 3) is supported by the machines in workstation C, Figure 5.1 may be employed to represent the situation.

FIGURE 5.1

Propagation of variability illustration.

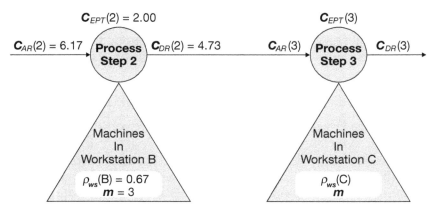

The values of the interarrival rate coefficient of variability and effective process time coefficient of variability are listed next to the circle representing process step 2. Under the assumptions cited earlier, all machines in this workstation (workstation B) support process step 2 and only that process step. In the triangle under process step 2, the occupancy rate of those machines ($\rho = 0.67$) and their number ($m = 3$) are specified. Using Equation (5.7), the coefficient of variability of the jobs leaving process step 2 is 4.7315.

This is shown above the arrow leading from process step 2 to process step 3. If the transit step between process step 2 and process step 3 has negligible variability and high capacity, the value of the coefficient of variability of interarrivals at process step 3 will be essentially equal to that of $C_{DR}(2)$.

By means of the three fundamental equations, we may approximate (where the key word is *approximate*) the cycle times of each process step, the variability propagated from one process step to another, and the average inventory at each process step. This, in fact, is precisely what was used to develop the 12- and 5-workstation models of Chapter 4, as well as the 12-workstation model to be employed in Chapter 6.

CAPACITY AND VARIABILITY

In Chapter 4 we saw that any increase in the throughput capacity of workstation B (recall Figure 4.6) resulted in an unexpected increase in overall factory cycle time. This happens to also be the case for any increase in the throughput capacity of workstation C. Given the three fundamental equations, particularly the third (the propagation of variability equation), this phenomenon may be explained.

In the 12-workstation factory, under its initial conditions, the values for the parameters of workstation C (which supports process step 3) are listed in Table 5.5.

Substituting the values in Table 5.5 into Equation (5.7), we obtain the following value for the squared coefficient of variability of the departures C_{DR} from workstation C (i.e., process step 3):

$$C_{DR}^2 = 1 + \left(1 - \rho^2\right) \bullet \left(C_{AR}^2 - 1\right) + \left(\frac{\rho^2}{\sqrt{m}}\right) \bullet (C_{EPT}^2 - 1)$$

$$C_{DR}^2 = 1 + \left(1 - 0.625^2\right) \bullet \left(4.7315^2 - 1\right) + \left(\frac{0.625^2}{\sqrt{3}}\right) \bullet (3^2 - 1)$$

$$= 15.5954 \text{ and thus } C_{DR}(3) = 3.9491$$

Now assume that we increase the maximum theoretical capacity EPR of each of the four machines of workstation C from their initial values of 8 jobs per day to, say, 18 jobs per day—a substantial increase in the capacity of the workstation. This would seem to be a good thing. The new data for workstation C are listed in Table 5.6.

TABLE 5.5

Workstation C Parameters

Parameter	Value	Comments
Process step supported by workstation C	3	—
Number of machines m	4	—
EPR per machine	8 jobs/day per machine	—
Throughput capacity (EPR per workstation)	32 jobs/day	4 machines times 8 jobs/day
Occupancy rate ρ (utilization) of workstation	0.6250	20 jobs/day factory throughput (takt rate) divided by 32 jobs/day capacity
C_{AR}	4.7315	—
C_{EPT}	3.0000	—

TABLE 5.6

Workstation C after Capacity Increase

Parameter	Value	Comments
Process step supported by workstation C	3	—
Number of machines m	4	—
EPR per machine Throughput capacity	18 jobs/day per machine	Increase in EPR
(EPR per workstation)	72 jobs/day	4 machines times 18 jobs/day
Occupancy rate ρ (utilization) of workstation	0.2778	20 jobs/day factory throughput (takt rate) divided by 72 jobs/day capacity
C_{AR}	4.7315	—
C_{EPT}	3.0000	—

Substituting the values in Table 5.6 into Equation (5.7), we obtain the following value for the new squared coefficient of variability of the departures C_{DR} from workstation C (i.e., process step 3):

$$C_{DR}^2 = 1 + \left(1 - 0.2779^2\right) \bullet \left(4.7315^2 - 1\right) + \left(\frac{0.2779^2}{\sqrt{3}}\right) \bullet (3^2 - 1)$$

$$= 20.9425 \text{ and thus } C_{DR}(3) = 4.5763$$

Note that by increasing the maximum theoretical capacity of workstation C (from 32 to 72 jobs per day), the coefficient of variability of the jobs departing workstation C (i.e., process step 3) has increased from 3.9491 to 4.5763. Consequently, via the second fundamental equation of manufacturing (Equation 5.4), the cycle time of the next process step (process step 4, supported by the machines in workstation D) must increase.

The data being employed for this illustration actually come from that used in the 12-workstation factory. As a consequence, it may be shown that the increase in $C_{DR}(3)$ of workstation C (i.e., supporting process step 3) from 3.9491 to 4.5763 will increase the cycle time of workstation D from 23.39 to 28.42 days; i.e., an increase of more than five days. It so happens that as a consequence, the cycle time of the entire factory will increase by somewhat less than five days (i.e., there is a decrease in workstation C's cycle time). Once again it is demonstrated that improving the performance of a single workstation may indeed degrade overall factory performance.

By means of the fundamental equations, we may determine when an increase in the throughput capacity of one workstation will either help or hurt overall factory cycle time. To accomplish this feat, though, we must have the data required to determine the coefficient of variability of both arrivals and departures. In Chapter 6 these essential data will be provided—allowing us to employ a more intelligent (and cost-effective) approach to factory cycle-time reduction for the 12-workstation factory.

CHAPTER SUMMARY

The impact of variability on process-step cycle time (and subsequently on factory cycle time) is evident from the second and third fundamental equations of manufacturing. With these equations, plus Little's equation (the first fundamental equation of manufacturing), one may investigate the impact of variability and throughput capacity (as well as occupancy rate) on factory performance.

Via extensions to the second and third fundamental equations, more complex factories may be modeled. These extended equations, however, are mostly of academic interest (a polite way of implying that they have limited practical value). Predictions of the performance of more complex factories are, at present, best achieved via discrete event simulation models or those employing fluid networks (Billings and Hasenbein, 2002) or electromagnetic networks (Ignizio, 2000). Even the most carefully crafted and detailed of these, however, still only provides rough estimates of the performance of large, complex factories (e.g., semiconductor fabricators).

The real importance of the fundamental equations lies in their ability to illustrate the impact of variability and complexity. Too much time, in fact, is wasted on attempts to derive precise values of factory cycle time, factory capacity, and the uncertainty about delivery times via the fundamental equations and their countless extensions when it can and should be more productively allocated to simply reducing factory variability and complexity. However, we shall continue our investigation of the simple 12-workstation factory in Chapter 6, where yet more insight into factory performance may be gained.

CASE STUDY 5: JUST WHO IS WINSTON SMITH?

Julia, Dan, and Brad are in Factory 7's largest meeting room, trying to make sure that everything is ready for Professor Leonidas's eight-hour presentation. At about ten to eight, the professor arrives.

"Here's the memory stick with my presentation," says Professor Leonidas. "But where's the audience?" he adds, staring at a nearly empty room.

"Don't worry, Professor," replies a very worried Julia Austen, "no meeting at Muddle ever starts on time. We'll have a full house, I assure you. All three plant managers promised me they'd be here, and if they come, the rest of the herd will follow."

At about ten past eight, a gaggle of department managers, Muddle Fellows, *LEAN* Forward team members, and senior factory engineers begin to arrive. Julia advises Dan to delay the introduction of Professor Leonidas until the three plant managers arrive. Some 15 minutes later, it is obvious to everyone that Tommy Jenkins and his fellow plant managers are not going to attend this meeting. When this realization sets in, all the factory department managers (with the lone and curious exception of Donna Garcia) make a hasty exit, followed by at least half the other members of the audience.

As those individuals leave the meeting room, one person does enter. He's a distinguished looking middle-aged gentleman with salt-and-pepper hair. When Julia sees him, she emits an audible gasp. Professor Leonidas has an entirely different reaction.

"Winston, my boy, what on earth are you doing here?" says Professor Leonidas as he extends his hand. "My goodness, the last I heard, you had decided to abandon academia and move to New Zealand and raise sheep."

"Hello, Professor," Winston replies. "I did indeed leave the Ivory Tower, but now I work for Muddle. It's a rather long story."

"Well, my boy, let's chat over lunch. Right now, if I correctly read the hand-waving of Miss Julia, it's time to start the presentation."

Following the introduction, Professor Leonidas walks to the podium and places his hand on the conference room laptop, ready to start the first slide of the presentation. At the same time, a frantic looking fellow with lots and lots of facial hair and a T-shirt reading, "Safety Rules," races to the podium and inserts himself between the professor and the laptop.

"Oh my gosh," whispers Brad, "that's Ed, the safety and ergonomics Nazi."

Ed insists that before the presentation is permitted to begin, the laptop must be raised (about half an inch) and that the mouse being used is replaced by one that satisfies the very latest, official Muddle ergonomic specifications. In the meantime, the professor stands aside, a bewildered look on his face.

Julia, Dan, and Brad are meeting in the company cafeteria. The professor's presentation was completed about an hour ago. Conversation among the threesome has been minimal to nonexistent since they bade their good-byes to the professor. Based on the pained expressions of their faces, things did not go well.

Dan breaks the silence. "Damn, what a disaster. Damn, damn, damn. Where were Tommy Jenkins and his pals? Damn it, he gave his word."

"I called Tommy's administrative assistant during the first coffee break," Julia replies, "It seems they 'just forgot' the meeting. Instead, they were doing a factory walk-through. That, by the way, is the code their administrative assistants use when the three of them are golfing. Based on the professor's performance today, however, I've got to say that I'm glad they passed on his presentation."

"Why's that?" asks Dan. "I thought that the professor made some very good points. He certainly seems up to speed on Muddle factories. His remarks about the impact of poorly written PM specifications sure hit home with me."

"You must have not been attending the same presentation as me," Julia replies, shaking her head. "The good professor was critical of just about everything we do. Weren't you listening when he asked Donna Garcia if she knew what the three fundamental equations of manufacturing are? Or when he asked if we used moves as a measure of factory performance and said that was quite possibly one of the worst metrics around? Good grief, he implied in no uncertain terms that we're doing just about everything wrong."

"So what?" says Dan. "He's spot on with his criticism. Julia, if we were doing things right, we wouldn't have such ridiculously long factory cycle times or so many unscheduled machine downs—or such a low stock price. Unless this company admits it has problems, how are we going to solve them?"

"Dan," Brad replies, "I love your enthusiasm. But Julia's right, the professor ticked off pretty much everybody but you. He may be spot on, but he's put everyone on the defensive. The people in this firm aren't used to that. When outsiders present here, they always tell us that we're doing great. Didn't you hear what Sally Swindel told us in the *LEAN* Forward course? She said that we were on the verge of greatness. All we needed to do was implement a few lean manufacturing concepts. And you know darn well she didn't mean it."

"Okay," says Dan, "so he wasn't very tactful. But do we want to have people tell us that things are fine when we know that our performance is terrible? I'd rather have an honest appraisal than have someone try to flatter me."

"That may be so," says Julia, "but he could have been a little more diplomatic. I'm betting that Donna Garcia is going to give Tommy Jenkins a blow-by-blow description of today's presentation. And her version, I promise you, will be even more critical than ours. Just wait and see."

"Oh my," says Dan. "Maybe we did make a mistake in inviting the professor. Although at least one fellow, that Winston Smith guy, sure seemed pleased to see him."

Dan's comment is met with frowns on the part of both Julia and Brad.

CHAPTER 5 EXERCISES

1. If the data in Table 5.1 were for batches (i.e., replace "Job" with "Batch" as the heading of the first column) consisting of *three* jobs per batch, what is the coefficient of variability of interarrival times?

2. A nonreentrant workstation supporting a single process step has the following performance characteristics. Determine its coefficient of effective process times.

$$MTBE = 50 \text{ hours}$$
$$MTTR = 10 \text{ hours}$$
$$C_{PT} = 0.1$$
$$C_{DE} = 2.0$$
$$PT = 2 \text{ hours}$$

3. A factory's average level of inventory at any given time is 50,000 units. Units flow through the factory at an average rate of 5,000 units per week. What is the factory's average cycle time in days?

TABLE 5.7

Data for Exercise 4

Parameter	Value
C_{AR}	4.0
C_{EPT}	3.0
Availability	90 percent
Arrival rate	7 jobs/hour
EPR	10 jobs/hour

4. Process step 19 of a process flow is supported by a single, nonreentrant machine. The performance parameters of that machine are provided in Table 5.7. Determine, using the second fundamental equation of manufacturing, the expected cycle time for process step 19.

5. If, in Exercise 4, it were possible to reduce the value of the coefficient of variability of interarrivals by half, what would be the expected cycle time?

6. Provide your personal assessment of the behavior of Professor Aristotle Leonidas in his presentation at Muddle. What might he have done, without compromising his integrity, to have softened the effect of his opinions?

CHAPTER 6

Running a Factory: In Three Dimensions

In Chapter 4 you were asked to reduce the cycle time of the 12-workstation factory, subject to a budget limitation of $13M. But the only data provided (e.g., in Figure 4.3) pertained solely to quantities (e.g., number of machines in the workstations) and averages (e.g., average *EPR* per machine and average occupancy rate per workstation). The data appearing in Figure 4.3 limited your options to either increasing the effective process rate of the existing machines in the workstation (via improvements in availability and/or process rates) or adding new machines. Still, by means of optimization, we were able to reduce the factory cycle time from 90.42 to 14.59 days after expending the entire $13M budget on increasing the effective process rates of the machines in each workstation.

In this chapter you have the same mission: Reduce factory cycle time. But now your budget is limited to just $0.50M (i.e., $500,000—which represents more than a 96 percent reduction in funding). You will, however, have one significant advantage. Rather than being limited to the first two dimensions of manufacturing (i.e., changing the physical features of the factory or its components), you now may extend your options into manufacturing's third dimension—changing factory protocols to reduce variability.

More specifically, you are now provided with data pertaining to variability and, by means of the three fundamental equations of manufacturing, permitted to allocate your funds to variability reduction. This reduction of variability, in turn, may be achieved by changes in the practices, policies, and procedures employed in the facility. For the time being, we shall simply assume that we may allocate funds to efforts that will identify and mitigate sources of variability in the factory. Specific recommendations on how to achieve these changes effectively in actual practice will be provided and illustrated in Chapters 10 and 11.

Figure 6.1 presents the particulars of the same 12-workstation factory as encountered in Chapter 4. This time, however, additional rows have been included.

FACTORY ATTRIBUTES

In Figure 6.1, (crucial) shaded rows 12 through 22 and 26 through 28 have been added. The contents of these new rows are defined in Table 6.1. The simulation model for employment may be found at

www.mhprofessional/Ignizio/12WS_Ch6

As before, you are to allocate funds either to increase the effective process rates of the machines in a workstation or to add machines to a workstation. In addition, however, you now also may allocate funds to reduce the coefficient of variability *CoV* of factory

FIGURE   6.1

Twelve-workstation factory simulation model, initial scenario.

TABLE 6.1

Factory or Workstation Attributes

Attribute	Value	From Cell	Comments
CoV of interarrival times C_{AR}	8.00	B12	Variability of arrivals at WS-A
Add $M to reduce C_{EPT}	0.00	B13:M13	Funds allocated thus far to reduce C_{EPT}
Original CoV of process times	8.00	B14	Initial C_{EPT} of each machine in WS-A
New CoV of process times	8.00	B15	New C_{EPT} of each machine in WS-A
CoV of departure times	6.17	B16	C_{DR} from WS-A
Mean work in process WIP at workstation	199.12	B17	Mean number of jobs at WS-A
Mean cycle time CT at workstation	9.96	B18	Initial CT at WS-A
Mean WIP in queue	194.12	B19	Mean number of jobs in WS-A queue
Mean CT in queue	9.71	B20	Initial mean CT in queue at WS-A
Mean WIP in processing	5.00	B21	Mean WIP processed in WS-A
Mean CT in processing	0.25	B22	Mean CT of processing in WS-A
Add $M to reduce CoV of starts	$0.00M	B26	Funds allocated thus far to reduce variability of factory starts
Original CoV of starts	8.00	B27	Initial variability of starts into factory
New CoV of factory starts	8.00	B28	New variability of factory starts

starts or to reduce the *CoV* values of the effective process times of the machines in each workstation. To reduce the variability of factory starts, you must assign funds to cell B26. To reduce the variability of effective process times, allocations of funds must be made to cells B13 through M13.

It is obvious that with a budget of just $500,000, there is no possibility of adding new machines to any workstation. Thus your only rational options are to (1) increase the effective process rates of the existing machines in one or more workstations, (2) reduce the variability of factory starts, or (3) reduce the variability of the effective process times of one or more workstations. We've previously discussed the way in which funds allocated to effective process rates (recall Equation 4.1) affect factory throughput capacity. We now need to appreciate how to allocate funds to the reduction of either the variability of factory starts or the variability of effective process times.

The new assumption to be employed in the 12-workstation model is that for every $10,000 ($0.01M) allocated, the coefficient of variability of either factory starts or effective process times is reduced by one unit. This is stated in Equation (6.1):

$$\text{New } CoV = \text{old } CoV - \$M/0.01 \tag{6.1}$$

For example, if the existing CoV is, say, 5.00 and we allocate $40,000 ($0.04M) to reduce its value, the new CoV value is given as

$$\text{New } CoV = 5.00 - \$0.04/0.01 = 5.00 - 4.00 = 1.00$$

In allocating funds to the reduction of CoV values, we also must follow certain rules. First of all, CoV values cannot be negative (e.g., in the preceding example, an allocation of $60,000 would indicate that the new CoV value is -1.00). Second, the cost of reducing variability becomes increasingly difficult if the desired CoV value is less than 1.0. Consequently, and for sake of discussion, we shall assume that CoV values will not be reduced to less than 1.0 (which is considered a moderate level of variability). Thus Equation (6.1) should be replaced with Equation (6.2):

$$\begin{aligned}\text{New } CoV &= \text{old } CoV - \$M/0.01 \\ \text{where } &\$M/0.01 \le \text{old } CoV - 1\end{aligned} \tag{6.2}$$

The factory simulation spreadsheet has in fact been set up to limit funding for variability reduction so that coefficient of variability values will never be less than 1.0. Again, the simulation model may be found at

www.mhprofessional/Ignizio/12WS_Ch6

GREEDY HEURISTIC SOLUTION

Figure 6.2 shows the resulting cycle time (of 9.18 days) after employing the first phase of a "greedy heuristic" (Ignizio and Cavalier, 1994). This phase of the heuristic simply allocates funds to reduction of the highest CoV values, where priority is given to the highest CoV values and those closest to the input of the factory. This is continued until all CoV values are 1.0 or funds run out.

Since the solution obtained in Figure 6.2 consumed only $400,000, we might improve on it by allocating the remaining funds ($100,000) to increasing effective process rates. One way to accomplish this is by allocating funds for EPR increases to the factory constraint workstations. The output of the second phase of the greedy heuristic, resulting in a cycle-time value of 3.94 days, is shown in Figure 6.3.

The solution obtained in Figure 6.3 is actually very close to that which would be obtained via optimization for this problem (i.e., 3.94 days for the heuristic versus 3.84 days for optimization). While the results obtained by the greedy heuristic are unlikely to always be this close, they are usually quite good. Considering the fact that the fundamental equations of manufacturing are approximations and that factory data are hardly perfect, the greedy heuristic provides an effective and practical means to improve factory performance. The two phases of the greedy heuristic for factory performance improvement are summarized below.

FIGURE 6.2

Twelve-workstation factory simulation model, reduced variability.

File Edit View Insert Format Tools Data Window Help OM_IE OR_MM

Copyright © 1994-2008 James P. Ignizio & Laura I. Burke

	WS A	WS B	WS C	WS D	WS E	WS F	WS G	WS H	WS I	WS J	WS K	WS L
Initialize	$6	$4	$4	$10	$6	$6	$4	$10	$6	$4	$10	$4
Workstation	WS A	WS B	WS C	WS D	WS E	WS F	WS G	WS H	WS I	WS J	WS K	WS L
Add $M to increase EPR_{ws}	0.00	0.00	0.00	0.00	0.00	0.00	0.00	0.00	0.00	0.00	0.00	0.00
Original EPR_m	4.00	10.00	8.00	4.10	9.50	2.50	11.00	10.20	5.20	10.00	10.20	10.00
New EPR_m	4.06	10.06	8.08	4.10	9.50	2.50	11.00	10.20	5.20	10.00	10.20	10.00
Add $M to increase machines	0.00	0.00	0.00	0.00	0.00	0.00	0.00	0.00	0.00	0.00	0.00	0.00
Original Machine Count	6.00	3.00	4.00	5.00	3.00	10.00	3.00	2.00	5.00	3.00	2.00	4.00
New Machine Count	6.00	3.00	4.00	5.00	3.00	10.00	3.00	2.00	5.00	3.00	2.00	4.00
Original TH capacity (EPR_{ws})	24.00	30.00	32.00	20.50	28.50	25.00	33.00	20.40	26.00	30.00	20.40	40.00
New TH capacity (EPR_{ws})	24.37	30.18	32.30	20.50	28.50	25.00	33.00	20.40	26.00	30.00	20.40	40.00
CoV of interarrival times	1.01	1.00	1.00	1.00	1.00	1.00	1.00	1.00	1.00	1.00	1.00	1.00
Add $M to reduce CoV of PTs	0.07	0.01	0.02	0.02	0.01	0.01	0.07	0.01	0.01	0.07	0.01	0.02
Orig CoV of process times	8.00	2.00	3.00	3.00	2.00	2.00	8.00	2.00	2.00	8.00	2.00	3.00
New CoV of process times	1.00	1.00	1.00	1.00	1.00	1.00	1.00	1.00	1.00	1.00	1.00	1.00
CoV of departure times	1.00	1.00	1.00	1.00	1.00	1.00	1.00	1.00	1.00	1.00	1.00	1.00
Mean WIP at Workstation	7.61	2.92	3.05	42.55	3.34	9.76	2.43	50.56	5.59	2.95	50.55	2.22
Mean CT at Workstation	0.38	0.15	0.15	2.13	0.17	0.49	0.12	2.53	0.28	0.15	2.53	0.11
Mean WIP in Queue	2.69	0.93	0.58	37.67	1.23	1.76	0.62	48.60	1.75	0.95	48.59	0.22
Mean CT in Queue	0.13	0.05	0.03	1.88	0.06	0.09	0.03	2.43	0.09	0.05	2.43	0.01
Mean WIP in Processing	4.93	1.99	2.48	4.88	2.11	8.00	1.82	1.96	3.85	2.00	1.96	2.00
Mean CT in Processing	0.25	0.10	0.12	0.24	0.11	0.40	0.09	0.10	0.19	0.10	0.10	0.10
Workstation "Utilization" (ρ_{ws})	0.82	0.66	0.62	0.98	0.70	0.80	0.61	0.98	0.77	0.67	0.98	0.50

Factory Throughput (lots per day)	20	
Add $M to reduce CoV of Starts	$0.07	
Orig CoV of Starts	8.00	
New CoV of Factory Starts	1.01	
Factory Cycle Time (CT_f)	9.18	89.86% Percentage Reduction in CT — Additional Cost for Cycle Time Reduction $0.40
Factory Inventory (WIP_f)	184	millions

FIGURE 6.3

Twelve-workstation model, second phase of greedy heuristic.

File Edit View Insert Format Tools Data Window Help OM_IE OR_MM

	WS A	WS B	WS C	WS D	WS E	WS F	WS G	WS H	WS I	WS J	WS K	WS L
Initialize	$6	$4	$4	$10	$6	$6	$4	$10	$6	$4	$10	$4
Workstation	WS A	WS B	WS C	WS D	WS E	WS F	WS G	WS H	WS I	WS J	WS K	WS L
Add $M to increase EPR_{ws}	0.0000	0.0000	0.0000	0.0333	0.0000	0.0000	0.0000	0.0333	0.0000	0.0000	0.0333	0.0000
Original EPR_m	4.00	10.00	8.00	4.10	9.50	2.50	11.00	10.20	5.20	10.00	10.20	10.00
New EPR_m	4.00	10.00	8.00	4.61	9.50	2.50	11.00	10.71	5.20	10.00	10.71	10.00
Add $M to increase machines	0.00	0.00	0.00	0.00	0.00	0.00	0.00	0.00	0.00	0.00	0.00	0.00
Original Machine Count	6.00	3.00	4.00	5.00	3.00	10.00	3.00	2.00	5.00	3.00	2.00	4.00
New Machine Count	6.00	3.00	4.00	5.00	3.00	10.00	3.00	2.00	5.00	3.00	2.00	4.00
Original TH capacity (EPR_{ws})	24.00	30.00	32.00	20.50	28.50	25.00	33.00	20.40	26.00	30.00	20.40	40.00
New TH capacity (EPR_{ws})	24.00	30.00	32.00	23.03	28.50	25.00	33.00	21.41	26.00	30.00	21.41	40.00
CoV of interarrival times	1.00	1.00	1.00	1.00	1.00	1.00	1.00	1.00	1.00	1.00	1.00	1.00
Add $M to reduce CoV of PTs	0.07	0.01	0.02	0.02	0.01	0.01	0.07	0.01	0.01	0.07	0.01	0.02
Orig CoV of process times	8.00	2.00	3.00	3.00	2.00	2.00	8.00	2.00	2.00	8.00	2.00	3.00
New CoV of process times	1.00	1.00	1.00	1.00	1.00	1.00	1.00	1.00	1.00	1.00	1.00	1.00
CoV of departure times	1.00	1.00	1.00	1.00	1.00	1.00	1.00	1.00	1.00	1.00	1.00	1.00
Mean WIP at Workstation	8.03	2.95	3.10	9.00	3.34	9.76	2.43	14.69	5.59	2.95	14.69	2.22
Mean CT at Workstation	0.40	0.15	0.16	0.45	0.17	0.49	0.12	0.73	0.28	0.15	0.73	0.11
Mean WIP in Queue	3.03	0.95	0.60	4.66	1.23	1.76	0.62	12.82	1.75	0.95	12.82	0.22
Mean CT in Queue	0.15	0.05	0.03	0.23	0.06	0.09	0.03	0.64	0.09	0.05	0.64	0.01
Mean WIP in Processing	5.00	2.00	2.50	4.34	2.11	8.00	1.82	1.87	3.85	2.00	1.87	2.00
Mean CT in Processing	0.25	0.10	0.12	0.22	0.11	0.40	0.09	0.09	0.19	0.10	0.09	0.10
Workstation "Utilization" (ρ_{ws})	0.83	0.67	0.62	0.87	0.70	0.80	0.61	0.93	0.77	0.67	0.93	0.50

Copyright © 1994-2008 James P. Ignizio & Laura I. Burke

Factory Throughput (lots per day)	20
Add $M to reduce CoV of Starts	$0.07
Orig CoV of Starts	8.00
New CoV of Factory Starts	1.00
Factory Cycle Time (CT_f)	3.94
Factory Inventory (WIP_f)	79

95.64% Percentage Reduction in CT

Additional Cost for Cycle Time Reduction $0.50 millions

- *Phase 1.* Allocate funds first to the reduction of variability (with priority given to the largest variability values) until all variability values have been reduced, where possible, to an *a priori* specified value (e.g., the value was 1.0 for the preceding example) or all funds have been expended. If there is a tie for the largest variability values, break it in favor of the process step farthest upstream (i.e., the one closest to the factory input).

- *Phase 2.* If any funds are left over, allocate them to increasing the effective process times (i.e., increase the availability and/or process rates of the machines) of the factory constraint workstations. If there is a tie for factory constraints, break it in favor of the factory constraint farthest upstream (i.e., the one closest to the factory input).

The real message of this exercise, however, is that the reduction of variability (wherever it exists and particularly in factory starts and effective process rates) is a cheap and effective way to improve factory performance. In Chapter 4, even with a budget of $13M, the best cycle time achieved was 14.59 days. Here, by allowing a focus on variability reduction, we achieved 3.94 days of cycle time (or less, had optimization been employed) while spending only $0.5M.

REDUCING VARIABILITY TRUMPS INCREASING CAPACITY

Examination of the second and third fundamental equations of manufacturing, coupled with observations from Chapters 4, 5, and 6, provides an important message: *Reducing variability anywhere in the production line always improves overall factory performance—particularly cycle time—whereas an increase in a single workstation's capacity may or may not provide an overall benefit to the factory.* Furthermore, in almost any real-world factory, it is almost always faster and less expensive to reduce variability than to increase capacity.

RETURNING TO THE FIVE-WORKSTATION PROBLEM

In Chapter 4, an investigation of the so-called fundamental premise of lean manufacturing was conducted by means of introducing a factory (the five-workstation model) that provided a counterexample. Recall that the fundamental premise of lean manufacturing is that a balanced production line with each workstation running at the takt rate minimizes factory inventory (and thus minimizes factory cycle time).

The five-workstation model of Chapter 4 demonstrated that a factory in which each workstation ran at its highest possible process rate produced inventory and cycle-time results that were superior to those attained by any balanced line. In this section, the comparison of balanced versus unbalanced lines—and the fundamental premise of lean manufacturing—is extended.

I will use the same five-workstation factory as in Chapter 4 to demonstrate some additional points. More accurately, the five-workstation factory to be employed here is *physically* identical to that of Chapter 4. That is, once again, the customer demand is 20 units per hour, and the ranges of process rates for the workstations are as before:

- Workstation A process-rate range: 10 to 25 jobs per hour
- Workstation B process-rate range: 10 to 40 jobs per hour
- Workstation C process-rate range: 10 to 100 jobs per hour

- Workstation D process-rate range: 10 to 25 jobs per hour
- Workstation E process-rate range: 10 to 60 jobs per hour

The simulation model in support of this version of the five-workstation model is provided at

www.mhprofessional.com/Ignizio/5WS_Ch6

Again, this factory is *physically* identical to that in Chapter 4. There is, however, a difference in terms of the protocols being employed to run the two factories (which, in turn, change the variability values within the factory). This difference will become evident if you attempt to compare the balanced-line versus unbalanced-line versions of the factory.

The best balanced line for the five-workstation factory of this chapter is, once again, a facility in which the process rate of each workstation is set to the maximum speed dictated by the factory constraint; that is, each workstation's process rate is set to 25 jobs per hour. The cycle time and inventory produced by the best balanced line are 65.78 hours and 1315.59 units, respectively. This is a very different result, however, from that produced by the five-workstation model in Chapter 4, where the cycle time and inventory were 9.39 hours and 187.76 units, respectively.

Why the quite large difference? The answer lies solely in the difference in factory starts and process time variability of the two versions of the five-workstation model.

Next, set the process rates of this version of the five-workstation model to their maximum values (i.e., 25, 40, 100, 25, and 60 units per hour, respectively) while maintaining a factory starts rate of 20 jobs per hour. If this is done, the resulting cycle time is 51.04 hours, and the corresponding inventory level is 1020.72 units. Once again, it has been demonstrated that an unbalanced production line, contrary to the fundamental premise of lean manufacturing, provides superior results to that of the best balanced line.

But, you should ask, is this the optimal setting for the process rates for the workstations for this version of the five-workstation factory? The answer is, in a word, "No." To demonstrate, try setting the process rates as follows:

- Workstation A process rate: 25 jobs per hour
- Workstation B process rate: 40 jobs per hour

- Workstation C process rate: **38.276 jobs per hour**
- Workstation D process rate: 25 jobs per hour
- Workstation E process rate: 60 jobs per hour

The sole difference between the process-rate settings in the optimal solution just cited and those used with the maximum-run-rate settings happens to be the setting for workstation C (i.e., 38.276 jobs per hour rather than its maximum process rate of 100 jobs per hour). With these latest settings, the cycle time and inventory levels are 50 hours and 1,000 units, respectively. While this represents just a 2 percent reduction over the maximum-run-rate settings for this version of the five-workstation factory, the message delivered is that the optimal production line for this factory is still unbalanced.

CHAPTER SUMMARY

At this point we may summarize the most important concepts of Chapters 4, 5, and 6. These are

- Reducing variability within a factory provides factory performance-improvement results that are most usually faster and cheaper to achieve than those obtained by increasing workstation throughput capacity.
- The theory of constraints has certain potentially serious limitations. Specifically, its fundamental assumption is that of a production line in which variability is essentially ignored and but a single, fixed factory constraint exists. Real-world factories, on the other hand, invariably have multiple migrating constraints and are affected by numerous sources of variability.
- Lean manufacturing, while representing a generally positive force, is not a panacea. Its fundamental premise— that a balanced production line operating at takt speed minimizes factory inventory and cycle time—is based on the implicit assumptions of synchronous systems in which variability may be ignored.
- For significant and sustainable factory performance improvement, the art of manufacturing (e.g., the theory of constraints, lean manufacturing, etc.) must be coupled with the science of manufacturing.

CASE STUDY 6: ROOM 101

It's Saturday, and Julia, Dan, and Brad are meeting once again with Professor Leonidas. The trio had agreed previously that no matter what opinion their colleagues may hold of him, it still would be wise to seek the professor's counsel with regard to their concerns about factory performance. It would seem, however, that the professor has some questions for them.

"What precisely is the situation with Winston Smith? He was awfully evasive about his appointment at Muddle."

Brad notices that Julia's eyes are downcast and decides that he should reply. "Professor, Winston Smith's position at Muddle is a bit of a mystery." Glancing again at Julia, he continues, "It seems that something he did a few years ago displeased management. Frankly, most of us thought he would be fired. Instead, they sent him to Room 101. After that, he's been pretty much invisible in the company, although he continues to show up for work."

"What a waste!" says Leonidas. "Winston Smith is not only a true genius, but he's one of the finest men I've ever known. From the little he said to me during my visit, my impression is that he's terribly unhappy. Why he stays with your company is beyond me."

"I think I can explain," Julia replies, sighing. "There are lots of rumors about Winston and me, and I might as well set the matter straight."

"Julia," Brad interjects, "there's really no reason for that."

"Thanks, Brad," says Julia, "but I want to. First of all, as Brad and some others know, Winston and I were engaged to be married at one time. Winston had tired of academia and moved to the United States to accept a position with Muddle. He had been assured that he would be a valuable source of advice in the running of our factories. And he was." Julia takes at deep breath and continues.

"Unfortunately, Winston reported to Ben Arnold, and Ben took credit for each and every recommendation made by Winston. Winston voiced his displeasure with senior management, and they made it clear that if he was to be a team player, he should be proud to make his immediate superior look good. I should add that Winston also made me look good. Thanks to his advice and guidance, I managed to get several major programs implemented. Winston allowed me to take credit for the results, even though they would never have happened without him. I felt a bit guilty about it, but I rationalized things. After all, this type of behavior was and is rampant in Muddle."

"You are sure right about that," says Brad. "But go on. Sorry for interrupting."

"You all need to understand that my dream, ever since I joined Muddle out of college, was to be appointed a Muddle Fellow. It may seem silly, but that was my goal, and unfortunately, I didn't let anything stand in my way, including my feelings for Winston. Each year they appoint a few people to Fellows ... "

"And promote about a hundred to vice presidents," Brad interjects.

Julia nods in the affirmative and continues, "I was one of the people nominated for a Fellow position. Winston wasn't. When he found out, he walked into Tommy Jenkins' office and demanded to know why he wasn't being considered for promotion to Muddle Fellow. Tommy flat out told him that he hadn't made any significant contributions, even though he must have known that wasn't true. Winston responded with a list of at least a dozen major contributions. Frankly, any one of them should have merited an appointment. Tommy's response was that he'd check into things and let Winston know his decision by the end of the week."

Julia's head sinks lower, and tears begin to appear. "I'm ashamed to say this, but when Tommy asked me about Winston's role in my projects, I inferred that he had been of some help but that I had come up with and implemented the ideas. Evidently, Ben Arnold was an even bigger liar. He told Tommy that Winston had played no role whatsoever in the projects that got Ben promoted. I'm quite sure that Tommy knew that wasn't true, but he sent Winston an e-mail telling him that he did not merit a nomination for Muddle Fellow. When I heard about that, I went straight to Tommy's office and told him that I hadn't given Winston the credit he deserved, and I was fully aware that Ben Arnold had taken advantage of Winston and used him as a means to get promoted to his present position."

"What was his response?" asks Dan. "Of course, based on the situation as it now exists, I can only guess that Tommy ignored your remarks."

"Not only did he ignore what I told him, but he had the audacity to send both Winston and me to Room 101. It was horrible."

"Okay," Dan replies, "I've heard rumors about this Room 101, but just what is it? What happened to the two of you there?"

"Room 101," Julia replies, "is where you are sent for what Muddle calls 'reeducation.' I was told that if I wanted to stay with

Muddle, I should keep my mouth shut and accept the nomination. Winston was warned that his actions could be interpreted as being sexist, that he was attempting to damage the career of a female employee. I agreed to keep quiet and spent the next six weekends in the Muddle reeducation program. It was dreadful, but what happened to Winston was worse."

Professor Leonidas shakes his head in disbelief. "I suspected that the corporate culture in your firm was dysfunctional, but this is just incredible. But you said that what happened to my friend Winston was worse. Would you elaborate?"

"Winston," says Julia, "was moved to a tiny cubicle in one of the parts and supplies buildings. He was threatened. The poor man was told that if he raised any further objections, Muddle would blackball him! He was told that he would never get another job anywhere if he persisted with his claims. He and I haven't spoken since then."

"But why," asks Dan, "didn't they just fire Winston?"

"Tommy, as well as other people in the executive offices, knows how brilliant Winston is and what he could do if he were hired by a competitor. They keep him here because they don't want any other firm to exploit his expertise. So he just sits in his little cube, except for one week a month. Then he's required to take a course on interpersonal relationships and business ethics. What a farce! I can never make it up to him."

"Perhaps," replies Leonidas, stroking his chin, "you can. I have an idea. Why don't the three of you team up with Winston? I'll continue to advise you on the science of manufacturing, and Winston can show you his special talents."

"I don't think that Winston would want to work with me," says Julia, "and I don't blame him."

"Nonsense," replies Leonidas, "this rift in your relationship has gone on long enough. It's time it was healed, and working together on one mission—the improvement of factory performance—could be the catalyst. Please, Julia, do consider it. I saw the way that Winston looked at you during my presentation. He stole glances at you whenever you weren't looking. It's quite obvious, even to an old man like me, that he still cares for you."

Brad schedules a meeting with Winston Smith. On Monday afternoon, he, Dan, and a very hesitant Julia approach Winston's diminutive cubicle in a remote and poorly lit corner of the parts and supply warehouse. After being assured that they will not reveal anything discussed in the encounter, Winston suggests they move the meeting to a small, windowless room in the rear of the building. A crudely fashioned plaque on its weathered door reads, "Authorized Personnel Only." Its interior is nothing like what Julia, Dan, or Brad expects.

Inside the room are a few chairs, several tables, and six computers—equipment Winston had rescued from the trash heap. The walls of the room are covered with graphs and plots. This, according to Winston, is his "war room."

"What, may I ask, do you do in here? Why so many computers?" asks Dan.

"I use this equipment to support my factory simulation efforts," replies Winston. "No one else ever comes here. In fact, no one in this company cares about what I do here—or its potential to help them."

"Are you running the firm's simulation package on those computers?" asks Brad. "I thought that software required the very latest, fastest computers. Those things I see appear to be at least 10 years old."

"Yes, they are old," Winston replies, "but I've rebuilt them, and no, I don't use Muddle's simulation software. First of all, I could never get approval to run that package. Second, I'm using a simulation approach based on fluid network modeling, a type of continuous simulation. It's enormously faster than Muddle's discrete event–based simulation, and it's better suited to my work."

"What exactly is your work?" asks Dan.

"I've built fluid network simulation models of all of Muddle's factories. I use these to experiment on. For example, what might happen if I increase the process rate of a workstation? Or what would factory performance be if I reduced the arrival-rate variability at a workstation? I can run a year's worth of simulations on an entire factory in a few minutes. If I used the Muddle simulation software, it would take hours or even days just to run a single replication. And, of course, for statistical significance, dozens of replications would be required. I don't have the level of detail in my models that Muddle's simulation group does, but I can get what I want in a fraction of the time—and cost."

"Impressive," says Brad, "could you give us an example of your findings?"

Pointing to a graph on the wall, Winston replies, "This plot contrasts the cycle time this factory now achieves versus what it could realize by nothing more than a declustering of factory starts. The time for an average product to pass through the factory could be reduced by anywhere between 2 and 30 percent just by means of smoothing out factory starts."

"Between 2 and 30 percent, you say," says Dan. "That's an awfully big range. Can't the model produce results that are more precise?"

"They could be a lot more precise," Winston replies, "if I just had certain data—like the coefficient of variability of job arrivals at our workstations or the variability of equipment downtimes. Unfortunately, I don't have access to the data I need to populate my models, and there's no way this company is ever going to allow me to gather those data. So, right now, I'm forced to just use a range of guesses."

"I think I can solve that problem," says Julia, avoiding eye contact. "I have access to all our factories' production-line data. I can provide you with those facts and figures, and with all of us working together; we could populate your simulation models with the data you need to get a better estimate of factory performance."

"That would be wonderful," Winston replies, "but it could get the three of you in a lot of trouble. I'm not someone you want to be seen with in this company."

"We'll just have to be careful," says Dan. "I'm game to spend some evenings and at least part of my weekend on this project."

"Me too," says Julia. "What about you, Brad?"

"I suppose I could spend some of my free time here," Brad answers without enthusiasm. "I'd definitely like to use Winston's models to test out the techniques that Professor Leonidas has been discussing, but I don't see much else in the way of a return on our investment."

"What do you mean by that?" asks Julia.

"Suppose that we try out the professor's concepts to improve the performance of Muddle's factories. Suppose that Winston's models validate those approaches. How is that going to help our careers? Someone else will take credit for all our hard work. This is, after all, the Muddle Corporation we're dealing with."

"Let's cross that bridge when we come to it," answers Julia. Dan nods in the affirmative. Brad shrugs his shoulders.

"Then I assume we're all in agreement," says Winston. "With Julia's assistance in obtaining the data, and with all of us working off-hours on this effort, we should be able to prove to Muddle's top brass that the science of manufacturing will solve this company's factory performance problems. In the meantime, we must be very discreet about this. No one outside the four of us in this room and Aristotle must know what we are doing."

Ben Arnold is working late. Putting the final touches on an e-mail, he presses SEND, and that interesting piece of correspondence is on its way to Jack Gibson, the junior member of the three plant managers at Factory 2. This, Ben thinks, could be the final nail in the coffin.

CHAPTER 6 EXERCISES

1. Employ, using your own tie-breaking rules, the greedy heuristic (phases 1 and 2) to reduce the cycle time of the 12-workstation simulation model (of Figure 6.1).

2. Employ, using your own tie-breaking rules, the greedy heuristic to reduce the cycle time of the 12-workstation simulation model (of Figure 6.1). This time, however, employ the second phase (e.g., allocate funds to increase workstation *EPR* values) first. Allocate no more than $250,000 to *EPR* increases, and then proceed to the allocation of funds to reduce variability.

3. Discuss the results obtained in Exercises 1 and 2. To what do you attribute the differences, if any?

4. What was the name of the main character in the classic novel, *Nineteen Eighty-Four,* by George Orwell? What fate did that character and his female friend suffer? What similarities are there between the world described in Orwell's book and the environment faced by employees of the Muddle Corporation?

Three Holistic Performance Curves

In Chapters 4 and 6 we explored the 12-workstation factory. In this chapter we use that same model to illustrate three factory performance curves by means of which we may fairly and objectively evaluate and compare factory performance (Ignizio, 1997).

The first curve presented is the factory *operating curve* (OC). The second is the factory *load-adjusted cycle-time efficiency* (LACTE) *plot*. The final curve is the factory *profit curve* (PC). Each of these curves reveals useful information with regard to the overall performance of a factory.

FACTORY OPERATING CURVE

A factory operating curve (a.k.a. *factory performance curve*) is a plot of factory cycle time versus factory loading, where loading is given by either (1) the factory throughput rate (e.g., flow rate of jobs introduced into the factory) or (2) the ratio of factory throughput rate to the upper bound of factory capacity (i.e., maximum theoretical capacity of the factory constraint). In Chapter 13, a means for computing the upper bound on factory capacity for the general case will be presented. However, since we are dealing with the simple, nonreentrant 12-workstation factory (e.g., the machines in each workstation are identical in terms of effective process rates, and each is capable of supporting the single process step), the upper bound of the capacity of each workstation may be found—*for this special case*—simply by adding the effective process rates of its machines.

To clarify, we return to the 12-workstation factory of Chapters 4 and 6. The initial factory conditions were shown in Figure 6.1 and are repeated here as Figure 7.1. Note that the upper bounds on the capacities of each workstation are listed in cells B11 through O11. For example, the upper bound (maximum theoretical capacity) of the capacity (i.e., EPR_{ws}) of workstation H is 20.40 jobs per day. Since workstation H is one of the factory constraints, 20.40 jobs per day also must be the upper bound on the capacity of the 12-workstation factory—at least under its initial configuration.

To derive the data required to plot the factory operating curve, we record the cycle times for various values of factory throughput (i.e., where those values are entered into cell B25). The resulting plot for the 12-workstation factory (for the initial scenario) is provided in Figure 7.2. Figure 7.3 is the same plot but employs, for easier reading, a truncated cycle-time scale.

It is clear from either Figure 7.2 or Figure 7.3 that as factory loading increases, cycle time increases (i.e., precisely as predicted by the Pollaczek-Khintchine equation). Further, as factory loading approaches the upper bound of factory capacity (i.e., 20.40 jobs per day in this case), cycle time turns exponential. In fact, just from

FIGURE 7.1

Twelve-workstation factory simulation model, initial scenario.

	A	B	C	D	E	F	G	H	I	J	K	L	M	O
	File Edit View Insert Format Tools Data Window Help OM_IE OR_MM										Type a question for help			
1	Initialize			Copyright © 1994-2008 James P. Ignizio & Laura I. Burke										
2		$6	$4	$4	$10	$6	$6	$4	$10	$6	$4	$10	$4	
3	Workstation	WS A	WS B	WS C	WS D	WS E	WS F	WS G	WS H	WS I	WS J	WS K	WS L	
4	Add $M to increase EPR_{ws}	0.00	0.00	0.00	0.00	0.00	0.00	0.00	0.00	0.00	0.00	0.00	0.00	
5	Original EPR_m	4.00	10.00	8.00	4.10	9.50	2.50	11.00	10.20	5.20	10.00	10.20	10.00	
6	New EPR_m	4.00	10.00	8.00	4.10	9.50	2.50	11.00	10.20	5.20	10.00	10.20	10.00	
7	Add $M to increase machines	0.00	0.00	0.00	0.00	0.00	0.00	0.00	0.00	0.00	0.00	0.00	0.00	
8	Original Machine Count	6.00	3.00	4.00	5.00	3.00	10.00	3.00	2.00	5.00	3.00	2.00	4.00	
9	New Machine Count	6.00	3.00	4.00	5.00	3.00	10.00	3.00	2.00	5.00	3.00	2.00	4.00	
10	Original TH capacity (EPR_{ws})	24.00	30.00	32.00	20.50	28.50	25.00	33.00	20.40	26.00	30.00	20.40	40.00	
11	New TH capacity (EPR_{ws})	24.00	30.00	32.00	20.50	28.50	25.00	33.00	20.40	26.00	30.00	20.40	40.00	
12	CoV of interarrival times	8.00	6.17	4.73	3.95	2.26	1.98	1.63	3.93	1.90	1.69	4.27	1.93	
13	Add $M to reduce CoV of PTs	0.00	0.00	0.00	0.00	0.00	0.00	0.00	0.00	0.00	0.00	0.00	0.00	
14	Orig CoV of process times	8.00	2.00	3.00	3.00	2.00	2.00	8.00	2.00	2.00	8.00	2.00	3.00	
15	New CoV of process times	8.00	2.00	3.00	3.00	2.00	2.00	8.00	2.00	2.00	8.00	2.00	3.00	
16	CoV of departure times	6.17	4.73	3.95	2.26	1.98	1.63	3.93	1.90	1.69	4.27	1.93	2.01	
17	Mean WIP at Workstation	199.12	22.06	11.97	467.74	7.71	14.97	22.34	473.57	10.48	33.85	541.17	3.42	
18	Mean CT at Workstation	9.96	1.10	0.60	23.39	0.39	0.75	1.12	23.68	0.52	1.69	27.06	0.17	
19	Mean WIP in Queue	194.12	20.06	9.47	462.87	5.61	6.97	20.53	471.61	6.63	31.85	539.21	1.42	
20	Mean CT in Queue	9.71	1.00	0.47	23.14	0.28	0.35	1.03	23.58	0.33	1.59	26.96	0.07	
21	Mean WIP in Processing	5.00	2.00	2.50	4.88	2.11	6.00	1.82	1.96	3.85	2.00	1.96	2.00	
22	Mean CT in Processing	0.25	0.10	0.12	0.24	0.11	0.40	0.09	0.10	0.19	0.10	0.10	0.10	
23	Workstation "Utilization" (ρ_{ws})	0.83	0.67	0.62	0.98	0.70	0.80	0.61	0.98	0.77	0.67	0.98	0.50	
24														
25	Factory Throughput (lots per day)	20												
26	Add $M to reduce CoV of Starts	$0.00												
27	Orig CoV of Starts	8.00												
28	New CoV of Factory Starts	8.00												
29	Factory Cycle Time (CT_f)	90.42		0.00% Percentage Reduction in CT					Additional Cost for Cycle Time Reduction				$0.00	
30	Factory Inventory (WIP_f)	1808											millions	

FIGURE 7.2

Factory operating curve for 12-workstation factory (initial).

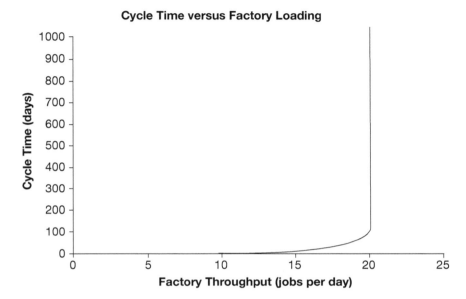

FIGURE 7.3

Factory operating curve for 12-workstation factory (truncated vertical axis).

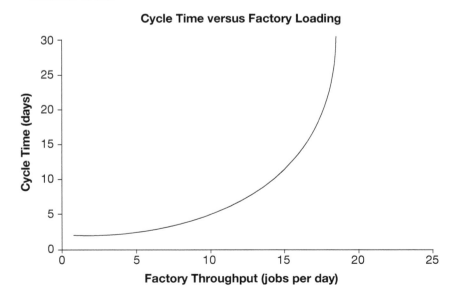

looking at Figure 7.3, I personally would be concerned about loading this factory at a rate of more than about 15 or so jobs per day.

The factory operating curve also provides a means to evaluate
the impact of either reducing or increasing factory variability.
Consider, for example, a reduction in the coefficient of variability
CoV of factory starts from 8 to 1 per day coupled with a reduction
in the *CoV* of the effective process times of all workstations (A
through L) to values of 1 (i.e., the same results that were obtained
by the first phase of the greedy heuristic and previously illustrated
in Figure 6.2). The resulting factory operating curve may be compared with the original factory operating curve (i.e., of Figure 7.2
or Figure 7.3). This is shown in Figure 7.4, where the solid line is
the factory operating curve for the initial scenario, whereas the
dashed line is the operating curve after reductions in the variability of starts and effective process times for workstation A (i.e., after
phase 1 of the greedy heuristic).

It is clear, or should be, from Figure 7.4 that simply by reducing factory variability (in this case the variability of both factory
starts and effective process times) we have improved factory

FIGURE 7.4

Before and after operating curves for the 12-workstation
factory.

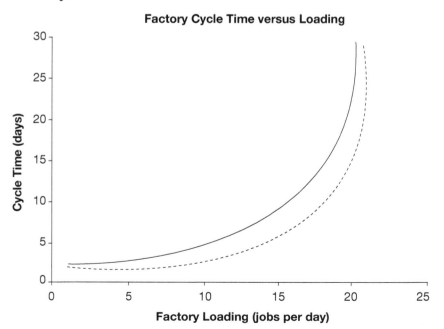

performance significantly. Prior to variability reduction, the cycle time for a factory loading of 20 jobs per day was 90.42 days. After reducing the sources of variability, the cycle time for the same loading is but 9.18 days (i.e., a reduction of about 90 percent).

It also should be noted that while the reductions in variability improved cycle times across all levels of factory loading, they did not change the upper bound on factory capacity (i.e., the *EPR* of the factory constraint workstation or workstations). Specifically, the upper bound on factory capacity (i.e., the maximum theoretical capacity) remains at 20.40 jobs per day.

What has been accomplished thus far is simply the conduct of the first phase of the greedy heuristic described in Chapter 6. If we employ the second phase (i.e., use any remaining funds, up to the $500,000 limit, to increase the *EPR* values of the factory constraints), the result is the factory depicted in Figure 6.3. The factory operating curve that may be developed after the second phase of the greedy heuristic is shown in Figure 7.5. In this figure, all three factory operating curves are shown, that is, that for the original scenario, for the reduction in variability (phase 1 of the greedy heuristic), and after both phases of the greedy heuristic.

FIGURE 7.5

Factory operating curves for the 12-workstation model.

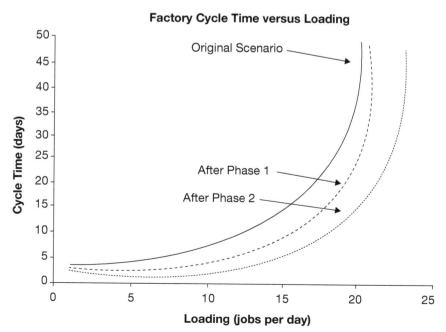

For both the initial 12-workstation factory scenario and the facility after phase 1 of the greedy heuristic, the upper bound on factory capacity is 20.40 jobs per day. Note, though, that after the second phase of the greedy heuristic, the upper bound on factory capacity increased to 21.41 jobs per day (see Figures 6.3 and 7.5). This is so because the second phase is focused on increasing factory capacity—while ignoring variability. Readers are invited to derive these results using the 12-workstation factory simulation model.

The factory operating curve is also useful for a rough estimation of the practical capacity of a factory (i.e., the maximum sustainable factory throughput rate beyond which cycle time would be unacceptably high). The maximum sustainable factory capacity may be estimated by visually examining the factory operating curve. More specifically, it is the maximum capacity exhibited on the operating curve occurring "somewhat prior" to the cycle time going exponential.

For example, in Figure 7.5, I would assert that the maximum sustainable factory capacities for the various scenarios are

- Initial scenario sustainable factory capacity: ~15 to 17 jobs per day
- Scenario after phase 1 of greedy heuristic: ~17 to 18 jobs per day
- Scenario after both phases of heuristic: ~20 jobs per day

The most important message presented by the factory operating curve is that the maximum sustainable capacity of a factory is determined in large part by the variability inherent in its production line. Simply by reducing that variability, the maximum sustainable capacity may be increased, sometimes substantially.

The derivation of the data required to plot the factory operating curve may be obtained by

- Running the actual factory at various loadings and recording cycle times or
- Running a simulation of the factory at various loadings and recording cycle times where the types of simulations that might be employed include
  - Discrete event simulation models (Taha, 2006)
  - Simulation models employing fluid nets (Billings and Hasenbein, 2002)
  - Simulation models employing electromagnetic nets (Ignizio, 2000)

○ Simulations employing queuing models (Ignizio and Gupta, 1975)

Clearly, attempting to derive factory operating curve data from experimentation on an actual factory may be impractical (and most likely will be). Consequently, the most typical approach to the development of the required data is by means of simulation.

LOAD-ADJUSTED CYCLE-TIME EFFICIENCY

Recall from Equation (3.23) that the cycle-time efficiency CTE of a factory is the ratio of its process time to its cycle time. The equation for the CTE of a factory is repeated below:

$$CTE_f = \frac{Process\ Time_f}{CT_f} \qquad (7.1)$$

For our purposes, we shall define a factory's *process time* as that which includes the time devoted to all value-added as well as non-value-added process steps. Alternative representations of factory cycle-time efficiency omit any non-value-added process step time (e.g., time consumed by transit, inspection, or test).

The problem—a particularly crucial one—with the CTE metric is the fact that it is not adjusted for factory loading. To illustrate, consider the 12-workstation factory operating curve in Figure 7.6. Assuming that the total process time required for the manufacture of the average product is 1.9035 days (which, indeed, is the case for the 12-workstation problem in its initial configuration), the cycle-time efficiencies for various values of factory loading are provided in Table 7.1.

It should be obvious that it would be patently unfair to compare the cycle-time efficiencies of two otherwise identical 12-workstation factories that are operating at different loadings. For example, the CTE_f of the factory at 73.53 percent loading (15 jobs per day) is 18.7 percent, whereas that of its twin, running at 98.04 percent loading (20 jobs per day), is just 2.11 percent. Despite this, I have seen, repeatedly, firms employ non-load-adjusted cycle-time efficiency (or, and even more often, non-load-adjusted cycle times) allegedly to compare the performance of several factories or allegedly to evaluate the results of the introduction of some new scheme for factory performance improvement.

If one is to employ cycle-time efficiency as a credible measure of factory performance, it *must* be adjusted for load. Furthermore,

FIGURE 7.6

Factory operating curve for 12-workstation factory (initial scenario).

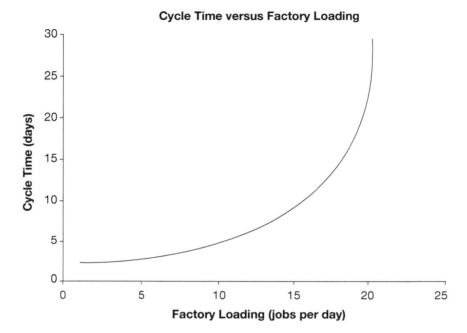

Cycle Time versus Factory Loading

TABLE 7.1

Factory Loadings versus Cycle-Time Efficiencies

Scenario	Loading (Jobs/Day)	Loading (Percent of Maximum Theoretical Capacity)	Factory Cycle Time (Days)	Sum of Process Times (Days)	CTE_f
1	0	0.0000	1.9035	1.9035	1.0000
2	1	0.0490	1.96	1.9035	0.9712
3	5	0.2451	2.78	1.9035	0.6847
4	10	0.4902	4.89	1.9035	0.3893
5	15	0.7353	10.18	1.9035	0.1870
6	19	0.9314	33.31	1.9035	0.0571
7	20	0.9804	90.42	1.9035	0.0211
8	20.39	0.9995	2249.23	1.9035	0.0008

the entire load-adjusted cycle-time efficiency (LACTE) *curve*—rather than just a point—must be employed.

Equation (7.2) is used to develop each point on the LACTE curve. More specifically, it may be used to compute LACTE values for various factory loadings.

$$LACTE_{\text{loading}} = \left(\frac{\text{factory process time}}{\text{factory cycle time}} \right) \bullet$$
$$\left(\frac{\text{factory throughput}}{\text{maximum theoretical factory capacity}} \right) \tag{7.2}$$

We may employ Equation (7.2) to compute the LACTE curve for the 12-workstation factory. To accomplish this, the initial factory scenario (e.g., Figure 7.1) will be employed. The computations required for development of this curve are summarized in Table 7.2.

Table 7.1 may be extended to include the factory loading percentage and, subsequently, to develop a number of *LACTE* point estimates. This is shown in Table 7.2. Note that a given *LACTE* value is found by multiplying the associated entry in column F by that in column C.

TABLE 7.2

Load-Adjusted Cycle-Time Efficiencies

A	B	C	D	E	F	G
Scenario	Loading (Jobs/Day)	Loading (Percent of Upper Bound of Capacity) =B/20.4	Factory Cycle Time (Days)	Sum of Process Times (Days)	CTE_f =D/E	$LACTE$ =F•C
1	0	0.0000	1.9035	1.9035	1.0000	0.0000
2	1	0.0490	1.96	1.9035	0.9712	0.0476
3	5	0.2451	2.78	1.9035	0.6847	0.1678
4	10	0.4902	4.89	1.9035	0.3893	0.1908
5	15	0.7353	10.18	1.9035	0.1870	0.1375
6	19	0.9314	33.31	1.9035	0.0571	0.0532
7	20	0.9804	90.42	1.9035	0.0211	0.0206
8	20.39	0.9995	2249.23	1.9035	0.0008	0.0008

The resulting LACTE curve is plotted in Figure 7.7. Note that the peak *LACTE* value of 19.08 percent is at a loading of 10 jobs per day (49.02 percent loading) and that this peak is at a point slightly skewed to the left on the LACTE curve.

To compare factory performance (i.e., of several factories or of a factory before and after changes), it is necessary to compare the LACTE *curves* for each factory. To illustrate, we return to the 12-workstation problem. This time, however, we plot the LACTE curve after phase 1 of the greedy heuristic (i.e., for the factory configuration presented in Figure 6.2). The LACTE curve for this instance is shown in Figure 7.8. Notice that the peak *LACTE* value of 59 percent occurs at a factory loading of about 74 percent (i.e., of the upper bound on capacity of 20.40 jobs per day). In this instance, the peak is at a point on the curve that is skewed to the right.

The LACTE curves for both the initial scenario and that developed after phase 1 of the greedy heuristic are plotted in Figure 7.9. The reduction in variability (phase 1) in the 12-workstation factory produces a LACTE curve that dominates, for any value of factory loading, the curve developed for the initial scenario.

FIGURE 7.7

LACTE curve for 12-workstation factory (initial scenario).

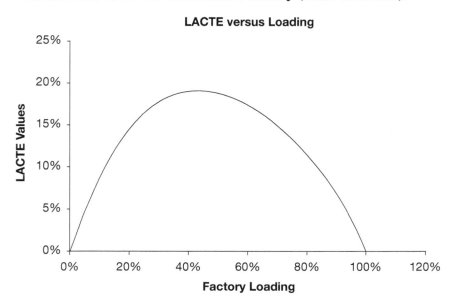

FIGURE 7.8

LACTE curve (after phase 1 of greedy heuristic).

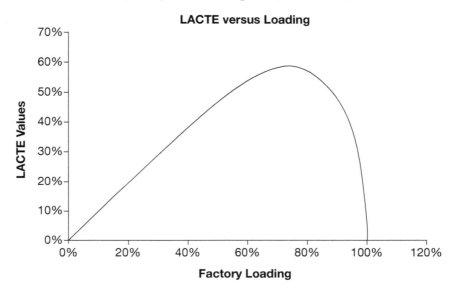

LACTE versus Loading

FIGURE 7.9

LACTE curves (before and after phase 1 of the greedy heuristic).

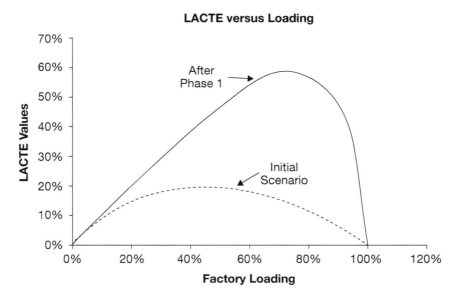

LACTE versus Loading

It is emphasized again that factory performance must be evaluated by a comparison of the LACTE *curves* rather than of point values. To illustrate, at a factory loading of 49 percent, the *LACTE* value associated with the initial scenario for the 12-workstation factory is approximately 19 percent. At a factory loading of 98 percent, the *LACTE* value associated with the factory after phase 1 of the greedy heuristic is about 15 percent. Clearly, it would be foolish to compare the before and after factory configurations using just these two *LACTE* point values because one would conclude erroneously that the initial configuration of the 12-workstation factory is the better performer.

Any LACTE curve for a factory in which the only changes are those owing to either reduction or variability increase must lie within the *LACTE envelope*. This is illustrated in Figure 7.10. The right triangle formed by the horizontal axis and the two straight lines form the LACTE envelope. Moreover, the LACTE envelope represents the utopian LACTE curve, that is, the curve that would be developed for a factory in which there is no variability whatsoever.

As a final illustration of the development and comparison of LACTE curves, consider Figure 7.11. In this figure, the LACTE

FIGURE 7.10

LACTE curves and the LACTE envelope.

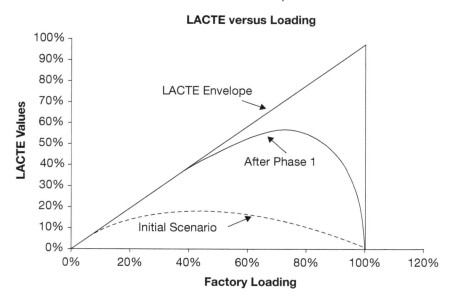

FIGURE 7.11

LACTE curves (after phases 1 and 2).

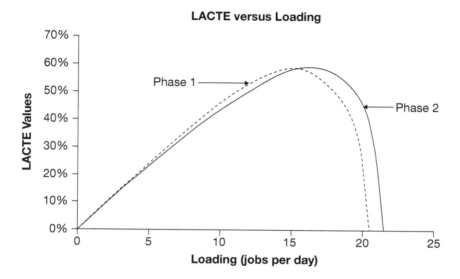

It may be seen in Figure 7.11 that the upper bound on factory
throughput capacity has increased (from 20.40 jobs per day to 21.41
jobs per day) as a result of the conduct of phase 2 of the greedy
heuristic. Typically, phase 2 (i.e., increasing factory capacity) will
not increase the peak value on the LACTE curve significantly but
will move the LACTE envelope to the right (i.e., increase the upper
bound on factory capacity).

FACTORY PROFIT CURVE

Some factory managers claim to want to minimize the cost of production. In fact, corporate-level management even may (and often
do) provide their factory managers with a cost-reduction goal. If,
however, cost reduction is truly the foremost factory goal, all one
has to do to minimize cost is to stop production, lay off all personnel, and sell all assets charged to the factory.

Despite the obsession of some MBA programs, many companies, and almost all Wall Street analysts with cost reduction, any
firm hoping to survive and prosper over the long run (e.g., such as

Toyota) must focus on increasing profit and market share. (This may require *increased* factory expenditures rather than reductions in cost.) To keep matters simple, I will focus herein solely on the goal of increased profit.

There is an unfortunate impression that profit is given by the following formula, wherein selling price and production costs are assumed to be constant:

Profit = units sold • selling price − units produced • unit cost

The fact is, however, that the selling price of a given product is seldom, if ever, constant. Instead, the price for which it may be sold typically decreases with time. (Consider, as just one example, the cost of large flat-screen television sets, DVD players, cell phones, and computer monitors.) Furthermore, the cost of manufacturing a product similarly is seldom, if ever, constant. Production cost typically decreases with time (e.g., as the bugs in the production line are worked out and as experience is gained by the workforce).

If the goal of a firm is, as it generally should be, to increase profit, then the factory loading for which profit is maximized should be computed. The factory profit curve serves to estimate that optimal level of loading. Derivation of the profit curve requires, as a first step, the development of estimates of profit over a given planning horizon.

Figure 7.12 presents the profit as a function of time curves for two different products, A and B. For sake of discussion, we will assume that product A is produced in a 12-workstation factory (designated as factory A) employing the configuration indicated in Figure 7.1 (i.e., the initial scenario of the 12-workstation factory). We further assume that product B is produced in a 12-workstation factory (designated as factory B) employing precisely the same configuration. It is clear from Figure 7.12 that the profit for product B decreases over time, at least initially, faster than that for product A. Our goal, then, is to determine the optimal level, in terms of profit, of factory loading for the two factories.

Simply by computing factory outs (i.e., the number of completed jobs leaving the factory) for each time period (or using a simulation model) and multiplying by the profit associated with that time period (i.e., from Figure 7.12), a graph of profit per factory loading may be easily derived. For the two factories and their two products, that graph is shown in Figure 7.13.

FIGURE 7.12

Profit versus time plots, products A and B.

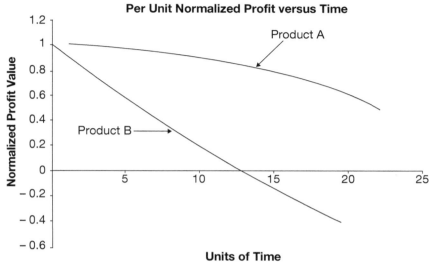

FIGURE 7.13

Factory profit curves for factories A and B.

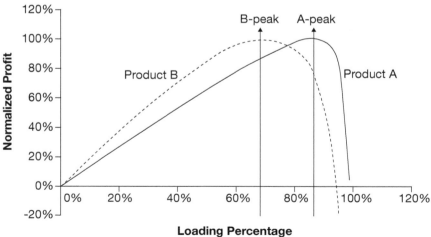

From Figure 7.13 we see that factory A should operate at about 88 percent of its upper bound on capacity. Factory B, on the other hand, should operate at roughly only 67 percent of its upper bound on capacity. In short, if the goal is to maximize profit, a factory might, depending on its profit function, best achieve this goal by underloading the factory—a decision that may be considered blasphemous by some factory managers.

CHAPTER SUMMARY

In this chapter, three holistic factory performance curves have been presented. (These metrics are holistic in that they attempt to evaluate the entire factory system rather than its parts.) The first, the factory operating curve, has received previous attention elsewhere in the literature (Aurand and Miller, 1997). The other two, the factory load-adjusted cycle-time curves and factory profit curves, have not been published previously in the open literature (Ignizio, 1997). When these curves, particularly the factory load-adjusted cycle-time and factory profit curves, are introduced into real-world factories, management is provided with the information necessary to direct resources and effort toward the most productive efforts in terms of improving factory performance. This is in marked contrast to the performance measures used by some firms.

In Chapter 8, a number of other, somewhat lower-level factory performance metrics will be presented. In addition, the limitations of some commonly employed metrics (e.g., moves, utilization, inventory turns, work-in-progress turns, etc.) will be discussed.

CASE STUDY 7: IN THE HOT SEAT

Tommy Jenkins shifts his weight on the rock-hard chair. He desperately hopes that his anxiety isn't evident. He truly hates whoever the fiend might be who designed the straight-backed chair in which he is sitting. Marvin Muddle, his eyes as cold as those of a great white shark, stares at him from across his massive desk, waiting for a response.

"I'm confident," says Tommy without any confidence whatsoever, "that my factory is competitive with any other Muddle factory anywhere. We're well along with the *LEAN* Forward program, and I'm positive that this quarter's figures will show that we've reduced costs."

Marvin thumbs through the latest report on Muddle factory performance. Pointing his finger at a graph of cycle-time comparisons, he answers, "Tommy, this graph indicates that your factory has the worst cycle time of any of our factories. Your customers are complaining about how long it's taking for delivery of their orders. These graphs don't lie, Tommy, so how can you still say everything is fine?"

Ben Arnold and Donna Garcia shift uncomfortably in their chairs. Tommy Jenkins' face is tomato red, and the veins on his forehead seem ready to pop out of his skull.

"I want to know," Tommy hisses, "just why I've not been told the truth about our situation. I don't ever, ever want to be chewed out by our CEO like I was yesterday. Now, which one of you is going to level with me?"

Ben Arnold clears his throat and responds, "Tommy, you've seen the before and after photos of our factory's workplaces. The CANDOs performed on our workspaces have reduced clutter. Pictures don't lie. And, by cleaning up those areas, we've reduced recordable injuries. Maybe our cycle time hasn't been reduced as of yet, but I'm told that it's bound to be shortened within the next six weeks."

"I don't care what you've been told, Ben. I want you to promise me that our factory cycle time will be the best in the company. Can you do that?"

"Tommy," Ben replies, "I can't promise you that. I can only tell you that is what I've been told. I've ..."

Donna Garcia interrupts, "Tommy, I can promise you that our cycle time will be the best in the firm. But it will require you to make a change in our factory starts."

Ben's eyes narrow. Tommy replies, "Why should I change our factory starts? You need to give me a damn good reason for that."

"Just give me a moment," says Donna, as she opens her laptop computer and places it on Tommy's desk. "I've got a copy of the slides that Professor Leonidas presented to the *LEAN* Forward team. I think you'll find one of them particularly interesting."

"How in the world did you get a copy of that man's slides?" asks Tommy. "Besides, you told me that his presentation was rubbish and that he spent the day bashing me and this company. So why should I even look at his slides?"

"First of all," replies Donna, "I had Ed, our safety and ergo director, divert the professor's attention before his presentation began. While Ed had his attention, I made a copy of the professor's slides on the conference room computer."

That's the girl, thinks Tommy. Our most recent slogan may be "*LEAN* Forward," but Donna realizes that our real slogan is "*Aufero absque dedecus.*"

"Second," Donna continues, "while the professor did indeed bash Muddle, and you in particular, he did make a few interesting points." Advancing the slides, Donna stops at one labeled, "Factory Operating Curve."

"How did your name get on those slides?" Tommy asks. "I expected to see the professor's name on them and even a copyright notice."

"I had one of the nerds in IT unlock the protection on the slides. He removed the copyright notice and the professor's name," says Donna. "I thought you'd approve."

"Good girl," says Tommy. Ben nods his head in agreement.

"Getting back to this slide," Donna continues, "notice that you can reduce factory cycle time by a significant amount by means of only a slight reduction in factory loading—at least if your factory is operating as poorly as ours. So, as I see it, the best way to reduce cycle time is for us to reduce factory starts."

"But," Tommy replies, "how can I convince headquarters to allow a reduction in factory loading? We've already told them that our capacity is 10,000 units per week. And even that is probably an underestimate."

"I think I can answer that," says Ben. "Just tell them that the figures provided to us on the capacity of our factory constraint workstation were wrong. Tell them that our true capacity is only 9,000 units per week. I'd also recommend that we put the blame for this error on one of the junior people in the Factory 7 capacity group and fire him or her."

"What about you, Donna?" Tommy replies. "Do you think Ben's plan will work?"

"I agree with Ben. Based on what the professor said, I believe that we can wind up with the best factory cycle time in the entire firm within six weeks. There's also something else we might want to consider—the matter of Winston Smith."

"Winston Smith?" asks Tommy. "I thought we had got rid of that problem a long time ago. What does he have to do with our dilemma with cycle time?"

"If you recall," Donna replies, "we promised Julia Austen that we wouldn't fire Winston if she accepted the Muddle Fellow appointment. Of course, we also promised Winston that we wouldn't fire Julia if he stayed on and kept his mouth shut. Winston has kept his side of the bargain, but for the past few years he's been sending his ideas and recommendations for factory performance improvement to your office. I've seen copies of his e-mails, and some of his ideas should, I think, at least be looked into."

"I have no idea of what you are talking about, Donna," says Tommy. "I've never seen any correspondence from Winston. What about that, Ben?"

"As your technical assistant, I filter out your e-mails, particularly those sent by such riff-raff as Winston Smith. Frankly, I didn't see anything of interest in the garbage he's been sending," says Ben, defensively.

"I disagree," says Donna.

"Okay, so you two disagree on Smith's input," Tommy replies. "Let's leave it at that for now. What I want, though, is to follow through with *my* plan for reducing factory starts. Ben, have someone in the capacity group take the blame for the overestimate, and have the poor sap fired. However, if we haven't achieved the best cycle time in the company within six weeks, I just may have to think about getting a new technical assistant—and a new factory operations department head. Do I make myself clear?"

"Clear, boss," says Donna and Ben in unison. "But," Donna adds, "what about the ideas Winston Smith has been sending in? Shouldn't someone at least look into those?"

"Have your people read his memos," says Tommy. "I also want you to keep an eye on that man. Mark my words, you should never trust an Englishman."

With the meeting concluded, Tommy turns his back on Donna and Ben. As a consequence, he misses the wink that Ben gives Donna.

When he hears the door of his office close, Tommy Jenkins swings his chair about and gazes out his corner office window. He's learned a few things in his time at Muddle, one of which is not to trust anyone. This might explain why he asked, months ago, that Ben keep tabs on Donna. He followed that up with a confidential meeting with Donna, asking her to keep her eye on Ben.

You can never, Tommy thinks, be too careful. Now, he thinks, I should make up a list of potential candidates to replace those two, should they not come up with some way, any way, to reduce our cycle time.

Two days later, Jenny Chen, a junior member of the factory capacity group, enters the security gate of the office complex at a Muddle factory campus. Her arrival time is 7:30 a.m., precisely 30 minutes early, as has been her habit for the two years she has been dutifully employed by Muddle. Jenny is taken aback to find that the security gate will not accept her badge and further surprised when an alarm sounds. And she is even more concerned when a half-dozen security personnel rush to the gate.

"Ms. Chen," says a security officer, "it is my duty to inform you that you are no longer an employee of the Muddle Corporation. You'll find your belongings in that cardboard box over there," he adds, pointing to a box outside the entranceway.

"But why?" asks Jenny. "What could have possibly happened to cause my firing? Can't I please speak to my manager? There must have been some terrible mistake."

Before Jenny can ask another question, two members of the security team forcibly escort her from the building. As heads turn, wondering just what all the commotion is about, Ben Arnold arrives. A few seconds later, he is on the elevator, feeling no remorse whatsoever about his role in the firing of Jenny Chen. This is, he thinks, what he gets paid for—and why he loves coming to work.

CHAPTER 7 EXERCISES

1. The total process time of a factory is 10 days. Its average factory cycle time is 30 days. What is its cycle-time efficiency?

2. The manager of the factory in Exercise 1 claims that among all the factories in the firm, her factory's velocity is the fastest (i.e., its cycle time is the lowest). Provide a response, in 25 words or less, that might serve to change her confidence in that statement.

3. Explain, in 25 words or less, why the comparison of factories on the basis of point estimates of their *LACTE* values is incorrect.

4. The factory manager of factory B (with regard to Figure 7.13) believes that his factory should be loaded at the same rate (i.e., 88 percent) as factory A. Which one of the seven wastes of lean manufacturing is he exhibiting?

CHAPTER 8

Factory Performance Metrics: The Good, the Bad, and the Ugly

In my work, I routinely encounter firms—particularly those involved in the manufacture of high-tech products—in which data for literally hundreds of factory performance metrics are collected. Such efforts provide these firms with an enormous amount of raw data and keep a sizable workforce of automation personnel, information technology (IT) people, and (alas) industrial engineers occupied.

In most instances, however, the data—once processed—provide little, if any, information. More distressing, many of the metrics developed and acted on actually are counterproductive; that is, they encourage employment of factory protocols that worsen rather than improve factory performance—or else they support decisions that could have been accomplished more cost-effectively. In short, substantial resources—in terms of human energy and funding—are devoted to ill-advised and non-value-added efforts because of a reliance on inferior metrics.

In this chapter I first introduce a number of useful, fair, valid, and credible factory performance metrics (i.e., the good metrics). These include the

- Waddington effect plot
- M-ratio metric
- Availability profile plot
- Cycle-time contribution factor (CTCF)
- Degree of reentrancy (DoR) metric

Illustrations of how to gather the data and compute each of these metrics are provided in the material to follow.

This chapter also includes a discussion of some widely employed but problematic metrics (i.e., the "bad" and the "ugly"). Included among these are inventory or work-in-progress (WIP) turns, moves, utilization (of personnel or machines), and cost—as well as any non-load-adjusted factory velocity (e.g., cycle time and X-factor) metric or any measure derived by means of an inadequate data sampling rate.

The employment of these "bad" and "ugly" metrics may be worse than not measuring anything at all because they encourage and lead to poor decisions. Old habits, even those that harm a firm's bottom line, are, however, difficult to break.

The chapter concludes with a discussion of ways in which metrics—even "good" metrics—may be inflated or otherwise "gamed." In some firms, more time and resources may be devoted to gaming metrics than to improving factory performance.

WADDINGTON EFFECT AND PLOT

In Chapter 2, mention was given to the role that operational research played in World War II. One of the topics cited there was that of the Waddington effect, a phenomenon I named in honor of C. H. Waddington (Waddington, 1973). Waddington's operational research team, assigned to the British Coastal Air Command, encountered and identified the Waddington effect during the conduct of an effort to increase the flying hours of the Coastal Air Command's beleaguered air fleet.

In essence, it was found that the preventive maintenance (PM) events being employed appeared to induce rather than reduce unscheduled repairs. This disturbing effect was particularly evident "shortly" after the conduct of a PM event.

While Waddington's team dealt with a fleet of aircraft, their findings apply equally well to the "fleet" of machines in a factory. Figure 8.1 is a Waddington effect plot for a single-machine workstation in an actual factory. The workstation in question was scheduled to undergo a major PM event, requiring shutdown of the machine, every 40 hours. The PM event then in use required, on average, five hours to conduct (i.e., the time represented by the shaded bars in Figure 8.1). Following the PM event, the solid black bars indicate unscheduled downs (e.g., unanticipated repairs and/or unscheduled recalibrations) and their duration in hours

FIGURE 8.1

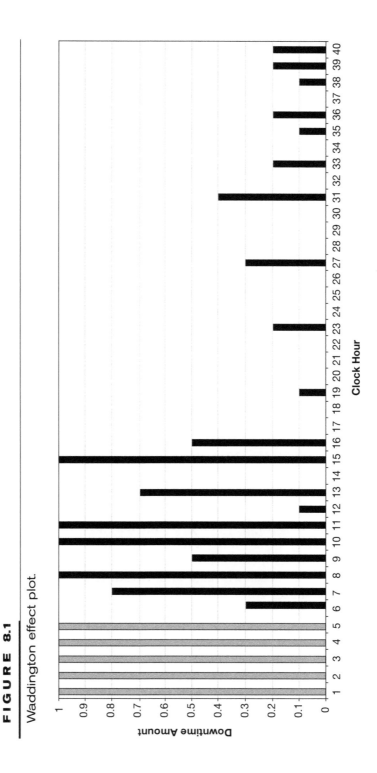

Waddington effect plot.

(see the vertical axis). For this machine, there were a total of five hours lost each 40-hour period to the major PM event and a further 9.2 hours lost to unscheduled downtime.

The Waddington effect may be recognized by an increase in unscheduled downtime *closely* following a PM event. In this illustration, a total of 6.4 hours of unscheduled downtime occurs within just 10 hours of completion of the PM event.[1] From then on, the profile of unscheduled downtimes decreases—until a similar pattern (not shown in the figure) is induced 40 hours later by the next major PM event.

Had the PM event accomplished its goal (i.e., to eliminate unscheduled downtime until the next PM event), the availability of this machine would be (we assume, for sake of discussion, that there is no blocked time)

$$A = \frac{(40-5)}{40} = 87.5 \text{ percent}$$

However, when the unscheduled downtime (9.2 hours in total) is included, the actual machine availability is just

$$A = \frac{(40-5-9.2)}{40} = 64.5 \text{ percent}$$

Furthermore, a full 16 percent of the machine's availability is lost to the unscheduled downtime in just the 10 hours following the PM event.

Waddington's group found that the unscheduled time lost closely following a PM event was a consequence primarily of poorly designed and/or poorly performed preventive maintenance (including scheduling PM events too frequently). The approach they developed (termed herein as a *Waddington analysis*) to eliminate or at least mitigate the Waddington effect will be described in Chapter 10.

To summarize, in an existing factory, data should be collected on the average time consumed by both scheduled (e.g., PM events) and unscheduled downtime (e.g., repairs and recalibrations) for

---

1 The downtime in the 10 hours following the conduct of the 5-hour PM event includes 0.3 hour in hour 6, 0.8 hour in hour 7, 1 hour in hour 8, 0.5 hour in hour 9, 1 hour in hour 10, 1 hour in hour 11, 0.1 hour in hour 12, 0.7 hour in hour 13, 0 hours in hour 14, and 1 hour in hour 15 for a total of 6.4 hours.

both individual machines and workstations. These data should be plotted against clock time (e.g., as in Figure 8.1). If visual inspection (or automated pattern-recognition analysis) indicates the existence of the Waddington effect, further action (to be described in detail in Chapter 10) most definitely should be taken.

M-RATIO

The *M-ratio* (a.k.a. *maintenance ratio*) is the ratio of scheduled downtime to unscheduled downtime—and it may be computed for either individual machines, workstations, or an entire factory. The formula employed to determine the M-ratio is[2]

$$\text{M-ratio} = \frac{\text{scheduled downtime}}{\text{unscheduled downtime}} \qquad (8.1)$$

Referring back to Figure 8.1, we see that the total unscheduled downtime over the period of interest (i.e., the 40 hours between PM events) was 9.2 hours, whereas the scheduled downtime was 5 hours. Assuming that these data represent averages typical of this workstation, its M-ratio is

$$\text{M-ratio} = \frac{5}{9.2} = 0.54$$

An M-ratio of 0.54 is in fact dreadful. It indicates that this workstation needs attention—and fast. For a typical factory (or machine or workstation), the M-ratio should be 9 or higher.

At an M-ratio of 9, the amount of unscheduled downtime is just 10 percent of the total downtime. In the preceding example, however, the amount of unscheduled downtime consumes 65 percent of the total downtime!

An M-ratio of less than 9 is usually an indication of a serious problem—most likely in the content, design, and implementation of PM events. Most often, however, factory engineers and managers would appear to want to believe that unscheduled downtime is caused by the design and/or operation of the machine, workstation, or factory (i.e., physical problems). While this may be the case, it is more likely that a low M-ratio is due to poor maintenance protocols.

---

2 An alternative form of the M-ratio equation may be developed by including blocked time in the denominator of Equation (8.1).

AVAILABILITY PROFILE PLOT

An *availability profile plot* is used to record and analyze the availability of either a single machine or an entire workstation versus time. Figure 8.2 presents the availability profile plot of a hypothetical multiple-machine workstation. Samples of the workstation's availability (i.e., percentage of machines up, running, and qualified to support the processing responsibilities of the workstation) were taken every hour. While hypothetical, the plot is typical and similar in shape to those found in firms that fail to recognize the importance of protocols (particularly maintenance protocols).

Readers may note that the availability profile plot repeats itself every 12 hours, that is, every shift. Figure 8.3 presents a typical availability profile plot for just a single shift for this factory. A visual examination of the profile in either Figure 8.2 or Figure 8.3 reveals the fact that workstation availability is high (on the order of 90 percent) at the beginning of each shift and then plummets to a little more than 50 percent about two or three hours into the shift. About five or six hours into the shift, workstation availability has recovered and remains in the range of roughly 80 to 90 percent for the remainder of the shift.

FIGURE 8.2

A hypothetical availability profile plot.

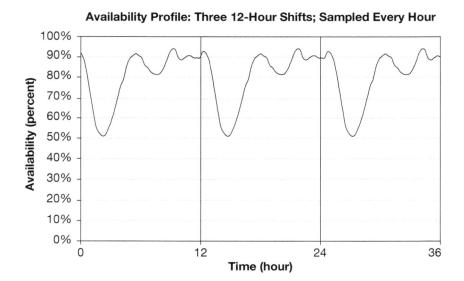

Availability Profile: Three 12-Hour Shifts; Sampled Every Hour

FIGURE 8.3

Availability profile plot, one shift.

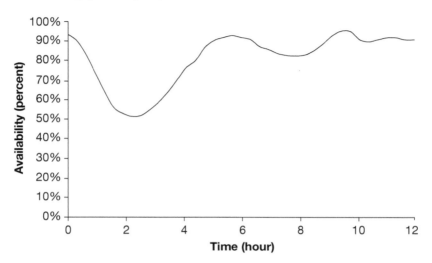

We may compute the average workstation availability and its coefficient of availability from the data employed to plot the preceding figures. The results are

- Workstation average availability $A = 81$ percent.
- Workstation coefficient of variance of availability $CoV(A) = 0.164$.

Given these statistics and the availability profile plots, the next step in the analysis is—or should be—to ask ourselves why the profile takes on the shape exhibited in the figures. In fact, this was the question I asked myself many years ago when I first encountered an availability profile plot very similar to the one in Figure 8.2.

By observing operations on the factory floor, the reason for the pattern became evident. The factory workers had been warned to complete as many maintenance and repair events within their shift as possible rather than having such events extend across shifts. Consequently, floor personnel routinely scheduled as many maintenance events as doable as early into their shift as possible. This in itself was the reason for the shape taken by the availability profile.

While the factory manager, factory engineers, and floor personnel were satisfied with the results, the practice of clustering maintenance events (in this case, early in the shift) is a bad habit that degrades factory performance and should be avoided. Simply by means of declustering workstation maintenance events (and after overcoming significant resistance to this "radical recommendation"), a significant improvement in factory performance (in terms of both effective capacity and cycle time) was achieved.

Before leaving the topic of availability profile plots, I must warn the reader that such plots can be—and too often have been— used improperly. Specifically, unless an adequate sampling rate is used, the plot is worthless. To illustrate, consider what would happen if instead of sampling availability every hour—as in Figures 8.2 and 8.3—we had sampled approximately every 12 hours (i.e., once per shift). Figure 8.4 shows the result of such a reduced sampling rate.

A visual examination of the new plot would suggest that workstation availability remains in a range between about 90 and 93 percent. The impression given is that this workstation is running very efficiently, whereas nothing could be farther from the truth.

We also may compute the average workstation availability and its coefficient of availability from the data employed to plot Figure 8.4. The results are

F I G U R E   8.4

Availability profile plot, samples taken every 12 hours.

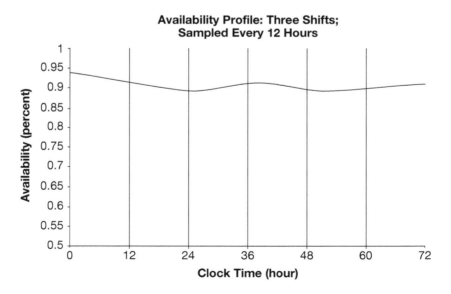

- Workstation average availability $A = 91$ percent, in contrast to 81 percent when an adequate sampling rate is used.
- Workstation coefficient of variability of availability $CoV(A) = 0.013$, in contrast to 0.164 when an adequate sampling rate is used.

Again, the impression is given of an efficient, stable workstation when, in fact, its actual performance is, at best, problematic. To summarize, unless the sampling rate employed to gather data is adequate, conclusions contrary to reality may be drawn.

CYCLE-TIME CONTRIBUTION FACTOR

The *cycle-time contribution factor (CTCF)*, while not infallible, provides a reasonably effective means to assign priorities to the dedication of resources for the improvement of factory performance. More specifically, this particular metric may be used to help decide how to best allocate resources among process steps so as to improve overall factory performance.

In Chapter 3, the *cycle-time efficiency (CTE)* metric was defined. Recall that the CTE of a given process step is found by means of Equation (8.2):

$$CTE_{ps} = \frac{PT_{ps}}{CT_{ps}} \qquad (8.2)$$

where PT_{ps} is the average raw process time of the process step, and CT_{ps} is the actual average cycle time of the step.

Consider, for example, the cycle-time efficiencies of two process steps at a specific level of factory loading. Assume for the moment that step X has a CTE of 10 percent, whereas that of process step Y is 20 percent. One may ask the question: To which of these two steps should priority be given to the dedication of resources for factory performance improvement at the existing level of factory loading?

While the CTE of process step X is less (and thus worse) than that of process step Y, it could be the case that dedicating resources to the improvement of the performance of step Y (e.g., by means of reducing the variability inherent in that step, by increasing the availability of the machines supporting that step, or by increasing their process rates) actually may be more beneficial to overall factory performance. This may be determined by means of computing the cycle-time contribution factor of the process steps in question.

To demonstrate, examine the reentrant factory of Figure 8.5. There are four workstations, each of which consists of one or more identical machines. The process flow is depicted in the figure. The degree of reentrancy (DoR) of the factory is 7/4, or 1.75.

We will assume that we know the raw process time *(RPT)* of each of the seven process steps and that we have expended the resources necessary to collect credible data on the average actual cycle times of these steps. These two sets of data are all that are required to determine the *CTCF* for each of the workstations' process steps.

The data are listed in Table 8.1 in the columns labeled *"PT"* and *"CT,"* respectively. We then use Equation (8.2) to derive the

FIGURE 8.5

Four-workstation reentrant factory.

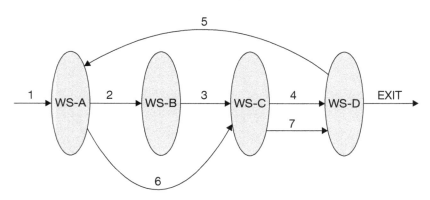

TABLE 8.1

Process step cycle-time contribution factors

Workstation	Process Step	PT	CT	CTE	CTCF
A	1	1	6	**0.167**	2.833
B	2	2	7	0.286	2.429
C	3	3	9	0.333	1.889
D	4	2	7	0.286	2.429
A	5	4	13	0.308	**1.308**
C	6	3	9	0.333	1.889
D	7	2	8	0.250	2.125

cycle-time efficiencies for each process step, as listed in the column headed by "CTE."

The final step in derivation of the cycle-time contribution factors is to employ Equation (8.3) for their derivation, where

$$CTCF_{ps} = \frac{\sum\limits_{ps=1}^{P} PT_{ps}}{CT_{ps}} \tag{8.3}$$

For example, the $CTCF$ for process step 5 is found by dividing 17 (the sum of all raw process times for all process steps) by the CT of the process step (i.e., 13).

It may be noted that although process step 1 has the worst CTE value (i.e., lowest CTE), the process step whose improvement likely will have the most impact on total factory cycle time is step 5 (i.e., the step having the lowest value of $CTCF$).

To repeat, the process step having the lowest $CTCF$ value typically is the highest-priority workstation in terms of the allocation of resources. In this instance, process step 5 of workstation A has the highest priority, followed by process steps 3, 6, 7, 2, 4, and 1 in that order. Thus, although process step 1 has the worst CTE, it likely has less impact on overall factory cycle time (again, for the specific factory loading level under consideration) than process step 5.

Given that process step 5 has the highest priority, just some of the actions that might be taken to increase the value of its $CTCF$ include

- Reduce the coefficient of variability of arrivals at process step 5.
- Increase the availability of the machines in workstation A that support process step 5.
- Reduce the coefficient of variability of the effective process times of the machines that support process step 5 (e.g., this might be accomplished by reducing the variability of the repair times of these machines).
- Increase the M-ratio of the machines that support process step 5 (e.g., this might be achieved via the conduct of a Waddington analysis).

Note that each of these actions should reduce the cycle time of process step 5 and thus increase the value of its $CTCF$.

DEGREES OF REENTRANCY

Readers were first exposed to the degree of reentrancy (DoR) metric in Chapter 3. As discussed, the DoR metric provides an indication of the complexity, as induced by reentrancy, of either a complete factory or any of its reentrant nests.

The ideal factory (approached to some degree by the Arsenal of Venice, the Ford Model T plant, or the Toyota production system) has a DoR of 1, that is, no reentrancy. Reentrancy in itself may, and usually does, induce variability—and it always increases complexity. One has only to observe the frantic (and mostly counterproductive) measures taken by engineers in a highly reentrant factory—say, a semiconductor wafer fabrication facility—in their attempts to dispatch jobs (a.k.a. *WIP management*) to reentrant workstations to appreciate the problems imposed by reentrancy.

Reentrant factories lead to countless mostly pointless and fruitless meetings in which the sole topic is that of the presentation of impassioned arguments for and against various WIP management schemes. Some personnel argue for "back-to-front" WIP management, some for "round-robin" (i.e., cyclic) dispatching, and others for the employment of "critical-ratio" WIP management, whereas others demand dynamic (as opposed to static) dispatching. The fact is, however, that given a reentrant or any other type facility, the only WIP management scheme that routinely and reliably improves overall factory performance is one that reduces the combination of batch forming times and departure-rate variability. This assertion should be obvious from a close examination of the second fundamental equation of manufacturing.

The optimal approach to the matter of WIP management is to focus on three factors: (1) reduce factory DoR, (2) reduce batch forming times, and (3) reduce the departure-rate variability from each process step. Subsequent chapters will deal with practical means to accomplish each of these goals.

SOME "BAD" AND "UGLY" PERFORMANCE METRICS

To qualify as "bad" and "ugly," a performance metric must be one that can and likely will lead to decisions that only worsen overall factory performance. Among the very worst of these are inventory (or WIP) turns, moves, and utilization, as well as (1) any non-load-adjusted factory velocity measure and (2) any metric derived from data collected at an inadequate sampling rate. Yet it is these measures, rather than the more valid and useful ones described previously [e.g., load-adjusted cycle-time efficiency (LACTE), factory operation curve, factory profit curve, Waddington effect plot, M-ratio, availability profile plot, cycle-time contribution factor, and DoR] that seem to be, alas, among the most commonly employed in actual practice. It should not be surprising, then, that the vast majority of factories (or supply chains and business processes) operate far below their potential.

Changing a factory manager's or engineer's mind, when it comes to these bad and ugly metrics, may prove to be an exceptionally difficult task. Hopefully, the discussion that follows will explain just why one should avoid (or, at the very least, appreciate the deficiencies of) the bad and ugly metrics. I begin with the metric known as *inventory* (or *WIP*) *turns*.

Inventory and WIP Turns

Inventory turns (or, alternately, WIP turns) are usually found by dividing average factory throughput *TH* by average factory inventory *WIP*. Thus one version of the formula for inventory turns is expressed as

$$\text{Inventory turns} = TH/WIP \qquad (8.4)$$

However, since Little's equation states that $WIP = CT \cdot TH$, Equation (8.4) may be transformed into

$$\text{Inventory turns} = TH/WIP = TH/(CT \cdot TH) = 1/CT \qquad (8.5)$$

Clearly, the shorter the cycle time (i.e., the faster factory velocity), the higher—and supposedly better—is the value of inventory turns.

An alternative representation of inventory turns, and one popular in the semiconductor manufacturing sector, is that of WIP turns, as given by

$$\text{WIP turns} = \frac{\text{number of value-added process steps}}{\text{cycle time}} \qquad (8.6)$$

For example, if there are 150 value-added process steps in the manufacture of a product and the average cycle time is 75 days, then the WIP turns are 150/75, or 2.

A few of the problems with using WIP turns include the following:

- It may be difficult to impossible to come to agreement as to the number of value-added process steps (e.g., which steps truly add value and which don't?).
- Some factories may produce products having inherently longer raw process times. This increases, at no fault of the factory, the minimum possible cycle time.
- Cycle time is a non-load-adjusted metric. Simply by just slightly reducing factory loading, one factory may, for example, be able to halve its cycle time.

Inventory turns, because they employ non-load-adjusted cycle time (Equation 8.2) in their computation, suffer from the same problem as noted in the second and third bullets in the preceding list.

Moves

There are factory managers who use moves as a performance metric. A number of them would seem to even rely on moves as their primary means for assessing performance. They evidently believe that the greater the number of moves (e.g., jobs processed per unit time through the factory, workstation, or machine or by a human), the better the entity in question is performing.

To explain why moves are such a poor and misleading metric, all one has to do is to consider a hypothetical factory having a single and fixed constraint, no loss owing to scrap, no reentrancy, and no variability whatsoever. Assume further that the constraint workstation has an upper bound on capacity (i.e., maximum throughput rate) of 5,000 jobs per week. Thus, if 4,000 jobs per week are entered into this factory, the average number of jobs out (i.e., moves per factory per week) would be 4,000. If the jobs started were 4,900 per week, the average number of moves per factory per week would be 4,900. A starts rate of 5,000 jobs per week would, in this perfect factory, produce 5,000 moves per factory per week.

So far, all is well and good. If, however, we increase the jobs rate to any level above 5,000 per week, the number of factory moves will remain at 5,000. Even if we increased jobs introduced into the factory to, say, 20,000 jobs per week, we still achieve just 5,000 moves—a value dictated by the factory constraint. Of course, with any job starts rate above 5,000, the factory inventory level would increase—ultimately to infinity. Correspondingly, the average job cycle time would increase to infinity. Not many customers would be pleased with that amount of lead time.

The employment of moves as a performance metric encourages factory overstarts (i.e., the introduction of jobs started at a rate higher than the maximum sustainable rate of factory throughput). If, however, management is ignorant or dismissive of the value and importance of reduced factory cycle time, moves actually may be employed as the preferred performance metric.

In short, moves are a poor measure of performance because their use encourages bad behavior and ignores factory cycle time and factory inventory buildup. The situation is even worse for a more realistic factory, that is, one having variability, multiple and migrating constraints, reentrancy, and losses owing to scrap.

Utilization

Whether we are talking about the utilization of machines or human beings, utilization is an unfortunate and counterproductive measure of performance. When a factory manager sets some level of utilization as a (or the) factory goal, he or she has fallen into the trap of relying on perception rather than reality.

Factories in which utilization is a primary performance goal encourage the "look busy" syndrome. When a factory manager or a corporate executive walks through such a factory, workers scramble to find something—anything—to do that will give them the appearance of being busy. I have observed, on more than one occasion, maintenance technicians actually stopping perfectly good machines and performing unnecessary and unscheduled maintenance—simply to appear to be doing something. In other instances, I have seen workers snatch jobs that had successfully finished processing on their workstation and reintroduce them (i.e., reprocess them) into the workstation. Perhaps the cleverest approach I have observed was that of a machine operator who hid a stockpile of unfinished jobs next to his machine so as to avoid ever having his machine idle in the event of a management walkthrough. There seems to be no end to ways in which to convince either a moves-or utilization-obsessed manager that a worker or workstation is busy.

Utilization is the first cousin of moves. Both metrics encourage the worst behavior of workers, and both do more harm than good.

Cost

The final member of the gang of "bad" and "ugly" metrics to be discussed is cost. Unfortunately, despite its problems and negative impact on decisions, cost is often the primary metric used by management (and Wall Street analysts) to measure a factory's or firm's performance. Just as with moves and utilization, however, an emphasis on minimizing cost encourages—and rewards—bad behavior and poor decision making.

As discussed in Chapter 7, the primary goal of a for-profit firm should be to maximize profit and market share and to do so over the long rather than the short term. Firms that emphasize cost minimization often do so while ignoring profit and market share— or the health of the company—over the long term. Unfortunately, the reduction of cost by a firm (e.g., via layoff of employees, consolidation of operations, outsourcing, etc.) is almost always both encouraged and well received by Wall Street.

Not only is corporate management encouraged to cut costs to achieve some short-term benefit, but also so are the firm's employees. Just one illustration of this was evident in a firm whose CEO demanded cost cutting as well as purchasing delays so as to avoid having to report a loss for the quarter. The CEO did not want to be the firm's first chief executive to have to report a quarterly loss, and he made his wishes clear to management.

In order to satisfy the CEO's short-term (and, as it proved to be, short-sighted) goal, management at all levels demanded that purchases of new machines be put off for one quarter and notified employees that they would be rewarded if they found ways to reduce the number of machines in each factory. Purchases were indeed delayed—resulting in increased factory cycle times and the displeasure of the firm's customers. Factory engineers, eager to satisfy the machine-reduction goal, conducted detailed (and mostly flawed) analyses to determine if any machines could be removed (and either sold for salvage or simply shut down for some period of time) without affecting factory capacity. One engineer discovered that a few machines could be removed from two of the workstations in the factory without any evident impact on capacity. A few months later, this engineer was recognized in a meeting of all factory personnel—and presented with a $20 coupon that could be used (within 30 days) at a local restaurant.

The primary results achieved by this firm's cost-reduction effort were as follows:

- Costs for the quarter were indeed reduced, and the firm avoided having to report a quarterly loss.
- Factory cycle times increased significantly.
- Lead times promised to the firm's customers could not be satisfied.
- Customer dissatisfaction increased significantly.
- Effective (as opposed to predicted) factory capacity decreased somewhat.
- Shortly after the "successful" cost-reduction effort, two of the firm's biggest customers switched either all or part of their business to the firm's major competitor.

While one would imagine that in a sane and rational world, this particular cost-cutting exercise would have taught this firm a lesson, cost reduction apparently remains—at least at this point in time—the firm's major concern. Cost reduction is still rewarded, the impact and importance of factory cycle time has yet to be fathomed, and factory managers remain convinced that there is no need to be knowledgeable about the science of manufacturing.

GAMES PEOPLE PLAY

It is all well and good to point out good, bad, and ugly factory performance metrics. Unfortunately, however, even the best metric may prove to be ugly—or even hideous—if management fails to insist on accountability and oversight in the collection, processing, and interpretation of the underlying data. A hands-off manager, particularly one who refuses to gain a tolerable level of appreciation of the science of manufacturing, invariably will fall victim to bogus information. To illustrate, I will now discuss just a few of the ways in which metrics may be (have been and—alas—are being) gamed.

Gaming LACTE

Load-adjusted cycle-time efficiency (LACTE), one of the three holistic factory performance measures described in Chapter 7, is—when employed and interpreted properly——one of the very best ways, if not *the* best way, to measure and compare factory performance. However, it is relatively easy to game this metric (this is true of any metric). Some of the approaches employed to misuse the LACTE metric include

- Ignoring the fact that a LACTE curve must be developed and using, instead, just a *LACTE* point value
- Intentionally or unintentionally understating actual factory capacity (e.g., assuming or pretending that the existing throughput of a factory employing inadequate or improper protocols represents the true, sustainable limit of its capacity)
- Intentionally or unintentionally inflating the value of the factory's raw process time

Gaming the Waddington Effect Plot and M-Ratio Metric

At one brief moment in time I had convinced myself that two metrics that could not be gamed were the Waddington effect plot and the M-ratio. However, I had underestimated the degree to which some individuals would go to produce bogus results.

In one firm, the engineers at one of its factories initially reported a very poor (i.e., low) M-ratio for their workstations. Once they discovered that their M-ratio performance (as, however, being computed correctly) was the worst in the firm, they found a way to triple the value of their M-ratio overnight. They simply omitted data produced by their poorest performing workstations, asserting that these were "outliers." The revised and bogus M-ratio value was cited in their next report. Other factories discovered the scheme and, in order to remain competitive, followed suit. Within a few weeks, all the factories in the firm had M-ratios anywhere from three to four times their true value. Management, ignorant of the practices being employed, congratulated everyone—and themselves—for achieving such excellent results in such a short time.

A similar rationale was employed subsequently in the development of factory Waddington effect plots. Unscheduled downtimes closely following a PM event were reclassified. Instead of being designated as unscheduled downs, many of these events were given such names as "pseudo-PM events" and "extended PM events." Thus, in one fell swoop—by means of self-deception—the Waddington effect was mitigated, and M-ratios were increased. The perpetrators of these practices, once again, were congratulated and rewarded for their "good work."

Gaming Cost

Since cost is such a popular metric, countless ways have been developed to report bogus cost reductions. Shifting expenditures into the future was discussed previously and remains a classic way to satisfy short-term cost-reduction goals.

With the proliferation of various management fads, some rather clever approaches to attributing cost reductions to the success of the fad *du jour* have been introduced. As just one illustration, a large multinational firm adopted a certain management cost-reduction fad [for the sake of discussion, let's call it *utopian management* (UM)] a decade or so ago. The firm's CEO stated that he wanted to see a reduction of at least 30 percent in costs as a consequence of the introduction of UM.

Not only was the 30 percent reduction goal achieved, but it was also surpassed. The cost reduction alleged to be achieved by the introduction of UM was on the order of 35 percent. This was accomplished, however, mostly by means of accounting trickery. Specifically, any cost reductions in the firm—achieved by any means—were attributed to the introduction of UM. For example, when one factory was shut down solely owing to obsolescence, UM was given the credit for the resulting reduction in cost. And when a factory engineer invented a new method for producing one of the firm's products, UM was given credit for the cost reduction.

As a result of the widespread reporting of the firm's alleged but mostly inflated success with UM, other firms eagerly adopted the fad. To their surprise, their results were not nearly so impressive. Such disappointments, however, have yet to slow the proliferation of articles, books, seminars, and courses on this particular fad.

Gaming Moves and Utilization

The metrics of moves and utilization are likely the most frequently abused measures of performance. The "look busy" culture that these metrics induce has been discussed.

Another way in which the moves metric is frequently abused is through the "cherry picking" of jobs to be introduced into a workstation. If management is imprudent enough to rely on moves, factory floor personnel soon will discover that given the choice between introducing a job that will take a long process time versus one that takes a short time, selecting the job requiring the shorter time will increase the number of moves.

The utilization metric may be and often is gamed by means of the introduction of unnecessary bureaucracy and red tape. At one firm, the approval of a minor, if not trivial change in the amount of supplies ordered for a workstation required the signatures of five different people. The requestor, a factory floor maintenance worker, hand carried the approval forms. The average time spent to obtain all five signatures was on the order of six hours—time that the requestor should have spent on the factory floor in support of the numerous unscheduled repair events the workstation encountered. Under this system, the average utilization of the workstation personnel was on the order of 80 percent.

This particular business process ultimately was changed—despite the resistance of floor personnel, who did not want to be seen as "less utilized." A clever but naive new hire on the factory floor conceived and developed an improved business process for the ordering of supplies. Despite the objections (and veiled threats) of his coworkers, he presented the concept to his supervisor. The method was approved and implemented soon thereafter. The new process, requiring a single approval—via e-mail—reduced the average approval time from six hours to less than an hour. The average availability of the associated workstation, as a consequence, increased from 74 to 86 percent. At the same time, the utilization of the workstation's personnel dropped significantly (i.e., the worker who had been spending much of his time gathering signatures was able to devote that time to the workstation).

Unfortunately, this story does not have a happy ending. About six months after introduction of the streamlined supply-ordering process, a "lean manufacturing" task force recorded the utilization of factory floor personnel. They found that the utilization of the floor personnel supporting the workstation in question was "only" about 60 percent—well below the 70 percent goal established by the firm's finance department. Failing to appreciate that lean manufacturing is, or should be, focused on more than cost reduction, the task force recommended a reduction in the number of personnel assigned to the workstation. As a consequence, the utilization of the workstation's floor personnel increased to more than 80 percent, and workstation availability decreased to roughly 75 percent. Factory cycle time took a similar hit. Perhaps even worse, the result confirmed the worst fears of the factory workforce, that is, that any improvements in business processes would be punished by reductions in workforce size and an increase in workload.

Gaming Is Widespread

Some readers may wonder if the practice of gaming is as insidious and widespread as I have implied. Perhaps, you may think, the preceding discussion has exaggerated such practices. Unfortunately, the gaming of performance metrics is all too common, whether in a factory, a mutual fund, a bank, or even the ranking of universities. As one example, in 2008, the *U.S. News & World Report* considered changing the way it ranks U.S. law schools (A. Efrati, "Law School Rankings May Change to Deter 'Gaming,'" *Wall Street Journal*, August 26, 2008, p. A1). The change considered attempts to deter a "popular practice" employed by law schools that involves channeling lower-scoring full-time applicants into part-time programs that don't count in the rankings.

The fact of the matter is that no matter what may be the results of any type of ranking (e.g., of factories, schools, or places to live), take these with a grain of salt. Unless there is a serious system for auditing and objectively analyzing such rankings, games can and will be played.

CHAPTER SUMMARY

If a factory performance metric is to be useful, it must satisfy certain conditions. These include

- The data employed to support the metric must be collected at an adequate sampling rate.
- If different factories are to be compared fairly or the changes in a factory's performance are to be evaluated properly, the metrics employed absolutely and positively must be load-adjusted.
- Discipline, accountability, and oversight (by those capable of doing so) are a necessity. Any performance metric, whether "good," "bad," or "ugly," is susceptible to gaming.

Factory performance metrics that do not satisfy these prerequisites encourage poor decisions and lead to degraded rather than improved performance.

My personal recommendations for performance metrics are

- Use holistic measures:
  - LACTE
  - Profit curve

- Use supporting measures:
  - Waddington effect plot
  - M-ratio
  - Availability profile plot
  - Degree of reentrancy

This said, I am convinced that far too much time and emotion are wasted on arguments concerning performance measures. Firms that most quickly achieve significant and sustained factory performance improvement focus the bulk of their efforts on simply reducing variability and complexity.

CASE STUDY 8: INTRIGUE IN THE PARTS WAREHOUSE

It's Saturday morning, and Winston is busy at work in his "war room." Sometime later, Julia and Dan arrive, announcing that Brad had told them that he might not be able to make it this morning.

"I do believe that Brad Simmons has something better to do this weekend," says Julia, grinning.

"What do you mean by that?" asks Dan. "What's up with Brad?"

"All I know," Julia replies, "is that I saw Brad and Sally Swindel having dinner at the Golden Goose last night. I've also been told that Sally asked her firm to transfer her to Hyperbola's local office—an office located about two blocks from here. Someone, I think, is going to be seeing a lot more of Sally Swindel."

"Wow," says Dan. "We could have a problem."

"I don't think so," Julia replies. "Brad's a good guy. If being with Sally Swindel makes him happy, then I'm happy for him."

Winston Smith clears his throat. "Brad may not be a concern, but we do have a problem. Walk with me to my cubicle, and you'll see what I mean."

Once the three are at Winston's cubicle, he points to another cubicle, located across the hall. "When I arrived at work yesterday, I noticed that someone had set up a cubicle, the one you see there. A few minutes later, a young man arrived and took a seat in the cubicle. He gave me a wave, I waved back, and that was the extent of our pleasantries. All day long, however, I caught him watching me. I don't think he's doing anything else. People, I think he's spying on me. We need to be very careful. Very careful."

Donna Garcia is also working this Saturday morning. She sits at the desk in her home office perusing the printouts of the e-mails that Winston Smith had sent to Tommy Jenkins—the same e-mails that were intercepted by Ben Arnold and had been considered to be of no value. Her efforts are interrupted by a phone call.

"Hello," says Donna. "Yes, I received your e-mail. Yes, it does seem that our Winston Smith has had a long relationship with Professor Leonidas. I've also found out that the professor was the person responsible for the turnaround of ToraXpress. Using his approach, they were able to reduce their factory cycle time by about 75 percent—without having to purchase any new machines. Somehow, they even increased their capacity. Then Muddle bought the company, forced our 'No Deviations' policy on them, and their performance turned rotten."

Donna pauses to listen to the other person on the line and then replies, "Don't worry. I've got someone watching Winston. I also had IT remotely download everything on his computer. We may find something there. In the meantime, I noticed that he sent e-mails to Tommy requesting approval to access the simulation software Muddle is using. He even asked if he could join forces with Muddle's simulation group. In one of the e-mails he claims that he is confident that we could reduce our factory cycle time by 60 percent or more."

Donna again pauses to listen. "Don't worry, Tommy is not going to know about any of this. Right now all the poor sap wants to do is to have the lowest cycle time of any of our factories."

Shortly after Donna Garcia hangs up her phone, Brad Simmons—on the other side of town—dials Sally Swindel's cell phone number.

CHAPTER 8 EXERCISES

1. The Waddington effect plots for two workstations in a factory indicate the existence of the effect for workstation A and no evidence of the effect for workstation B. Their

average availabilities, however, are identical. Why should one be concerned with workstation A?

2. Return to Exercise 4 of Chapter 3 and compute the M-ratio for the machine described.

3. An availability profile plot of a workstation in a factory indicates that its average availability is in the range of 85 to 90 percent for the night shift but lies in the range of 40 to 80 percent for the day shift. What might be the cause of this difference? What should be done?

4. A firm samples the availability of its workstations at the end of each shift (the value recorded is the average availability of each workstation over the entire shift). What argument would you present to the factory manager that might convince him or her to be wary of the results presented via such a practice?

5. List some of the ways in which the following performance metrics might be gamed. Try to come up with tricks not mentioned in this chapter.

   - M-ratio
   - Utilization
   - Availability profile plot
   - Factory operating curves

CHAPTER 9

A Transition: From Words to Deeds

The purpose of the preceding eight chapters was to present you with an introduction to and appreciation of the fundamentals that serve to determine factory performance. An awareness of factors that do and don't directly affect factory cycle time, capacity, and lead time is an essential first step toward taking the actions necessary to improve the performance of a factory or, for that matter, a business process or organization.

Now that this initial step has been taken, we may transit from history, terminology, equations, and concepts to a discussion of pragmatic and cost-effective means to achieve significant and sustainable factory performance enhancement in the real world. Simply put, the purpose of this brief chapter is to provide a transition from words to deeds.

The actions required do not necessarily stem from current philosophies or fashions (e.g., lean manufacturing, Six Sigma, or reengineering) or slogans or buzzwords. Rather, they are the tools of implementation—formed via a combination of experience and science—necessary to most effectively achieve the desired results.

The section that follows provides a brief recapitulation of the material covered in the preceding eight chapters. This is followed by a similarly brief introduction to the approach required to move from words to deeds—topics that will be addressed in detail in Chapters 10 through 15.

CHAPTERS 1 THROUGH 8: A LOOK BACK

One must never forget that the three enemies of factory performance, in terms of operations and maintenance (i.e., the actual running of the facility), are complexity, variability, and lackluster leadership. Attempting to improve performance by means of addressing topics other than these is almost always a waste of time and resources.

While there is much to be said for the notions encompassed in such efforts as lean manufacturing, Six Sigma, and the Toyota production system, and while—if applied properly—positive results may be achieved, their names themselves may get in the way of attaining significant and sustainable results. What, for example, does it really mean to achieve a "lean" factory? Depending on the conscious or subconscious intent of management, "getting lean" may mean anything from reducing the workforce to reducing cost to increasing utilization. These, however, are goals—and not necessarily the right goals. Goals, even if selected properly, are meaningless without (1) an understanding and appreciation of the factors that determine performance and (2) a practical plan (i.e., means) for achieving the goals.

While the title of this book, *Optimizing Factory Performance: Cost-Effective Ways to Achieve Significant and Sustainable Improvement,* is not intended to be cute, clever, or sexy, it summarizes precisely what is required for factory performance improvement in the complex and perplexing environment of the real world. Specifically, we must both appreciate and exploit the third dimension of manufacturing. Furthermore, three factors (i.e., politics, art, and science) must be considered if improved production-line operation is to be achieved and sustained. Moreover, if factory performance improvement is to be accomplished, it must be done in an intelligent (as opposed to a strictly emotional) and systematic manner.

In addition—as revealed in the 12-workstation problem of Chapters 4 and 6—without an appreciation of the three fundamental equations of manufacturing, one must substitute experience, judgment, guesses, hunches, intuition, speculation, and luck in place of science. The three fundamental equations, on the other hand, indicate precisely what factors determine capacity, cycle time, and the propagation of variability. Most important, they encourage a focus on actions that most likely will improve performance while avoiding less effective or even counterproductive decisions based on hunches and intuition.

While the forms of the three fundamental equations illustrated previously are appropriate only for very simple factories (e.g., those in which there is an absence of reentrancy, job-to-machine dedication, batching, and cascading), they may be and have been extended to more realistic and complex facilities. Such extensions are mostly of academic interest, however, and one need only comprehend the most basic forms of the three equations (i.e., those presented in Chapter 5) to gain the necessary appreciation of how factory performance is determined. For example, it now should be clear that

- A reduction of variability (e.g., of job arrivals, process times, down events, or wait times) always improves all aspects of factory performance.
- An increase in capacity (e.g., via faster process rates or increases in availability) may or may not improve all aspects of factory performance.
- Exploitation of the third dimension of manufacturing (i.e., changes in manufacturing protocols) provides a means to improve performance that is generally faster, cheaper, and more sustainable than decisions confined to the first or second dimension (i.e., physical changes).
- While balanced production lines running at the takt rate (i.e., the fundamental premise of lean manufacturing) may be appropriate for synchronous facilities (e.g., bottling plants and automotive assembly lines), they are often inappropriate for certain modern-day factories (i.e., asynchronous production lines, such as found in semiconductor manufacturing) (Stecke and Solberg, 1985).
- The theory of constraints provides an interesting and insightful supposition but has limited utility in real-world factories, where there exist multiple migrating constraints operating within a dynamic environment of variability and change.
- Complexity induces variability, which, in turn, degrades performance.
- Any reduction in complexity improves production-line performance and reduces stress on the workforce.
- An ideal factory should eliminate or at least reduce batching and cascading, incorporate the simplest production line possible (e.g., minimize DoR), and keep the

size of each machine ideally not more than four times the size of the job (or lot or batch) it processes—unless otherwise dictated by the laws of physics.

- The most overlooked means of improving a firm's bottom line is through reduction of factory, business process, and supply-chain cycle time.
- Since a factory is a nonlinear dynamic system with feedback, one's intuition is almost always wrong.
- Absent the support and involvement of management (up to and including the firm's CEO), any effort directed toward performance improvement is less likely to be successful and almost certainly will not be sustainable.

We also have discovered that many factory performance measures do not, in fact, do a particularly good job in objectively, fairly, and accurately assessing performance and, in fact, are likely to be counterproductive. Furthermore, organizations too often waste vast amounts of time and resources in never-ending arguments as to which metrics to use, how to collect the data, how to present the data, and even—alas—how to game the results.

In my experience, firms that have achieved real and lasting factory performance improvement devoted the bulk of their efforts to directly and effectively addressing the three enemies of performance rather than in purposeless and seemingly endless meetings. In short, there is far too much time wasted on words and far too little devoted to action.

The following section presents a brief introduction to the real-world implementation of the art and science of manufacturing. This discussion will be illustrated and elaborated on in the chapters that form the remainder of this book.

CHAPTERS 10 THROUGH 15: A LOOK FORWARD

The fundamental equations of manufacturing and (1) a familiarity with the history of manufacturing, (2) an acquaintance with the most effective measures of factory performance, and (3) an appreciation of the scope and limitations of both the art and science of manufacturing provide a solid foundation for the selection and implementation of the actions necessary to most quickly and effectively improve production-line performance. These actions, in turn, consist of those dedicated to

- The reduction of complexity
- The reduction of variability
- A more accurate determination of workstation and factory capacity
- Realization of the leadership necessary to overcome the political obstacles faced by any effort that involves change

Chapter 10 presents guidelines and illustrations of the most effective means to reduce the complexity of the protocols employed within the factory. Coverage includes the means to achieve a reduction in

- The number of process steps
- The factory's degrees of reentrancy
- The complexity (and ambiguity) of maintenance and operations specifications
- Clutter and confusion in the workspace
- Complexity of workstation run rules (a.k.a. *dispatch rules*)

Reduction of the sources and impact of variability is the focus of Chapter 11. The chapter provides illustrations and discussions of the reduction of variability in such areas as

- Variability induced through the clustering of
  - Factory starts
  - Maintenance activities
- Variability induced by the inefficient assignments of personnel to tasks (e.g., the allocation of maintenance personnel to workstations) and subsequent wait times
- Variability induced by the inefficient location and stocking of spare parts and supplies
- Variability induced by (invariably futile) attempts to chase work-in-progress (WIP) bubbles (i.e., the perils of reactive as opposed to proactive decision making)
- Variability induced by inappropriate job-to-machine dispatch (WIP management) rules (Ignizio, 2003b)
- Variability induced by batching and cascading operations
- Variability induced by the failure of management to act expediently and consistently and to provide the means and guidance necessary to manage change

Chapter 12 presents a simple example—using a modification of the original 12-workstation factory model—that serves to illustrate the way in which one may use the material in previous chapters to improve factory performance significantly. Rather than mathematical methods and models, only the guidelines for complexity and variability reduction need be employed. In essence, this chapter serves to put together, in one illustration, most of the ideas presented in previous chapters. For many readers, this may prove to be the most useful chapter in this book.

Chapter 13 provides an overview of the methods and models that should be employed to determine the true upper bound of workstation (and factory) capacity. When combined with the discussion of variability presented in Chapters 5 and 11, this chapter allows you to more accurately predict both maximum theoretical and sustainable capacity. The models and methods employed also may be extended to encompass, among other matters, the analysis of optimized job-machine dispatch rules and personnel-to-task assignments.

If the implementation approaches presented in Chapters 10 through 13 are to be successful, there must be a vision, a plan, a capable (and preferably experienced) team, the means to implement the plan, and first-rate leadership. In addition, consideration must be given to the politics of the organization and, in particular, any resistance to change. Chapter 14 deals with these topics.

Finally, Chapter 15 recalls the attributes of the ideal factory and provides a current example of a firm that appears to have incorporated, independently, the main concepts outlined in this book. This Spanish firm has turned conventional wisdom on its head and in so doing has achieved a corporate cycle time (i.e., time from the inception of a new product to its delivery to retail outlets) that is 95 percent less than that of its best-in-class competition.

CHAPTER SUMMARY

Having completed Chapters 1 through 8, you have attained the background necessary for practical, real-world, cost-effective factory performance improvement. You are now prepared to address the plans, decisions, and modes of implementation necessary to overcome the three enemies of factory performance—and to do so in the real world.

If only the Muddle Company would follow these guidelines!

CASE STUDY 9: EVERYBODY'S DOING IT!

Some six weeks after his unfortunate meeting with Marvin Muddle, Tommy Jenkins is presented with the latest performance numbers for Muddle's factories. A nervous pair of toadies waits as the facts sink in.

"What the heck is going on?" asks Tommy. "Our factory's cycle time decreased by 20 percent, but in the same time period Jack Gibson's factory's cycle time—Factory 2—dropped by 30 percent! I thought you two promised me that our cycle time would be the best in the firm by now. And just look at Factory 2's per-unit cost—that's been reduced by 20 percent!"

Donna replies, "Tommy, somehow Jack Gibson found out about our plan to reduce factory starts. He claimed—or lied, just as we did—that his factory capacity was lower than previously estimated and received permission to reduce his starts. That's how he achieved the reduction in cycle time. He also did something else. He ordered his people to cut costs by reducing their inventory of parts and supplies. They've pushed out their purchase requests until the next quarter. He also stopped funding activities like retirement parties, retirement gifts, and team building. He's even curtailed virtually all travel. Boss, he's really making us look bad."

"Two can play at that game," says Tommy. "Ben, send out an order to our department managers. Tell them that I want our expenses cut by at least 30 percent. In addition, I want to announce a 'Hurry Up' program. I want to see everyone on the factory floor busy all the time. And you, Donna, find out who leaked our plans to reduce factory starts. I want that person drawn and quartered!"

"You've got it, boss," Donna replies, barely suppressing a giggle.

Behind Tommy's back, Ben gives her the "thumbs up" sign.

It's 9 p.m., and we find Julia, Dan, and Winston busy in the "war room." Dan has noticed that the coolness between Julia and Winston has lessened. Right now they are sitting next to one another examining the results of the latest simulation exercise. Dan's attention is diverted by a message on his cell phone.

"Winston," says Julia, "just look at what's been achieved by no more than a reallocation of maintenance technicians. My goodness, the simulation shows that our factory cycle time could be reduced by a third."

"Not only that," adds Winston, "there's an opportunity to reduce maintenance personnel by at least 10 percent and still maintain the same improved cycle time. I bet that Marvin Muddle would love that. The man's obsessed with cost cutting."

"I hate to burst your bubble," says Dan, addressing the pair, "but I just received an e-mail on my BlackBerry from Professor Leonidas. It seems that Donna Garcia has asked him to teach her about the science of manufacturing. She offered to pay him $10 an hour for his services."

"Good grief," says Julia, "that's not much more than minimum wage. Can she be serious? Did the professor accept her 'generous' offer?"

"No," says Dan. "He said that he thanked her for her interest but just didn't have the time. She didn't take that well."

"This is strange," says Winston. "Why has Donna Garcia taken such a sudden interest in the science of manufacturing? She's about the last person in this company who I think would be interested in anything having to do with science."

"Something is up, that's for sure," says Julia.

"There's more," adds Dan. "Donna expressed a lot of interest in reducing cycle time and in factory operating curves. She also asked his opinion on simulation via fluid models."

"Something is fishy," says Winston. "I sent some e-mails to Tommy Jenkins about fluid models months ago. Like all the other e-mails, I got no response. Now, all of a sudden, one of Tommy's toadies is asking Aristotle about fluid models."

"Do we have," asks Dan, "anyone we can trust? Someone who might provide us with some information? We seem to be treading on dangerous ground."

"There is one person," says Julia. "Bridget Wallace is Ben Arnold's administrative assistant. Bridget also happens to be Brad Simmon's cousin. I know for a fact that she despises Ben. If it weren't for the money and medical coverage, she'd be long gone. We need to see if Brad can convince her to keep her eyes open."

"I'm not sure about that option," says Winston. "Brad seems preoccupied with this Sally Swindel person. Besides, have you ever given any thought to the fact that Brad may have gone over to the dark side? Perhaps your friend is the one leaking information to Donna Garcia."

"I don't believe that for a minute," Dan replies angrily, "Brad's not that kind of guy."

"I agree," says Julia. "Brad Simmons is a decent and honorable person. There's no way he would be trying to hurt us."

"But," says Winston, "if you recall, Brad wondered out loud as to what all our work here would do for us. As I recall, he implied that this is a waste of time, that someone else will take credit for our work."

CHAPTER 10

Reducing Complexity

The pioneering figures of scientific management, industrial engineering, and operational research emphasized, in their work, the reduction of complexity in the operation and control of factories, supply chains, business processes, and entire organizations. This focus also was evident in the efforts of the more enlightened nineteenth- and early-twentieth-century industrial firms—particularly the Ford Motor Company of the early 1900s.

As discussed in earlier chapters, the Toyota production system (a.k.a. *lean manufacturing*) systematized, revised, and enhanced many of these contributions. Toyota put together a unified package of numerous concepts and methods that ultimately led them to a world-class status in automobile manufacturing. Unfortunately, "waste walks" (i.e., identifying sources of waste by means of visits to the factory floor), "CANDO" (i.e., *c*leaning up, *a*rranging, *n*eatness, *d*iscipline, *o*ngoing improvement, a.k.a. *5S* or *workplace organization*), and "process-step reduction" form, for many firms, the main—and alas, sometimes sole—thrust of their attempts to introduce lean manufacturing.

When conducted by the right people with the right training in the right manner on the right problem, waste walks, CANDO, and process-step reduction can and usually do lead to performance improvement—at least over the short run. Such efforts represent, however, only a limited subset of the undertakings necessary to deal most effectively with all sources of factory complexity. The more insidious forms of waste escape detection when lean is limited to just these approaches.

The following sections provide discussions and illustrations of complexity-reduction efforts. The chapter concludes with an example that illustrates the implementation of a Waddington analysis, a tried, true, practical, and cost-effective methodology that reduces or eliminates most of the typical sources of complexity, be they in a factory or, as to be described, for improvement of the operating and maintenance protocols of the legendary "Brown Bess" musket (Antil, 2006; Wikipedia, Brown Bess Musket). We begin with the task of reducing unnecessary process steps.

PROCESS STEPS

A common thread of most efforts directed toward the reduction of complexity is their empirical, as opposed to scientific, basis. The reduction of complexity in the process steps of a production line is no exception. More specifically, complexity reduction typically is an art enhanced by experience and practice. Some individuals ultimately are able to become experts—true artists—whereas others, regardless of their training and actual experience, never progress beyond the ordinary.

Whatever one's skill level and natural gifts, the first step in the reduction of process steps is to develop a process flowchart, preferably a process-step-centric flow path. Recall that the development of such plots was illustrated in Chapter 3.

Unfortunately, it is rare to find a firm that has developed flow-charts at the level required for effective process-step reduction. This means that the organization or some outside consultant must construct the necessary flowcharts. The steps recommended for establishing a process-step-centric flowchart include the following:

1. Locate the individual or individuals in the firm who have detailed knowledge of and demonstrable expertise in the production-line process flow.[1]

2. Combine visits to the factory floor with carefully structured discussions with the firm's process flow experts. Use these visits and discussions to establish a preliminary, mutually agreed upon process-step-centric flowchart.

---

1 Guidance on how to identify and work with experts and on the task of knowledge acquisition in general is provided in Chapter 5 of Ignizio (1991). One way to identify a domain expert (e.g., in the domain of process-step flow) is to determine the domain-expert bottleneck, that is, the person or persons who are busiest fielding questions and assisting in solving problems in the domain of interest.

3. Once satisfied that the process-step-centric flowchart reflects the true nature of the process flow, identify and list the steps that are the most likely candidates for either elimination (i.e., outright removal) or refinement (i.e., reduction in the complexity of the individual process step). Agreement on this matter should be accomplished jointly with the firm's process-step experts. The most common process steps for reduction or refinement are

   - Inspection steps
   - Inspection sampling rates
   - Transit steps (i.e., movement from one process step to the next)
   - Unnecessarily complex or superfluous process steps of any type

4. Evaluate the consequences of removal or refinement of the process steps identified in step 3. Ideally, this should be accomplished by exercise of a credible and validated simulation model. Absent the existence of such a model, the most effective alternative for evaluation is by means of a carefully planned and controlled pilot study on the actual factory floor.

Based on readings, discussions, and personal experience, I have noted that anywhere from 10 to 40 percent of the process steps employed by a typical firm may be eliminated or refined. One reason for unnecessary steps is the fact that it is not atypical to encounter a production line employing the same or nearly the same process-step flow as originally implemented (possibly years or even decades ago) for a given product. This is particularly true for inspection steps.

Typically, the initial inspection steps (and associated sampling rates) employed for a new product are conservative, that is, likely excessive. Fear, timidity, and unwarranted concern may serve to defer any thought of changes in these steps. Alternately, the potential improvement possible by changing the inspection steps simply may not be recognized. Once, however, confidence in the machines and methods employed to support a given step has been established, action (in the form of an analysis and evaluation of the consequences) should be taken to remove or refine the associated inspection step. Such an effort almost always will pay for itself many times over.

The reduction in the complexity of transit steps typically involves determining shorter, less complex routings between non-transit process steps. This may be extended to substituting transit via automated means (e.g., robots, conveyors, or monorails) for manual transportation (e.g., hand carries or movement by push-carts). It should be noted, however, that the automation of transit may not necessarily produce less complexity or even improve performance. In fact, there have been instances in which a change to automated transit actually increased complexity, cost, and factory cycle time.

The ultimate impact of the reduction or refinement of process steps is determined very much by the parameters and configuration of the production line in question. Reduction in factory cycle times of anywhere from 5 to 20 percent appear to be typical, however. In at least one instance I am familiar with, process-step reduction and refinement reduced factory cycle time by more than a third.

DEGREES OF REENTRANCY

As discussed previously, reentrancy induces complexity (which, in turn, increases variability) and thus the ideal factory should have a degree of reentrancy (DoR) of 1. Engineers at the Ford Motor Company achieved significant and sustainable improvements in the cycle time for the Model T automobile "simply" by transforming their original reentrant flow path into a serial nonreentrant path. This was accomplished by locating each of the machines supporting a given process step according to the sequence of process steps.

Factory engineers and plant managers often are hesitant to follow Ford's example. Their intuition (and remember my caution about intuition) evidently tells them that this approach to reducing reentrancy will degrade rather than improve performance.

Much of this misplaced concern is based on the assumption that the more machines in a given workstation, the better is its (and the factory's) performance. It seems obvious that the more machines in a workstation, the greater is its availability and flexibility. This assumption, however, may be invalid when the workstation supports reentrancy. This may be demonstrated by means of the following example.

Figure 10.1 depicts a four-workstation factory with a DoR of 3.25 (i.e., 13 operations supported by four workstations). The rate of arrivals at this factory (i.e., arriving at workstation A) is 1.5 jobs

FIGURE 10.1

Four-workstation factory (DoR = 3.25).

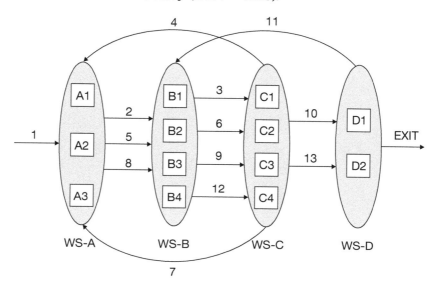

per hour. Transit time between operations will be assumed, for sake of simplicity, to be zero. We also will assume that there is no rework or scrap, and thus, if the factory is to be effective (and not allow the buildup of an unsustainable length queue), its output also should be 1.5 jobs per hour. The maximum theoretical capacity of each machine in each workstation is listed in Table 10.1. (The availability of all the machines in the factory has been assumed to be 90 percent.)

Note in Table 10.1 that the effective process rate (*EPR*) for process step 1 by any machine in workstation A is 1.5 jobs per hour, whereas the *EPR* for process step 7 by any machine in workstation A is 1.636 jobs per hour. Wherever blank spaces occur in the table (e.g., the machines in either workstation B, C, or D for process step 1), we interpret this to mean that those workstations do not support that particular process step.

While Table 10.1 lists maximum theoretical capacities by machine type and process step, Table 10.2 summarizes the maximum theoretical capacity of each workstation. It also serves to list the specific process steps supported by each workstation, the composite arrival rate of jobs at each workstation, and the workstation occupation rate ρ.

TABLE 10.1

Machine Maximum Theoretical Capacities

Effective Process Rates per Machine Type (Lots/Hour)				
Process Step	A Machines	B Machines	C Machines	D Machines
1	1.5	—	—	—
2	—	1.5	—	—
3	—	—	1.5	—
4	1.5	—	—	—
5	—	1.636	—	—
6	—	—	1.8	—
7	1.636	—	—	—
8	—	1.5	—	—
9	—	—	1.5	—
10	—	—	—	1.5
11	—	1.5	—	—
12	—	—	1.5	—
13	—	—	—	1.8

TABLE 10.2

Workstation Maximum Theoretical Capacities EPR_{ws}

Workstation	Process Steps Supported	Composite Arrival Rate (Lots/Hour)	Workstation Theoretical Capacity (EPR in Lots/Hour)	Workstation Occupation Rate ρ
A	1, 4, 7	4.5	4.628248	0.972290
B	2, 5, 8, 11	6.0	6.127341	0.979220
C	3, 6, 9, 12	6.0	6.260870	0.958330
D	10, 13	3.0	3.272727	0.916670

The derivation of the values listed in Table 10.2 may be explained as follows:

- Composite arrival rate = the sum of the arrival rates of the jobs to be processed. For example, workstation A processes three steps (1, 4, and 7), and the rate of flow of each of these is 1.5 jobs per hour. Thus the composite arrival rate at workstation A is 3 • 1.5 = 4.5 jobs per hour.
- Workstation (maximum) theoretical capacity = the product of the number of machines in the workstation and the

harmonic mean of the effective process rates for every operation of each machine in the workstation. For example, the maximum theoretical capacity of workstation A is given by multiplying 3 (machines) by the harmonic mean of 1.5, 1.5, and 1.636. The spreadsheet representation of this is 3*Harmean(1.5, 1.5, 1.636), with a result of 4.628248. (Note that simply adding the individual *EPR* values of the machines in a workstation, as used in the 12-workstation demonstration, is appropriate only if the workstation supports a single operation, whereas the harmonic mean is appropriate if the workstation supports multiple operations, and every machine in the workstation has identical machine-to-operation process rates. For more general situations, the methods of Chapter 13 must be employed.)

- Workstation occupation rate = the ratio of the workstation's composite arrival rate and its maximum theoretical capacity. The occupation rate of workstation C, for example, is given by 6 divided by 6.26087, resulting in $\rho = 0.95833$.

Since the occupation rate of each workstation is less than 1, it is (at least theoretically) possible that the factory can support the process flow. Whether this is practical or not (i.e., in terms of maximum acceptable factory cycle time) depends on the variability imposed by factory starts, interarrival rates, and effective process times.

Now that the original, fully coupled version of this factory has been analyzed, we may proceed with an effort to reduce its DoR, that is, either fully or at least partially decouple the factory depicted in Figure 10.1. For sake of discussion, we shall partially and arbitrarily decouple this factory by means of adding three machines, one each to workstations A, B, and C, and then assign the machine-to-process-step dedications shown in Table 10.3. In this table, the three new machines are labeled as "Anew," "Bnew," and "Cnew." The decoupling has, as may be noted, resulted in three new virtual workstations: A′, B′, and C′.

The resulting workstation-centric flow plot for the reconfigured factory is shown in Figure 10.2. This partially decoupled factory has a DoR of 13/7, or 1.86. The nest, composed of workstations A′, B′, C′, and D, has a DoR of 10/4, or 2.5. The original factory had a DoR of 3.25, and thus the partial decoupling has resulted in a substantial reduction in the factory DoR (i.e., from 3.25 to 1.86).

TABLE 10.3

Workstation Process-Step Dedications for Partial Decoupling

Workstation	Machines	Process Steps
A	A1, A2	1
B	B1, B2	2
C	C1, C2	3
A′	A3, Anew	4, 7
B′	B3, B4, Bnew	5, 8, 11
C′	C3, C4, Cnew	6, 9, 12
D	D1, D2	10, 13

FIGURE 10.2

Partially decoupled factory.

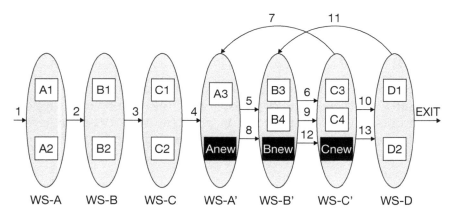

As accomplished previously for the original factory configuration (see Table 10.2), we may determine the composite arrival rates, maximum theoretical capacities, and occupation rates for the partially decoupled factory. The results are provided in Table 10.4.

So, having reduced the factory's DoR, have we improved its performance? The answer to this may be determined by either simulation or a pilot study. A simulation-generated comparison of the performance of the original versus the partially decoupled factory is shown in Table 10.5. (It should be noted that the availabilities and performance measures, as well as variability, were assumed identical in each factory configuration.)

TABLE 10.4

Workstation Maximum Theoretical Capacities EPR_{ws}

Workstation	Process Steps Composite Supported	Composite Arrival Rate (Lots/Hour)	Workstation Theoretical Capacity (Lots/Hour)	Workstation Occupation Rate
A	1	1.5	3.000000	0.500000
B	2	1.5	3.000000	0.500000
C	3	1.5	3.000000	0.500000
A′	4, 7	3.0	3.130000	0.958466
B′	5, 8, 11	4.5	4.629000	0.972132
C′	6, 9, 12	4.5	4.765000	0.944386
D	10, 13	3.0	3.272727	0.916590

TABLE 10.5

Comparison of Original and Partially Decoupled Factory

	Original Factory	Partially Decoupled Factory
Mean cycle time (hours)	30.050	23.480
Standard deviation of cycle time	6.270	4.400
Coefficient of variability of cycle time	0.210	0.189

By adding three machines to reduce factory DoR, factory cycle time has been reduced by 22 percent, whereas the variability in factory outs is reduced by about 10 percent. The question as to whether or not the reduction of DoR is worthwhile depends on a comparison of the cost of the additional machines versus the increase in profit (and customer satisfaction) resulting from the reduction in cycle time.

In a real situation, as opposed to this illustration, it may indeed be worthwhile to add machines to decrease cycle time, cycle-time variability, and customer lead time. For example, the cost imposed on a product over its lifetime by one additional day of cycle time in the semiconductor wafer fabrication industry is estimated (based on data in the open literature) to range from $5M to $100M depending on market conditions. Using the lower, more conservative value, a reduction in factory cycle time of, say, 10 days reduces cost by about $50M. If this offsets the cost of any additional machines, it would be worthwhile to reduce the DoR.

To more fully appreciate the potential benefit of DoR reduction, consider its implementation in an actual factory. This particular factory had an initial DoR of approximately 5.0. It was estimated that for every day of reduction in factory cycle time, the firm could—conservatively—increase its overall profit by \$10M. Given data on the costs of any additional machines, an optimization procedure (Ignizio, 1992b) was employed to determine the optimal factory configuration for various budget constraints (i.e., constraints on the amount of money that could be spent on additional machines). The results of the optimization then were validated by means of factory simulations. The savings achieved via DoR reduction are shown in Figure 10.3.

This figure indicates that each reduction in factory DoR, from its original value of 5.0 down to 3.0, monotonically increases overall factory cost savings (i.e., considering both the cost of additional machines and the profit increase as a consequence of cycle-time reduction). Once, however, the DoR is reduced below about 3.0, the cost of the additional machines (i.e., those required to reduce the DoR to 3) begins to reduce the benefits from its maximum level of \$100M. Clearly, it is unwise to ignore the potential benefits of a reduction in factory DoR.

FIGURE 10.3

Savings via process-step decoupling.

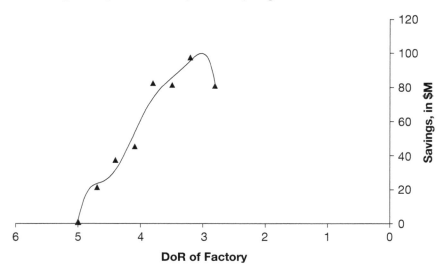

MAINTENANCE SPECIFICATIONS

The allocation of maintenance resources is one of the least appreci-ated and most underestimated factors in factory performance. I have labeled maintenance the "thankless science" because it receives so little respect and support in many firms. Yet improvements in maintenance protocols—and their supporting documentation—pro-vide an enormous lever for the potential enhancement of factory per-formance (Duffuaa, Raouf, and Campbell, 1999; Robinson and Ginder, 1995).

Because of a failure to appreciate the importance of preventive maintenance (PM), maintenance costs often are substantially higher than need be, and maintenance resources are misdirected and overall factory performance suffers. Based on related surveys and personal experience (Anderson, no date; Ignizio, 1999), it is estimated that

- More than half the unscheduled downtime of machines is caused by errors in the most recent or previous PM activity.
- Because of poorly written PM specifications, time must be devoted to passdowns between factory shifts and to even the repeat of PM steps.
- A significant portion of unscheduled machine downtime is a result of a "hurry up" mentality (e.g., hurry a PM event so as to complete it before the end of a shift or before the lunch break).
- Calendar-based PM events (e.g., weekly, monthly, or quarterly) are employed mostly, if not solely, for convenience. If such events were scheduled less frequently (e.g., every nine days instead of weekly or every 35 days instead of monthly), most facilities could reduce maintenance costs by 10 to 20 percent—with no measurable impact on factory performance.
- Even in factories where maintenance activities are carried out relatively effectively, the personnel used to conduct the efforts are often misallocated (resulting in increased wait time as well as variability in downtime).
- Rarely is management aware of problems in maintenance protocols. Instead, managers tend to attribute poor machine

availability to physical sources (i.e., their focus is restricted to just the first two dimensions of manufacturing).

Anderson, in a Web-hosted paper summarizing a survey of this topic (Anderson, no date), notes that

- 30 to 40 percent of PM costs are spent on assets with negligible failure impact.
- A review of preventive maintenance activities indicated that
  - Only 13 percent of existing maintenance activities were worthwhile.
  - 19 percent of PM activities were a waste of time.
  - 30 percent of PM activities were carried out too frequently.
  - 70 percent of PM costs were incurred by just 25 percent of the PM activities.
  - Just under half of PM activities accounted for 90 percent of PM costs.

Such problems often are attributed to nothing more than abysmal (in terms of both content and language) PM specifications. One of the cheapest and most effective ways to improve factory performance is, in fact, to strive for C^{4}U-compliant maintenance specifications. Recall that C^{4}U-compliant specifications must be

- Clear
- Concise
- Complete
- Correct
- Unambiguous.

The trick, of course, is to translate these five adjectives into actions. This may be accomplished by the techniques employed by C. H. Waddington's group during World War II (Waddington, 1973) combined with lessons learned in later military and space programs (particularly the Apollo manned moon landing effort).

C^{4}U-compliant maintenance specifications may be achieved by following these steps and guidelines:

1. Cite the precise goal or goals the maintenance effort in question is intended to accomplish. (If you cannot cite the precise purpose of a maintenance specification, it is

unlikely that the resulting document will support the primary intent of preventive maintenance, for example, to avoid unscheduled downtime.[2])

2. Recognize that the developer of the maintenance specification must be thoroughly familiar with the machine or machines for which the specification is to be designed. (Too often maintenance is the thankless science in a factory, and thus it is assumed that anyone can develop a specification.)

3. Develop the initial specification, and then refine and validate it by means of a series of dry runs (i.e., carefully structured practice runs). Repeat these until the developer believes that no further improvement is possible.

4. Once the developer is satisfied with the specification, have someone other than the developer engage in additional dry runs. (Despite what the maintenance expert and specification developer may think, vital steps invariably will be omitted, and ambiguities will be present. These are best caught by a novice in his or her attempt to follow the steps of the specification.)

5. Use the previous two steps to eliminate unnecessary steps and avoid unsafe actions. Document every known deviation, ambiguity, and problem encountered, and revise the specification accordingly.

6. Repeat steps 3, 4, and 5 until the specification is deemed safe, credible, and effective—and the need for any passdown or explanation is, hopefully, eliminated.

7. After completing step 6 (and not until that step has been completed), take any actions necessary to ensure that the workspace is organized to support the final, refined specification.

8. Monitor the performance of each PM activity, and revise and refine the associated specifications (and subsequent workspace organization) whenever necessary. No matter what type of factory or what type of machine, continual improvement in PM specifications is a necessity.

---

2 In discussions with factory personnel at more than two dozen factories, I found that the specific goal of a random sample of their PM specifications could *not* be cited more than 60 percent of the time. In many cases there was no agreement whatsoever on the purpose of a given specification. Much of the time, in fact, I was informed that a PM spec was conducted simply because "it had always been conducted."

There is one other matter that must be considered if a firm is to achieve C^{4}U-compliant PM specifications and benefit from them. Specifically, the firm must recognize the importance of the development of such specifications and adequately and publicly reward their developers. It must be made crystal clear that the development and continual refinement of PM specifications are a high priority and valued assignment.

Unfortunately, in too many cases the opposite impression is given to factory floor workers and engineers. In some firms, personnel actually may believe (a belief quite possibly based on experience) that they will be punished if they request a refinement to a PM specification. To provide just one example, I received an e-mail from a factory floor technician in which he cited a problem with a particular PM specification at his firm. He and his coworkers had discovered numerous (and obvious) errors in the specification 15 years ago and proposed changes to correct the deficiencies. The changes were ignored by superiors because any alterations in a specification had to be approved by some seven individuals in the factory and then sent to a virtual factory committee (consisting mostly of managers bent on reducing costs rather than technical experts) for final approval. The red tape, bureaucracy, and lack of interest in changes in documentation ultimately served to silence even the most dedicated and conscientious employee.

The preceding guidelines and steps have cited the actions required to produce a C^{4}U-compliant PM specification. There are also, however, certain guidelines and goals for determining if the effort in question actually has produced such a specification. Among these are

- The spec must be capable of being conducted successfully by other technicians, ideally without the need for input or a passdown.
- The spec must be shown, to the degree possible, not to induce unscheduled downs and must satisfy all safety, ergonomics, and human factor requirements.
- The spec must be shown to enable the right components to be examined, replaced, or repaired at the right time by the right people using the right tools as located in the right place and applied in the right order.
- The conduct of the spec must make a measurable and positive difference. (This is typically noted by improvements in availability and mitigation of the Waddington effect and

an improvement of the M-ratio.) If not, one must ask, "Why is this specification being performed?"

- A mechanism for anonymous input must have been provided.

What is always surprising to those who dismiss the importance of maintenance—particularly something so seemingly mundane as maintenance documentation—is the fact that a dedication to the development of C^4U-compliant PM specifications can and will provide significant, sustainable, and cost-effective improvements in factory performance.

OPERATING SPECIFICATIONS

Precisely the same points made with regard to the development of C^4U-compliant PM specifications hold true for the specifications that guide factory operations. This remains true even as more and more manual operations are automated (e.g., dispatching of jobs to machines, insertion of the jobs, and removal of the completed jobs).

One of the more overlooked areas for factory performance improvement is, in fact, that of the conversion of manual operations to automated methods. What is too often done is nothing more than the automation of existing manual operations. Unfortunately, if what is being accomplished manually is inefficient or even incorrect, all that automation accomplishes is the ability to do the wrong thing faster.

WORKSPACE ORGANIZATION (DECLUTTERING)

One of the most widely promoted tools of lean manufacturing is the process designated as *CANDO* (or *5S*). The purpose of this concept is to encourage cleanliness, order, and safety in the workspace. A further objective is to improve a workstation's ability to support the operations and maintenance activities in the factory. These are admirable intentions and definitely worthy of consideration by any firm.

While I encourage all companies to conduct workspace organization efforts, whether they are called CANDO, 5S, plain-old industrial engineering, or whatever, two critical factors are often overlooked. First of all, workspace organization is most definitely an art. One's ability to perform a useful workspace organization effort depends on one's motivation, training, and—in particular—experience. As such, it is vital to seek the guidance of those with experience and a successful track record.

While the conduct of a workspace organization effort—even by novices—may and likely will produce exciting before and after photographs, the impact on factory performance may not be nearly so exhilarating. Unless the effort serves to directly support the correct procedures to be used in the workstation's maintenance or operations, the results will be either less momentous than expected or even counterproductive. This unfortunate result may be avoided by acknowledging a second critical factor.

Specifically, it is important to make sure that a workspace organization effort is conducted *after* first completing the process of achieving C⁴U-compliant specifications (either maintenance or operations, as appropriate). This was called out in the seventh step in the guidelines given in the preceding section.

The importance of performing the workspace organization effort *after* determining the existence of C⁴U-compliant specifications—and the difficulty in selling such an idea—may be illustrated by means of a real-world example.

In one firm, a newly formed lean manufacturing team was eager to demonstrate its effectiveness to management. Team members identified one exceptionally cluttered and chaotic workplace (one that supported the maintenance operations for a particular workstation) and conducted a CANDO effort. Once this effort was completed, the workplace was as clean, tidy, and orderly as the most immaculate hospital operating room one would hope to find.

The before and after photos of the workspace were posted throughout the factory and presented to the factory manager. Duly impressed, she authorized support for the continuation of CANDO efforts.

One skeptic—let's call him Thomas—however, carefully examined the performance of the workstation both before and after the CANDO event. He discovered that the workstation's availability, cycle time, and departure-rate variability were as bad as before the cleanup effort. A plot of the Waddington effect showed, in fact, that the phenomenon still existed and was as pronounced as before. In short, the CANDO effort simply had made it easier to conduct a set of particularly dreadful PM events faster.

When Thomas's results were presented to the lean manufacturing team, they were met with open resentment. The lean team had photographic "proof" of the effectiveness of their effort—proof readily and eagerly accepted by the factory manager. Pictures, they reminded the chagrined Thomas, do not lie. Besides, as they informed him, they were too busy conducting CANDO events to bother with the thankless and time-consuming task of improving PM specifications.

The message in this example is most definitely not that CANDO is a bad idea. Rather, if one is to take full advantage of any workplace organization effort, it is wise to first achieve C^4U-compliant specifications—and then organize the workstation to support those specs.

WORKSTATION RUN RULES

The run rules [a.k.a. *dispatch rules* or *work-in-progress* (WIP) *management methods*] employed at a workstation can have a significant impact on the performance of both the workstation and the entire factory. This impact is even more pronounced (and complex) when the workstation supports multiple process steps and reentrancy.

Consider, for example, the implant machines (i.e., ion implantation) used in the semiconductor manufacturing industry. Such machines ionize dopant atoms, which then are isolated, accelerated, formed into a beam, and bombarded on the surface of a semiconductor wafer (Van Zant, 2000). Gases typically serve as the dopants, and these are usually fluorine-based. The typical implant machine is large and expensive.

The machines in the workstation that serve to conduct ion implantation characteristically support numerous implant operations, each of which may employ a different ionization source. Some operations, however, cannot be performed on the same machine owing to the incompatibility of the sources. In other instances, there may be a requirement to wait several minutes—or even hours—before one operation (using one type of source) can be safely followed by another (using another type of source).

Attempting to dispatch jobs to such machines manually is extremely complicated and confusing to human operators. Even the automation of such run rules may not (and typically does not) result in optimal or even near-optimal workstation performance.

The ideal solution would be to have each operation supported by a unique machine or set of machines (i.e., establishment of implant machines in a sequence identical to the sequence of implant operations). Such a fully decoupled implant process, however, would likely require the purchase of many additional machines and might be impractical because of both the cost and size of such machines.

A more practical alternative may be accomplished by partial decoupling via use of optimized operation-to-machine dedications. In most semiconductor firms, however, the operation-to-machine dedications of implant machines (as well as those of lithography machines, etc.) are accomplished heuristically. That is, the dedications are determined by some combination of expert judgment, experience, intuition, and luck.

Unfortunately for these firms, heuristic dedications are invariably (and substantially) inferior to optimized dedications. I will defer this discussion to Chapter 13 because optimized operation-to-machine (i.e., process-step-to-machine) dedications may be best accomplished by an extension of the mathematical model to be employed for the determination of workstation capacity.

"BROWN BESS" AND WADDINGTON ANALYSIS

I discovered more than a decade ago that many, if not most, of the concepts introduced in this chapter may be illustrated by means of a discussion of the evolution and refinement of the operation and maintenance protocols employed for the "Brown Bess," a 0.75-caliber musket of the eighteenth and nineteenth centuries (Antil, 2006). Rudyard Kipling does an admirable job of introducing this legendary weapon in a poem (a sonnet enhanced by a number of double entendres):

> In the days of lace-ruffles, perukes, and brocade
> Brown Bess was a partner whom none could despise
> An out-spoken, flinty-lipped, brazen-faced jade,
> With a habit of looking men straight in the eyes
> At Blenheim and Ramillies, fops would confess
> They were pierced to the heart by the charms of Brown Bess.
>
> —Rudyard Kipling, 1911 "Brown Bess"

Any reader who at this point may be wondering how on earth a discussion of an antique firearm could possibly add insight to the running of a factory must bear with me. I can only assure you that the Brown Bess discussion provides a concise and simple analogy that may be used to explain the purpose of a Waddington analysis (i.e., the procedure recommended for reducing complexity in operations and maintenance specifications and procedures).

First, however, I need to provide a brief overview of the Brown Bess musket—a "machine" considerably simpler than most readers would find on the factory floor, but one requiring very much the same type of support.

The Brown Bess was relatively reliable and cheap to manufacture and maintain and was not replaced until introduction of the percussion cap (in place of a flintlock) and rifles (i.e., a rifled barrel as opposed to the smooth bore and thus less accurate barrel of a musket). The musket, as a consequence of its poor accuracy and limited range, typically was employed by a force of musketeers arranged in carefully positioned ranks of men two to three deep. Firing of the musket, a black powder weapon, was conducted via a simultaneous volley of shots emanating from either all or just one row of men at a time.

Using such a system, and despite the weapon's inaccuracy (or any lack of sharpshooting skills by the musketeers), at least some of the enemy forces should be struck (i.e., "pierced to the heart by the charms of Brown Bess") in each volley. The primary components of such a musket are its wooden stock, smooth-bore metal barrel, rammer, and lock mechanism. The lock mechanism, the heart of the weapon, consists of a hammer (designed to hold a piece of flint), a priming pan (into which a priming charge of black powder was placed), and a frizzen (an L-shaped metal plate that, when closed, covered the priming pan and charge). Next to the priming, or flash, pan is a touch hole drilled through the barrel into the space where the main black powder charge is loaded.

When the trigger is pulled, the hammer snaps forward, causing the flint to scrape against the face of the frizzen, which, in turn, throws the frizzen back to expose the powder in the flash pan. The force of the flint on the metal produces a shower of sparks that are released into the pan, thus igniting the powder and sending flames through the touch hole. This results in ignition of the main charge of black powder in the barrel and fires the musket ball from the barrel.

Unlike the carefully planned, systematic, and focused conduct of a (properly designed and efficiently performed) Waddington analysis, enhancement of the operating and maintenance protocols of the Brown Bess evolved over decades through, in many cases, nothing more than trial and error or the inspiration of an individual musketeer. The operation of the musket is reflected in the steps required for its employment in battle. One early set of these steps (comprising the drill used in both training and battle) for a force consisting of two lines of musketeers (typical of the British) is as follows:

1. Order: "Prime and load" (accompanied by drumbeat). *Note:* In each step, the musket is held in the left hand while the right hand performs the operations.
2. Bring musket diagonally across your front, holding it midlength with the left hand (muzzle is high and to your left and does not point forward—a safety procedure).
3. Push the frizzen forward to open the priming pan (i.e., the flash pan).
4. Move the hammer to half cock.
5. Insert a charge of an "appropriate" amount from your powder horn into the musket priming pan.
6. Shut the pan with the frizzen so as to contain the priming powder in place.
7. Cast about, bringing musket diagonally across body in the opposite direction (muzzle is now high and to your right).
8. Use your powder horn to place a "sufficient" amount of gunpowder into the muzzle.
9. Remove a musket ball from its container (e.g., located in a bag carried in various locations on the soldier's person), and insert the ball into the barrel of the musket.
10. Stuff paper into the muzzle to serve as wadding (i.e., to keep the musket ball from rolling out of the barrel).
11. Seize the end of the rammer, and withdraw it from its storage location under the barrel of the gun.
12. Reverse the rammer, and ram down the ball on top of the charge (repeat this three times).
13. Withdraw the rammer and replace it in its storage location.
14. Bring musket to "Poise." It should be high on your left side, trigger facing out, held at neck by the left hand, with the right hand resting against it. Wait for next command. *Note:* With the musket at poise, the next order might be to "Shoulder," "Advance," or "Trail."
15. If the musket is to be fired, the next order is "Make ready," in which you bring the hammer to full cock using your right thumb.

16. If you are in the front rank, stand ready at "Poise." On the command "Make ready," kneel on your right knee, bring the hammer to full cock, and rest the musket butt on the ground near your knee.

17. Next order is "Present." Level your musket, and point it horizontally in front of you.

18. You may be ordered to "Oblique left" or "Oblique right," in which case all muskets point to either the left or the right.

19. At the order "Fire," pull trigger and then return the musket diagonally across your body, muzzle high and to the left; that is, return to step 2 and make ready for a repeat of the steps.

Now imagine, if you will, the training, practice, and nerve required to follow each of these steps in the face of a frontal attack by a column of determined French infantry, each shouting *"Vive l'emperor"* and accompanied by the rallying roll of their drummers. Add in the deafening roar of the muskets in the lines in front or behind you, coupled with the thick, acrid smoke of those black powder weapons, and you have a situation that definitely requires some precise and effective operating and maintenance protocols.

In addition, and vital to the effective conduct of the battle, was the cycle time of the musketeers, that is, the number of shots that could be fired per minute. During training exercises, a rate of fire of four shots per minute usually could be achieved. During an actual battle, however, the rate of fire might be as low as two shots per minute—unless shortcuts could be found to increase the effectiveness of the troops.

In short, the military was (or should have been) always alert for ways to reduce and/or refine the process steps employed in the drill. Stated another way, a reduction in the complexity of the drill (i.e., its process steps) was a primary goal—precisely as it is (or should be) in factory operating and maintenance "drills."

Over the years, the input of soldiers in the field and their officers and the inventions of weapons makers achieved a reduction in complexity and an increase in effectiveness. Some of this reduction was achieved by subtle physical changes; others by equally delicate changes in protocols. Just a few of these are as follows:

- In place of loose musket balls and separate strips of wadding, a paper (to be used later as wadding) twisted at the ends and enclosing a musket ball, the priming charge, and the powder to be inserted into the musket barrel was developed. The paper container itself was designated as a "cartridge."

- A container for the cartridges was designed and held in place on the right side of the musketeer (remember, the right hand was used for all operations and the left for holding the musket). This allowed for the replacement of powder horns with cartridge belts and, later, cartridge boxes (again, placed on the right side of the soldier).
- Instead of removing the musket ball and holding it in your hand, place it between your teeth (i.e., "bite the bullet"), and once powder has been inserted into the musket's barrel, spit the bullet into the barrel opening.[3]
- In actual battle and under extreme conditions, the soldier might ignore the loading and tamping of the wadding into the barrel. Instead, he would tap the butt of the musket against the ground to seat the bullet. (While this increased the rate of fire, it also reduced the velocity and range of the bullet.)

These refinements in the operating drill ultimately produced a reduction in process steps by about 20 percent and a subsequent increase in shots fired per minute.

Another change in protocols that may have achieved an even more substantial increase in the firing rate was accomplished in sixteenth-century Japan. Oda Nobunaga, a warlord credited with the introduction of firearms into Japan, used a unique and effective set of musket drill protocols.

This change in protocols turned Nobunaga's forces into particularly efficient killing machines. Nobunaga's favorite saying, by the way, was, "If a bird doesn't sing, kill it."

Nobunaga's musketeers worked in teams of loaders and shooters. Three muskets, plus the necessary powder, bullets, and supporting accoutrements, were assigned to each team. Immediately

---

3 There are conflicting views as to whether or not the musketeer actually spat the bullet into the barrel. Some believe that this is a myth and that the soldier actually removed the bullet from between his teeth and manually inserted it into the barrel. Insertion was accomplished in this way, it is alleged, because after repeated firing, the musket barrel would be too hot to touch to one's lips. In lieu of either photographic evidence or a live (and exceptionally old) musketeer from that time period, I will leave it to readers to decide which view is correct.

after each shot, a cocked and loaded weapon was handed to the shooter by a loader. This protocol substantially increased the rate of fire of each musketeer.

While such a team effort was employed in Japan, for whatever reason, it never took hold in Europe or America.[4] Tradition, it would seem, can be a significant obstacle to change.

It should be noted that Frank Gilbreth developed an analogous team-based operating scheme in the early 1900s for protocols in hospital operating rooms. Gilbreth observed and took movies of actual operations. He noted that the "cycle time" of the surgeon was a major factor in the successful outcome of any operation. During steps of the operation, the surgeon would take his eyes off the patient and reach for whatever surgical instrument was needed for the next step. In fact, the surgeon would spend more time searching for instruments than in performing the operation. Gilbreth recommended that the surgeon focus on the operation and let a nurse hand him instruments. By nothing more than this simple change, the time required to complete an operation was reduced dramatically.[5]

The same team-based method, sometimes designated as the *nurse-surgeon-operation room* (NSOR) concept can and has been employed in factories and maintenance facilities. For example, an apprentice maintenance technician may serve as the "nurse," while the expert technician is the "surgeon." The expert focuses his or her attention on the maintenance event, while the apprentice reads off the steps of the specification and hands the expert the appropriate tool at the appropriate time.

When one factory agreed to implement a pilot study of the NSOR concept, the time to conduct PM events in several workstations was reduced by anywhere from 20 percent to nearly 50 percent. Equally important, the variability about these PM events was reduced by roughly two-thirds. Unfortunately for the

---

4 One reason for the hesitancy to adopt such a team-based approach evidently was the belief that every man on the battlefield should be firing a weapon. This conclusion conveniently ignored the fact that much of the time the musketeer was engaged in reloading, repairing, or maintaining his gun. A modern-day team-based approach for the firing of a weapon is employed by sniper teams. One individual serves as the spotter (and also may estimate distance and wind direction and strength). Another is the shooter, the individual tasked with actually firing the sniper rifle at the target specified by the spotter.

5 Like so much of Gilbreth's work, this concept has been rediscovered and renamed by those with little or no appreciation of the contributions of the pioneers of scientific management.

firm, the factory was unionized, and the effort was halted owing to the concerns of union leaders. They believed (possibly with good reason) that the reduction in time to conduct the PM events would result in a corresponding reduction in the maintenance workforce.

But let's return to the discussion of Brown Bess. The discourse until now has dealt with the reduction in the complexity of the musket drill (i.e., the operating steps). Equally important was the reduction in the complexity (and downtime variability) of the maintenance and repair of the musket, particularly in the heat of battle.

Both scheduled (i.e., more accurately, usage-based events) and unscheduled maintenance events were to be expected before, during, and following a firefight. These included such events as

- Loss or breakage of the flint
- Buildup of residue on the flint (with a subsequent reduction in the intensity of the sparks emitted)
- Blockage of the touch hole (a small hole that permitted the powder explosion in the flash pan to detonate the powder charge under the musket ball in the barrel of the musket)
- Jamming (i.e., the musket ball and wadding might become wedged partway down the musket barrel)
- Caking of residue in the musket barrel (after a number of shots, the residue left by the black powder would build up in the barrel and have to be removed)

The musketeer was, by necessity, both the operator and maintainer of his musket. Through training, observation, and word of mouth, a set of maintenance procedures was developed (e.g., the best-known methods for quickly and reliably replacing the flint, cleaning the flint, unblocking the touch hole, dislodging jammed musket balls, and removing residue in the barrel). There is, by the way, nothing like being shot at to encourage a speedy way to return one's weapon back to service.

It is important to recognize that the conduct of these maintenance events served to promote changes in the organization of the musketeer's "workspace." For example, over a period of time, the tools needed for maintenance and repair were identified, and their precise placement on the musketeer's person was determined. Each of these tools was placed in the soldier's cartridge box in precisely specified positions. The tools (and spare parts) necessary for maintenance consisted of

- A rag or brush to clean the flint and flash pan
- Spare flints
- A vent pick (to clean the touchhole)
- A screwdriver (to replace or adjust the flint)
- A bullet extractor (to remove jammed musket balls)

Over time, the bullet extractor evolved into a combination hammer, vent pick, and screwdriver (i.e., an early "all-in-one" tool set).

One other truly inspired approach to maintenance process-step reduction should be mentioned. As noted earlier, after prolonged firing, the barrel of the musket would become caked with powder residue. Furthermore, it should be pointed out that water boys were used to carry water to the dehydrated musketeers during breaks in the firing. As a result of drinking the water, the musketeers, quite naturally, found it necessary to relieve themselves.

A few ingenious musketeers found that they could both relieve themselves and remove the residue built up in the musket barrel. Simply and bluntly, they urinated into the barrel of the musket. By combining two "maintenance" steps into one, the downtime of the Brown Bess was reduced.

The reader should note that the story of the Brown Bess confirms the importance of improving a maintenance (or operating) specification *before* performing a workplace organization effort (e.g., CANDO). The organization of the workplace (in this case, the cartridge box and tools carried by the musketeer) was determined by and after changes in the operating and maintenance protocols employed rather than the other way around. While there is considerable resistance to this argument, history and successful improvements in factory performance prove its correctness.

At any rate, the reduction and refinement of operating and maintenance steps served to increase the firing rate of the musketeers substantially. The motivation behind these improvements was literally one of life and death. The motivation behind factory performance improvement may well be one of the life and death of the manufacturing firm. The faster the reduction in complexity of operating and maintenance procedures and specifications is accomplished, the quicker the factory will achieve (and exceed) world-class manufacturing status.

CHAPTER SUMMARY

This chapter discussed some of the more obvious sources of complexity within the factory. They are, however, by no means the only ones. There are, in fact, forms of complexity even more widespread and sometimes more damaging. Among these are

- Complexity in the factory's and firm's business processes
- Complexity in the firm's supply-chain network and protocols
- Complexity in terms of the inconsistency and ambiguity in the firm's mission statements, goals, requests, and pronouncements
- Complexity induced by frequent changes in the firm's goals, measures of performance, and mission
- Complexity in terms of the retrieval of data and information
- Complexity in the number of steps and red tape required to make a change in maintenance and operation protocols

In other words, any team involved in complexity reduction (whether labeled a lean team, industrial engineers, factory performance team, a *kaizen* group, etc.) should look beyond the more obvious factory protocols and flow paths. Furthermore, the same concepts that may be employed to reduce complexity in these areas may be extended to virtually all other facets of the firm, and vice versa.

CASE STUDY 10: MIDCOURSE CORRECTION

Ben and Donna take a seat and wait, apprehensively, for Tommy to announce the reason for the meeting. Tommy, for his part, simply sits there, glaring at them. Donna decides to break the uncomfortable silence.

"I couldn't convince that stupid professor to tell us anything about simulating by means of fluid models. But I did have one of my people look into the matter. He says that it's pretty straightforward, but it would take a long, long time to construct such a model for this factory. I figure we can convince Winston Smith to do the grunt work on that matter. But I'm not quite sure just what we do with the model once it's been built."

Tommy continues to glare.

"Folks," says Ben, "all we need to do is to threaten Winston once again. Just tell him that if he doesn't explain how building this fluid model will decrease our cycle time, we'll get rid of Julia."

"You two idiots," Tommy replies, "I've already checked with our director of manufacturing, and he says that the introduction of a simulation package other than what has been authorized would be a violation of the 'No Deviations' policy. Besides, this firm is no longer concerned with reducing cycle time. What Marvin Muddle wants us to do now is to increase our capacity, and to hell with cycle time. It seems that every factory in our system has reduced its factory starts so as to reduce cycle time. We all may be fast now, but we're not able to fulfill our customers' orders. Every Muddle factory has been ordered to increase factory starts. Cycle time is now a moot point. So now, you two geniuses, our mission is to increase factory capacity. Ben, send out an e-mail to our factory managers. Tell them we have to increase our starts to 11,000 units per week. And you, Donna, forget about that idiot professor and this nonsense about fluid models. I want you to increase workstation availability and utilization by 20 percent. This meeting is over."

A day later we find Julia, Winston, Dan, and even Brad in the "war room." Julia has some news.

"Fellows, Tommy Jenkins has ordered his department managers to forget about factory cycle time. The mission now is to increase capacity to 11,000 units per week. He also has demanded an increase in workstation availability and utilization. I guess we shouldn't be surprised. Marvin Muddle has a short attention span. It's cycle time one day, capacity the next, then moves, and then Marvin Muddle's all-time favorite, cost reduction."

Winston rolls his eyes and replies, "The maximum sustainable capacity of this factory, under near-perfect conditions, is about 10,000 units per week. They may start whatever number they want, but the weekly output will be no more than 10,000 units. Besides, within a few weeks, there will be no room for the inventory that will be built up in the queues in front of the factory workstations. This will just be one more disaster. Don't they ever learn?"

"Apparently not," Julia replies. "But is there any rational way to increase our factory's capacity? Can we use your fluid models to investigate that?"

"Certainly," says Winston. "There are a number of ways to increase capacity, some better than others. As you may have learned in your lessons with Aristotle, there is a cost-effective way to improve factory performance. Just reduce complexity and variability. Do that, and you're guaranteed to improve overall factory performance, including both cycle time and capacity."

"You've shown that the declustering of factory starts will reduce cycle time. I noticed that it also results in a slight increase in capacity. Is there something else that could improve capacity even more?" asks Dan.

"Yes," Winston replies. "One almost sure-fire way to increase workstation availability is to employ a Waddington analysis. In particular, you want to have PM and operating specifications that are C^4U-compliant. The only problem is that you can't demonstrate this change with any type of simulation model. Another thing you can do is to optimally allocate maintenance personnel. These things, and others, will increase availability. If you simultaneously reduce complexity and increase availability, you can get some truly substantial increases in factory capacity. Hasn't Aristotle discussed these approaches with you?"

"Yes, he has," says Dan, somewhat sheepishly. "I have to admit that I had forgotten about it. But how do we get an approval to conduct a Waddington analysis?"

"I can answer that," says Julia. "It isn't going to happen. There's no way we'd be able to convince management that we should assign people to improve our maintenance and operating specs or to even consider the reallocation of our maintenance technicians. These are all serious violations of the 'No Deviations' policy. Besides that, the quality control group would go wild. It's not going to happen."

"Julia's right," says Brad. "The only way we could get an approval for any of this is to introduce an educational effort—have the professor and Winston present the material on the science of manufacturing. Maybe then they'd finally listen."

"That's not going to happen either, Brad," Julia replies. "Management is not going to permit courses on the science of anything. We'd have to condense everything into a slogan and maybe 7 to 10 principles. And those would have to be made as simplistic as possible."

"So," says Dan, "what do we do? Nothing?"

"Let's talk to Aristotle," says Winston. "Maybe he has some ideas. In the meantime, did any of you notice that the cubicle that was put in a few days ago, along with its occupant, has suddenly vanished?"

CHAPTER 10 EXERCISES

1. Given the four-workstation factory in Figure 10.1 and the data in Table 10.1, develop a *fully* decoupled factory capable of handling the 1.5 jobs per hour arrival rate.
2. Compute the occupancy rates of each workstation in the fully decoupled factory of Exercise 1.
3. List at least three actual examples of accidents that resulted (or likely resulted) from a failure to develop C^4U-compliant PM specifications. (*Hint:* Look into accidents in the space program, airlines, automobiles, and construction.)
4. Perform the following experiment: First, ask a colleague to add paper to a copy machine. Then record, in detail, the steps followed. Next, determine if there is a more efficient way (e.g., by reducing the number of steps).

Reducing Variability

While complexity indirectly (and sometimes substantially) induces variability, there are other more direct (i.e., first- and second-order) sources of this particular enemy of factory performance. As noted in Chapter 5 and exhibited in the 12-workstation demonstrations of Chapters 4 and 6, variability increases cycle time, increases factory inventory, and subsequently serves to reduce the factory's maximum sustainable capacity. The three sources of variability explicitly cited (i.e., first-order sources) in the second and third fundamental equations of manufacturing are

- Variability in arrival times (i.e., interarrival rates) of jobs entering into the queue in front of a process step and designated as C_{AR}
- Variability in departure times (i.e., interdeparture rates) of jobs exiting a process step and designated as C_{DR}
- Variability of the process-step effective process times and designated as C_{EPT}

These three principal sources of variability are themselves determined by a variety of second-order causes, including but not limited to batch sizes, factory starts protocols, macro and micro work-in-progress (WIP) management protocols, operating protocols, maintenance protocols, and spare parts and supplies protocols.[1] The most practical and cost-effective means to reduce factory

---

1 For example, the variability about effective process times C_{EPT} is determined in part by a second-order source of variability, the variability about repair and maintenance events, that is, C_{DE}.

variability must address these second-order causes and are the subject of the sections that follow.

BATCH SIZES AND VARIABILITY

Batching serves to increase both arrival- and departure-rate variability. Recall the example in Chapter 5 in which batching (with a relatively small batch size of four) at a previous process step increased arrival-rate variability (i.e., C_{AR}) at the subsequent process step by more than three times what it had been with no batching. The larger the batch size used by the machines supporting a given process step, the greater is the arrival-rate variability at the next process step.

As a consequence, a particularly effective way to reduce variability is simply to reduce batch sizes throughout a factory. If, however, a process step (e.g., such as heat treating) takes a long time, say, eight hours, to complete, the temptation (and "quick and easy solution") is to use batching. For example, the heat-treatment furnaces employed in semiconductor manufacturing may use batches of wafer lots of sizes four, five, or more. Furthermore, each individual lot of semiconductor wafers may contain a dozen or more wafers (lot sizes of 25 wafers are not uncommon).

Thus, if a batch size of six lots (of 25 wafers per lot) is employed, the total time to process the 150 wafers would be eight hours. However, if the same furnace were used to process just a single wafer at a time, the 150 wafers would require 1,200 hours (i.e., 50 days) in total—just for this one heat-treatment step.

Consider, however, what is at this time the Holy Grail of semiconductor manufacturing: single-wafer processing (SWP) (Ignizio, 2004; Wood, 1995). As noted earlier, if we had to rely on conventional furnaces, SWP would not be practical. Advances in furnaces using rapid thermal processing (RTP), though, may be used to make SWP not just feasible but advantageous.

Consider what a strictly hypothetical reduction in the process-step time of the furnace from 8 hours to, say, 10 minutes would accomplish. The six-lot batch (of 25 wafers each) discussed previously could be heat treated, one wafer at a time, in 25 hours in total if RTP were employed. This, of course, is still more than the 8 hours required with batching. However, since a RTP furnace is of smaller size (and, hopefully, lesser cost), we might employ 10 (or more) RTP furnaces for every conventional one. If this were done, the total process time of the 150 wafers using 10 RTP furnaces would be just 2.5 hours—a significant reduction over the 8 hours required for this process step using a conventional batching furnace. Quite possibly more important, however, is the reduction in variability achieved by SWP over batch processing.

The message is that whatever can be done to reduce (or, better yet, eliminate) batching should be considered. SWP coupled with RTP plus other advances offer one hope for the reduction of overall process time and variability via the elimination of batching—or at least a reduction in batch sizes. Another, even simpler way to improve factory performance is to reduce the variability imposed by inferior (and, unfortunately, rather typical) factory starts policies.

FACTORY STARTS PROTOCOLS AND VARIABILITY

One of the easiest and quickest ways to reduce variability is simply to decluster factory starts. A declustered factory starts protocol is one in which jobs (i.e., in either single units or, if necessary, lots or batches) are introduced into the factory in such a way as to minimize the coefficient of variability (CoV) of the interarrival rate of jobs into the queue in front of the very first workstation. This may be accomplished if jobs are introduced in a *smoothed* manner.

For example, if the desired factory output is 480 jobs per a 24-hour day, then the ideal time between the insertion of one job and the next would be 3 minutes. That is, we divide the number of jobs to be started each day (480) by the number of hours in the workday (24) and achieve a result of 20 jobs per hour or—using a smoothed starts protocol—one job every 3 minutes.

Few factories I have encountered, however, employ a smoothed starts protocol. Instead, mainly for reasons of alleged convenience, jobs are clustered. For example, in the preceding illustration, the goal was 480 jobs to be started per day. Some factories simply may insert 480 jobs in front of the first process step at the beginning of the day. Others might make a feeble attempt to decluster by, for example, introducing 160 jobs every 8 hours. While the first scheme will impose considerable interarrival-rate variability, the second (i.e., 160 jobs every 8 hours) is likely to be only marginally better.

Firms that have taken the time to decluster factory starts have seen substantial reductions in factory cycle time (particularly in the front end of the factory). Furthermore, if a declustered factory starts protocol is combined with an effective factory starts *load-management scheme,* reductions in total factory time will be even more pronounced.

A factory load-management scheme, in turn, is a protocol for reducing or increasing (i.e., synchronizing) the jobs started into the factory in accordance with the health of the factory (e.g., according to reasonably accurate predictions of the factory's constantly changing sustainable capacity). One of the worst mistakes made by a firm is to blindly follow some *a priori* quota for starts while ignoring the fact that the environment within any real-world factory is in a constant state of flux.

For example, if the quota established (by whomever, too often by the dictates of the finance department) happens to be 5,000 jobs per week, but the factory is only capable of handling 4,500 jobs this particular week (perhaps owing to the need to conduct preventive maintenance or repair on a bottleneck workstation), all we would achieve by unbendingly adhering to the quota is to diminish factory performance. Inventory and queues will increase, variability will increase, and factory velocity will decrease. And even if the factory's real capacity is returned to something greater than 5,000 jobs per week, it could take weeks to work off the inventory and queues built up in that single week of factory overstarts.

A word of warning: One of the potential reactions to any proposal for the smoothing of factory starts—or of synchronizing the imposed factory load in accordance with actual factory capacity—is to be told, "This will require too much time and thought." (One might be tempted to respond that if the goal is to reduce time and thought, why not just shut down the factory? Hopefully, however, any urge to voice such an imprudent reply will be resisted.) The usual reason a smoothed factory starts protocol is opposed is because such a change requires more oversight and planning than that of simply dumping the jobs to be started for the day in front of the first workstation at the beginning of each day. This resistance sometimes may be overcome by conducting either a simulation or a carefully structured pilot study (e.g., one that employs a smoothed starts policy for a month or more, followed by a comparison of the results with the original, clustered protocol).

Firms that have been convinced of the need for a smooth starts policy, coupled with a rational factory loading scheme, have seen reductions in factory cycle time by as much as 50 percent. When combined with the next topic, the smoothing of preventive maintenance (PM) events, reductions of as much as 70 percent sometimes have been achieved.

MAINTENANCE EVENT SCHEDULING AND VARIABILITY

Declustering of factory starts, as discussed above, is a quick, easy, and effective way to reduce variability. The same holds true for the declustering of PM activities. A declustered factory maintenance protocol is one in which maintenance events are scheduled in such a way as to minimize any induced variability and increase effective workstation availability. This may be accomplished if PM events are scheduled in such a way as to evenly spread out their resulting machine and workstation downtimes.[2]

In Chapter 8, a factory performance metric designated as the *availability profile plot* was introduced and illustrated by means of two graphs, repeated here as Figures 11.1 and 11.2. As may be seen, there are sharp decreases in workstation availability at the beginning of each 12-hour shift.

FIGURE 11.1

Hypothetical workstation availability profile plot.

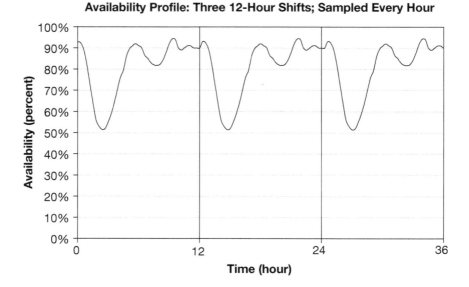

2 A formal optimization method for the achievement of smoothed PM event scheduling (i.e., a method for the establishment of a PM schedule that simultaneously minimizes any overlap of PM events at a workstation *and* evenly spreads out these events) has been developed (Ignizio, 1978, 1992a, 1999).

FIGURE 11.2

Workstation availability profile plot, one shift.

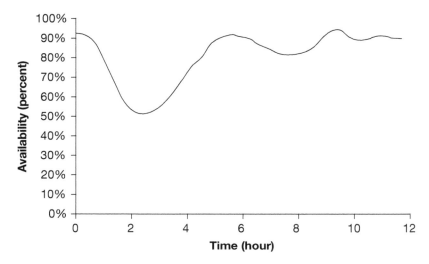

As discussed in Chapter 8, a possible reason (one that actually has been identified in several firms) for a sharp dip in a workstation's availability at the beginning of a shift is the desire on the part of the workforce assigned to that station to avoid having a PM event extend into the next shift. Perhaps in the past workers in the next shift have complained to management about the number of incomplete PM events being passed on to them. Perhaps there is a desire on the part of the workforce on every shift to avoid lengthy passdown meetings between shifts (e.g., to list the PM events that have yet to be completed and discuss their status). Perhaps the workers want as many PM events as possible completed before a lunch break. Or perhaps the PM specifications are so poorly written (i.e., they are not C^4U-compliant) that the maintenance technicians on the next shift are not confident that the PM steps presumably completed by the preceding shift have been conducted (or documented) properly. Any or all of these reasons serve to motivate the clustering of PM events at the beginning of a shift.

Time- or usage-based PM events usually are conducted during some window of time rather than at a fixed time. For example, a time-based PM event (say, event X on workstation A) may be scheduled for every 40 hours, but the actual window for the conduct of event X might be anywhere between 35 to 45 hours since the last time event X was conducted on a given machine. Given that workstation A consists of several machines, each having been in operation a certain number of hours since the last PM event X, the goal should be to evenly spread out the performance of these events while still staying within their desired window of conduct.

To clarify the concept of a smoothed (i.e., truly declustered) versus a clustered schedule of PM events, consider an example. To keep matters simple, assume that we have a workstation consisting of five machines. During the forthcoming eight-hour shift, each of the machines must undergo some type of PM event. Furthermore, assume that all these PM events must be initiated within the first five hours of the shift.

Table 11.1 lists the predicted time (i.e., ignoring variability and assuming ideal conditions) required to conduct each of the PM events. Note that the specific type of PM event may differ during the time period of interest for each machine (e.g., the PM required for machine 1 is different—in this shift—from that required for machine 2 and, for these cases, consumes 1.00 and 1.50 hours, respectively).

There are an infinite number of possible schedules for these five events, but Figure 11.3 presents the three most pertinent to this discussion. In Figure 11.3a, all five events are started at time zero (i.e., at the start of the shift), and as a consequence, the events are both overlapping and clustered. Such a schedule might be motivated simply by the desire to get the PM events conducted as soon as possible in the shift. Of the three schedules to be discussed, this is the worst possible choice. Unfortunately, for some firms, it is the first and only choice.

In Figure 11.3b, the PM events of the second approach have been scheduled to minimize (or, if possible, to eliminate) any overlap. The motivation for such a schedule likely would be to complete all maintenance events as soon as possible while maintaining as many machines in operation at any one time as feasible.

TABLE 11.1

PM Event Times per Machine

PM Event	Time Required (Hours)
Machine 1 PM event	1.00
Machine 2 PM event	1.50
Machine 3 PM event	0.30
Machine 4 PM event	1.00
Machine 5 PM event	0.80

FIGURE   11.3

Clustered, minimized overlap, and declustered PM event
schedules.

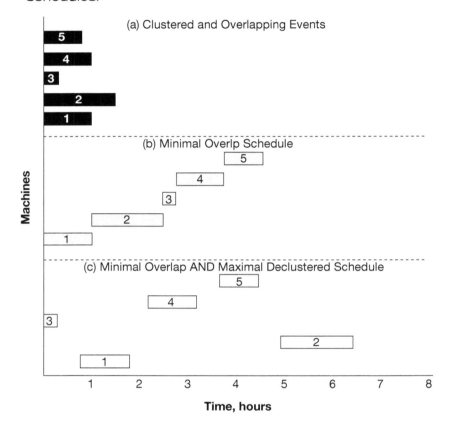

Finally, in Figure 11.3c, a truly declustered schedule has been
established. The difference between simply minimizing overlap
and truly declustering PM events is apparent when the schedule of
Figure 11.3b is compared with that of Figure 11.3c. While the schedule in Figure 11.3b has no overlap, it is still clustered; that is, the PM
events take place contiguously between 0 and 4.6 hours, followed
by 2.4 hours in which no events occur. Consequently, the PM
events of Figure 11.3b are clustered, although not as severely as in
Figure 11.3a, within the initial portion of the shift.

Now consider the impact on workstation availability of each of
the three schedules shown in Figure 11.3. Whatever the schedule
employed, the predicted workstation availability is 88.5 percent.
Consequently, the factory manager or factory engineers (particularly
if their primary focus is on average workstation availability) may be

lead to believe that it doesn't make any difference as to the schedule employed. Thus, under the illusion that the maximally clustered schedule of Figure 11.3*a*, the minimal overlap schedule of Figure 11.3*b*, or the truly declustered schedule of Figure 11.3*c* result in identical workstation availabilities, they may see no reason to consider declustering the PM events.

If so, they are ignoring two significant factors. First, the PM event times in Table 11.1 are predictions—based on ideal conditions. However, unless there are a sufficiently large number of maintenance technicians (MTs), the actual PM times that will be experienced by either the maximally clustered or minimal overlap schedules typically will exceed those that are predicted. For example, in the maximally clustered schedule of Figure 11.3*a*, there must be enough MTs to simultaneously start and conduct the five PM events on the five different machines. This likely would require the firm to employ far more MTs than necessary.

A somewhat similar argument holds for the minimal overlap schedule in Figure 11.3*b*. While this schedule might require fewer MTs, it assumes that they can transit from a PM event on one machine to one on another in zero time. This is obviously unrealistic.

The second significant factor that serves to present problems when either a maximally clustered schedule or a minimal overlap schedule is employed is that of the likely buildup of a queue in front of the workstation because of such schedules. This will induce additional variability in the departures of jobs exiting the workstation. (This particular impact may be best illustrated by means of simulation.)

In summary, an improvement in factory performance may be achieved by declustering PM events. While one should expect some resistance to this "radical" notion, it is important to gain management and workforce support for declustering. The benefits of declustering overwhelm any real or imagined obstacles.

MAINTENANCE PERSONNEL ALLOCATION

The allocation of maintenance personnel to workstations plays a particularly significant role in factory performance. Inferior allocation schemes increase the time wasted in waiting for an MT or team of MTs to arrive and conduct a PM event or repair. This both decreases workstation availability and increases factory variability. The guidelines that should be employed, or at least seriously considered, with regard to the allocation of MTs to workstations include the following:

- Care should be taken to train the MTs properly and to equip them most effectively and efficiently to perform their duties.
- A factory cannot afford to tolerate the employment of any MT who either cannot or will not exhibit the skills necessary to perform his or her duties effectively and efficiently. Oversight and firm actions in support of this goal must be established.
- Consideration should be given, wherever and whenever possible, for the cross-training of MTs. Cross-training can play a significant role in reducing wait-for-MT times and variability.
- Avoid the allocation of MTs according to the "squeaky wheel syndrome." The "owners" or advocates of a given workstation may well be louder and/or more eloquent in their demands for MTs, but emotions and marketing skills should not be the basis for MT allocation. The focus always must be on the improvement of overall factory performance.
- An increase in factory capacity might be (and likely will be) accomplished by the allocation of additional MTs to constraint workstations (or, more properly, to the machines supporting the constraint process steps).
- The workstations receiving the highest priority for the allocation of MTs, however, should be the ones whose downtimes have the greatest impact on overall factory performance.

The last point in this list may be best achieved by means of an optimization model (Ignizio, 2004). Alternately, a reasonably effective MT-to-workstation allocation may be accomplished by adhering to a set of heuristic rules.

To illustrate, a hypothetical factory configuration—one in which each machine in a given workstation has performance identical to any other machine in that workstation—is employed. Assuming the existence of a valid factory simulation model—one that considers the allocation of MTs to workstations—the basic steps to be followed by the heuristic approach for this type of factory are as follows[3]:

---

3 We shall let *CAP* represent the maximum theoretical capacity of the entity, that is, its *EPR* value. Later, once a more precise estimate for maximum sustainable capacity (*SC*) is developed in Chapter 13, then *CAP* may be replaced by the *SC* of the entity.

- Determine the value of the following parameters:
  - $m(ws)$ = number of machines in each workstation.
  - $CAP_m(ws)$ = capacity of each machine in the given workstation.
  - $CAP(ws)$ = capacity of all the machines in the given workstation (i.e., the sum, in this case, of the individual capacities).
- Let the bottleneck workstation's capacity be designated $CAP(bn)$, where bn denotes a bottleneck (i.e., a constraint).
- $CAP(ws,-1)$ = capacity of the workstation if one machine goes down.
- Determine the first weighting factor, designated $w(ws,1)$, for each workstation, where
  - If the workstation is a bottleneck, set its first weighting factor to a value of 1; that is, $w(bn,1) = 1$.
  - If the workstation is not a bottleneck, determine the value of x as follows:
    - $x = CAP(ws,-1) - CAP(bn)$
    - If $x \geq 0$, then $w(ws,1) = 1$.
    - If $x < 0$, then $w(ws, 1) = \dfrac{CAP(ws)}{CAP(ws) + x}$.
- Determine the second weighting factor, designated $w(ws,2)$, for each workstation, where m is the number of machines in the workstation of interest:
  - $w(ws, 2) = \dfrac{m}{m-1}$ if $m > 1$; otherwise, $w(ws,2) = 1$
- Determine the third weighting factor, designated $w(ws,3)$, for each workstation, where NO is the number of operations performed by the workstation of interest:
  - $w(ws,3) = \sqrt{NO}$
- Determine the fourth weighting factor, designated $w(ws,4)$, for each workstation as follows:
  - If the workstation is a bottleneck, then $w(ws,4) = 3$.
  - If the workstation is not a bottleneck, then $w(ws,4) = 1$.
- Determine the fifth weighting factor, designated $w(ws,5)$, for each workstation as follows:
  - $w(ws,5) = 1.5$ if the workstation directly feeds a bottleneck.
  - $w(ws,5) = 1$ otherwise.

- The composite weighting factor, designated $W(ws)$, assigned to workstation ws is given by

  - $W(ws) = \displaystyle\prod_{s=1}^{5} w\,(ws, s)$

- Determine (or estimate) the expected arrival rate (designated λ) of machine downs per unit of time for each workstation (e.g., if a machine fails every 50 hours, the arrival rate is 0.02 machines per hour).
- Determine (or estimate) the expected repair or maintenance rate (designated μ) per machine for each workstation (e.g., if it takes on average four hours to repair a machine, the rate is 0.25 machines per hour).

To illustrate, consider a workstation, say, workstation, with four machines and located within a factory employing a 168-hour workweek, where

- Each machine is capable of processing 500 widgets per week (i.e., $EPR_m = 500$).
- The number of operations supported by this workstation is nine.
- The workstation is not a bottleneck and does not directly feed a bottleneck.
- The capacity (EPR) of the bottleneck workstation is 1,900 widgets per week.

Thus, for this workstation, the pertinent parameters are

$$CAP(3) = 4 \bullet 500 = 2,000$$
$$x = (2,000 - 500) - 1,900 = -400$$
$$w(3,1) = \frac{2,000}{2,000 - 400} = 1.250$$
$$w(3,2) = 4 / (4 - 1) = 1.333$$
$$w(3,3) = \sqrt{9} = 3.00$$
$$w(3,4) = 1$$
$$w(3,5) = 1$$

Consequently, the composite weighting factor is

$$W(3) = 1.25 \bullet 1.333 \bullet 3 \bullet 1 \bullet 1 = 5$$

The same process may be used to compute the composite weighting factor for all the workstations in the factory. Once this is done, you may use the λ and μ values of each workstation to compute expected wait times for the MTs. Assume that $\lambda = 1.2116$ and $\mu = 23.02$ (i.e., each machine in the workstation goes down at an average rate of one every 138.66 hours, and each maintenance event has an expected duration of 7.3 hours per machine).[4] Using the queuing theory, the expected time in hours spent in the maintenance queue for the workstation may be computed (Taha, 2006; Hillier and Lieberman, 2005).

Once the preceding analysis has been performed for each workstation, then you can conduct a series of factory simulations. Whenever factory performance is less than desired, reallocate the MTs—from the workstations having the lowest priority to those having the highest priority (with priority established by the values of the workstation composite weighting factors combined with the results of the supporting queuing analysis).

One way in which to determine this priority is to rank the workstations according to their composite weighting factors—and (as an option) factor in the queuing theory results. For example, a workstation with both the highest composite weighting factor and the most wait time for maintenance might be assigned the highest priority for a reallocation of MTs (e.g., move an MT from the lowest-priority workstation to the highest-priority workstation). Continue this procedure until no further improvement in factory performance appears feasible.

To demonstrate the importance of the proper allocation of MTs to workstations, consider the difference between optimal MT allocation and the traditional MT assignment policy employed by a firm. The total number of MTs, as deduced by the traditional method, was used as a baseline for comparison. These MTs also were allocated in the traditional manner (i.e., hunches, guesses, averages, and the "squeaky wheel syndrome"). This number was lowered gradually, and the cycle time for each reduction (i.e., in terms of the percent of original number of MTs) was computed by means of factory simulations.

Using the same total number of MTs, an optimization model (Ignizio, 2004) was employed for the MT-to-workstation

---

4 These values are determined by (1) dividing 168 hours by λ and (2) dividing 168 hours by μ.

assignments. The total number of MTs then was reduced sequentially and their allocation reoptimized. Figure 11.4 summarizes the results.

The figure shows as a solid line the cycle time of the factory using the traditional method of MT-to-workstation allocation. At 100 percent of the number of MTs (as computed or conjectured via traditional means), the factory cycle time is 71 days. If headcount is reduced to 87 percent of the original number, the factory cycle time is 74 days (but the factory becomes highly unstable). For any further reduction, the factory "breaks"; that is, cycle time goes ballistic.

On the other hand, by using the optimal allocation of MTs to workstations, the cycle time for the factory at 100 percent of the original number of MTs (again, as computed via the traditional method) is just 45 days. In fact, the total number of MTs (as computed via the traditional allocation) may be reduced by about 45 percent, and the factory's cycle time will be the same as that of the traditional method at 100 percent of MT headcount.

When the optimization method for MT-to-workstation allocation has been employed, factories have seen significant reductions in cycle times—anywhere from a 20 to 50 percent reduction—over

FIGURE 11.4

Comparison of cycle times.

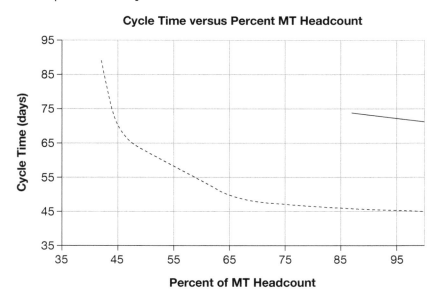

that experienced under their previous heuristic approaches. The optimization method offers not just substantial factory performance improvement but also the opportunity to reduce factory headcount.

SPARES AND SUPPLIES LOCATION AND VARIABILITY

Just as an inefficient number and allocation of MTs to workstations degrades factory performance, so will an inappropriate number and location of spares and supplies. The case study in Chapter 1 (recall Dan Ryan's frantic attempts to obtain spare parts for his workstation) provided a hypothetical illustration of the problems a factory will face if it has too few locations from which to dispatch spare parts and supplies. While that story is fiction, the consequences of an inadequate number of dispatch stations are definitely real. The same consequences hold true if the dispatch stations are not optimally or at least nearly optimally located.

Specifically, inadequate numbers and/or inferior locations of dispatch stations increase the duration and variability of the wait times inflicted on workstations needing parts and supplies. Unfortunately, as in the case study in Chapter 1, some firms may believe that a reduction in the number of dispatch stations will save money—or that the locations of these stations do not play a significant role in factory performance. Such reasoning, however, is wrong on both counts.

A solution to determining locations and number of dispatch stations may be found by means of a well-designed simulation effort (assuming that the impact of dispatch station location is credibly portrayed in the simulation). A faster and more accurate means for deciding these matters is available through either optimization or heuristic models specifically designed for this problem. Adoption of such methods usually will result in significant and sustainable improvement in factory performance and also will indicate the impact of either reducing or increasing the number of dispatch stations. Certain heuristic approaches in particular are fast and simple to employ (e.g., the only mathematical operations in one are addition, subtraction, and comparison). More details on these methods, as well as numerical illustrations of their implementation, may be found in the references (Francis and White, 1974; Ignizio, 1971; Ignizio and Cavalier 1994).

SPARES AND SUPPLIES INVENTORY LEVELS AND VARIABILITY

Even if the spares and supplies dispatch stations are sufficient in number and positioned optimally, wait times will be incurred if there is insufficient inventory. The two most effective ways to determine spares and supplies inventory levels are by means of either simulation (where, again, the impact of inventory levels on factory performance must be modeled appropriately) or through the employment of analytical inventory-level models (Ignizio and Gupta, 1975; Hillier and Lieberman, 2005; Jensen and Bard, 2003; Taha, 2006). It should be noted, however, that the development of analytical models for factories with a large number of machines (and thus a large number of part and supply types) is hardly a trivial matter.

Whether you employ simulation or an analytical model, there is one mistake that you must take care to avoid. This is the matter of ignoring the importance of, and impact on wait time for, each specific type of part or supply. This is analogous to the perils of ignoring the importance of, and impact on the wait time for, the arrival of the MTs assigned to each specific workstation.

For example, if the number of spare parts stocked is based solely or mainly on historical mean-time-to-fail (MTTF) data, one might conclude that a particular part, say, part X of machine type A, fails so seldom that only one spare of this type needs to be stocked at any given time. Following this (questionable and indefensible) logic, one might further decide that part Y of machine type B fails so frequently that a large number of spares of part Y should be kept in inventory.

Unfortunately, this line of reasoning ignores the importance and impact of a failure of both parts X and Y on the performance of the factory. Continuing this illustration, assume that machine A is the sole machine contained within workstation A. Thus, if part X of machine A fails, the entire workstation will go down for repair. Further, if machine A is repaired, using the single unit of spare part X, and that part happens to fail before the inventory of part X is restocked, the impact on factory performance may be truly substantial.

Just as in the case of assigning MTs to workstations, determination of the number of spares (and amount of supplies) in support of each workstation must explicitly consider the importance of and impact on the overall performance of the factory. In fact, the general methodology discussed for the allocation of MTs to workstations—either optimally or heuristically—may be modified to encompass this situation. For the simple case (i.e., workstations consisting of identical machines), either the optimization model or the heuristic method described for MT allocation may be revised to deal with spares and supplies inventory levels. One complication to either of these approaches is the fact that storage space for spares and supplies is limited (as is the budget for purchase and storage of spares and supplies). However, this can be handled by means of constrained optimization (Ignizio and Cavalier, 1994).

An alternate approach is to employ a simulation model that incorporates spares and supplies inventory levels. After each simulation of the factory, the level of spares and supplies is revised (typically by means of a version of the greedy heuristic)—considering storage limitations—and the simulation is rerun. Continue this procedure until no further increase in factory performance seems feasible. While this approach is highly unlikely to reach even a near-optimal solution, it generally produces a "good enough" result.

Unfortunately, some firms ignore the importance and impact on factory performance of each type of spare part or supply. One such example is that of a firm that sought to reduce factory costs by reducing the number of spares kept in inventory. The spares inventory policy of the firm was to determine the average number of each type of spare part that had been required in each quarter and then multiply that number by an arbitrary weighting factor. The number of spares of each type then was established—with ad hoc consideration given to the limitations of the storage space for the inventory of spares.

After a "suggestion" by the CEO that production costs must be trimmed (including the costs of storing the inventory of spare parts), it was decided to reduce the number of *all* spare parts by one-third. More specifically, a reduction of one-third of each and every type of spare parts was dictated. It was clearly not recognized that an across-the-board reduction of spares was nonsensical. What should have been done was to prioritize parts by their importance and impact on factory performance.

Furthermore, as in many instances of factory decisions, no consideration was given to the value of cycle time. Therefore, while the cost of spares and supplies was reduced, the more important negative impact on factory performance and the firm's bottom line was substantial.

CHASING WIP BUBBLES AND VARIABILITY

Jay Forrester, in his pioneering work in systems and industrial dynamics (Forrester, 1999), demonstrated the futility of attempting to contain the oscillations of stochastic systems by means of conventional wisdom (and hasty reaction). A factory is just one type of stochastic system, and the fluctuation of its inventory levels represents one example of oscillation. Forrester, by means of simulations and feedback theory, showed that many, if not most, of the decisions taken in an attempt to stabilize a system (e.g., a factory or a supply chain) may only serve to make matters worse. This observation holds true in instances in which factory personnel engage in the ill-advised but all too common practice of chasing WIP bubbles.

A *WIP bubble* is an unanticipated increase in the number of jobs (i.e., a bubble) flowing toward a specific section of the production line. Consider, for example, a factory in which the expected number of jobs arriving at a given process step (say, process step X) previously has been estimated to be on the order of 10 jobs per hour. For some time that prediction has held; that is, the average arrival rate at process step X has been approximately 10 jobs per hour with minimal standard deviation. Unfortunately, one day several machines (which happen to have very fast process rates) in the front portion of the production line incur unexpected downtimes. Consequently (and amplified by a lack of a factory starts load-adjustment policy), a large queue forms in front of the afflicted machines. Ultimately, the machines are repaired, and as a consequence of their fast processing rate, they soon will send a much higher than usual number of jobs to the machines supporting process step X.

The reaction on the part of some factory managers and engineers may be to shift resources to the machines supporting process step X, the machines that soon will be "slammed" by the WIP bubble. For example, personnel assigned to other machines may be reassigned to support the process step X machines. Or if these machines support multiple process steps (e.g., a reentrant factory, such as a semiconductor wafer fabrication facility), a decision may be made to reassign the priority and dedications of the machines to process step X. Either way, there is a shift of resources from the support of some process steps to the step that is to soon receive the WIP bubble. Such an action, one manager informed me, is only natural. "We can't," he went on to say, "just sit back and do nothing."

Such actions, however, will only either make matters worse or simply move the impact of the WIP bubble to the machines supporting process steps farther downstream. Most likely this will increase the variability of arrival rates of machines supporting process steps downstream. And by now we know that such an increase in variability will degrade overall factory performance.

When I bring this subject up or demonstrate it by means of simulation in real-world factories, there is a predictable reaction. What, I am asked, are we supposed to do in the face of WIP bubbles? Nothing?

Frankly, doing nothing is sometimes the best course of action. If the factory has been designed properly and employs the manufacturing protocols outlined in this book, the impact on factory performance will be transient, and performance soon should return to an acceptable level. In fact, if any action is to be taken, it should be to reduce factory starts to maintain the level of inventory in the factory at a prespecified level—the level required to retain factory cycle time at the desired value (e.g., according to the first fundamental equation of manufacturing, i.e., Little's equation).

Reducing the impact of WIP bubbles and attaining a desired level of factory performance may be achieved by

- Avoiding the temptation to chase WIP bubbles by reassigning resources
- Employing appropriate manufacturing protocols, including a factory starts protocol linked to factory health and loading
- Using scientifically based WIP management (e.g., job-dispatch) rules

The latter concept is discussed in the following section.

WIP MANAGEMENT SCHEMES AND VARIABLITY

Some firms, particularly those having highly reentrant factories, such as in semiconductor manufacturing, expend enormous amounts of time, energy, and funds on the development of WIP management schemes, that is, the rules employed to dispatch jobs to the machines within a workstation. A factory starts protocol, as discussed previously, represents a type of macro-level WIP management scheme. When dealing with job-to-machine dispatch rules, the problem exists at a micro level (i.e., workstation or process-step level), and that is the matter of interest in this section.

The schemes commonly employed in WIP management at the workstation level are identical to those discussed in the literature on the general topic of sequencing and scheduling (Baker, 1974). These include first in, first out (FIFO); last in, first out (LIFO, or back-to-front); cyclic (a.k.a. *round robin*); critical ratio (CR); and on and on. Sometimes the WIP management scheme is static; that is, no matter what, the same scheme is used for the workstation. Other times the schemes are dynamic (and even frantic), changing from one set of rules to another depending on the real or perceived condition of the workstation or factory. Schemes of a dynamic nature are seen often in factories involved in chasing WIP bubbles and have the same problems as discussed in the preceding section.

WIP management (a.k.a. *job-machine dispatching*) must be employed with care. First, the type of production line must be factored into any decision made concerning a WIP management scheme. Consider, for example, a synchronous production line (e.g., a bottling plant or automobile assembly line). Such a production line is, at least for the assembly of discrete items, the closest we come to the ideal factory. There is (normally) no batching, cascading, or priority jobs. As such, the only WIP management scheme that should be required is FIFO; that is, the first job to arrive at a workstation is the first job to be selected for processing.

Another common type of production line is that which supports several types of jobs, and each job type may follow a different process-step flow through the facility. Some workstations may support several job types, whereas others may be limited to a single type. In this type of factory, customer due dates are of definite importance. Consequently, some form of the CR WIP management scheme may be appropriate.

Consider, for example, a workstation that is shared by two different job types, type A and type B. For the sake of discussion, assume that one type A job and one type B job are in the queue awaiting processing at this workstation. The decision to be made, as soon as a machine in the workstation becomes available, is which of the two jobs should be sent to it. This decision may be made by selecting the job with the smallest critical ratio.

The CR of a job is found, in turn, by dividing the time remaining (the due date of the job minus the current time) by the predicted processing time remaining for the job. Given our example with two jobs, assume that the current time is time zero. Further assume that job A is due 20 hours from now, whereas job B is due in 10 hours.

The predicted processing time remaining for job A is 14 hours, whereas that of job B is 9 hours. Table 11.2 summarizes these data and lists the associated CRs. As may be seen, job B has the smallest CR and should be the next job to be assigned to the next idle machine in this workstation.

While the CR WIP management scheme is often the most effective scheme for a multiproduct, multiple-process-step-flow, shared-workstation facility, high-volume production lines with few products and reentrancy are better served by another approach. This WIP management scheme, designated herein as the *minimal variability dispatch method* (MVDM), dispatches jobs so that the variability of the departures from the workstation (and subsequent variability of arrivals at the workstation or machines supporting the next process step) is minimized.

The most basic and simplest form of the MVDM WIP management scheme may be illustrated by means of an example. Assume that several jobs are in the queue in front of a workstation that supports multiple operations. Some of these jobs require one operation, whereas others require some other operation. The decision that must be made is: Which of these jobs should be sent to the next available machine in this workstation?

The job that minimizes the arrival-rate variability at the machines supporting the next process step should be the job selected for processing. One way to roughly approximate this is to select the job to be processed at this workstation that was least recently processed at its next process step. Thus, if the situation is as depicted in Table 11.3, the job to process next is job 3.

Schemes exist (somewhat more complex schemes) that reduce departure/arrival-rate variability more effectively, but this example

TABLE 11.2

Computation of CR Values

	Job A	Job B
Due date	20 hours from now	10 hours from now
Processing time remaining	14 hours	9 hours
CR	$(20 - 0)/14 = 1.43$	$(10 - 0)/9 = 1.11$

TABLE 11.3

Minimal Variability WIP Management Scheme Approximation

Jobs in Queue	Job Type	Hours Since the Last Job of This Type Was Processed at the Next Process Step
1	X	3 hours
2	X	3 hours
3	Y	6 hours
4	Z	2 hours

should indicate the general concept. There also may be an advantage in combining the MVDM scheme with the CR approach. For example, should there be a tie in the selection of jobs for dispatch, based on minimization of variability, the tie may be broken by selecting the job having the minimum CR value.

Before leaving this topic, another WIP management scheme should be discussed. Some firms assign priorities to the jobs to be processed. Priority jobs, however, always degrade overall factory performance (Clason, 2003). A higher-priority job may jump the queue and be processed before a lower-priority job that actually has been waiting in the queue longer. It may even be the case that a workstation is kept idle, even though there are other jobs in queue, so that it is immediately available when a high-priority job is expected to arrive.

If a factory has been designed properly, and if the appropriate manufacturing protocols have been implemented, there should be no need to employ priority jobs. They only serve to complicate matters, induce variability, and degrade factory cycle time for the nonpriority jobs. The larger the volume of priority jobs, the worse is the situation.

Consider, for example, a facility that originally had priority-job cycle times of 20 days and non-priority-job cycle times of 90 days. By implementing enhanced manufacturing protocols and eliminating the prioritization of jobs, the cycle time for all jobs was reduced to 22 days. As such, the average cycle time of any job was almost the same as that of the priority jobs in the factory's original configuration.

To repeat, avoid whenever possible the prioritization of jobs in high-volume reentrant factories, and in general, never allow the volume of priority jobs in such a facility to exceed 5 percent of the total.

CHAPTER SUMMARY

Complexity and variability are two of the three enemies of factory performance. Chapter 10 presented guidelines for the reduction of complexity. This chapter introduced guidelines useful for reducing variability. Chapter 12 provides a brief overview of the implementation of these guidelines by means of a return to the 12-workstation model.

CASE STUDY 11: HURRY UP ... AND PAY THE PRICE

Tommy issued several follow-on orders in an attempt to bolster his "Hurry-Up" campaign. All leaves, with the exception of those for pregnancy, and all vacations were canceled for factory floor personnel. To further increase factory output, he demanded that all PM events and efforts be halted. "Run," Tommy said, "until the machines break down, and then fix them."

The "Hurry-Up" effort appeared to work, at least at first. Frantic factory floor personnel managed to up the factory outs to almost 11,000 units a week. Marvin Muddle seems placated, at least for the moment. When it seemed that the capacity problem had been licked, Tommy held a rally in the complex's cafeteria. Everyone was given his or her choice of a free ice cream sandwich or soft drink.

Unfortunately for Tommy, now—two months later—chaos reigns. And Tommy seems to be receiving the full force of the blame.

"Have you seen the latest figures on factory performance," says Dan. "It seems that our cycle time is worse than it has ever been, and factory inventory is enormous. They can't find anyplace to store the in-process work. That 'Hurry-Up' program has destroyed the factory and antagonized most of the floor personnel. From what I hear, the best people have either left or are looking for other jobs. What a mess!"

"If you recall," says Julia, "that's precisely what Professor Leonidas said would happen. His exact words were, if I recall correctly, 'You can only ask so much of people and machines. Anyone foolish enough to try to defy the laws of physics and human nature is begging for trouble.' And trouble is exactly what we are seeing."

"I talked to one of my friends, a factory floor supervisor for a workstation in the front end of the production line," says Brad. "He told me that the machines are in terrible shape. As a result of putting off their PM events, a number of critical and costly machines were ruined. Others are off-line while the maintenance and repair crews do what they can to get them back up and running. But I think that the 'Hurry-Up' program broke one thing that will never be fixed—the trust and morale of the people who had to endure this short-sighted campaign."

"I even heard that some of the members of the *LEAN* Forward team have left," says Dan. "And there was even a fistfight between a couple of their people and some members of the quality control team. But hey, what the heck, I did get a free ice cream sandwich."

"People," says Brad, "I've got an announcement to make. I hate to leave you all in the lurch, but I've had enough. I see no point in trying to get Muddle interested in science. This place is run by the seat-of-the-pants, and that's never going to change. I turned in my resignation this morning. Two weeks from now I'll no longer be an employee of Muddle. I wish you all the best, but I just can't take it anymore."

"I'm sorry to hear that," says Julia. "Can you tell us where you are going? Do they need anyone with my background? And I mean that seriously."

"Sally Swindel and I have decided to pursue, as they say, other interests. We intend to form our own management consulting firm once we return from our honeymoon."

"Congratulations, Brad," says Dan, trying to contain his shock. "What type of management consulting will you two be doing, if I may ask?"

"You may. Sally and I came up with an idea for a book on leadership some time ago. I've put together a rough draft and hope to have the book finished in a few months. Once that's done, Sally is going to do her thing. She's going to market the book and the associated training courses. As you know, she can be pretty per-suasive."

"What's the title of the book?" asks Winston.

"The tentative title is *Leadership Principles of the Donner Party: How to Overcome Any Obstacle.*"

"The Donner party?" asks Dan. "Isn't that the group of emi-grants who sought their fortune in the West and tried to make their way to California? Isn't that the same group of pinheads that got caught in a blizzard and resorted to cannibalism? Didn't about half those poor souls die?"

"You've got it," says Brad, grinning broadly. "Sally and I are convinced that the book will be a best-seller and that we can charge top prices for our training courses."

Winston could only wonder if those training courses would take place in the dead of winter without anything to eat but your fellow attendees. I guess, Winston thinks, that I will never understand the management consulting business.

CHAPTER 11 EXERCISES

1. Batching induces variability in a factory. Suggestions to reduce batch sizes, however, are met with resistance. The arguments made for not reducing batch sizes are
   - If batch sizes are reduced, the full capacity of the batching machines will not be exploited.
   - Smaller batch sizes produce the need for more setups.
   These arguments against smaller batch sizes are valid. So why might smaller batch sizes still improve *overall* factory performance, and how could you prove it?
2. The arguments against declustering of factory starts are that declustering will require more oversight as well as more trips to the factory starts site. What is your counterargument?
3. How do clustered and minimal overlap PM activities induce variability?
4. You have developed an optimized MT allocation scheme for a factory, but it is met with resistance on the part of the factory floor supervisor for the workstation that has, in the past, always been the factory constraint. The machines in that workstation are also by far the most expensive in the factory. In the past, 25 percent of the MTs on each shift were allocated to this workstation. Your optimal plan reduces that proportion to just 20 percent. The floor supervisor demands a reallocation based on the traditional allocation rate. What is your counterargument?
5. Whether it is for spare parts or supplies, what is your counterargument for those who believe that if any reductions are to be made, they must be across the board (e.g., "equal pain")?

6. In one firm there are daily operations meetings in which the state of the factory is discussed. The primary output of these meetings is recommendations for the shift of resources from one workstation or set of machines to another based on predictions of incoming WIP bubbles. Explain why such frequent changes are usually counterproductive. Explain why such a practice is so attractive to factory management and engineers.

The 12-Workstation Model Revisited

Several of the guidelines for improving factory performance (i.e., described in the preceding two chapters) may be illustrated by means of a revised version of the 12-workstation factory. In this form of the model, our primary objective is to maximize profit rather than simply minimize factory cycle time.

THE ATTRIBUTES OF THE FACTORY

The basic configuration of the revised 12-workstation factory is similar to that of the models presented in Chapters 4 and 6. The only significant differences are as follows:

- Workstation D now has, in its initial state, 6 machines rather than 5.
- Workstation F now has, in its initial state, 12 machines rather than 10.
- The effective process rates (EPRs) of the machines in each workstation have been separated into two components: their raw process rates and the availability achieved via the choice of the number of maintenance technicians allocated to the workstations.
- Every day that factory cycle time decreases below that attained in the initial scenario increases profit by $1M.

The objective of this exercise is to allocate funding to (1) purchase additional machines, (2) increase the raw process rates of the machines, (3) increase or decrease the number of maintenance technicians (MTs) allocated to each workstation, or (4) reduce the variability imposed by either the factory starts protocol or effective process times of the workstations—and do so to maximize profit (i.e., rather than just minimize factory cycle time, as was the objective in Chapters 4 and 6).

Figure 12.1 presents the revised workstation-centric flowchart for the 12-workstation factory. As before, there are zero transit times between workstations and no reentrancy or scrap. The blocks within each workstation, as before, indicate the number of machines that exist initially in the associated workstation. The arrows show direction of job flow from workstation to workstation.

Assuming, as before, that every machine in a given workstation is qualified to support the (single) process step conducted by that workstation, an equivalent process-step-centric model may be constructed for the 12-workstation factory. That model is shown in Figure 12.2. In that figure, the machines supporting each process step are listed in the triangle under the associated process step. For example, process step 2 is supported by machines B1, B2, and B3 (i.e., B1 through B3, designated in the figure as B1–B3) of workstation B.

The numbers in parentheses above each transit-step arrow indicate that the throughput flow rate of jobs through the factory (and through each workstation in the factory) is—as in the original model—an average of 20 units per day. Additional details about the attributes of the factory are presented in the next section.

FIGURE 12.1

Workstation-centric flowchart for revised 12-workstation factory.

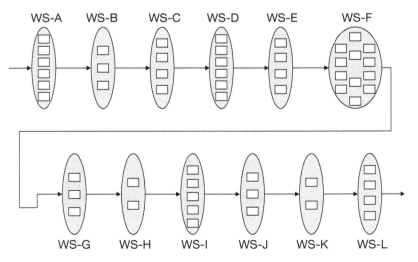

FIGURE 12.2

Process-step-centric flowchart for revised 12-workstation factory.

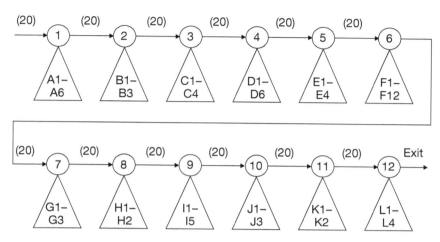

PROBLEM STATEMENT

Presently, the cycle time of the factory is 211.76 days—which is assumed to be much, much worse than that of your competition (and even worse than the initial factory configurations of Chapters 4 and 6). Now, however, maximizing profit is your primary goal (and reduction of factory cycle time is secondary).

Your mission is to maximize profit by means of one or more of the following actions:

- Allocate the funds necessary to add additional machines to one or more of the workstations.
- Increase or reduce the MTs assigned to each workstation (which, in turn, affects availability), where the cost of an MT is assumed to be $1M ($100,000) each.
- Allocate funds to increase the raw process rates (PR) of the machines in a workstation.
- Allocate funds to decrease the primary sources of factory variability (i.e., the coefficient of variability values determined by either factory starts or effective process times).
- Or use some combination of the preceding.

Any of these alternatives involves money, and for sake of discussion, we will assume that our total budget is limited to $15M.

Figure 12.3 serves to summarize, in virtually the same matrix form as employed earlier, the present condition of the factory. Before proceeding further, however, we should discuss the impact of the number of MTs on the availability (and subsequent *EPR*) of the workstation.

Row 7, cells B7 through M7 list the availability of each workstation as a function of the number of MTs assigned in cells B4 through M4 and subject to failure rate λ and repair rate μ values in rows 5 and 6 (cells B5:M5 and B6:M6). For example, the failure rate of the machines in workstation A is 0.014 (i.e., 0.014 failures per machine per hour). The inverse of this value is 1/0.014, or 71.4 hours, and represents the mean time to failure (MTTF).

The repair (or service) rate of the machines in workstation A is shown as 0.030 (i.e., the average service rate is 0.030 machines per hour). The inverse of this value is 1/0.030, or 33.33 hours, and is the mean time to repair (MTTR) for each machine in workstation A.

Given the number of MTs (e.g., servers) and the arrival-rate and service-rate values, the queuing theory may be used to compute the

FIGURE 12.3

Twelve-workstation model for profit maximization, initial scenario.

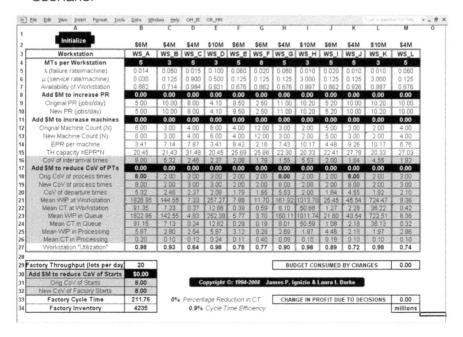

workstation availability values (Hillier and Lieberman, 2005; Taha, 2006). This is precisely what has been used in the figure. The availability value thus computed then is used to determine the *EPR* of each machine and the throughput capacity (*TH*) of each workstation. Other than this, the 12-workstation model performs in an identical fashion to that employed in Chapter 6.

PROBLEM SOLUTION

The objective of the solution process is to perform resource allocation and reallocation in a manner that maximizes profit. Readers are encouraged to attempt to accomplish this task before proceeding further. The spreadsheet for the model may be found at

www.mhprofessional.com/Ignizio/12WS_Ch12

Once you have completed this exercise, proceed to the next paragraph and compare your results with those achieved here.

If we apply the guidelines indicated in Chapters 10 and 11, our first step (phase 1) is to allocate funds to reduce variability. As in Chapter 6, we assume that we will attempt to reduce the coefficient of variability (*CoV*) values of factory starts and process times to values of 1.0 or until funds run out. Priority is given to reducing the *CoV* values that are the largest and closest to the factory input. The result of funding to reduce variability is presented in Figure 12.4. Note that with an expenditure of $0.4M ($400,000), we are able to reduce all *CoV* values to 1.0 with an associated value for profit and factory cycle time of $199.27M and 12.08 days, respectively. This represents a 94 percent reduction in cycle time. All this was accomplished simply (and cheaply) by reducing factory variability!

Our next step (phase 2) is to reallocate the MTs assigned to each workstation. While this could be accomplished by means of optimization (Ignizio, 2004; Ignizio and Cavalier, 1994), we will follow the heuristic guidelines from Chapter 11. More specifically, priorities will be established via the heuristic introduced in Chapter 11, and using these, the MTs will be reallocated. Note carefully, however, that if the number of MTs assigned to a workstation is insufficient to avoid development of an infinite queue, the cell associated with workstation utilization will turn red. In such an instance, increase the number of MTs for that workstation until the color of that cell is again white.

FIGURE 12.4

Twelve-workstation model for profit maximization, phase 1.

		A	B	C	D	E	F	G	H	I	J	K	L	M	0
1															
2	**Initialize**		$6M	$4M	$4M	$10M	$6M	$6M	$4M	$10M	$6M	$4M	$10M	$4M	
3	Workstation		WS_A	WS_B	WS_C	WS_D	WS_E	WS_F	WS_G	WS_H	WS_I	WS_J	WS_K	WS_L	
4	MTs per Workstation		5	3	5	3	5	8	5	3	5	5	3	5	
5	λ (failure rate/machine)		0.014	0.050	0.015	0.100	0.060	0.020	0.060	0.010	0.020	0.010	0.010	0.060	
6	μ (service rate/machine)		0.030	0.125	0.900	0.500	0.125	0.125	0.125	3.000	0.125	0.125	3.000	0.125	
7	Availability of Workstation		0.682	0.714	0.984	0.831	0.676	0.862	0.676	0.997	0.862	0.926	0.997	0.676	
8	Add $M to increase PR		0.00	0.00	0.00	0.00	0.00	0.00	0.00	0.00	0.00	0.00	0.00	0.00	
9	Original PR (jobs/day)		5.00	10.00	8.00	4.10	9.50	2.50	11.00	10.20	5.20	10.00	10.20	10.00	
10	New PR (jobs/day)		5.00	10.00	8.00	4.10	9.50	2.50	11.00	10.20	5.20	10.00	10.20	10.00	
11	Add $M to increase machines		0.00	0.00	0.00	0.00	0.00	0.00	0.00	0.00	0.00	0.00	0.00	0.00	
12	Original Machine Count (N)		6.00	3.00	4.00	6.00	4.00	12.00	3.00	2.00	5.00	3.00	2.00	4.00	
13	New Machine Count (N)		6.00	3.00	4.00	6.00	4.00	12.00	3.00	2.00	5.00	3.00	2.00	4.00	
14	EPR per machine		3.41	7.14	7.87	3.41	6.42	2.16	7.43	10.17	4.48	9.26	10.17	6.76	
15	TH capacity =EPR*N		20.45	21.43	31.48	20.45	25.68	25.86	22.30	20.33	22.41	27.78	20.33	27.03	
16	CoV of interarrival times		1.00	1.00	1.00	1.00	1.00	1.00	1.00	1.00	1.00	1.00	1.00	1.00	
17	Add $M to reduce CoV of PTs		0.07	0.01	0.02	0.02	0.01	0.01	0.07	0.01	0.01	0.07	0.01	0.02	
18	Orig CoV of process times		8.00	2.00	3.00	3.00	2.00	2.00	8.00	2.00	2.00	8.00	2.00	3.00	
19	New CoV of process times		1.00	1.00	1.00	1.00	1.00	1.00	1.00	1.00	1.00	1.00	1.00	1.00	
20	CoV of departure times		1.00	1.00	1.00	1.00	1.00	1.00	1.00	1.00	1.00	1.00	1.00	1.00	
21	Mean WIP at Workstation		32.48	10.81	3.14	39.41	3.49	9.03	6.64	60.54	9.24	3.31	60.54	3.00	
22	Mean CT at Workstation		1.62	0.54	0.16	1.97	0.17	0.45	0.33	3.03	0.46	0.17	3.03	0.15	
23	Mean WIP in Queue		28.48	8.81	0.64	34.54	1.39	1.03	4.82	58.58	5.39	1.31	58.58	1.00	
24	Mean CT in Queue		1.42	0.44	0.03	1.73	0.07	0.05	0.24	2.93	0.27	0.07	2.93	0.05	
25	Mean WIP in Processing		5.87	2.80	2.54	5.87	3.12	9.28	2.69	1.97	4.46	2.16	1.97	2.96	
26	Mean CT in Processing		0.23	0.10	0.12	0.24	0.11	0.40	0.09	0.10	0.19	0.10	0.10	0.10	
27	Workstation "Utilization"		0.98	0.93	0.64	0.98	0.78	0.77	0.90	0.98	0.89	0.72	0.98	0.74	
28															
29	Factory Throughput (lots per day)	20							BUDGET CONSUMED BY CHANGES					0.40	
30	Add $M to reduce CoV of Starts	$0.07													
31	Orig CoV of Starts	8.00				Copyright ©: 1994-2008 James P. Ignizio & Laura I. Burke									
32	New CoV of Factory Starts	1.00													
33	Factory Cycle Time	12.08		94% Percentage Reduction in CT				CHANGE IN PROFIT DUE TO DECISIONS					199.27	
34	Factory Inventory	242		15.3% Cycle Time Efficiency										millions	

One of several alternative reallocations is shown in Figure 12.5. Notice that the total number of MTs has been reduced from 55 to 49. The subsequent profit and factory cycle time has been changed slightly to $199.89M and 12.07 days, respectively. We have, however, reduced the cost of the changes to −$0.2M (i.e., a savings of $200,000 over the original factory configuration).

The third phase of the effort is to allocate funds for either adding machines or increasing raw process rates. If we prioritize the workstations that are either constraints or that feed constraints, one possible allocation of funds produces the matrix shown in Figure 12.6. In this final phase of the heuristic process, the profit has increased to $205.72M, whereas factory cycle time has been reduced to just 3.74 days (and a quite impressive *CTE* of 47 percent).

Our result, obtained by means of the heuristic guidelines (depending on tie-breaking rules, even better solutions are possible), may be compared with that found by optimization (i.e., via the first phase of a genetic algorithm). This optimal solution is shown in Figure 12.7. It may be noted that the optimal solution has a profit of only a little more than 1 percent greater than that

FIGURE 12.5

Twelve-workstation model for profit maximization, phase 2.

	A	B	C	D	E	F	G	H	I	J	K	L	M
2	Initialize	$6M	$4M	$4M	$10M	$6M	$6M	$4M	$10M	$6M	$4M	$10M	$4M
3	Workstation	WS_A	WS_B	WS_C	WS_D	WS_E	WS_F	WS_G	WS_H	WS_I	WS_J	WS_K	WS_L
4	MTs per Workstation	6	3	4	3	4	9	3	3	3	5	2	4
5	λ (failure rate/machine)	0.014	0.050	0.015	0.100	0.060	0.020	0.060	0.010	0.020	0.010	0.010	0.060
6	μ (service rate/machine)	0.030	0.125	0.900	0.500	0.125	0.125	0.125	3.000	0.125	0.125	3.000	0.125
7	Availability of Workstation	0.682	0.714	0.984	0.831	0.676	0.862	0.676	0.997	0.862	0.926	0.997	0.676
8	Add $M to increase PR	0.00	0.00	0.00	0.00	0.00	0.00	0.00	0.00	0.00	0.00	0.00	0.00
9	Original PR (jobs/day)	5.00	10.00	8.00	4.10	9.50	2.50	11.00	10.20	5.20	10.00	10.20	10.00
10	New PR (jobs/day)	5.00	10.00	8.00	4.10	9.50	2.50	11.00	10.20	5.20	10.00	10.00	10.00
11	Add $M to increase machines	0.00	0.00	0.00	0.00	0.00	0.00	0.00	0.00	0.00	0.00	0.00	0.00
12	Orignal Machine Count (N)	6.00	3.00	4.00	6.00	4.00	12.00	3.00	2.00	5.00	3.00	2.00	4.00
13	New Machine Count (N)	6.00	3.00	4.00	6.00	4.00	12.00	3.00	2.00	5.00	3.00	2.00	4.00
14	EPR per machine	3.41	7.14	7.87	3.41	6.42	2.16	7.43	10.17	4.48	9.26	10.17	6.76
15	TH capacity =EPR*N	20.45	21.43	31.48	20.45	25.68	25.96	22.30	20.33	22.40	27.78	20.33	27.03
16	CoV of interarrival times	1.00	1.00	1.00	1.00	1.00	1.00	1.00	1.00	1.00	1.00	1.00	1.00
17	Add $M to reduce CoV of PTs	0.07	0.01	0.02	0.02	0.01	0.01	0.01	0.01	0.01	0.07	0.01	0.02
18	Orig CoV of process times	8.00	2.00	3.00	3.00	2.00	2.00	8.00	2.00	2.00	8.00	2.00	3.00
19	New CoV of process times	1.00	1.00	1.00	1.00	1.00	1.00	1.00	1.00	1.00	1.00	1.00	1.00
20	CoV of departure times	1.00	1.00	1.00	1.00	1.00	1.00	1.00	1.00	1.00	1.00	1.00	1.00
21	Mean WIP at Workstation	32.21	10.81	3.14	39.41	3.49	9.03	6.64	60.54	9.27	3.31	60.54	3.00
22	Mean CT at Workstation	1.61	0.54	0.16	1.97	0.17	0.45	0.33	3.03	0.46	0.17	3.03	0.15
23	Mean WIP in Queue	26.21	8.91	0.84	34.54	1.39	1.03	4.82	58.58	5.42	1.31	58.58	1.00
24	Mean CT in Queue	1.41	0.44	0.03	1.73	0.07	0.05	0.24	2.93	0.27	0.07	2.93	0.05
25	Mean WIP in Processing	5.87	2.80	2.54	5.87	3.12	9.28	2.69	1.97	4.46	2.18	1.97	2.96
26	Mean CT in Processing	0.20	0.10	0.12	0.24	0.11	0.40	0.09	0.10	0.19	0.10	0.10	0.10
27	Workstation "Utilization"	0.98	0.93	0.64	0.98	0.78	0.77	0.90	0.98	0.89	0.72	0.98	0.74

29	Factory Throughput (lots per day)	20	BUDGET CONSUMED BY CHANGES	-0.20
30	Add $M to reduce CoV of Starts	$0.07	
31	Orig CoV of Starts	8.00	Copyright © 1994-2008 James P. Ignizio & Laura I. Burke
32	New CoV of Factory Starts	1.00	
33	Factory Cycle Time	12.07	94% Percentage Reduction in CT	CHANGE IN PROFIT DUE TO DECISIONS	199.89
34	Factory Inventory	241	15.4% Cycle Time Efficiency	millions

achieved by the heuristic method. Cycle time and *CTE* for the optimal solution are also only a bit better. What is of most interest, however, is that by means of following the guidelines laid out previously, a simple heuristic has obtained a solution very close to optimal.

Now that we have the solution to the problem by means of either heuristic guidelines or optimization, we should examine the mechanism of the heuristic approach in more detail. For example, just how do we reduce factory variability in phase 1?

HEURISTIC PROCESS IN DETAIL

The initial configuration of the 12-workstation factory was provided in Figure 12.3. The first phase of the heuristic approach is that of reducing the inherent variability of the factory by adding funds to projects that should reduce the *CoV* of factory starts and effective process times. It is a general rule that the emphasis in either reducing variability or increasing effective capacity should be placed on a change of protocols in the front end of the

FIGURE   12.6

Twelve-workstation model for profit maximization, phase 3.

	A	B	C	D	E	F	G	H	I	J	K	L
Initialize	$6M	$4M	$4M	$10M	$6M	$6M	$4M	$10M	$6M	$4M	$10M	$4M
Workstation	WS_A	WS_B	WS_C	WS_D	WS_E	WS_F	WS_G	WS_H	WS_I	WS_J	WS_K	WS_L
MTs per Workstation	6	3	4	3	4	9	3	3	5	3	2	4
λ (failure rate/machine)	0.014	0.050	0.015	0.100	0.060	0.020	0.060	0.010	0.020	0.010	0.010	0.060
μ (service rate/machine)	0.030	0.125	0.900	0.500	0.125	0.125	0.125	3.000	0.125	0.125	3.000	0.125
Availability of Workstation	0.682	0.714	0.984	0.831	0.676	0.862	0.676	0.997	0.862	0.926	0.997	0.676
Add $M to increase PR	0.50	0.50	0.00	0.50	0.00	0.00	0.00	0.50	0.00	0.00	0.50	0.00
Original PR (jobs/day)	5.00	10.00	8.00	4.10	9.50	2.50	11.00	10.20	5.20	10.00	10.20	10.00
New PR (jobs/day)	5.87	10.87	8.00	4.97	9.50	2.50	11.00	11.07	5.20	10.00	11.07	10.00
Add $M to increase machines	0.00	0.00	0.00	0.00	0.00	0.00	0.00	0.00	0.00	0.00	0.00	0.00
Original Machine Count (N)	6.00	3.00	4.00	6.00	4.00	12.00	3.00	2.00	5.00	3.00	2.00	4.00
New Machine Count (N)	6.00	3.00	4.00	6.00	4.00	12.00	3.00	5.00	5.00	3.00	2.00	4.00
EPR per machine	4.00	7.78	7.87	4.13	6.42	2.16	7.43	11.03	4.48	9.26	11.03	6.76
TH capacity =EPR*N	24.02	23.29	31.48	24.80	25.68	25.86	22.30	22.07	22.41	27.78	22.07	27.03
CoV of interarrival times	1.00	1.00	1.00	1.00	1.00	1.00	1.00	1.00	1.00	1.00	1.00	1.00
Add $M to reduce CoV of PTs	0.07	0.01	0.02	0.02	0.01	0.01	0.07	0.01	0.01	0.07	0.01	0.02
Orig CoV of process times	8.00	2.00	3.00	3.00	2.00	2.00	8.00	2.00	2.00	8.00	2.00	3.00
New CoV of process times	1.00	1.00	1.00	1.00	1.00	1.00	1.00	1.00	1.00	1.00	1.00	1.00
CoV of departure times	1.00	1.00	1.00	1.00	1.00	1.00	1.00	1.00	1.00	1.00	1.00	1.00
Mean WIP at Workstation	5.46	5.12	3.14	5.95	3.49	9.03	6.64	10.17	9.24	3.31	10.17	3.00
Mean CT at Workstation	0.27	0.26	0.16	0.30	0.17	0.45	0.33	0.51	0.46	0.17	0.51	0.15
Mean WIP in Queue	2.06	3.28	0.84	1.92	1.39	1.03	4.82	8.36	5.39	1.31	8.36	1.00
Mean CT in Queue	0.10	0.16	0.03	0.10	0.07	0.05	0.24	0.42	0.27	0.07	0.42	0.05
Mean WIP in Processing	5.00	2.58	2.54	4.84	3.12	9.28	2.69	1.81	2.16	1.81	1.81	2.98
Mean CT in Processing	0.17	0.09	0.12	0.20	0.11	0.40	0.09	0.09	0.19	0.10	0.09	0.10
Workstation "Utilization"	0.83	0.86	0.64	0.81	0.78	0.77	0.90	0.91	0.89	0.72	0.91	0.74

Factory Throughput (lots per day)	20		BUDGET CONSUMED BY CHANGES	2.30
Add $M to reduce CoV of Starts	$0.07			
Orig CoV of Starts	8.00		Copyright © 1994-2008 James P. Ignizio & Laura I. Burke	
New CoV of Factory Starts	1.00			
Factory Cycle Time	3.74	98% Percentage Reduction in CT	CHANGE IN PROFIT DUE TO DECISIONS	205.72
Factory Inventory	75	47.0% Cycle Time Efficiency		millions

production line. As such, the first source of variability that should be dealt with is factory starts. We may devote funding up to $0.07M for reducing that CoV from its present value of 8.0 to the desired value of 1.0.

Reducing factory starts variability may be achieved by using a declustered factory starts protocol (coupled with, where possible, a factory loading scheme synchronized with factory health). Once this has been achieved, we move to the remaining largest sources of variability, with priority again given to the sources closest to the factory input. Thus we deal with the variability of the effective process time of workstation A (devoting $0.07M to that effort).

The source of variability within an effective process time of a workstation may be actual variability in the raw process rate of the machines in the workstation—a matter that may require physical changes—or, more likely, problems with operating or maintenance protocols. If the workstation requires manual operation and the presence of human operators, the cause of the variability may be too few operators, poorly trained operators, or operating specifications that are not C^4U-compliant. It is more likely (particularly in

FIGURE 12.7

Optimal solution.

Workstation	WS_A	WS_B	WS_C	WS_D	WS_E	WS_F	WS_G	WS_H	WS_I	WS_J	WS_K	WS_L
Initialize	$6M	$4M	$4M	$10M	$6M	$6M	$4M	$10M	$8M	$4M	$10M	$4M
MTs per Workstation	4	3	1	2	2	3	3	1	2	1	1	3
λ (failure rate/machine)	0.014	0.050	0.015	0.100	0.060	0.020	0.060	0.010	0.020	0.010	0.010	0.060
μ (service rate/machine)	0.030	0.125	0.900	0.500	0.125	0.125	0.125	3.000	0.125	0.125	3.000	0.125
Availability of Workstation	0.679	0.714	0.983	0.814	0.643	0.849	0.676	0.997	0.855	0.915	0.997	0.673
Add $M to increase PR	0.27	0.20	0.06	0.38	0.13	0.21	0.19	0.47	0.10	0.02	0.44	0.03
Original PR (jobs/day)	5.00	10.00	8.00	4.10	9.50	2.50	11.00	10.20	5.20	10.00	10.20	10.00
New PR (jobs/day)	5.77	10.72	8.57	4.92	10.16	3.23	11.72	11.06	5.83	10.47	11.05	10.49
Add $M to increase machines	0.00	0.00	0.00	0.00	0.00	0.00	0.00	0.00	0.00	0.00	0.00	0.00
Original Machine Count (N)	6.00	3.00	4.00	6.00	4.00	12.00	3.00	2.00	5.00	3.00	2.00	4.00
New Machine Count (N)	6.00	3.00	4.00	6.00	4.00	12.00	3.00	2.00	5.00	3.00	2.00	4.00
EPR per machine	3.92	7.66	8.42	4.01	6.54	2.74	7.92	11.02	4.99	9.59	11.01	7.06
TH capacity =EPR*N	23.53	22.97	33.67	24.05	26.15	32.89	23.76	22.05	24.95	28.76	22.02	28.25
CoV of interarrival times	1.01	1.01	1.00	1.00	1.00	1.00	1.00	1.00	1.00	1.00	1.00	1.00
Add $M to reduce CoV of PTs	0.07	0.01	0.02	0.02	0.01	0.01	0.07	0.01	0.01	0.07	0.01	0.02
Orig CoV of process times	8.00	2.00	3.00	3.00	2.00	2.00	8.00	2.00	2.00	8.00	2.00	3.00
New CoV of process times	1.02	1.00	1.00	1.00	1.00	1.00	1.00	1.00	1.00	1.00	1.00	1.00
CoV of departure times	1.01	1.00	1.00	1.00	1.00	1.00	1.00	1.00	1.00	1.00	1.00	1.00
Mean WIP at Workstation	5.99	5.62	2.80	6.49	3.14	8.37	4.34	10.26	5.43	2.99	10.39	2.68
Mean CT at Workstation	0.30	0.28	0.14	0.32	0.18	0.32	0.22	0.51	0.27	0.15	0.52	0.13
Mean WIP in Queue	2.53	3.75	0.47	2.43	1.17	0.17	2.63	8.45	2.00	1.08	8.58	0.17
Mean CT in Queue	0.13	0.19	0.02	0.12	0.06	0.01	0.13	0.42	0.10	0.05	0.43	0.04
Mean WIP in Processing	5.10	2.61	2.38	4.99	3.06	7.30	2.53	1.81	4.01	2.09	1.82	2.83
Mean CT in Processing	0.17	0.09	0.12	0.20	0.10	0.31	0.09	0.09	0.17	0.10	0.09	0.10
Workstation "Utilization"	0.85	0.87	0.59	0.83	0.76	0.61	0.84	0.91	0.80	0.70	0.91	0.71

Factory Throughput (lots per day)	20	BUDGET CONSUMED BY CHANGES	0.00
Add $M to reduce CoV of Starts	$0.07		
Orig CoV of Starts	8.00	Copyright ©: 1994-2008 James P. Ignizio & Laura I. Burke	
New CoV of Factory Starts	1.01		
Factory Cycle Time	3.33	98% Percentage Reduction in CT	CHANGE IN PROFIT DUE TO DECISIONS — 208.43
Factory Inventory	67	49% Cycle Time Efficiency	millions

highly automated factories), however, that the source of variability in effective process times is inferior maintenance protocols. This calls for an examination of the preventive maintenance (PM) specifications, development of an availability profile plot, and computation of the M-ratio.

Consequently, to reduce the CoV of the effective process times of workstation A, we may have to develop C⁴U-compliant PM specs, decluster maintenance events, evaluate the location and levels of spares and supplies, or reallocate MTs (the latter is accomplished via the second phase of the heuristic). In short, a Waddington analysis should be considered.

Once we have reduced the CoV of the effective process times of workstation A, we move on to workstations G, J, C, D, L, B, E, F, H, I, and K in that order. The same approach to CoV reduction as described for workstation A applies to these workstations.

Before proceeding to phase 2, it should be pointed out that the 12-workstation model does not include batching and assumes that the only source of variability, other than factory starts, is effective process times. In an actual factory, we also should consider the variability caused by job arrivals at each workstation and machine and allocate the resources necessary to reduce the variability about arrivals to a reasonable level. For example, batching at a preceding process step will induce variability in the arrival rate at the next process step. Steps thus should be taken to reduce batch sizes whenever possible.

Another matter that is not dealt with in the 12-workstation factory model is that of "victim" and "villain" workstations. In a real-world factory, a specific workstation (or set of machines supporting a specific process step) might be perceived as a problem because of a higher than expected cycle time. It is all too common to jump to the conclusion that resources should be allocated to the (apparently) poorly performing workstation when, in actuality, it is the victim of a workstation supporting the preceding process step (or steps).

Remember the third fundamental equation of manufacturing, the propagation of variability. It may well be that the feeder workstation is delivering jobs to the next workstation with a high level of arrival-rate variability. This means that it is the workstation to which resources should be allocated rather than the victim workstation. While this is not dealt with in the 12-workstation factory model, it is a matter that always should be considered in practice.

Phase 2 of the heuristic approach involves the reallocation of MTs as well as a possible increase or decrease in total MT headcount. While the optimization procedure may be used here, let's restrict our discussion to implementation of the heuristic guidelines of Chapter 11. Rather, however, than computing the weighting factors and queues, as was described there, an even simpler approach may be employed. While not as effective, this simpler method is often "good enough." The approach may be summarized as follows:

Observe, at all times, the impact on profit (cell M29) of any action taken. If the action reduces profit, do not take it. Observe, at all times, the color of the cells in row 27 (cells B27 to M27). If an action taken (e.g., reducing the number of MTs at a workstation) results in a cell turning red, do not take that action.

If the number of MTs exceeds the number of machines in the workstation (and under the assumption that only one MT is required for an event), reduce that number to the number of machines. (Thus the number of MTs assigned to workstation C may be reduced to a value of 4, those to E to 4, those to G to 3, those to J to 3, those to K to 2, and those to L to 4.)

In the next step, allocate additional MTs (up to the number of machines in the workstation—again under the assumption that only one MT is required for an event) to the workstations having the highest utilization (workstations A, D, H, and K). If, however, the addition of MTs fails to reduce the utilization value (i.e., occupation rate), return the number of MTs to the original value. For this factory, at this step, additional MTs at any workstation will not improve profit.

We next attempt to reduce the number of MTs at each workstation. If the reduction improves profit while not turning a cell in row 27 red, then take that action.

Following the reallocation of MTs, we move to phase 3. In phase 3, we employ a theory of constraints–influenced approach and allocate funds to increase the capacity of constraint and near-constraint workstations, with priority given to the constraints closest to factory input. Since increasing the process rate of a machine (e.g., by modifying its physical components) is usually cheaper than adding machines, priority normally should be given to process-rate increases.

If the allocation of funds to increasing process rates or machines increases total profit, take that action. Otherwise, return to the previous factory state.

At the conclusion of these three phases, a solution close to the optimal solution (in terms of profit) should have been achieved. The result, for the steps just outlined, is even better in terms of profit (although worse in terms of cycle time and CTE) than was obtained previously. This is shown in Figure 12.8.

Considering the fact that there are invariably errors in collected data and that estimates of costs for projects (e.g., increasing raw process rates or reducing variability) and of the value of a day of cycle time are predictions, we probably should be satisfied with implementation of the heuristic approach to factory performance improvement. This is certainly evident in this example.

CHAPTER SUMMARY

The guidelines of Chapters 10 and 11, combined with the lessons from previous chapters, provide the basis for a practical, straightforward heuristic approach to factory performance improvement. Key to such improvement is, as demonstrated repeatedly, reducing variability (as well as any complexity serving to induce variability) in the factory.

F I G U R E   12.8

A second heuristic solution.

	A	B	C	D	E	F	G	H	I	J	K	L	M
2	**Initialize**	$6M	$4M	$4M	$10M	$6M	$6M	$4M	$10M	$6M	$4M	$10M	$4M
3	Workstation	WS_A	WS_B	WS_C	WS_D	WS_E	WS_F	WS_G	WS_H	WS_I	WS_J	WS_K	WS_L
4	MTs per Workstation	5	2	1	3	2	2	2	1	2	1	1	2
5	λ (failure rate/machine)	0.014	0.050	0.015	0.100	0.060	0.020	0.060	0.010	0.020	0.010	0.010	0.060
6	μ (service rate/machine)	0.030	0.125	0.900	0.500	0.125	0.125	0.125	3.000	0.125	0.125	3.000	0.125
7	Availability of Workstation	0.682	0.706	0.983	0.831	0.643	0.792	0.664	0.997	0.855	0.915	0.997	0.643
8	Add $M to increase PR	0.50	0.00	0.00	0.50	0.00	0.00	0.00	0.50	0.00	0.00	0.50	0.00
9	Original PR (jobs/day)	5.00	10.00	8.00	4.10	9.50	2.50	11.00	10.20	5.20	10.00	10.20	10.00
10	New PR (jobs/day)	5.87	10.00	8.00	4.97	9.50	2.50	11.00	11.07	5.20	10.00	11.07	10.00
11	Add $M to increase machines	0.00	0.00	0.00	0.00	0.00	0.00	0.00	0.00	0.00	0.00	0.00	0.00
12	Original Machine Count (N)	6.00	3.00	4.00	6.00	4.00	12.00	3.00	2.00	5.00	3.00	2.00	4.00
13	New Machine Count (N)	6.00	3.00	4.00	6.00	4.00	12.00	3.00	2.00	5.00	3.00	2.00	4.00
14	EPR per machine	4.00	7.06	7.86	4.13	6.11	1.98	7.31	11.03	4.45	9.15	11.03	6.43
15	TH capacity =EPR*N	24.01	21.18	31.45	24.80	24.45	23.75	21.92	22.07	22.24	27.46	22.07	25.73
16	CoV of interarrival times	1.00	1.00	1.00	1.00	1.00	1.00	1.00	1.00	1.00	1.00	1.00	1.00
17	Add $M to reduce CoV of PTs	0.07	0.01	0.02	0.02	0.01	0.01	0.01	0.07	0.01	0.01	0.07	0.02
18	Orig CoV of process times	8.00	2.00	3.00	3.00	2.00	2.00	8.00	2.00	2.00	8.00	2.00	3.00
19	New CoV of process times	1.00	1.00	1.00	1.00	1.00	1.00	1.00	1.00	1.00	1.00	1.00	1.00
20	CoV of departure times	1.00	1.00	1.00	1.00	1.00	1.00	1.00	1.00	1.00	1.00	1.00	1.00
21	Mean WIP at Workstation	5.47	12.76	3.15	5.95	3.98	10.09	7.66	10.17	9.73	3.38	10.17	3.30
22	Mean CT at Workstation	0.27	0.64	0.16	0.30	0.20	0.50	0.38	0.51	0.49	0.17	0.51	0.17
23	Mean WIP in Queue	2.06	10.76	0.65	1.92	1.88	2.09	5.84	8.36	5.89	1.38	8.36	1.30
24	Mean CT in Queue	0.10	0.54	0.03	0.10	0.09	0.10	0.29	0.42	0.29	0.07	0.42	0.07
25	Mean WIP in Processing	5.00	2.83	2.54	4.84	3.27	10.10	2.74	1.81	4.50	2.19	1.81	3.11
26	Mean CT in Processing	0.17	0.10	0.12	0.20	0.11	0.40	0.09	0.08	0.19	0.10	0.09	0.10
27	Workstation "Utilization"	0.83	0.94	0.64	0.81	0.82	0.84	0.91	0.91	0.90	0.73	0.91	0.78

Factory Throughput (lots per day)	20	BUDGET CONSUMED BY CHANGES : -0.70
Add $M to reduce CoV of Starts	$0.07	
Orig CoV of Starts	8.00	*Copyright ©: 1994-2008 James P. Ignizio & Laura I. Burke*
New CoV of Factory Starts	1.00	
Factory Cycle Time	4.29	98% Percentage Reduction in CT CHANGE IN PROFIT DUE TO DECISIONS : 208.17
Factory Inventory	86	41.2% Cycle Time Efficiency millions

CASE STUDY 12: PAY THE PIPER

Tommy Jenkins receives his notice of termination by e-mail. It simply states that his services are no longer required and that, by 1 p.m. this day, he is to be escorted from the Factory 7 campus. As he gathers his belongings, limited to those that can fit in a single book box as per Muddle regulations, his office door swings open—without the courtesy of a knock.

"Are you ready, Tommy?" asks Ben Arnold, struggling to suppress a smile. "It's almost 1 p.m., and I've been asked to escort you from the premises."

Tommy Jenkins restrains his anger, tries hard to keep his feelings masked, and simply nods in the affirmative. There are no further words exchanged as Ben walks Tommy to the exit of the office complex.

As he turns the key in his plush Mercedes-Benz CL600, one word runs through Tommy's mind: *Unfair, unfair, unfair, unfair.*

Back in what had been Tommy's office, three words run through Ben's mind: *I did it! I did it! I did it!*

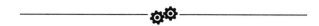

Donna Garcia is in a bad mood. Tommy Jenkins's removal had only been made possible by the coordinated efforts of her, Ben Arnold, and Jack Gibson. Their plan had worked perfectly, as far as the dismissal of Tommy had gone and his replacement by Ben. But one promise, a solemn promise made by both Ben and Jack, has not been honored.

They had promised her that once they were rid of Tommy, she would be promoted to the position of Ben's technical assistant. Instead, as she learns through a tersely worded e-mail, she is to be sent to Room 101 for reeducation. If that six-week course is completed successfully, she is to be reassigned to an aging Muddle factory site in, of all places, Fargo, North Dakota. There she will be responsible for decommissioning the facility. Her future after that has been left unspecified. There is, she thinks, no way I'm going to either Room 101 or Fargo.

Some 200 miles away, Jack Gibson, the junior factory manager for Factory 2, is informed that he has been promoted to the position of senior vice president and director of manufacturing, replacing William "Wild Bill" Barlow. This doesn't come as a surprise to Jack.

With the departure of Tommy Jenkins and the resignation of Donna Garcia, the leadership of the *LEAN* Forward team in Factory 7 is effectively gutted, at least in terms of its existence on the formal organization chart. This proves to be no problem because Marvin Muddle and the MRC conclude—*without any actual evidence*—that lean manufacturing has done absolutely nothing to improve the performance of their factories.

After much discussion, it is decided to disband the lean effort and to consider another approach—increased factory moves. The only, and most difficult, decision remaining is the choice of a new slogan and logo.

Marvin Muddle picks, from among the dozen or so slogans proposed, "Fast Mover." The new logo will consist of the word *Muddle* located above a stylized drawing of a roadrunner. To most people, however, it just looks a lot like a confused and frightened bird.

An order is issued to all plant managers that, henceforth, the new measure of factory performance will be a count of moves per week through the machines in each factory. At the end of each quarter, the factory with the highest number of moves will be presented with the coveted "Muddle Badge of Merit" plus six-figure bonuses to the plant managers, along with funds sufficient to provide a free soft drink to each and every factory floor worker.

Ben Arnold is determined to win the award each and every quarter. He issues a memo to his department managers demanding that factory moves be increased by at least 20 percent. The department managers and factory floor personnel have already devised some rather ingenious methods for accomplishing, if not surpassing, those goals.

Julia Austen has called a meeting, and its participants have arrived at Winston Smith's "war room." She provides a brief summary of the situation now facing Factory 7, as well as the Muddle Corporation.

"Guys," says Julia, "the good news is that Tommy Jenkins, Donna Garcia, and Bill Barlow are no longer with the firm. The bad news is that Ben Arnold is now our senior plant manager. But you already know all that. What you may not have heard is that Ben's first order of business has been to demand that we increase factory moves by 20 percent or more. Naturally, he hasn't explained just how this will be done. On the other hand, the good news is . . ."

"That's insane," Winston interrupts. "Focusing solely on factory moves, as we all know, is quite possibly the worst thing a factory can do. Besides, an increase in moves of 20 percent will overload this factory. If you think our performance is bad now, you ain't seen nothin' yet."

"I'm sure we all agree," says Julia. "But there is some good news, or at least I hope so. With all the fuss about the reorganizations, firings, and resignations, I think we can operate under the radar. Ben and his people are too busy with more important matters than to pay much attention to the three of us. We should be able to continue our work. At least that's my opinion. One thing we might want to look into is the 20 percent increase in factory moves. I'd like to recommend we use Winston's models to investigate the impact of moves on the factory. Once that's done, why don't we just bite the bullet and present our findings to Ben and the other Factory 7 plant managers?"

"Frankly, I don't think we have anything to lose," says Dan. "We may be under the factory's radar at the moment, but sooner or later I'm sure the three of us will be looking for other jobs."

"I agree," says Winston. "We may as well give it a try. Who knows? Perhaps a miracle will happen. Perhaps we'll actually be able to convince management that we can vastly improve factory performance simply by reducing complexity and variability. That reminds me, I'm in the process of developing an executive summary of our findings. It's even better than I had thought."

"What's the bottom line?" asks Dan. "Just how much improvement did the simulation models indicate?"

"When we combine just four of Professor Leonidas' methods for reducing complexity and variability in the Factory 7 simulation model, we get a 72 percent reduction in factory cycle time and a 65 percent reduction in the variability of factory outs. In addition, mainly by the reduction in variability, we achieve a 9 percent increase in effective factory capacity. I'm also convinced that if we performed a Waddington analysis and brought our operating and maintenance specifications up to C^4U compliance, we could increase effective factory capacity by at least 20 percent—all this without having to buy any additional machines or hire any more personnel."

"Wow," says Julia, "that's amazing. "Fellows, we should put a slide-show presentation together. If these results don't convince plant management, nothing will."

CHAPTER 12 EXERCISES

Using the 12-workstation factory simulation model of this chapter, perform the following exercises.

1. Employ the greedy heuristic to find the maximal profit solution, but reverse the order of the first two phases (i.e., first reallocate maintenance personnel and then reduce variability).
2. Defend the use of a heuristic procedure (i.e., the greedy heuristic) as opposed to an optimization procedure.

The Fundamental Model of Manufacturing

In preceding chapters I introduced, discussed, and illustrated the three fundamental equations of manufacturing. These equations, in turn, provided the foundation necessary for developing the pragmatic and cost-effective guidelines listed and illustrated in Chapters 10, 11, and 12. In this chapter I deal briefly with the fundamental model of manufacturing. Using this model, we shall be able to determine, precisely, the maximum theoretical capacity of a workstation (and thus a factory). By combining this model with an appreciation of variability, we will be better able to forecast the maximum sustainable capacity of a workstation or factory. Furthermore, by means of straightforward extensions to the fundamental model, it is possible to develop models that solve such problems as the optimization of operation-to-machine assignments (a.k.a. *dedications*).

While preceding chapters required only a limited appreciation of mathematics and employed only the most basic mathematical operations, readers should be forewarned that the fullest understanding of the material in this chapter is best achieved via at least a modest background in mathematical modeling and optimization [e.g., linear programming (Ignizio and Cavalier, 1994)]. Consequently, some readers may want to peruse the material, whereas others may have the background—and interest—sufficient to obtain a more complete appreciation of the fundamental model.

A REVIEW OF CAPACITY

The maximum theoretical capacity of a workstation was computed in preceding chapters, in certain instances, simply by adding the effective process rates (*EPRs*) of each machine. On another occasion, the harmonic mean was employed. In either case, the approach presented was limited to special cases. More specifically, we simply may sum the *EPRs* of the machines in a workstation to determine its maximum theoretical capacity if and only if

- The workstation supports only a single operation (i.e., process step).
- Each machine supports that single operation (even if at different process rates).

Table 13.1 presents data for a multiple-machine, single-operation (MM/SO) workstation in which the effective process rates may be added. Consequently, this workstation's *EPR* is 1.800 + 1.125 + 1.020 + 1.848 = 5.793 lots per hour.

The harmonic mean, in turn, may be employed in instances in which

- The workstation supports multiple operations (i.e., process steps).
- Every machine in the workstation has the same process rate for a given operation (e.g., if machine A has a *PR* of 5 lots per hour on operation 4, then all other machines in the workstation must have a *PR* of 5 lots per hour on that particular operation).

Table 13.2 presents data for a multiple-machine, multiple-operation (MM/MO) workstation for which derivation of the capacity through employment of the harmonic mean is appropriate. This is

TABLE 13.1

Maximum Theoretical Capacity of an MM/SO Workstation

Machine	Process Rate (Lots/Hour)	Availability (Percent)	EPR (Lots/Hour) = PR • A
A	2	90	1.800
B	1.5	75	1.125
C	1.2	85	1.020
D	2.1	88	1.848

TABLE 13.2

Maximum Theoretical Capacity of an MM/MO Workstation

Machine	Operation 1 (Lots/Hour)	Operation 2 (Lots/Hour)	Operation 3 (Lots/Hour)	Harmonic Mean (*HM*)	Availability (*A*) (Percent)	EPR (Lots/Hour) = *HM* • *A*
A	2.0	1.2	1.8	1.5882	90	1.4294
B	2.0	1.2	1.8	1.5882	90	1.4294
C	2.0	1.2	1.8	1.5882	90	1.4294
D	2.0	1.2	1.8	1.5882	90	1.4294

so because the process rates for each operation (the numerical values in columns 2, 3, and 4) are the same for each machine. In other words, each machine is identical in terms of its process rate per operation type.

The maximum theoretical capacity of the workstation whose data are shown in Table 13.2 is found by summing the effective process rates of each machine (where these, in turn, must be determined by multiplying their harmonic means by their availability). Thus the maximum theoretical capacity of this workstation is 4 • 1.4294, or 5.7176 lots per hour.

THE FUNDAMENTAL MODEL

The fundamental model, or general capacity model (GCM), as developed by Ignizio (1992a, 1992b), may be employed in either of the two special cases described earlier or—more important—for the completely general case, that is, where

- The workstation supports one or more operations.
- Not every machine in the workstation necessarily has identical process rates for associated operations and even when some machines are not qualified (e.g., dedicated) to support certain operations.

Frankly, the GCM is so easy to formulate and solve (given access to a supporting linear programming software package such as SOLVER, which is a free add-on in the Microsoft Excel package) that the safest course of action is to always employ the GCM when computing workstation or overall factory maximum theoretical capacity. I shall initially illustrate application of GCM on the example originally provided in Table 13.2. While the harmonic mean happens to be appropriate for that workstation, it will be instructive to employ the GCM as an alternate (and preferred) approach.

For construction of the general form of the model, I shall impose a few initial assumptions, *each of which may be relaxed ultimately*. These initial assumptions are

- The average number of lots processed per hour through each operation is equal. (For example, if the workstation supports three operations and the average number of lots, requiring any of the three operations, is six lots per hour, then the average number of lots processed by each individual operation is two per hour.)
- Only one type of product is processed by the workstation.
- There is no scrap or loss owing to yield loss.

Under these initial assumptions, the maximum theoretical capacity of a workstation may be determined simply by maximizing the total number of lots per hour of any one of the operations supported by the workstation. Thus, if we let *OP1* represent the number of lots requiring operation 1 supportable by the workstation, our objective may be stated simply as "maximize *OP1*."

Other parameters used to construct the optimization model include

- i = machines ($i = 1, 2, \ldots, m$)
- j = operations ($j = 1, 2, \ldots, n$)
- $x(i,j)$ = number of hours devoted by machine i to the conduct of operation j
- $PR(i,j)$ = process rate in lots (or jobs or batches) per hour for the performance of operation j on machine i
- $OP(j)$ = total number of lots (or jobs or batches) requiring operation j that the workstation processes each hour

Employing these definitions, we may construct the form of the GCM for the situation depicted in Table 13.2. The resulting model is listed in Equations (13.1) through (13.10). As noted, these equations form a special type of optimization model known as a *linear program* (LP) (Ignizio and Cavalier, 1994).

$$\text{Maximize } OP1 \tag{13.1}$$

subject to

$$x(A,1) + x(A,2) + x(A,3) \leq 0.90 \tag{13.2}$$

$$x(B,1) + x(B,2) + x(B,3) \leq 0.90 \tag{13.3}$$

$$x(C,1) + x(C,2) + x(C,3) \leq 0.90 \tag{13.4}$$

$$x(D,1) + x(D,2) + x(D,3) \leq 0.90 \tag{13.5}$$

$$OP1 = PR(A,1) \bullet x(A,1) + PR(B,1) \bullet x(B,1) +$$
$$PR(C,1) \bullet x(C,1) + PR(D,1) \bullet x(D,1) \tag{13.6}$$

$$OP2 = PR(A, 2) \bullet x(A, 2) + PR(B, 2) \bullet x(B, 2) +$$
$$PR(C, 2) \bullet x(C, 2) + PR(D, 2) \bullet x(D, 2) \tag{13.7}$$

$$OP3 = PR(A, 3) \bullet x(A,3) + PR(B,3) \bullet x(B,3) +$$
$$PR(C,3) \bullet x(C,3) + PR(D,3) \bullet x(D,3) \tag{13.8}$$

$$OP1 = OP2 = OP3 \tag{13.9}$$

$$x(A,1), x(A,2), \ldots, x(D,2), x(D,3) \geq 0 \tag{13.10}$$

Each of the functions listed in the LP model may be defined as follows:

- Equation (13.1) is the LP objective function wherein we seek to find the maximum value of $OP1$, the number of lots supportable by the machines capable of processing operation 1. We could have just as well sought to maximize $OP2$ or $OP3$ because these variables are equal in value under our initial set of assumptions.
- Equations (13.2) through (13.5) state that the time devoted by a given machine (e.g., machine A in Equation 13.2) must be equal to or less than that available on the machine on average each hour. For example, in Equation (13.2), the time devoted by machine A to each of the three operations each hour must be equal to or less than the machine's average availability (i.e., 0.90 of an hour).
- Equations (13.6) through (13.8) serve to define the number of lots processed per hour for operations 1, 2, and 3, respectively.
- Equation (13.9) indicates that the number of lots processed per hour for each of the three operations must be equal (i.e., under the initial assumptions).
- Finally, Equation (13.10) says that the model's *decision variables* (i.e., hours allocated by each machine to each

operation) must be nonnegative. In other words, none of the hours allocated to an operation may have a negative value.

If we define one more parameter, we may derive the general form for this LP. We will let $TA(i)$ represent the time available on machine i per hour for processing. This will be equal to the availability of the machine. The LP model for the MM/MO single-product workstation in general form then is: Find $x(i,j)$ so as to maximize $OP1$ (or $OP2$, $OP3$, etc.) such that

$$\sum_{j=1}^{n} x(i,j) \leq TA(i) \qquad \text{for all } i \text{ machines}$$

$$OP(j) = \sum_{i=1}^{m} \left[PR(i,j) \bullet x(i,j) \right] \qquad \text{for all } j \text{ operations}$$

$$OP(s) = OP(t) \qquad \text{for all } s \text{ and } t$$

$$x(i,j) \geq 0 \qquad \text{for all } i \text{ and } j$$

SOLUTION VIA SOLVER

If you have access to an LP software package, the solution to the LP model (i.e., for the maximum theoretical capacity of a given work-station) may be found easily. To illustrate, examine how the model for Table 13.2 (i.e., Equations 13.1 through 13.10) is entered into an EXCEL spreadsheet and then solved by the SOLVER add-on. The associated spreadsheet problem representation is presented in Figure 13.1. Cell I20 contains the maximum theoretical capacity per operation, as determined by optimization, and has a value of 1.9059 lots per hour per operation. The maximum theoretical flow through all three operations is given in cell I21: 3 • 1.4059, or 5.7176 lots per hour per workstation.

When we employed the harmonic mean for this situation, we computed the exact same maximum theoretical capacity for the entire workstation (i.e., 5.7176 lots per hour). Thus, at this point, the difference between the GCM and harmonic mean model is not apparent. I will deal with that matter later. First, however, examine Figure 13.2, which shows the formulas embedded in the spread-sheet.[1] The initial values of the decision variables (cells C9 through

---

1 In Figures 13.1 and 13.2, the cells containing *ETLT* simply indicate that the values to the left should be equal to or less than (i.e., *ETLT*) those on the right. These *text entries* do not actually need to be included on the spreadsheet and have been inserted only as a reminder of the form of the corresponding constraints.

FIGURE 13.1

Spreadsheet representation of MM/MO capacity example.

Machine	Op 1 (lots/hr)	Op 2 (lots/hr)	Op 3 (lots/hr)	Availability (fraction)
A	2.00	1.20	1.80	0.90
B	2.00	1.20	1.80	0.90
C	2.00	1.20	1.80	0.90
D	2.00	1.20	1.80	0.90

Machine	x(i,1)	x(i,2)	x(i,3)
A	0.0529	0.6882	0.1588
B	0.0000	0.9000	0.0000
C	0.0000	0.0000	0.9000
D	0.9000	0.0000	0.0000

Machine	Actual Time		TA(i)
A-time	0.90	ETLT	0.90
B-time	0.90	ETLT	0.90
C-time	0.90	ETLT	0.90
D-time	0.90	ETLT	0.90

OP1 Lots	1.9059
OP2 Lots	1.9059
OP3 Lots	1.9059

Maximum Capacity per Operation =	1.9059	lots per hour
Total Lot Flow per Hour (all Operations) =	5.7176	lots per hour

FIGURE 13.2

Spreadsheet formulas for example.

Machine	Op 1 (lots/hr)	Op 2 (lots/hr)	Op 3 (lots/hr)	Availability (fraction)
A	2	1.2	1.8	0.9
B	2	1.2	1.8	0.9
C	2	1.2	1.8	0.9
D	2	1.2	1.8	0.9

Machine	x(i,1)	x(i,2)	x(i,3)
A	0	0	0
B	0	0	0
C	0	0	0
D	0	0	0

Machine	Actual Time		TA(i)
A-time	=SUM(C9:E9)	ETLT	=F3
B-time	=SUM(C10:E10)	ETLT	=F4
C-time	=SUM(C11:E11)	ETLT	=F5
D-time	=SUM(C12:E12)	ETLT	=F6

OP1 Lots	=C3*C9+C4*C10+C5*C11+C6*C12
OP2 Lots	=D3*D9+D4*D10+D5*D11+D6*D12
OP3 Lots	=E3*E9+E4*E10+E5*E11+E6*E12

Maximum Capacity per Operation =	=C20	lots per hour
Total Lot Flow per Hour (all Operations) =	=3*I20	lots per hour

E12) have been set to zero in the spreadsheet. (Readers are advised to replicate this model and then employ SOLVER for its solution.)

The settings required in SOLVER are listed in Figures 13.3 and 13.4. (Not shown in Figure 13.3 is the final constraint: C21 = C22.)

There is one final important aspect of the solution found by the GCM that should be mentioned. Note in Figure 13.1 that the total number of nonzero-valued decision variables $x(i,j)$ is six in the final solution. That portion of the spreadsheet is repeated in Table 13.3

FIGURE   13.3

SOLVER settings (objective, decision variables, and constraints).

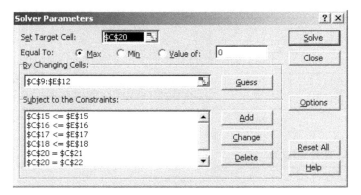

FIGURE   13.4

SOLVER option settings

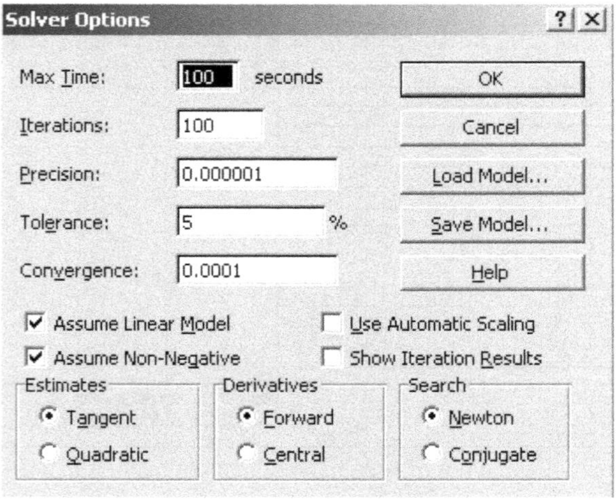

TABLE 13.3

Decision Variables, Optimal Solution

Machine	$x(i,1)$	$x(i,2)$	$x(i,3)$
A	0.4742	0.0000	0.4258
B	0.0000	0.8000	0.0000
C	0.0000	0.1284	0.7516
D	0.9200	0.0000	0.0000

TABLE 13.4

Workstation Performance Data

Machines \ Operations	1 (Lots/Hour)	2 (Lots/Hour)	3 (Lots/Hour)	Availability (A) (Percent)
A	1.00	1.50	1.50	90
B	0.80	1.70	1.25	80
C	0.80	1.70	1.25	88
D	1.20	1.40	1.60	92

(where the variables taking on nonzero values are shown in the shaded cells).

The total number of nonzero variables, each representing the amount of time devoted by machine i to operation j, has an upper limit—in any optimal solution—to the total number of constraints in the LP model. Note that in Figure 13.3 (SOLVER settings) there are exactly seven constraints (recall that the seventh, C21=C22, is not displayed). Consequently, an optimal solution cannot have more than seven nonzero decision variables in the final solution. It will be shown later in the chapter that this is an important point in the development of solutions to such problems as optimally allocating jobs or operations to machines. First, however, let us examine a problem for which the employment of the harmonic means is *not* appropriate. Table 13.4 lists the performance data for a workstation consisting of four machines and supporting three operations.

Notice carefully that the machines do not, as was the case in Table 13.2, have identical process rates for their associated operations. For example, machine A has a process rate of 1 lot per hour for lots requiring operation 1, whereas machine B has a process rate of 0.8 lot per hour for that same operation. In this general case, you must employ the GCM if you hope to determine the correct value of the maximum theoretical capacity.

The optimization model for this problem is listed in Equations (13.11) through (13.20). Other than for the availability values and process rates, the model is identical to that solved previously.

$$\text{Maximize } OP1 \tag{13.11}$$

subject to

$$x(A,1) + x(A,2) + x(A,3) \le 0.90 \tag{13.12}$$

$$x(B,1) + x(B,2) + x(B,3) \le 0.80 \tag{13.13}$$

$$x(C,1) + x(C,2) + x(C,3) \le 0.88 \tag{13.14}$$

$$x(D,1) + x(D,2) + x(D,3) \le 0.92 \tag{13.15}$$

$$OP1 = PR(A,1) \bullet x(A,1) + PR(B,1) \bullet x(B,1) + \\ PR(C,1) \bullet x(C,1) + PR(D,1) \bullet x(D,1) \tag{13.16}$$

$$OP2 = PR(A,2) \bullet x(A,2) + PR(B,2) \bullet x(B,2) + \\ PR(C,2) \bullet x(C,2) + PR(D,2) \bullet x(D,2) \tag{13.17}$$

$$OP3 = PR(A,3) \bullet x(A,3) + PR(B,3) \bullet x(B,3) + \\ PR(C,3) \bullet x(C,3) + PR(D,3) \bullet x(D,3) \tag{13.18}$$

$$OP1 = OP2 = OP3 \tag{13.19}$$

$$x(A,1), x(A,2), \ldots, x(D,2), x(D,3) \ge 0 \tag{13.20}$$

SOLUTION TO SECOND EXAMPLE

Employing the same approach as described previously, the model based on Table 13.4, that is, Equations (13.11) through (13.20), may be solved. The associated spreadsheet representation for the optimal solution is shown in Figure 13.5. Cell I20 contains the maximum theoretical capacity per operation, as determined by optimization, and has a value of 1.5782 lots per hour per operation. The maximum theoretical flow through all three operations is given in cell I21: 4.7347 lots per hour per workstation. The setup of the SOLVER menus happens to be, for this problem, identical to that employed in the preceding model.

F I G U R E   13.5

Spreadsheet representation of MM/MO capacity example.

	A	B	C	D	E	F	G	H	I	J	K
1											
2		Machine	Op 1 (lots/hr)	Op 2 (lots/hr)	Op 3 (lots/hr)	Availability (fraction)		Harmonic Mean	EPR		
3		A	1.00	1.50	1.50	0.90		1.2857	1.1571		
4		B	0.80	1.70	1.25	0.80		1.1371	0.9097		
5		C	0.80	1.70	1.25	0.88		1.1371	1.0007		
6		D	1.20	1.40	1.60	0.92		1.3808	1.2704		
7								Sum =	4.3379		
8		Machine	x(i,1)	x(i,2)	x(i,3)			Max Theor Capacity			
9		A	0.4742	0.0000	0.4258			via Harmonic Mean =	4.3379		
10		B	0.0000	0.8000	0.0000						
11		C	0.0000	0.1284	0.7516						
12		D	0.9200	0.0000	0.0000						
13											
14		Machine	Actual Time		TA(i)						
15		A-time	0.90	ETLT	0.90						
16		B-time	0.80	ETLT	0.80						
17		C-time	0.88	ETLT	0.88						
18		D-time	0.92	ETLT	0.92						
19											
20		OP1 Lots	1.5782					Maximum Capacity per Operation =	1.5782	lots per hour	
21		OP2 Lots	1.5782					Total Lot Flow per Hour (all Operations) =	4.7347	lots per hour	
22		OP3 Lots	1.5782								

For purposes of comparison, the maximum theoretical capacity that would be computed if we erroneously (as indicated in the shaded cells in the top right-hand corner of the spreadsheet) employed the harmonic mean is given in cell I9 and is 4.3379 lots per hour through the workstation, or 1.4460 lots per hour per operation.

The correct maximum theoretical capacity of the workstation actually is 9 percent higher than that computed via the harmonic mean. In other words, if your firm employs the harmonic mean (or any capacity formula based on that mean), you would significantly underestimate the maximum theoretical capacity of this workstation.

MULTIPLE MACHINES, OPERATIONS, AND PRODUCTS

As promised, the GCM may be extended easily to encompass any type of workstation (e.g., multiple machines, multiple operations, multiple products, scrapped lots, inspection lots, etc.). This may be illustrated by means of modeling a problem involving multiple machines, multiple operations, and multiple products. The data for the problem used to illustrate the procedure are listed in Table 13.5.

The problem now faced involves two products, X and Y. We assume that product X must comprise 80 percent of the total volume supported by the workstation, whereas product Y forms the

TABLE 13.5

Multiple Machines, Operations, and Products

Machines \ Operations	Product X			Product Y		
	1 (Lots/Hour)	2 (Lots/Hour)	3 (Lots/Hour)	4 (Lots/Hour)	5 (Lots/Hour)	Availability (A) (Percent)
A	1.00	1.50	1.50	1.80	1.60	90
B	0.80	1.70	1.25	0.00	0.00	80
C	0.80	0.00	1.25	1.20	1.40	88
D	1.20	1.40	1.60	1.00	1.00	92

FIGURE 13.6

Optimal solution to multiproduct example.

	A	B	C	D	E	F	G	H	I	J	K	L
1												
2			*Product One Operations*			*Product Y Operations*						
3		Mach	1	2	3	4	5	Avail				
4		A	1.00	1.50	1.50	1.80	1.60	0.90				
5		B	0.80	1.70	1.25	0.00	0.00	0.80				
6		C	0.80	0.00	1.25	1.20	1.40	0.88				
7		D	1.20	1.40	1.60	1.00	1.00	0.92				
8												
9		Mach	x(i,1)	x(i,2)	x(i,3)	x(i,4)	x(i,5)					
10		A	0.286	0.020	0.400	0.193	0.000					
11		B	0.000	0.800	0.000	0.000	0.000					
12		C	0.000	0.000	0.632	0.000	0.248					
13		D	0.920	0.000	0.000	0.000	0.000					
14												
15		Mach	Actual Time		TA(i)							
16		A-time	0.900	ETLT	0.90							
17		B-time	0.800	ETLT	0.80							
18		C-time	0.880	ETLT	0.88							
19		D-time	0.920	ETLT	0.92							
20												
21		Op1 Lots	1.390									
22		Op2 Lots	1.390	Product X operations								
23		Op 3 Lots	1.390									
24		Op 4 Lots	0.348	Product Y operations								
25		Op 5 Lots	0.348									
26												

remaining 20 percent. Product X requires three operations (1, 2, and 3), whereas product Y involves two (4 and 5). While machines A, C, and D may be used to support the operations of either product, machine B may be used only in support of product X (note the shaded cells for machine B and operations 4 and 5). Finally, machine C is unable to support operation 2 of product X (indicated by the shaded cell under operation 2).

The optimal solution—the maximum theoretical capacity of this workstation—is shown in Figure 13.6. Given the condition that products X and Y comprise, respectively, 80 and 20 percent of the volume of product types supported by the workstation, the maximum theoretical capacity for each of the three operations associated with product X is 1.390 lots per hour, whereas that for each of the two operations for product Y is 0.348 lots per hour. Multiplying each of these results by the number of operations per product, we find that the maximum theoretical capacity of the entire workstation is, for the given product mix, 4.866 lots per hour.

The optimization model for this multiproduct example is shown in Equations (13.21) through (13.36). These equations follow the same pattern as employed in the solution of the MM/MO single-product workstation. Particular attention, however, should be paid to Equations (13.31) through (13.35). These serve to maintain the 80–20 proportions of the two products.

$$\text{Maximize } OP1 \qquad (13.21)$$

subject to

$$x(A,1) + x(A,2) + x(A,3) + x(A,4) + x(A,5) \leq 0.90 \qquad (13.22)$$

$$x(B,1) + x(B,2) + x(B,3) + x(B,4) + x(B,5) \leq 0.80 \qquad (13.23)$$

$$x(C,1) + x(C,2) + x(C,3) + x(C,4) + x(C,5) \leq 0.88 \qquad (13.24)$$

$$x(D,1) + x(D,2) + x(D,3) + x(D,4) + x(D,5) \leq 0.92 \qquad (13.25)$$

$$OP1 = PR(A,1) \bullet x(A,1) + PR(B,1) \bullet x(B,1) + PR(C,1) \bullet x(C,1) + PR(D,1) \bullet x(D,1) \qquad (13.26)$$

$$OP2 = PR(A,2) \bullet x(A,2) + PR(B,2) \bullet x(B,2) + PR(C,2) \bullet x(C,2) + PR(D,2) \bullet x(D,2) \qquad (13.27)$$

$$OP3 = PR(A,3) \bullet x(A,3) + PR(B,3) \bullet x(B,3) + PR(C,3) \bullet x(C,3) + PR(D,3) \bullet x(D,3) \qquad (13.28)$$

$$OP4 = PR(A,4) \bullet x(A,4) + PR(B,4) \bullet x(B,4) + PR(C,4) \bullet x(C,4) + PR(D,4) \bullet x(D,4) \qquad (13.29)$$

$$OP5 = PR(A,5) \bullet x(A,5) + PR(B,5) \bullet x(B,5) + PR(C,5) \bullet x(C,5) + PR(D,5) \bullet x(D,5) \qquad (13.30)$$

$$OP1 = OP2 = OP3 \tag{13.31}$$

$$OP1 = 4 \bullet OP4 = 4 \bullet OP5 \tag{13.32}$$

$$OP2 = 4 \bullet OP4 = 4 \bullet OP5 \tag{13.33}$$

$$OP3 = 4 \bullet OP4 = 4 \bullet OP5 \tag{13.34}$$

$$OP4 = OP5 \tag{13.35}$$

$$x(A,1), x(A,2), \ldots, x(D,4), x(D,5) \geq 0 \tag{13.36}$$

Readers may wish to enter the equivalent mathematical model into SOLVER and employ that package to determine the solution—and compare those results with the results presented in Figure 13.6. The modeling process and SOLVER menus follow a format similar to those employed in the two preceding examples. The problem, in this case, is simply a bit larger in terms of the number of variables and constraints. It should be noted, however, that solutions to models larger than those dealt with thus far may require a different version of SOLVER (e.g., Premium SOLVER) or other LP software capable of dealing with more variables and constraints.

THE FALLACY OF FLEXIBILITY

If we examine the optimal solutions depicted in either Figures 13.1, 13.5, or 13.6, one thing should stand out. This is the fact that the capacity of a workstation is maximized without the need to have every machine dedicated to the support of every operation. This conclusion may fly in the face of conventional wisdom, wherein it may be believed that for the sake of both capacity and *flexibility*, every machine must be capable of supporting every operation assigned to a workstation if its capacity is to be maximized.

The results indicated in Figures 13.1, 13.5, and 13.6 demonstrate that this is not the case; that is, the maximum theoretical workstation capacity was achieved even though some machines were not assigned to the support of some operations. It may be (and has been) demonstrated by means of factory simulations, in fact, that overall factory performance may be improved—sometimes significantly—through the employment of workstation operation-to-machine allocations in which not every machine supports every operation.

These optimal operation-to-machine allocations may be achieved by means of extensions of LP-based models (the GCM model) discussed previously. In this case, however, the models are no longer strictly linear and require software capable of dealing with integer and, in some cases, even nonlinear mathematical models.

OPERATION-TO-MACHINE DEDICATIONS: AN OVERVIEW

In a factory employing reentrancy, determining the allocation of operations to machines (e.g., machine dedications or qualifications) may play a large role in determining workstation and factory performance. In many firms, this decision would appear to be accomplished by heuristic means—most of which seem to have little basis other than judgment and luck. There is a better way. First, however, consider the inherent complexity of the operation-to-machine dedication problem.

Examine, for example, an extremely simple workstation consisting of two machines and two operations. Given no other restrictions, the 16 possible operation-to-machine dedication schemes are listed in Table 13.6. For example, in the first operation-to-machine

TABLE 13.6

Allocation Schemes, Two Machines and Two Operations

Operation-Machine Scheme	Machine 1	Machine 2
1	None	1,2
2	None	1
3	None	2
4	None	None
5	1	None
6	1	1
7	1	2
8	1	1, 2
9	2	None
10	2	1
11	2	2
12	2	1, 2
13	1, 2	None
14	1, 2	1
15	1, 2	2
16	1, 2	1, 2

allocation, machine 1 supports no operations, whereas machine 2 supports two. The fourteenth scheme has machine 1 supporting both operations, whereas machine 2 supports only operation 1.

While not all these schemes are feasible (i.e., schemes 2, 3, 4, 5, 6, 9, and 11 do not provide support for all operations), the table begins to indicate the fact that the operation-to-machine allocation problem is not nearly so simple as it might first appear. More specifically, the operation-to-machine allocation problem is a type of problem known to be *NP-complete,* or in other words, it is *combinatorially explosive.* In plain English, this means that for almost any real-world situation (e.g., a highly reentrant factory), this is an extremely difficult problem to solve.

In general, given M machines and O operations, the total number of operation-to-machine allocation schemes is given as

$$\text{Number of schemes} = 2^{M \bullet O}$$

Thus, in a somewhat more realistic workstation consisting of, say, 16 machines and 12 operations, the number of allocation schemes would be

Number of Boolean (0/1) variables = $M \bullet O = 12 \bullet 16 = 192$
Number of operation-to-machine schemes = 2^{192}
or roughly 6.28e+57.

Consequently, even if we employed one of the world's fastest computers (e.g., running at 35,600 gigaflops per second, i.e., 35,600 billion floating-point operations per second), and even if that supercomputer could evaluate each allocation scheme via only a single floating-point operation (in reality, it would take far more operations), it still would take more than $5.6 \bullet 10^{36}$ years to evaluate all possible allocations. Clearly, the determination of operation-to-machine allocation schemes is not a trivial problem.

The number of constraints that must be employed to describe the problem fully further increases its complexity. For example, any schemes that do not provide support for all operations must be ruled out immediately. In addition there may be operation-to-operation conditions or conflicts. For example, operations X and Y always may have to be performed on the same machine, whereas perhaps operations A and B never can be performed on the same machine.

Another possible constraint may be a result of the physical limitations of the machines in the workstation. For example, there may be a limit on the number of chemicals for which a machine is plumbed. This situation occurs, for example, with photolithography machines, in which no more plumbing than for, say, four different photoresists may be accommodated. Consequently, any operation-to-machine allocation scheme that requires more than four photoresists for that machine would be infeasible.

There are also practical limitations to how many operations should be supported by a given machine and the fact that it takes time and personnel to perform and maintain the operation-to-machine qualifications (e.g., periodic tests, calibrations, etc.) within the respective process specifications. Taken together, the number of possible schemes coupled with practical limitations may serve to form a massively large problem of combinatorial optimization.

Simply put, there is little likelihood that any heuristic approach to the allocation of operations to machines will come close to optimal. In fact, it is almost certain that heuristically derived schemes will be far less effective than the optimal allocation. As such, it would seem reasonable to find an effective, practical way in which to optimally allocate operations to machines.

The following section presents the general mathematical model describing the operation-to-machine problem. While it is based on the GCM of preceding sections, the problem is considerably more complex—as is the mathematical model. In addition, we are no longer able to employ the simple LP model and associated software cited previously. There are, however, a number of commercially available software packages that may be employed to derive optimal or near-optimal solutions. I now proceed to a description of the model for a fairly typical operation-to-machine allocation problem.

OPERATION-TO-MACHINE DEDICATIONS: THE BASIC MODEL

It should be noted that the general form of mathematical model to be presented is not new. The model was developed originally for the representation and solution of reentrant networks (such as certain business processes and supply chains) in the 1990s (Ignizio, 1992b).

While a reentrant business process or supply chain and a reentrant factory would seem to be quite different, their mathematical representations are similar (i.e., either may be represented by a network that includes feedback/reentrant loops). As a consequence, the same fundamental Boolean optimization model (a model in which the variables may take on values of only 0 or 1) employed for supply chains may be employed for the operation-to-machine allocation model.

A quite basic form of the Boolean optimization model that serves to define the operation-to-machine allocation problem is presented below. It is assumed that the problem involves jobs that arrive in the form of lots and that the time period of interest is a 168-hour week. I begin, however, with definitions of the parameters that serve to support the model.

Definitions

- $r(i,j,k)$ = a Boolean variable where $r(i,j,k)$ is 1 if operation k is performed on machine i of lot j during the week and is 0 otherwise.
- $y(i,k)$ = a Boolean variable where $y(i,k)$ is 1 if operation k is qualified on machine i and is 0 otherwise.
- $x(i,r)$ = a Boolean variable where $x(i,r)$ is 1 if machine i uses a chemical (e.g., photoresist) r and is 0 otherwise.
- $\theta(r)$ = the set of operations that require a chemical of type r.
- $R_{max}(i)$ = the maximum number of chemicals of any type that may be allocated to machine i.
- $a(i,k)$ = time required (in hours) for performance of operation k per lot on machine i. Note that this includes any additional average time for rework, test lots, and setups.
- $TA(i)$ = time available per week for performance of any and all operations assigned to machine i. (*Note:* Assume this is 168 hours per week times the availability of the machine.)
- $T(k)$ = the minimum amount of time that must be made available each week for the conduct of operation k, including additional time for rework at the operation (this, in turn, is a function of the desired throughput of the factory).
- gap = minimum gap across all the machines (note that the gap is defined as the difference between the time available on the machine and the time consumed by the operations performed by the machine).
- λ = a small multiplier (e.g., 0.0001 in our case) used to control the values of $x(i,r)$, that is, used in the support of the transformation of a nonlinear function into a linear function.
- M = a large multiplier (e.g., 1,000 in our case) used in support of the transformation of a nonlinear function into a linear function.

- And where
  - $k = 1, \ldots, K$ $i = 1, \ldots, m$ $j = 1, \ldots, n$ $r = 1, \ldots, R$

With these definitions behind us, the formulation of the model to be employed may be presented:

$$\text{Maximize } [gap - \lambda \bullet x(i,r)] \tag{13.37}$$

subject to

$$\sum_{k=1}^{K}\sum_{j=1}^{n}\left[r(i, j, k) \bullet a(i, k)\right] + gap \leq TA\,(i) \quad \text{for all } i \tag{13.38}$$

$$y(i,k) \bullet M \geq \sum_{j=1}^{n} r(i, j, k) \quad \text{for all } i \text{ and } k \tag{13.39}$$

$$\sum_{i=1}^{m} y(i,k) \geq 2 \quad \text{for all } k \tag{13.40}$$

$$\sum_{k=1}^{K} y(i,k) \leq \frac{\text{maximum number of operations on machine } i}{\text{for all } i} \tag{13.41}$$

$$\sum_{i=1}^{m}\sum_{j=1}^{n}\left[r(i, j, k) \bullet a(i, k)\right] \geq T(k) \quad \text{for all } k \tag{13.42}$$

$$\sum_{i=1}^{m} r(i, j, k) = 1 \quad \text{for all } j \text{ and } k \tag{13.43}$$

$$\sum_{k=\theta(r)} y(i,k) \leq x(i,r) \bullet M \quad \text{for all } j \text{ and } r \tag{13.44}$$

$$\sum_{r=1}^{R} x(i,r) \leq R_{\max}(i) \tag{13.45}$$

where $x(i,r)$ and $y(i,k)$ are 0–1 (i.e., Boolean) variables.

We also may add numerous other conditions such as those one would encounter in a real-world factory. For example:

- $y(i,5) + y(i,7) \leq 1$; that is, operations 5 and 7 cannot both be performed on machine i.
- $y(3,3) - y(3,9) = 0$; that is, if operation 3 is performed on machine 3, then operation 9 also must be performed on machine 3.

Each of the functions in the model is described briefly in Table 13.7, and this is followed by a numerical illustration.

TABLE 13.7

Model Components Definitions

Function	Description
(13.37)	Objective function: We seek to maximize the minimum gap across the workstation; that is, balance the workload across the set of machines to minimize factory variability. Subtracted from this is the number of chemicals across the workstation multiplied by some small number (e.g., to set the number of chemicals per machine to zero unless absolutely required to support the constraint set).
(13.38)	Constraint: Limit the time devoted to all the operations on a given machine for the week to less than the total time available on that machine.
(13.39)	Constraint: Ensures that a dedication is made to a machine only if necessary.
(13.40)	Constraint: Ensures that at least two machines are qualified for every operation to maintain redundancy (this number may be adjusted as desired).
(13.41)	Constraint: Limits the maximum number of dedications on each machine.
(13.42)	Constraint: Requires that the time devoted to the operations on the lots equals or exceeds the minimum time required for that week.
(13.43)	Constraint: Ensures that every operation of every machine is supported.
(13.44)	Constraint: Ensures that the variable $x(i,r)$ is set to a value of 1 if and only if this is necessary to satisfy other constraints.
(13.45)	Constraint: The total number of chemicals employed by each machine must be less than its maximum plumbed capacity.
Others	Other constraints (e.g., limitations on the minimum or maximum number of machines qualified per operation or operations qualified per machine).

OPERATION-TO-MACHINE DEDICATIONS: AN ILLUSTRATION

Figure 13.7 presents the final solution for a moderately sized operation-to-machine allocation problem. There are 12 machines in a workstation that happens to support 12 operations. Jobs arrive in batches, with each batch consisting of 4 jobs. Given the process rates and other supporting data (not shown), a 0 in the qualification matrix indicates that the associated machine is not to be qualified for the given operation (e.g., machine 1 will not support operation 1), whereas a 1 means that there is an operation-to-machine allocation (e.g., machine 1 should be qualified to support operation 2).

FIGURE 13.7

Optimal operation-to-machine dedications,

Number of Machines = 12
Number of Operations = 12
Number of Batches = 48
Batch size= 4

QUALIFICATIONS PER MACHINE

	Op 1	Op 2	Op 3	Op 4	Op 5	Op 6	Op 7	Op 8	Op 9	Op 10	Op 11	Op 12	Ops per Mach		TB(I)	GAP(I)
Mach 1	0	1	0	0	0	0	0	1	0	0	0	1	3	TB(1)	132.384	20.610
Mach 2	0	0	0	1	0	0	0	0	0	0	1	1	3	TB(2)	132.384	20.346
Mach 3	0	1	1	1	0	1	0	0	0	1	0	0	5	TB(3)	132.384	20.601
Mach 4	0	1	0	0	0	0	0	1	0	1	0	0	3	TB(4)	132.384	21.557
Mach 5	0	0	1	0	0	1	0	1	0	0	0	1	4	TB(5)	132.384	21.296
Mach 6	1	1	0	1	0	1	0	0	0	0	0	0	4	TB(6)	132.384	21.030
Mach 7	0	0	1	0	0	0	0	0	1	0	1	0	3	TB(7)	132.384	20.352
Mach 8	1	0	0	0	1	0	1	0	0	0	0	0	3	TB(8)	132.384	20.352
Mach 9	0	1	0	0	1	0	1	1	0	0	0	0	4	TB(9)	132.384	20.557
Mach 10	0	0	1	0	0	0	1	0	1	0	1	0	4	TB(10)	132.384	20.472
Mach 11	1	0	1	0	1	0	0	0	0	0	0	0	3	TB(11)	132.384	21.179
Mach 12	0	0	1	0	0	0	1	0	1	1	1	0	5	TB(12)	132.384	20.712
Machines per Layer	3	5	6	3	3	3	4	4	3	3	4	3	44		Min Gap=	20.346

	T(1)	T(2)	T(3)	T(4)	T(5)	T(6)	T(7)	T(8)	T(9)	T(10)	T(11)	T(12)
T(k)	98.2	102.9	98.2	102.9	98.2	93.7	98.2	93.4	98.2	93.4	98.2	93.4
Actual	114.0	121.4	113.6	121.1	111.1	107.3	111.1	106.2	111.1	105.9	110.9	105.9

Note that only 44 of the possible 144 qualifications (i.e., all 12 machines qualified for all 12 operations) are employed in the optimal solution.

Based on extensive simulations, the employment of optimal operation-to-machine dedications in place of more common approaches (e.g., intuition, guesses, etc.) indicates that factory performance is often improved anywhere from 5 to 20 percent through the optimization of operation-to-machine dedications. The reason for this lies primarily in the balance in the loading of the individual machines in the workstation.

This approach to balance should not be confused with the notion of balanced production lines, however (i.e., the so-called fundamental premise of lean manufacturing). Here we are striving to produce equal gaps (differences between the time available on individual machines and the time consumed in processing). Balanced production lines, on the other hand, seek to have equal cycle times among all the workstations in the production line.

To conclude our discussion, I now indicate how to estimate the maximum sustainable capacity of a workstation. This may be done once the maximum theoretical capacity has been determined, as has been described.

ESTIMATING MAXIMUM SUSTAINABLE CAPACITY

The GCM provides us with an accurate determination of the maximum theoretical capacity of a workstation and, by extension, that of the factory. By combining it with the three fundamental equations of manufacturing, we may—at least in theory—estimate the maximum sustainable capacity.

Consider, for example, the most simple factory type, one in which there is no batching, no reentrancy, and only one machine supports a given process step. The formula for the cycle time of such a process step is given by the most basic form of the second fundamental equation of manufacturing:

$$CT_{ps} = \underbrace{\left(\frac{C_{AR}^2 + C_{EPT}^2}{2}\right) \bullet \left[\frac{\rho}{(1-\rho)}\right] \bullet \left(\frac{1}{EPR_{ps}}\right)}_{\text{wait in queue time}} + \underbrace{\left(\frac{1}{EPR_{ps}}\right)}_{\text{effective process time}} \quad (13.46)$$

Recall from Chapter 3 that the occupancy rate (i.e., utilization) of these machines is expressed by

$$\rho = \frac{AR}{EPR} \quad (13.47)$$

By using Equations (13.46) (and assuming that arrival rate and effective process-time variability are known) and (13.47), it may be shown that the maximum permissible value of the arrival rate for the maximum tolerable cycle time of the process step is

$$AR_{max} \leq EPR \bullet \rho_{max} \quad (13.48)$$

The value for ρ_{max} is found by substitution into Equation (13.46) (given the maximum permissible value for the cycle time of the process step). The value of EPR is found by means of the GCM. Thus, assuming that ρ_{max} is 90 percent and the value of EPR is 3 lots per hour, the maximum permissible arrival rate is

$$AR_{max} \leq EPR \bullet \rho_{max} = 0.90 \bullet 3 \text{ lots/hour} = 2.7 \text{ lots/hour}$$

In other words, the maximum sustainable capacity at this process step is 2.7 lots per hour.

To determine the maximum sustainable capacity of the entire production line would require the summing of the formulas of cycle times for each of the process steps—given the maximum permissible value of total factory cycle time. For a simple factory with relatively few process steps, this could, in practice, be computed. More realistic factories with many process steps would be more involved, but the solution still would be possible theoretically.

In the real world, the time and effort involved most likely would not be worthwhile or even necessary. More specifically, virtually all the terms in the fundamental equations are estimates—some of which may be very rough estimates. As such, rather than attempting to determine the maximum sustainable capacity of a workstation precisely, it is, I believe, more rational to employ an approximation.

Table 13.8 lists approximations that have produced more than adequate results for certain classes of real-world factories (and decent approximations for most all types). The values for the coefficients of variability (CoV) for the last three columns are found by finding the average of the CoV of job arrivals at a processing entity (e.g., a workstation) and that of the effective process times of the machines forming that entity.[2]

To illustrate, assume that a workstation in the factory of interest has a maximum theoretical capacity (found by means of the GCM) of 4,000 units per week. Furthermore, the average coefficient of variability of job arrivals at the workstation is 1.4, whereas the average coefficient of variability of its effective process times is 2.2. The average of these two values (i.e., $2.2 + 1.4 \div 2$) is 1.8. This means that the factor that should be used is, from Table 13.8, a value of 0.90. To estimate the maximum sustainable capacity, we multiply the maximum theoretical capacity by this factor. The

TABLE 13.8

Maximum Sustainable Capacity Factors

	CoV < 1	1 ≤ CoV < 2	2 ≤ CoV < 3
Factor	0.93	0.90	0.87

2 Alternately, you may use the average of the CoV values of job arrivals (e.g., at a factory) and job departures. This also seems to produce reasonable estimates.

result (4,000 jobs per week $\times$ 0.9) is 3,600 jobs per week and represents a reasonable estimate of the maximum sustainable capacity of the workstation. The maximum sustainable capacity of the factory, in turn, is simply the minimum of those of all the workstations in the factory.

While numerous other extensions of the GCM may be developed, I conclude the discussion of this topic here.

CHAPTER SUMMARY

The GCM may be used to determine the maximum theoretical capacity of a given workstation and thus the maximum theoretical capacity of an entire factory. Extensions of the GCM permit the modeling and solution of a number of important factory problems, including a determination of the optimal operation-to-machine qualification problem. Finally, by means of an adjustment factor, one may develop reasonably accurate estimates of the maximum sustainable capacity of a workstation or an entire factory.

CASE STUDY 13: IT'S SHOWTIME

Ben Arnold and his two fellow plant managers are uncharacteristically quiet during Winston's presentation. Not only does Winston claim that factory performance may be improved immensely by means of a few straightforward and inexpensive efforts, but he also has the audacity to state that an increase in factory moves—by itself, as ordered by Ben—will absolutely destroy performance. Finishing the presentation, Winston asks if there are any questions.

Ben, smirking, responds, "Are you three out of your mind? Just because those weird ideas worked on your simulation models means absolutely nothing. None of you has ever run a real factory, just those silly simulation models. My intuition, and it never fails me, is that your nutty proposal likely will destroy us."

"But," argues Dan, "Winston has just showed you that increasing factory moves definitely will destroy this factory. Don't you remember what happened when Tommy Jenkins increased factory starts? What will it take to convince you? Do you really want to help this company?"

"Mr. Ryan," says Ben, "you're fired. I want you off this campus by the end of the workday."

Winston and Julia realize that there is no point in any further discussion. Each is convinced that he or she will be the next to be fired.

"As for you two," says Ben, pointing to Julia and Winston, "you've used unauthorized simulation models in support of your efforts. That's a clear violation of this firm's 'No Deviations' policy. You've also rebuilt company computers, computers that could have been sold for scrap. That's likely a felony, although I'll have to check with our corporate lawyers."

"Are we all fired?" asks Julia.

"For the moment, only Mr. Ryan is terminated," Ben replies. "My colleagues and I will discuss the matter. You'll have our decision by the end of the week."

Julia and Winston are in the "war room." The silence is broken by a question from Julia.

"Winston, why didn't they just fire us on the spot, like they did with Dan?"

"My guess is that they may be concerned that we might hire on to one of Muddle's competitors. I'm guessing that's what they're discussing right now."

"Winston, dear Winston, why don't *we* make this decision? Why wait for them? Why on earth should we stay with this company? As long as it's run by people like Marvin Muddle, Jack Gibson, and Ben Arnold, nothing is going to change."

CHAPTER 13 EXERCISES

1. Employ LP (e.g., the SOLVER package) to check and verify the results obtained for the maximum theoretical capacities of the workstations depicted in Tables 13.2, 13.4, and 13.5.

2. A factory has a coefficient of variability for factory starts of 3.0 and an average coefficient of variability for effective process times of 2.3. The maximum theoretical capacity of the factory's constraint is 10,000 units per week. What is its estimated maximum sustainable capacity?

CHAPTER 14

The Elements of Success

As has been emphasized repeatedly, the three enemies of factory performance are variability, complexity, and lackluster leadership. The preceding chapters have dealt mostly with ways in which to identify and mitigate variability and complexity. Less coverage has been devoted, however, to dealing with lackluster leadership or, in particular, the specific details of how to conduct an efficient, successful, and sustainable factory performance-improvement effort. I attempt to rectify these omissions in this chapter.

DOS AND DON'TS

There are certain fundamental rules that must be adhered to if any effort toward factory performance improvement is to produce significant and sustainable results. Some of these are summarized in the following list of dos and don'ts:

- Do seek to find the cause of and cure for factory performance problems. Don't seek simply to soothe the symptoms.
- Do focus your efforts on reducing variability and complexity while recognizing that there invariably will be resistance and skepticism within the typical organization toward virtually any change.
- Do seek the approval and, hopefully, involvement of senior management up to and including the firm's CEO; but don't expect this to happen without either a successful "marketing" effort (i.e., an effort taken to convince

management of the crucial importance of performance
improvement) or solid and impressive evidence of some
success (e.g., via a pilot study or relatively small-scale
performance-improvement effort).

- Do select the right individual to lead the effort, that is, an
individual with the education, experience, vision, and
fortitude necessary to successfully implement the protocols
necessary for performance improvement.
- Don't choose a performance-improvement leader whose
only—or main—"strengths" are self-promotion, cronyism,
and the propagation of unsubstantiated claims. In particular,
don't select a leader who has a habit of taking credit for the
ideas of others—particularly if they are the ideas of his or
her subordinates. (While this would seem to be obvious, it is
a sad fact that the culture inherent in some firms virtually
ensures that such dodgy individuals are selected.)
- Do provide the necessary education and training for
members of the group advancing the factory performance-
improvement effort. Don't expect this to be accomplished
in a day, week, or even a month. Do recognize that
management may resist this crucial step and be prepared
to advance arguments that support the need for education
and training.
- Do recognize the obstacles that will be faced in any
attempt to achieve significant and sustainable performance
improvement within an organization that happens to be
void of leadership and encumbered by a culture that not
only resists but also fears change. While success may be
possible in such an organization, it will require an
immense amount of patience, passion, endurance, courage,
and conviction.
- Don't separate improvement efforts in maintenance
from those in operations. Do recognize that the same
three enemies of manufacturing and the same three
fundamental equations of manufacturing hold just as true
for maintenance.[1]

---

1 Factory performance-improvement efforts must focus on improving the *overall*
performance of the entire factory. Dividing performance-improvement efforts into,
say, those focused on cost reduction, those dealing with operational protocols, and
those fixed on maintenance serve only to divide and degrade what could and
should be a unified effort. Such a division is a recipe for failure.

- Do learn from the mistakes of others, including the fictional blunders described in the Muddle case studies.
- Don't limit your focus in terms of performance improvement to cost reduction. Do recognize that sustainable increases in profit, market share, and customer satisfaction should be a firm's primary goals.
- Do take the time and effort necessary to appreciate the history of manufacturing so as not to, as just one example, blindly accept the promises of the promoters of the latest manufacturing or management fad.

A CENTER FOR MANUFACTURING SCIENCE

The most promising and cost-effective path that may be taken to achieve overall performance improvement in a factory is to launch a center for manufacturing science. Obtaining approval to establish such a center may meet with resistance, though. It even may be perceived as a threat to the status quo. Ironically, although not surprisingly, the worse the performance of a firm's factories and the more lackluster its leadership, the harder it may be to gain management support for such an institute.

One way to gain the necessary backing for such a center is to mimic the marketing techniques employed by successful (at least in terms of receiving recognition and exorbitant fees) management consultants and motivational speakers. Even when they have little or nothing of substantive value to offer an organization—and even when there is no credible evidence whatsoever that their proposals will provide significant and sustainable improvement—they may, and often do, receive a rousing reception by top management, desperate for a quick and easy solution to the firm's woes.

By no means, however, am I suggesting that you lie, exaggerate, or make promises you know you cannot keep. What one needs to recognize, and what the most successful management consultants and motivational speakers provide an example of, is that you must package and market your product properly. The product in this case is the need for science in manufacturing and an appreciation of the powers of production-line protocols, that is, the benefits that may be accrued via exploitation of the third dimension of manufacturing.

Some managers may react negatively to any suggestion of a need for science, and thus rather than calling it a center for manufacturing science, you might want to call it a center for improved factory performance or possibly something even more alluring (and vague) such as a center for excellence in factory performance. *Excellence*, it would seem, is a noun that few are able to resist—just look at the titles of some of the most successful management books. Of course, as a last resort, you may have to name the unit the center for cost reduction. Hopefully, it won't come to this, but sometimes desperate measures are needed to deal with desperate situations.

You will be more likely to have such a center approved if you propose to begin relatively small, that is, no more than 6 to 12 personnel and modest requests for space and other support. The key to the ultimate success of such a center lies in two factors: (1) finding a corporate champion and (2) the qualifications and motivation of the team assembled. Before even considering seeking approval for such a center, both these matters should be considered.

The corporate champion should be someone who is approachable, open to new ideas, and hopefully, aware of the need for improvement in the firm's factories. The champion must have direct access to senior management and ideally the firm's CEO. In addition, the champion must recognize that the status quo will no longer suffice and that real, meaningful change is required. You must realize that if this champion is to stick his or her neck out for you, he or she must have confidence in your team's ability to obtain results. The champion wants to enhance his or her stature in the organization. Consequently, this person must be convinced— by your business plan and marketing skills—that the establishment of such a center will result in significant and visible results (e.g., evident all the way up to the CEO). In short, you want to convince this champion—perhaps without coming right out and saying it— that the center will serve to make the champion "look good."

Even before seeking out a corporate champion, you will be well served to establish a list of potential members of the center. Just as with the corporate champion, you must be able to persuade them that this endeavor will enhance their experience and job satisfaction and, if successful, advance their career prospects. This is something that you should be able to do if you are comfortable with the material presented in this book.

It should be noted that you or whomever the person may be who is advancing the idea of factory performance improvement and a center for excellence in manufacturing may not be the person best suited to lead such an effort. As Clint Eastwood said in his role as Dirty Harry, "a man's got to know his limitations."

If this person is a leader, then he or she may want to seek the position as leader of the group. If, however, the person is more comfortable with and more proficient at actually implementing the art and science of manufacturing, he or she might want to be the team's technical advisor or technical expert. In any event, if the individual is not comfortable with marketing the center, he or she should consider a position that will enhance the team rather than pursue what are possibly unrealistic aspirations.

Ultimately, the center's primary technical advisor (a.k.a. *internal consultant*) will determine the actual success of the center and the performance-improvement efforts. First, however, the need for the center must be marketed successfully, and later, its successes must be publicized (tastefully yet effectively). Hopefully, the leader selected for the center will be a person who gives credit where credit is due. If not, the morale, cohesion, and retention of the team assembled will be at extreme risk.

The remaining members of the team should be individuals selected on the basis of their motivation, willingness to work as a team, and technical qualifications. Perhaps the most important of these three attributes is motivation. Even if a team member is not an international expert in the politics, art, and science of manufacturing and its third dimension, he or she must have the motivation, discipline, and desire to become sufficiently well educated in these areas. He or she also should have an ancillary skill that directly supports the efforts of the center. Particularly helpful skills include

- Data collection, processing, and interpretation
- Simulation model development, exercise, and analysis
- Statistical analysis and the modeling of stochastic systems
- Operational research, systems engineering, and/or industrial engineering
- Knowledge acquisition and knowledge engineering
- Safety engineering and ergonomics
- Finance
- Human and organizational dynamics
- An appreciation of (and, as a distinct plus, actual factory floor experience in) the firm's factory operations, processes, and procedures

Ideally—and hopefully—the personnel comprising the team should be among the best and brightest of the firm's people. Unfortunately, there may be a temptation among management to

assign personnel who at the moment "have no significant responsibilities" (these are, alas, code words to describe individuals in the
firm who have shown so little motivation and skill as to not have
made a positive impact on the organization—and are unlikely to
do so in the future).

The final matter to be determined is that of the prioritization
of the factory performance efforts to be undertaken. Management
is typically, if not invariably, impatient for results, so the efforts initially undertaken should be those that (1) may be conducted relatively quickly, (2) are expected to produce significant results, and
(3) are most likely to be concluded successfully. Efforts possessing
such favorable attributes include

- Improvements in the factory starts protocol (e.g., starts
  declustering)
- Allocation of maintenance technicians to workstations
- Declustering of preventive maintenance (PM) events
- Removal or refinement of the production-line process steps
- Reduction of batch sizes

Ultimately, an educational outreach effort should be undertaken as early as possible in the life of the center. Short courses introducing the third dimension of manufacturing should be provided
company-wide. Attendance should include employees at all levels
and, in particular, plant managers, factory department managers,
and senior factory engineers. Those attending these short courses
should be encouraged to ask questions and explore possible causes
of performance degradation within their factories and/or business
processes. Rather than the presentation of a "course" in which the
attendees are passive observers of PowerPoint slides, each person
should be expected to participate.

In lieu of the establishment of a center for excellence in manufacturing, adoption and retention of the methods and philosophy
of the topics contained in this book are less likely—at least until the
present generation of managers moves on. However, there have
been a few "grassroots" efforts that have achieved some degree
of success.

In at least one factory within one multinational firm, the sheer
doggedness and determination of a few individuals, coupled with
the encouragement of a factory manager, resulted in a truly significant improvement in overall factory performance. While there has
yet to be (at least at the time these words are being written) adequate

appreciation of these efforts across the firm, there is at least some hope that over time the methods employed will receive the acceptance due them.

LEADERS VERSUS MANAGERS

One of the three enemies of performance is lackluster (or absence of) leadership. Of all the obstacles faced in factory performance improvement, this is by far the most difficult to overcome. Furthermore, while you might get away with informing corporate management that its factories are beset with unnecessary complexity and variability, it is unlikely that these same individuals will take kindly to any hint that they lack the attributes necessary for leadership.

First of all, however, it is important to recognize that leaders are not necessarily managers and managers are not necessarily leaders. Advancement to management positions within a firm are often a result of exceptional performance (or at least exceptional as perceived by one's superiors) in the management of a group, program, or project. For example, if a program is accomplished on time and within budget, this may be a sign of a person with good management skills, that is, the ability to assign personnel, schedule events, hold meetings, and overcome the obstacles common to almost any complex effort. While such a person may possess the necessary qualifications to be a manager, he or she may fall short of those required to be a leader.

The qualities that distinguish leaders from simply managers are not easy (and some would say impossible) to specify. Some leaders also may be competent managers. Many managers, however, lack the charisma, vision, and communication skills necessary to lead. As a consequence, some managers may focus their attention and efforts toward the development of mission plans, the invention of slogans, the establishment of goals (e.g., particularly short-term financial and market-share goals that appeal to Wall Street analysts), and the maintenance of their power and position (e.g., by means of currying favor with their superiors or populating the board of directors with those of a like mind).

Managers of this ilk are little more than departmental or corporate caretakers, advocates of the status quo, and they usually fail to inspire their subordinates and employees. While they can play an important role in the organization, they are more likely to push rather than to lead.

A leader, on the other hand, is willing to take reasonable risks and provide the means to accomplish the organization's goals (as opposed to simply voicing them and demanding results) and is able to inspire those he or she leads—as well as gain their loyalty. This does not necessarily mean that everyone in the organization will always agree with the vision and decisions of the leader. In fact, if this were the case, there probably would be no need for leadership.

It is also important to recognize that some leaders set their followers on precisely the wrong path (e.g., Hitler, Mussolini, Stalin, and Jim Jones of Jonestown infamy). They may have the charm, magnetism, and verbal gifts to attract a following, but they have chosen the wrong path. As such, it is vital that a leader have a vision that will enhance the organization (and possibly the state, the nation, and even the world) rather than advance a hallucination that leads to degradation and despair.

Another important, if not crucial, attribute of a successful leader is a willingness to listen to opposing viewpoints. Individuals in a position of power who refuse to hear anything with which they disagree guarantee a dysfunctional culture.

Saddam Hussein, for example, was able—through treachery, deceit, unbridled force, and outright terror—to become the president of Iraq. Like other tyrants before him, he had a vision—one in which he and a favored few prospered while most of his people suffered. While some have claimed that Hussein was a leader, consider his unwillingness to tolerate any views other than those he already espoused. If you were foolish enough to tell Hussein something that might well be true but counter to his personal belief, you risked having your tongue cut out or worse.

If you are to be successful in gaining the support of senior management and, hopefully, the CEO, you would be well advised to determine whether you are dealing with a manager or a leader. Managers are generally more risk adverse, less approachable, and more resistant to new ideas than leaders. If you recognize this and advance and package your proposal (e.g., for factory performance improvement or the initiation of a center for excellence in manufacturing) accordingly, your chances of obtaining the approval and resources necessary to initiate a meaningful improvement effort will be enhanced. Furthermore, if you are dealing with a manager rather than a leader, you must be able to (discreetly) convince him or her that the advancement of your proposal will benefit the manager directly.

On the other hand, if you are dealing with a leader, your plan for the advancement and acceptance of your proposal may have to be adapted to that which will appeal to this type of individual. While the typical manager will be more receptive to proposals that benefit his or her position and maintain or enlarge his or her sphere of influence, a leader may be more positively inclined to consider a proposal that will serve to achieve—or at least advance—the leader's vision.

This is not meant to imply that managers have huge egos and leaders are altruistic, selfless, and noble. Leaders can and often do have massive egos (e.g., George Patton, Napoleon, and Wellington). A difference between a manager and a leader is that a manager's ego is enhanced by maintaining and enhancing his or her power and position, whereas a leader's ego is most often fed by events that prove his or her vision to be the right one.

In the real world, you rarely, if ever, meet a pure manager or a pure leader. Most managers have at least some degree of leadership ability. Most managers—unlike some of those discussed in the Muddle Corporation case studies—are decent, honest, intelligent, and creative, but most exhibit the attributes and inclinations of a manager more so than those of a leader. Most leaders, on the other hand, have an ability to manage but prefer to lead.

These distinctions should be kept in mind if you have been given the opportunity to present your case for factory performance improvement to a firm's CEO and/or senior officers. They also should be considered when deciding on the leadership of the center for excellence in manufacturing.

EDUCATION AND TRAINING

As discussed in Chapter 1, it is my personal opinion that few academic or corporate training programs provide the education necessary to accomplish significant and sustainable improvement in factory performance. As just one example, consider today's academic programs in industrial and manufacturing engineering. While there are classes in a variety of useful topics, courses in classical industrial engineering and scientific management—the very foundation for the Toyota production system/lean manufacturing—became almost passé by the 1970s, replaced by classes that were considered to be more scholarly and more in step with modern times.

As a consequence, one could—and many did—graduate with a degree in industrial or manufacturing engineering with little or no appreciation of the contributions of Frederick Taylor, Frank and Lillian Gibreth, Harrington Emerson, Walter Shewhart, W. Edwards Deming, and Joseph Juran. Academic amnesia has reached such a point that it is believed by many that the Toyota production system emerged on its own and that the fundamental concepts of lean manufacturing are brand new.

Some have gone so far as to term this the *Topsy syndrome,* in reference to a quote from the unfortunate young slave girl in the novel, *Uncle Tom's Cabin.* When asked about her parents, Topsy replied, "I s'pect I just growed. Don't think nobody never made me." Her ignorance of her origin was sad but understandable. Ignorance of the history of manufacturing, however, should not be tolerated. The individuals and concepts that "made" the Toyota production system must be recognized, along with events, successes, and failures in the evolution of manufacturing.

As such, the history of manufacturing must be encompassed in any educational program for members of a factory performance-improvement team. No one finishing such a program should ever go away believing that the Toyota production system/lean manufacturing "just growed."

This book was written with the intention of providing material for support of the educational program advocated by me. Other excellent books exist (Hopp and Spearman, 2001; Levinson, 2002; Meyer, 1993; Standard and Davis, 1999) that may serve to augment this effort. The important point to be recognized, however, is that the educational program must provide attendees with a solid basis for an appreciation of the need for factory performance improvement and the means to achieve it in actual practice. Furthermore, it must be recognized that it takes more than cute slogans, clever diagrams, empty promises, and vague guidelines to achieve improvement.

Some firms have assumed, alas, that the educational process may be accomplished by a few hours or few days of exposure to PowerPoint slides. This naive notion (and mind-numbing approach) is a recipe for failure. While such a program—if limited to an hour or two and very carefully developed—might suffice to introduce senior management to the bare fundamentals of the art and science of manufacturing and its third dimension; it cannot possibly provide an adequate foundation for successful efforts in factory performance improvement.

One of the biggest mistakes management can make is to equate a course in manufacturing's third dimension to one in, say, how to position your computer's flat screen on your desk or how to fill out a purchase order. This sends a message to the firm's employees that management has equated the degree of knowledge required to improve factory performance to that necessary to perform an ordinary, mechanical, and mundane task. It also reveals the fact that any manager making such a statement has no experience in (and possibly no interest in) conducting any meaningful improvement efforts.

For those who will lead and/or directly participate in such efforts, a program extending over at least two weeks (and classes of six to eight hours per day) is recommended. Most important, the presentations/lectures must consist of something more than PowerPoint slide shows. Questions must be asked of attendees by instructors competent to do so—and instructors must be prepared to provide thoughtful and intelligent answers to the questions posed by attendees.[2] This requires something more—something far more—than the ability to hit the PowerPoint presentation advance key on the computer.

Ideally, quizzes and comprehensive exams should be part of the course. In an academic environment, this is expected. In a company training course, this practice may come as a rude shock—and even frighten away those who might benefit most from the material. To mitigate this reaction, it has been my practice to grade the quizzes and exams while assuring attendees that the grades will be kept absolutely confidential. This practice may be met with skepticism, but student feedback, in terms of graded papers, serves a vital, if not essential, role in education. It also discourages course attendees from "multitasking" (e.g., pretending to listen while surfing the Web on their laptops or responding to or sending e-mails) during course presentations. And trust me, without quizzes, exams, and class participation, multitasking will be the norm.

Once the formal course has been completed (or at least the majority of key points covered), attendees should be involved in meaningful and carefully planned exercises outside the classroom. Walks through the factory, development of process-step-centric flowcharts (possibly limited to just a segment of the production

---

2 Individuals who "instruct" by means of nothing more than advancing the slides in a PowerPoint presentation are not instructors; they are readers.

340   CHAPTER 14

line), examination and discussion of existing operating and maintenance specifications, collection of data such as the arrival times of jobs at a workstation, and assessment of such matters as factory start protocols are excellent first steps.

These relatively simple events often lead to observations and recommendations that serve to measurably improve factory performance—and lend credibility to the leverage potentially achievable by a simple change in factory protocols. Equally important, these experiences invariably serve to impress on attendees the importance and validity of the classroom experience.

Whatever the recommendations made by novice factory performance-improvement personnel, the instructor always should ask certain questions of the novice; that is,

- What motivated the recommendation (e.g., observation of data or observations on the factory floor)?
- Why does the novice believe the change will improve performance?
- Is the novice able to present a defense of his or her argument?
- What is the scientific foundation for the recommendation (e.g., how and why might it reduce variability)?

In other words, the novice must be capable of justifying any changes proposed. And this justification must be based on more than just hunches, past experience, and intuition. Until the novice is able to provide a solid, defensible rationale for any recommendations for changes, that person will remain a novice and should not be entrusted with the sole leadership of a performance-improvement effort.

WHAT ABOUT LEAN MANUFACTURING, ETC.?

If you have read and understood the material in the preceding chapters, you already should have the answer to the question, "What about lean manufacturing, Six Sigma, total productive maintenance, etc.?" In case you need a refresher, however, the answer will be summarized briefly in this section.

The fundamental concepts found in lean manufacturing, Six Sigma, total productive maintenance, theory of constraints, and a host of other proposals for factory performance improvement are encompassed within the material you have already (or should have already) covered. One difference, however, has been that of terminology. I have—definitely, intentionally, and unapologetically— avoided the use of Japanese words and phrases (e.g., *muda, mura, muri, kaizen, poke-a-yoke*, etc.) and instead have employed the words and phrases originated by the pioneers of scientific management (and only later translated into Japanese).

The primary difference, however, has been a matter of emphasis. Advocates of lean manufacturing, for example, typically focus their attention on a subset of the causes of complexity and variability and most often avoid any discussion of the culture and politics of the organization. Advocates of total productive maintenance focus their attention primarily on maintenance while mostly ignoring the fact that isolating maintenance protocols from nonmaintenance activities within a factory is counterproductive. This arbitrary separation may and often does build a wall between maintenance and operations that leads to decisions in one sector that have a negative impact on performance in the other.

The fact is that these concepts (i.e., lean manufacturing, Six Sigma, theory of constraints, total productive maintenance, and whatever might be the next "hot thing") represent a segmented reincarnation of the notions and practices embodied within their broader predecessors, that is, scientific management and classical industrial engineering. None of these "new" concepts is actually new, but each has a role to play, and each—if pursued properly— leads to improvements in factory performance.

One purpose of this book is to gather these fragments together under a unifying theme, that is, the politics, art, and science of production as practiced within the third dimension of manufacturing. Such unification should avoid the failure and disappointment rate now faced by these concepts when used in isolation. In short, the ideas and notions encompassed within lean manufacturing, theory of constraints, total productive maintenance, Six Sigma, and reengineering are important but are far more likely to achieve significant and sustainable improvement in factory performance if they are presented and employed in a unified fashion. Hopefully, this conclusion—and paragraph—will correct any misperception that I oppose the use of these methodologies. What I do oppose is their use in isolation and—in particular—where it is assumed that they are *the* answer.

OUTSIDE CONSULTANTS

As a final note on the elements required for a successful factory performance-improvement effort, we should consider the employment and role of outside consultants. An outside consultant, if chosen carefully, may serve to advance performance-improvement efforts significantly. Unfortunately, the wrong outside consultant—one who relies on slogans and has only a superficial comprehension of the complexity of a factory—can and will do more harm than good.

There is one thing that an outside consultant often can accomplish that is less likely to be achieved by the corporation's rank and file. This is the consultant's ability to find an audience with the firm's top management and perhaps even its CEO. There is a certain mystique about outside consultants. While they may be nothing more than a reasonably articulate person (with slides) who resides at least 100 miles away, they often are perceived to have knowledge that doesn't exist within the organization. This may be true, even though far more knowledgeable—and capable—individuals may reside in virtual obscurity within the firm's cubicles.

An outside consultant who is perceived as "the answer" is often able to convince management of the need to initiate certain efforts that simply would not be considered if proposed by a member of the firm's rank and file. Unfortunately, this also means that the consultant may be able to persuade management to undertake efforts that are counterproductive. Intriguingly, managers often seek the advice of outside consultants who have—never once—managed any effort or program of any meaningful size or complexity. This is akin to asking a stranger, a person who has never once played tennis, to teach your children how to become proficient at that game.

Consultants have the luxury of giving advice, receiving their compensation, and walking away. By the time their recommendations have been implemented (and have either succeeded or failed), they are on their way to their next consulting or speaking engagement.

This is not to imply that there are not some very capable consultants—individuals whose advice will advance the fortunes of their clients. The difficulty is, however, in determining whether a consultant will prove worth the expense or not.

One way to separate the good from the bad is to carefully evaluate the consultant's achievements, either real or perceived.

Selection of a consultant should require the same amount of time, effort, and investigation as selection of, say, a member of the board of directors or a senior executive. After all, a poor choice can inflict considerable damage to the firm. (Consider, for example, the immense damage that some "reengineering" consultants inflicted on their clients in the 1990s.) In short, some degree of skepticism is warranted in the selection and use of an outside consultant.

As someone who actually has served as a manager, I developed a list of red flags that I employed when considering the hire of an outside consultant. Anyone who exhibited the majority of these red flags was immediately shown the door. Those who exhibited several were assigned to the "suspect list." These red flags include

- Indications of the "one-trick-pony syndrome," that is, assertions that the particular concept being advanced is *the* answer—to whatever the situation
- Promises of quick-and-easy solutions
- Name dropping
- Record of hopping from one management or manufacturing fad to another
- Lack of knowledge of the history of manufacturing
- Lack of knowledge of or a reluctance to discuss alternate approaches
- Reliance on slogans and the proposal of vacuous guidelines
- Reluctance to participate in the actual implementation of any efforts that might be recommended
- Authorship of books and speeches long on promises but short on specifics
- Inability to cite specifics and get to the point when asked a direct question
- Unwillingness to admit to not knowing the answer to every question
- Unwillingness to spend any significant time on the factory floor and observing existing protocols
- Lack of awareness of or interest in the fundamental equations of manufacturing or an outright dismissal of their importance
- Inability to differentiate methods appropriate for synchronous factories from those designed for asynchronous facilities

- Excessive employment of such fuzzy and faddish terms as *excellence, robust, Pareto, strengths, actionable, bandwidth, multitasking, best practices, drill down, low-hanging fruit, learnings, paradigm shift, synergy,* and *teaming.*

CHAPTER SUMMARY

The successful accomplishment of any and all efforts devoted to improving factory performance requires more than the simple assignment of a team to a task (particularly if it is implied that the effort is to be in addition to the conduct of their existing activities). A corporate champion is a necessity in most firms, and the establishment of a center (e.g., center for excellence in manufacturing) is highly desirable. These basic elements, coupled with adequate education and training in the art and science of manufacturing, are the first steps toward success.

CASE STUDY 14: WHAT'S THE WEATHER LIKE IN FARGO?

Professor Aristotle Leonidas has invited Julia, Winston, and Dan to his home. He has as yet given no reason for the gathering. Each person seems lost in his or her own thoughts, and the only sound to be heard is that of a distant waterfall.

"Children," says the professor, breaking the silence, "what are your plans now that you're no longer employed by the Muddle Corporation?"

"Winston and I are considering starting our own consulting company," Julia answers. "We're convinced that the methods you've taught us could be put to use in supply-chain performance improvement. After all, as you told us, the underlying mathematical models of supply chains and factories are nearly identical. Reduce the complexity and variability in a supply chain and you've found the answer to improved performance."

"What about you, Dan?" asks the professor.

"I'm thinking about going to work for one of Muddle's competitors. Most of them operate just as inefficiently as Muddle. Maybe one of those firms will be more receptive to the methods you've taught us."

"Those are all good ideas," says the professor. "But I'd like to offer the three of you another option. One of Muddle's older, smaller factories has been sold to a group of investors. They're looking for people to get it up and running and to operate it efficiently. It doesn't produce Muddle's primary product, but it has been used to manufacture a supporting part. I think the new owners would look favorably on hiring any one or all three of you. Julia would make a fine plant manager, Winston would more than fill the bill as director of research and development, and Dan would be my choice for director of manufacturing. So, children, what about it?"

Julia is the first to answer. "Professor, it sounds like a great opportunity. But are you referring to Muddle's old Factory 1A, the one in Fargo?"

"I am," the professor answers. "Is that a problem?"

"I've never been to Fargo," Julia replies, "but I've seen the movie by the same name. As I recall, all it does there is snow. What about you, Winston, how do you feel about Fargo? Wherever we go, we go together."

"I happen to have been to Fargo," says Winston, "and they definitely have some hard winters. But they have some fine people. I'm all for applying for a job there if you are."

"Okay," says Julia, "let's get our résumés updated."

"And you, Dan, any interest in Fargo?" asks the professor.

"I'm game," Dan replies, "and I've already got my résumé updated."

"Excellent," says the professor, "but there's really no need to work on your résumés. As one of the investors in the Fargo facility, and having been authorized to hire its management, I can tell you that the three of you are, as of this moment, hired. Congratulations."

Ben Arnold can barely contain his anger. Freddy Mertz, the new factory floor operations manager, is sweating profusely. The two junior plant managers have turned pale. The other meeting attendees have averted their eyes, sensing that they are about to witness a "train wreck."

"Freddy," says Ben, "let me stop you right there. You're telling us that the moves through the factory have been increased by almost 20 percent, our goal, but that you're convinced the figures are bogus?"

"That's right," Freddy replies, wiping his brow. "It seems that the people on the factory floor have figured out a way to increase moves while decreasing factory outs. They're using all kinds of tricks."

"What tricks?" screams Ben. "Who is doing this? I want them fired."

"First of all," says Freddy, "you'd have to fire pretty much everyone on the factory floor. Second, the tricks that are being used include everything from changing data to reworking perfectly good in-process units. They've also discovered that one clever way to increase moves is just to run those parts that take the least process time. Another thing that has happened is that we've now got a huge inventory of in-process units—too many to keep in the factory. The factory just can't handle the increased load, so people have been removing in-process units from the factory floor and storing them in the parts and supplies warehouses. Ben, it's out of control. This factory simply can't cope with your goal. It's just not physically possible."

"Don't go blaming me for your failure," shouts Ben. "You're fired."

Freddy Mertz simply shrugs his shoulders and leaves the conference room.

"You, Juan," says Ben, "as of this moment you're the new factory floor operations manager. I want you to . . ."

Before Ben can finish his sentence, Juan Gonzalez takes off his badge, tosses it to the floor, and follows Freddy Mertz from the room.

CHAPTER 15

Summary and Conclusions

THE IDEAL FACTORY

Based on the material covered in the preceding chapters, we may conclude that the ideal (i.e., utopian) factory should possess the following attributes:

- Single-piece, continuous process flow, as achieved by the elimination of
  - Batching or cascading
  - Priority jobs
  - Reentrancy
  - Need for rework
- Small, inexpensive, and relatively simple machines
- Adherence to the guideline (e.g., as set forth by Toyota) that the size of each machine should not be more than four times the size of the job it processes—unless otherwise dictated by the laws of physics
- Strict control and oversight over all links of the supply chain
- Impossible to produce a defect
- Impossible to induce an accident or injury
- Use of intelligent automation (e.g., the machines must be capable of monitoring and correcting their own performance)
- The employment of intelligent predictive maintenance

- A corporate culture that encourages human creativity and is receptive to change
- A single point of oversight with regard to operations and maintenance (e.g., an established center for factory performance improvement)
- C^4U-compliant operations and maintenance specifications
- The elimination of slogans
- The elimination of any temptation to chase fads and fashions

It also might be noted that if such a factory could be established, there would be no need for work-in-progress (WIP) management (i.e., job dispatch rules).

APPROACHING THE IDEAL

At this time, synchronous factories (e.g., automobile assembly lines and bottling plants) are closer to achieving the utopian goals just listed than are asynchronous production lines (e.g., semiconductor manufacturing facilities and certain pharmaceutical factories). Neither, of course, is likely to arrive at the ideal state in the foreseeable future—if ever. However, this should not deter us from establishing these goals and comparing an existing factory's performance with its ultimate but as yet unattainable form.

Some of the ideal performance measures may be reached—or at least significantly improved upon—by means of physical changes to the factory and its components. For example, progress in developing rapid thermal processing machines (e.g., for heat treatment) provides the means to reduce batch sizes, if not eliminate batching entirely. Higher-precision machines reduce the need for rework as well as inspection. And artificial intelligence (e.g., neural networks) could be and is being employed in the support of predictive maintenance. The importance of evolutionary and revolutionary changes in the physical components of a factory is undeniable. However, it still appears that the most promise toward achieving the ideal factory is through increased exploitation and understanding of the third dimension of manufacturing, that is, enhanced operating and maintenance protocols.

An awareness of the three enemies of factory performance, with at least some appreciation of the factors found in the three fundamental equations of manufacturing, serves as a guide toward improving performance by means of changes in protocols.

At all times we must measure and compare factory performance by means of metrics that are objective, normalized, and subject to oversight and audit. Such measures were introduced in Chapters 7 and 8.

The guidelines for enhancing factory protocols were laid out and illustrated in Chapters 10 through 12. The factors critical to the practical implementation (and acceptance) of the third dimension of manufacturing were covered in Chapter 14.

ZARA: A MANUFACTURING ROLE MODEL

I have presented examples of factories that have, to some degree, approached the ideal factory by means of exploitation of the third dimension of manufacturing. These included the Arsenal of Venice, the Ford Motor Company, and Toyota. One other firm should be considered because it provides a more current—and possibly even more intriguing—role model for any manufacturing firm seeking significant and sustainable improvement.

Spain's Inditex, a clothing manufacturer, has spent more than 30 years independently perfecting a strategy that incorporates virtually every fundamental concept proposed in this book. Zara is Inditex's wildly popular chain of clothing stores that serves as a retail link of Inditex's manufacturing efforts. The company, as of 2009, had either tied or surpassed The Gap as the world's largest clothing retailer. Since 2000, the firm had "nearly quadrupled sales, profits, and locations" (Capell, 2008).

Recall from Chapter 1 of this book that many of the manufacturing firms in the United States have either partially or wholly moved their factories to developing countries in a seemingly never-ending search for low wages and loose regulations. It also was mentioned that *approximately 96 percent of all clothing purchased in the United States is now produced outside the country*. Conventional wisdom among U.S. clothing manufacturers is that they have no choice but to produce apparel in developing countries. Inditex would seem to take issue with this assessment.

Inditex has turned conventional wisdom on its head. Rather than establishing factories in developing countries such as China, Inditex produces about half its clothing in factories in Spain and the nearby countries of Portugal, and Morocco. Factory workers in Spain, by the way, earn, on average, $1,650 per month in wages compared with $200 a month in China (and even less in other countries). Furthermore, Inditex supplies every market from its

warehouses in Spain rather than locating those elements of it supply chain in other countries.

The approach employed by Inditex allows its Zara chain to
receive new designs in its retail stores *within two weeks or less* while
still remaining competitive. The best of Inditex's competition, on
the other hand, require *eight months* between design conception
and delivery to retail outlets.

As was the case with the Arsenal of Venice and Ford Motor
Company, Inditex maintains control over every link in its supply
chain—thus reducing complexity. This is coupled with the production of small batch sizes and the continuous pursuit of fast cycle
times. In short, Inditex has explicitly or implicitly recognized and
defeated two of the three enemies of manufacturing—complexity
and variability. Furthermore, its owner (Amancio Ortega Gaona)
has exhibited the attributes necessary to overcome the third and
most difficult enemy—lackluster leadership. While Senor Ortega
may be reclusive (there are only two known public photographs of
him), the man definitely has a vision.

Ortega believes that market flexibility and minimal inventory
levels are more important than cheap labor. While business
schools—desperate for some means to describe the Inditex production system—cite the employment of lean manufacturing and
just-in-time as the basis for Zara's success, they are missing the
point. Zara's success is due almost entirely to the mitigation of
complexity and variability coupled with the vision, persistence,
and patience of Ortega. It's as simple as that.

CONCLUSION

If significant and sustainable factory performance improvement is
to be achieved, it will require an approach that combines the art
and science of manufacturing while considering at all times the
impact of the culture and politics of the organization. While such
concepts as lean manufacturing, Six Sigma, and total productive
maintenance offer the potential to support such an effort, they
should be part of a unified approach rather than implemented sep-
arately or in isolation. The emphasis of any manufacturing firm
seeking significant and sustainable performance improvement
should be on reducing complexity and variability—something that
can only be accomplished by expertise in the science of manufacturing coupled with real leadership at the top.

CASE STUDY 15: FIVE YEARS LATER

The case studies and their characters that have been presented are, as has been noted, strictly fictional. They do, however, reflect to a degree the types of behaviors I and others have witnessed in some real-world factories. Fortunately, few real-world firms are as dysfunctional as the Muddle Corporation, and even fewer have managers the likes of which we encountered in the case studies. Most managers are, in fact, smart, honest, diligent, and dedicated. While some people do work their way up the corporate ladder through intrigue, back stabbing, and co-opting the ideas of others, they are—hopefully—in the minority.

Unfortunately, whatever the manufacturing firm and whomever might be in charge, it is all too common to encounter resistance to any proposal for changes that might require what may be considered "too much work." Some managers are at their most creative when it comes to making up excuses for avoiding change—of any type. Proposals for the inclusion of the third dimension of manufacturing in decision making and for changes in manufacturing protocols are often perceived to be "too difficult" mainly, if not solely, because they differ from the more typical "quick and easy" proposals traditionally delivered to management.

Sadly, it is far easier to convince management to accept a proposal that is based almost solely on sloganeering, vague guidelines, empty promises, and noble principles than one that requires serious thought and the conviction necessary for a change in corporate culture. It is also far easier for management unaware of the third dimension of manufacturing to purchase more machines and hire more personnel rather than to deal more cost-effectively with an underperforming factory. But, before you despair, let me assure you that it can be done.

There are some firms that, like Muddle, can never be convinced to change their ways. When faced with a problem, even a problem of immense proportions, some firms simply cannot seem to alter their ingrained response (e.g., note the plight of the "big three" American automobile manufacturers). Rather than admit that they have followed the wrong path, they continue to rely on the very same things that caused their problems in the first place; that is, they focus on cutting costs, closing plants, outsourcing, and—like Muddle—changing logos and slogans. These firms deserve the fate that awaits them, and there is little point in expending much time and effort in an attempt to convince them that there is a better way.

Fortunately, if you are patient (and knowledgeable about the third dimension of manufacturing), you should be able to convince management of a more receptive firm to give you at least an opportunity to prove your promises, be it via simulations or pilot studies. It does, however, require tact and diplomacy, attributes that are not emphasized nearly as much as they should be in the classroom.

Let's conclude the stories of the Muddle Corporation with a brief summary of the fortunes and misfortunes of some of the characters in the story five years from now.

Brad Simmons and Sally Swindel-Simmons

Brad and Sally's wildly popular book, *The Leadership Principles of the Donner Party*, reached number one on the list of best-selling business and management books. Sally is in great demand as a speaker and counts most of the Fortune 500 firms as her customers. Her fee, for an hour-long speech, is now $150,000. Brad, on his part, has discovered a passion for writing books on leadership. Buoyed by the success of *The Leadership Principles of the Donner Party*, he is hard at work on a new book, *The Leadership Principles of General George Armstrong Custer*. One may rest assured that it will receive a wide audience among managers desperate for advice that doesn't require any changes of consequence.

Julia Austen-Smith and Winston Smith

This happy pair was so effective in the startup and operation of the Fargo facility that they have now been placed in charge of three more factories. While they are now successful, their most prized possession is their job satisfaction.

Dan Ryan

Dan decided that before he could accept Professor Leonidas' offer, he should go back to school. He has now completed his dissertation and is ready to take on the duties as director of the center for manufacturing science at the professor's firm. One of the more interesting things he learned at university was the fact that he already knew considerably more about running a factory than his professors. He decided, however, to keep that fact to himself.

Professor Aristotle Leonidas

The good professor recently celebrated his ninety-third birthday. The professor claims, with a wink, that his longevity is due to a life free of complexity and variability. Prominent among the celebrants at his birthday party were Brad, Sally, Julia, Winston, and Dan.

Benedict "Ben" Arnold

Ben Arnold was promoted to the position of CFO of the Muddle Corporation. Considering the truly abysmal performance of Factory 7 under his reign, this actually may have been a good move for Muddle. Shortly after that promotion, Ben was hired by an alternative energy (wind turbines) firm to serve as its CEO. Between the stock options he received and his generous salary, Ben is doing quite well, thank you. One moral here is that the "bad guys" sometimes may win on the corporate battlefield.

Donna Garcia

Donna ultimately gave up looking for a comparable appointment at one of Muddle's competitors. At this time, her whereabouts are unknown.

Tommy Jenkins

Fewer than six months after his termination, Tommy managed to secure a factory manager position with one of Muddle's competitors. That factory's performance, since his arrival, has been on a downward spiral. Rumor has it that Tommy may be looking for a new job in the near future. He remains convinced, however, that there is no need for science in the operation of a factory.

Marvin Muddle

The Muddle Corporation continues to control the market for its primary product. This required, however, a fierce price war with its competitors and the use of some dubious marketing practices. The firm is faced with countless law suits in the United States and elsewhere citing unfair practices. Marvin Muddle remains the firm's CEO, although less and less is seen of him. There have been some unsubstantiated claims that Marvin, much like Howard Hughes in the 1950s, has become a recluse. At this point in time, it is rumored that he is working on the design of yet another new logo for his firm.

Bibliography

Alford, L. P., and H. R. Beatty, *Principles of Industrial Management*, revised edition, Ronald Press, New York, 1951.

Anderson, D., "Reducing the Cost of Preventive Maintenance," *www.plant-mainte nance.com/articles/PMCostReduction.pdf*, no date.

Antil, P., "Baker Rifle," a description of the Brown Bess musket that may be found at *www.historyofwar.org/articles/weapon_brown_bess.html*, February 4, 2006.

Arthur, J., *Lean Six Sigma Demystified*, McGraw-Hill, New York, 2007.

Aurand, S. S., and P. J. Miller, "The Operating Curve: A Method to Measure and Benchmark Manufacturing Line Productivity," in *Proceedings of the Advanced Semiconductor Manufacturing Conference and Workshop*, September 10–12, 1997, pp. 391–397.

Baker, K. R., *Introduction to Sequencing and Scheduling*, Wiley, New York, 1974.

Barnes & Noble Classics, *Sun Tzu, The Art of War*, Barnes & Noble Books, New York, 2003.

Billings, R., and J. J. Hasenbein, "Heuristic Methods for Near-Optimal Wafer Fab Scheduling and Dispatching Using Multiclass Fluid Networks," in *Proceedings of the International Conference on Modeling and Analysis of Semiconductor Manufacturing*, Tempe Arizona, April 10–12, 2002, pp. 200–205.

Bodek, N., *Kaikaku: The Power and Magic of Lean*, PCS Press, Vancouver, WA, 2004.

Buzacott, J. A., and J. G. Shanthikumar, *Stochastic Models of Manufacturing Systems*, Prentice-Hall, Englewood Cliffs, NJ, 1993.

Capell, K., "Zara Thrives by Breaking All the Rules," *BusinessWeek*, October 20, 2008, p. 66.

Clason, T., *Fast Cycle Production*, 1st Books Library, Bloomington, IN, 2003.

Coman, K., *Industrial History of the United States*, Macmillan, New York, 1930.

Cooke-Taylor, R.W., *History of the Factory System*, Richard Bentley & Son, London, 1886.

Del Angel, C., and C. Pritchard, "Behavior Tests Six Sigma," *Industrial Engineering Magazine*, August 2008, p. 41.

Duffuaa, S. O., A. Raouf, and J. D. Campbell, *Planning and Control of Maintenance Systems*, Wiley, New York, 1999.

Encyclopedia Britannica, "Matthew Boulton," *Encyclopedia Britannica*, 2008.

Ford, Henry, in collaboration with S. Crowthers, *My Life and Work*, Garden City Publishing, New York, 1922.

Forrester, J. W., *Industrial Dynamics*, Pegasus, Waltham, MA, 1999.

Francis, R. L., and J. A. White, *Facility Layout and Location: An Analytical Approach*, Prentice-Hall, Englewood Cliffs, NJ, 1974.

Galileo, G., *Discorsi e dimonstrazioni matematiche intorno a du nuove science*, 1638.

George, M. L., *Lean Six Sigma*, McGraw-Hill, New York, 2002.

Gilbreth, F. B., *Bricklaying System*, Myron C. Clark Publishing, New York, 1909.

Gilbreth, F. B., *Motion Study*, Van Nostrand, New York, 1911.

Goldberg, D. E., *Genetic Algorithms*, Addison-Wesley, Reading, MA, 1989.

Goldratt, E., and J. Cox, *The Goal*, North River Press, Great Barrington, MA, 1984.

Gross, D., and C. M. Harris, *Fundamentals of Queuing Theory*, Wiley, New York, 1998.

Hillier, F. S., and G. J. Lieberman, *Introduction to Operations Research*, McGraw-Hill, New York, 2005.

Hirano, H., and M. Furuya, *JIT Is Flow*, PCS Press, Vancouver, WA, 2006.

Hitomi, K., *Manufacturing Systems Engineering*, Taylor & Francis, London, 1996.

Hopp, W. J., and M. L. Spearman, *Factory Physics*, McGraw-Hill, New York, 2001.

Hounshell, D. A., *From the American System to Mass Production, 1800–1932*, John Hopkins University Press, Baltimore, 1984.

Ignizio, J. P., "Saturn S-II Telemetry Antennas: Ground Test Procedures," *North American Aviation S&ID Report*, Downey, CA, 1962.

Ignizio, J. P., "A Heuristic Solution to Generalized Covering Problems," Ph.D. dissertation, Virginia Tech, Blacksburg, VA, 1971.

Ignizio, J. P., "Solving Massive Scheduling Problems by Minimizing Conflicts," *Simulation*, March 1978, pp. 75–79.

Ignizio, J. P., "The Third Dimension in Manufacturing," technical paper, Pennsylvania State University, 1980.

Ignizio, J. P., *Introduction to Expert Systems*, McGraw-Hill, New York, 1991.

Ignizio, J. P., "The General Capacity Model," technical paper, Resource Management Institute, 1992a.

Ignizio, J. P., "Extensions of the General Capacity Model," technical paper, Resource Management Institute, 1992b.

Ignizio, J. P., "Metrics for the Evaluation of Factory Performance," technical paper, Resource Management Institute, 1997.

Ignizio, J. P., "Integrating, Cost, Effectiveness, and Stability," *Acquisition Review Quarterly* 5(1):51–60, 1998.

Ignizio, J. P., "An Optimization Model for the Declustering of Preventive Maintenance Scheduling," technical paper, Resource Management Institute, 1999.

Ignizio, J. P., "Fluid and Electromagnetic Network Simulation Models," technical paper, Resource Management Institute, 2000.

Ignizio, J. P., "Optimal Factory Tool Portfolios," *IEEE International Symposium on Semiconductor Manufacturing,* September 30–October 2, 2003a, pp. 31–34.

Ignizio, J. P., "The Implementation of CONWIP in Semiconductor Fabrication Facilities," *Future Fab International* 14, 2003b.

Ignizio, J. P., "Optimal Maintenance Headcount Allocation: An Application of Chebyshev Goal Programming," *International Journal of Production Research* 42:201–210, 2004.

Ignizio, J. P., "What Are the Alternatives to 450-nm Wafers?" *Future Fab International* 25:61–64, 2008a.

Ignizio, J. P., "Lean Manufacturing in the Semiconductor Industry: Proceed with Caution, Part I, *Fab Engineering & Operations* 3:37–44, 2008b.

Ignizio, J. P., "Lean Manufacturing in the Semiconductor Industry: Proceed with Caution, Part II, *Fab Engineering & Operations* 4:42–48, 2008c.

Ignizio, J. P., and J. N. D. Gupta, *Operations Research in Decision Making,* Crane Russak, New York, 1975.

Ignizio, J. P., and T. M. Cavalier, *Linear Programming,* Prentice-Hall, Englewood Cliffs, NJ, 1994.

Jensen, P. A., and J. F. Bard, *Operations Research: Models and Methods,* Wiley, New York, 2003.

Kennedy, J. B., and A. M. Neville, *Basic Statistical Methods for Engineers & Scientists,* IEP, New York, 1964.

Khade, S. B., and J. P. Ignizio, "A Heuristic for Batch Selection in Production Planning of Flexible Manufacturing Systems," in *Proceedings of Decision Sciences Institute,* Vancouver, Canada, 1990, pp. 363–366.

Levinson, W. A., *Henry Ford's Lean Vision,* Productivity Press, New York, 2002.

Liker, J. K., *The Toyota Way,* McGraw-Hill, New York, 2004.

Little, J. D. C., "A Proof for the Formula $L = \lambda W$," *Operations Research* 9:383–387, 1961.

Meyer, C., *Fast Cycle Time,* Free Press, New York, 1993.

Nolan, J., "Willow Run and the Arsenal of Democracy," *The Detroit News,* January 28, 1997 (also see *www.strategosinc.com/willow_run.htm*).

Paton, S. M., "Juran: A Lifetime of Quality," *Quality Digest,* August 2002.

Pegels, C., *Japan vs. the West: Implications for Management,* Kluwer-Nijhoff Publishing, Boston, 1984.

Popkin, J., and K. Kobe, "U.S. Manufacturing Innovation at Risk," *Council of Manufacturing Associations Report,* February 2006.

Robinson, C. J., and A. P. Ginder, *Implementing TPM,* Productivity Press, New York, 1995.

Roethlisberger, F. J., and W. J. Dickson, *Management and the Worker,* Harvard University Press, Cambridge, MA, 1939.

Sato, N., J. P. Ignizio, and I. Ham, "Group Technology and Material Requirements Planning: An Integrated Methodology for Production and Control," *CIRP Annals* 27(1):471–473, 1978.

Standard, C., and D. Davis, *Running Today's Factory,* Hanser Gardner Publications, Cincinnati, OH, 1999.

Stecke, K. E., and J. J. Solberg, "The Optimality of Unbalancing Both Workloads and Machine Group Sizes in Closed Queuing Networks of Multiserver Queues," *Operations Research* 33:882–910, 1985.

Taha, H., *Operations Research: An Introduction,* Prentice-Hall, New York, 2006.

Taylor, F. W., *The Principles of Scientific Management,* Harper, New York, 1911.

TECHNEWS, "Japanese Computer Chips Made at Too High Quality to Be Competitive on World Market," *www.technologynewsdaily.com/node/29238,* May 17, 2006.

Usher, A. P., *Industrial History of England,* Houghton Mifflin, Boston, 1920.

Van Zant, P., *Microchip Fabrication,* McGraw-Hill, New York, 2000.

Waddington, C. H., *OR in World War 2: Operational Research Against the U-Boat,* Elek Science, London, 1973.

Walton, M., *The Deming Management Method,* Berkley Publishing Group, New York, 1986.

War Production Board, Bureau of Training, "Training Within Industry Report," September 1945, p. 92.

Wikipedia, "Brown Bess Musket," *http://en.wikipedia.org/wiki/Brown_Bess.*

Wills, G., *Venice: Lion City,* Washington Square Press, New York, 2001.

Womack, J. P., and D. T. Jones, *Lean Thinking,* Free Press, New York, 2003.

Womack, J. P., D. T. Jones, and D. Roos, *The Machine That Changed the World: The Story of Lean Production,* HarperCollins, New York, 1991.

Wood, S. C., "The Impact of Single-Wafer Processing on Fab Cycle Time," in *Electronics Manufacturing Technology Symposium,* 1995, pp. 488–494.

Index

A

Aircraft production, 44–49
Alighieri, Dante, 39–40
American system of manufacturing, 1
Analytical inventory-level models, 276
Anderson, D., 242
Apollo moon landing program, 51–52
Arrival rate:
  process-step, 91
  variability in, 261, 281
Arrival times, variability in, 261
Arrivals, coefficient of variability of,
  141–144
Arsenal of Venice, 38–40, 42n.6, 55, 57
Art of manufacturing, 6
Art of War (Sun Tzu), 37
Arthur, Jay, 128
Assembly jobs, 68, 77
Assembly lines, 38, 40, 131, 234
Asynchronous factories, 76, 131, 348
Automation of operations, 245
Availability:
  of machines, 92–93, 202
  of workers, 86–87
  of workstations, 97–98, 265–269
Availability profile plot, 202–205,
  265–266
Averages, reliance on, 87

B

B24 bombers, 44–49
Back-to-front WIP management,
  208, 280
Bacon, Francis, 69n.1
Bad decisions, rectifying, 36
Balanced production line, 128–131,
  167–169
Balanced workload, 127–128
Batches, 78
Batching, 59
  coefficient of variability of arrivals
    in, 142–144
  protocols for, 8
  and reduction of variability, 262–263
  types of, 78
Bethlehem Steel, 1
Blocked state (machines), 83, 84
Blocked time, 83, 84
Boeing Commercial Aircraft, 1
"Bomber an Hour" effort, 44
Boolean optimization model, 319–322
Bottlenecks, 37, 38
Boulton, Matthew, 40–41, 42n.6
British Air Coastal Command,
  44–47, 198
"Brown Bess," 248–252, 254–255
Business processes, models for, 69

About the Author

James P. Ignizio received a Ph.D. in Industrial Engineering and Operations Research from Virginia Tech in 1971. He is a fellow of the Institute of Industrial Engineering, a fellow of the British Operational Research Society, and a fellow of the World Academy of Productivity Science.

Dr. Ignizio is the author of nine books and more than 350 publications, including over 150 peer reviewed papers in international professional journals. In 1980 he was awarded The First Hartford Prize by the U.S. National Safety Council for his contributions to this country's manned moon-landing program. Dr. Ignizio was also a fellow and senior research associate for the National Research Council from 1982–1983. In 2002 Dr. Ignizio was inducted into the Academy of Distinguished Alumni of the Department of Industrial and Systems Engineering at Virginia Tech.

Dr. Ignizio has held the positions of professor and chair: University of Virginia; professor and chair: University of Houston; professor: Pennsylvania State University; visiting professor: Naval Postgraduate School; visiting professor: U.S. Army ALMC; and distinguished adjunct professor: Helsinki School of Economics. His efforts in the fields of Industrial Engineering, Operational Research, and AI have received international recognition and his textbooks on these topics have been widely adopted in the United States and abroad. Dr. Ignizio's short courses on Operational Research, Industrial Engineering, Manufacturing Science, and Artificial Intelligence have been attended by several thousands of industrial, governmental, and military sector personnel over the past 30 years.

Prior to his 30-plus year academic career, Dr. Ignizio served as a program manager for the Apollo manned moon-landing mission. He was also deputy director of the Apollo/Saturn Integration Committee—with a focus on Fast Cycle Time. Dr. Ignizio has also served as a consultant to numerous industrial and governmental organizations in both the United States and abroad, including the U.S. Army, U.S. Air Force, U.S. Navy, NASA, SDI ("Star Wars"), Litton, Exxon, Texaco, Boeing, SAI, GRC, SRI, Bell Labs, Finland's Ministry of Economics, Quantas Airways, KAIST, Virginia Manufacturing Institute, Chase Bank, the Commercial Bank of Greece, and various semiconductor manufacturing firms.

CPSIA information can be obtained
at www.ICGtesting.com
Printed in the USA
BVHW062002300122
627175BV00002B/38

9 780071 632850